Dynamic Commodity Models: Specification, Estimation, and Simulation

Dynamic Commodity Models: Specification, Estimation, and Simulation

WALTER C. LABYS

Graduate Institute of International Studies
Geneva

Lexington Books
D. C. Heath and Company
Lexington, Massachusetts
Toronto   London

658.5
L 127

Library of Congress Cataloging in Publication Data

Labys, Walter C   1937–
    Dynamic commodity models.

    Bibliography: p.
    1. Commercial products—Mathematical models.
    2. Coconut oil. 3. Palm-oil. I. Title.
    II. Title: Commodity models.
    HF1040.7.L32   658.5   73–986
    ISBN 0-669-81877-1

Published simultaneously in Canada.

Printed in the United States of America.

International Standard Book Number: 0-669-81877-1

Library of Congress Catalog Card Number: 73-986

To Jane, Paulo, and Lottie

Contents

List of Figures

List of Tables

Preface

From time to time during the development of economic theory and methods, a plateau is reached. Progress can best follow when recent advances are synthesized so as to provide a uniform body of thought from which new research can then flow. This monograph attempts to serve that end in its effort to draw together the many different facets of commodity model building which have recently appeared and to provide a foundation from which improved commodity models can be constructed and applied. It became evident to me that such a study was needed when I began analyzing a number of commodity and econometric developments as a preparation to constructing an econometric model for the international lauric oils market. Another incentive was provided by the kind of problems treated in an earlier book, *Speculation, Hedging, and Commodity Price Forecasts*, where I was concerned with explaining commodity price fluctuations of a very short run nature.

The present study deals with the theory and methods required for specifying, estimating, validating, and applying commodity models which describe behavior of a quarterly or annual nature, though certain material is relevant for explaining monthly behavior as well. These models are being employed increasingly by governments, firms, manufacturers, producers, and traders to reduce the large amount of uncertainty that surrounds commodity decision making.

The organization of the study is in three parts. I first deal with the behavioral components of commodity models. These components are then incorporated into complete commodity models, and finally the application of these models is discussed. Essential to each part is the examination of basic theories, relevant econometric methods, and empirical applications. I realized from the outset that it would be difficult to integrate these aspects of modeling into a single study, yet it seemed necessary to do so and I hope that the resulting inadequacies will be overlooked. Among other difficulties encountered, I wished to strike a balance between international and domestic models, though many of the studies discussed relate to international markets. Synthesis also requires selecting only the more important studies in a field. Where a study has been omitted, either it gave way to the need to reduce the size of this monograph or it was not brought to my attention, and I hope that such omissions will be forgiven. Furthermore, it was necessary to concentrate only on the equilibrium form of models, this form usually providing the basis from which programming and systems models follow. Finally, it appeared best to examine the application of the various theories and methods based on the experience of a single commodity; however, in demonstrating these applications in the form of the lauric oils model, one must keep in mind that it is only a first generation model with additional research and experimentation necessary.

I believe that the study will be of interest to a wide audience, including commodity model builders, commodity enthusiasts, econometricians, micro-theorists, and students. *Commodity model builders* will be interested in the practical approach to building and applying commodity models as well as in the empirical results provided for certain commodities. *Commodity enthusiasts* may want to test the strength of their trading tactics against trading prescriptions that could be obtained through forecasting from simple models. This monograph, with its emphasis on application of methods and theory, should be of use as a supplementary text to *econometricians* teaching at the graduate level. The same could be said for *micro-theorists* who are teaching courses in applied theory or in model building. Lastly, it is hoped that *graduate students* and *research workers* will find new techniques and results to employ in their own efforts.

Many of the ideas and concepts presented here arose while I was first working on the lauric oils model under Alfred Maizels of the U.N. Conference on Trade and Development in Geneva. I am grateful to him for the encouragement and interest which he gave me. Gerry Adams of Wharton introduced me to the policy simulation approach and offered many suggestion as to how commodity models could be improved and better applied; he also facilitated my interaction with other members of the Economic Research Unit who were working on various aspects of model building. Jim Matthews of the Economic Research Service, U.S.D.A. discussed some of the fine points of the study with me and widened my understanding of the different models being constructed in his Division. Jim Burrows also provided helpful recommendations and Ivar Strand lent a hand in preparing Chapter 7.

I also would like to express my gratitude to the many economists whose works I have quoted and which have helped stimulate the present effort. Of the persons who helped in different ways with the present manuscript, I would like to thank: Dennis Bender, Chris Yandle, Henry Arthur, Grant Taplin, Phil Howrey, Ray Leuthold, Dennis Meadows, Mary Lee Epps, Arthur Lysons, and Clive Granger. Many others helped and I am grateful to them as well. If one appreciates the different places which contribute the backdrop to a written work, the present list includes Geneva, London, Rome, Manila, Colombo, Djakarta, New Delhi, Singapore, Les Diablerets, and Jamestown (Rhode Island).

Lastly, I would like to express my gratitude to my wife Jane and to my children to whom this book is dedicated. Jane provided help in revising the many drafts; the time that all three gave was precious.

The preparation of the manuscript was supported in part by a grant from the International Center for Marine Resource Development at the University of Rhode Island; Lucien Sprague is to be thanked in this regard.

During the year which I taught at the University of Rhode Island, Rick Sabatino placed the facilities of the Economics Department at my disposal. To the many typists, I am also appreciative.

The views and opinions expressed are, of course, mine, and for them I take full responsibility.

WALTER C. LABYS

Dynamic Commodity Models: Specification, Estimation, and Simulation

1 Introduction to Commodity Models

This monograph attempts to present a cohesive econometric approach to specifying and estimating dynamic commodity models as well as to simulating them for historical explanation and prediction. There presently exist a number of building blocks in the form of theories and research results that need to be synthesized to improve our modeling capabilities. These building blocks stem not only from recent econometric research in commodity economics and model building but also from such research in other areas of microeconomics and in macroeconomics.

I have chosen in this study to develop an approach to commodity modeling in three distinct parts. In the first part we examine the components or separate behavioral relationships necessary for constructing a commodity model—i.e., demand, supply, inventories, and prices. The second part considers how these different relationships can be incorporated into a complete econometric commodity model, taking into account model specification, estimation, and validation. In the third part we show how commodity models can be applied to a variety of policy problems utilizing both multiplier analysis and simulation analysis. All sections of the study are drawn together to some extent by demonstrating how the theories and methods can be applied to a single model, that describing the international lauric oils (coconut oil and palm kernel oil) market.

Any attempt to synthesize existing research by including both theoretical and empirical results is obviously subject to limitations. First of all, a synthesis helps us to see existing material in a new and helpful way, but obviously is limited in any original contributions. Also, since each commodity faces different demand, supply, and market situations, the methodology presented cannot be expected to be valid for all commodities. One must also take into account the important issue of the gap existing between the complexities and realities of commodity markets and the simplified nature of the relationships and models adopted. Commodity model building is still in its infancy, for our ability to explain real market behavior is limited. Where possible, I shall point out the techniques that can be used to better interpret these complexities. But recent progress despite its gains needs to be tempered with an awareness of the problems remaining to be solved.

Presentation of the material follows a fairly uniform pattern from chapter to chapter. Each chapter begins with a brief introduction to the historical background of the theories to be presented. The basic theories are then discussed and formulated, emphasis being given to their econometric aspect. Empirical examples are presented that demonstrate the strengths or weaknesses

1

of these theories. To advance from the simplicity of theory to the exigencies of available estimation techniques and on to the complexities of empirical application is a difficult task, but such an approach is essential if one wants to discuss model building in a practical sense. Each chapter concludes with practical suggestions on research methodology, indicating which developments seem of most value and which problems require further study.

Part I, dealing with the specification of component behavioral relationships to be incorporated into a complete commodity model, consists of Chapters 2 through 5. Chapter 2 concentrates on explaining commodity demand not only from the partial adjustment approach but also from the differential or continuous time adjustment approach. Suggestions are offered for analyzing and formulating appropriate substitution mechanisms which reflect the influence of competing commodities and synthetics on commodity demand.

In Chapter 3 the behavioral relationships underlying commodity supply are examined. The types of relationships considered are much more diverse than for commodity demand simply because the inherent production conditions are more diverse. Supply can be classified as regular, annual, perennial, or cyclical, depending on whether the commodities of interest are: for example, minerals, grains, tree crops, or livestock. Accordingly, the supply relationships studied include static and dynamic, annual and perennial adjustment, and cyclical types.

Chapter 4, in attempting to explain the development of theoretical inventory relationships, probably raises more questions than it answers. Explaining commodity inventory behavior is the weakest link in the network of relationships needed to construct a commodity model. This appears to result from the general lack of good commodity inventory data as well as from the lack of theoretical research. To help offset these difficulties I have given careful attention to the research that has already been done. This includes applications of the flexible and modified flexible accelerator to consumer inventories, and applications of the supply of storage theory to total inventories.

The analysis of price relationships contained in Chapter 5 requires delving into an area where theory also has not caught up with the empirical evidence to be explained. Theoretical approaches differ according to whether we are concerned with short or long run behavior. For the most part, we concentrate on price behavior of quarterly or annual intervals, and price theories appropriate to these intervals are presented. A framework is provided for determining which theory might be most useful based on either a competitive or a noncompetitive market structure. Among the theories examined and empirically evaluated are the inverted demand theory, theories of stock and flow adjustment, and the supply of storage theory.

Part II, dealing with the specification, estimation, and validation of complete commodity models, consists of Chapters 6 and 7. Chapter 6, perhaps the most important in the monograph, concentrates on the development of the econometric equilibrium form of commodity model. This form is also contrasted with process, trade, industrial dynamics, and systems forms of models. Procedures for specifying model structures are given, and the problem of causality is taken up and related to the selection of estimation procedures. Other criteria are also presented for determining which estimation procedure might be most appropriate for a particular commodity model. Especially useful are the suggestions given regarding the trade-off that must be made between computational convenience and the desired properties of estimates. A complete version of the lauric oils model is also presented.

Chapter 7 discusses the validation of commodity models from the viewpoint of stability or internal consistency. Appropriate to determining the stability properties of dynamic models are the methods of analytical solution and computer solution. These methods are analyzed according to the combination of characteristics a commodity model may have: linear or nonlinear, stochastic or nonstochastic. Also included are applications to particular models.

Part III, concerned with the application of commodity models, consists of Chapters 8 and 9. Chapter 8 deals with the forms of multipliers which have been used in policy analysis with commodity models. These include static short and long run multipliers as well as dynamic delay and cumulative multipliers. Also presented is the concept of dynamic discrepancy, which explains deviations from the long run equilibrium path of the endogenous variables resulting from continuous changes in the exogenous variables. The principal difficulty in using static or dynamic multipliers for making projections is that computation becomes inefficient when lagged values of dependent variables or nonlinearities in the endogenous variables enter the model. One way of dealing with these difficulties is to analyze multiplier effects using simulation analysis.

Simulation analysis as discussed in Chapter 9 provides both the background and theory of using computer simulation procedures with dynamic commodity models. Particular methods of simulation examined relate to both the reduced form and the structural form of model solution. Problems of nonconvergence are discussed and model validation is again taken up, now considering a wider range of criteria. Examined are parametric and nonparametric tests for evaluating the correspondence of actual and simulated data, with certain tests recommended for the sample and for the post-sample periods of estimation.

The conclusions presented in Chapter 10 contrast the developments relevant to commodity model building against the major problems remaining to be solved. An attempt is made to assess the current state of the art and technology of commodity modeling, and guidelines are provided for organizing future research.

Vital to the reader in carrying out his goals of commodity model building are an appendix of model listings and a bibliography, which complete the book. Appendix C provides for the first time, a comprehensive list of recently constructed commodity models. Although by no means exhaustive, the bibliography lists a large number of studies valuable to model building and application. So vast a field cannot be covered in a single monograph, and so references to additional models and studies should facilitate further reading and investigation of important topics.

Part I
Components of Commodity Models

2 Demand

This chapter examines commodity demand from the viewpoint of both static and dynamic behavior. Static behavior is described utilizing both linear and nonlinear relationships. Dynamic behavior is described with relationships that vary according to the nature of the underlying adjustment processes: partial adjustment in discrete time and differential adjustment in continuous time. Among the other factors introduced as essential to explaining demand is the influence of the demand for other commodities classified as either substitutes or complements. Demand is also examined as it relates to imports rather than domestic consumption and estimation methods relating to single demand equations are discussed. Empirical results are presented for cobalt, zinc, wool, and lauric oils.

Demand Relationships

Background

Probably no other aspect of the specification and estimation of commodity behavioral relationships has received as much attention as that of demand. Among the numerous theoretical and empirical studies which have appeared, we concentrate only on the major developments. The beginnings of empirical demand analysis are associated with the work of Moore, Working, and Schultz.[1] Moore in 1919 introduced the statistical estimation of commodity relationships as an essential part of economic analysis. This was followed in 1922 by Working's study involving the estimation of a number of commodity demand equations, and in 1938 by the monumental study of Schultz that combined both the economic and statistical theory of dealing with commodity demand curves.

Ensuing developments are associated with the work of the Cowles Commission; some of the more difficult problems encountered in using single equation models such as autocorrelation and multicollinearity were studied, as well as problems relating to systems of equations including identification and simultaneity. Of the published papers resulting from this effort, an important one is that of Haavelmo in 1943, which presented a comprehensive approach to estimating simultaneous sets of equations.[2]

Both the single and the simultaneous equation approach to explaining demand received further development throughout the 1950s as is reflected in the publications of Wold and Jureen, Hood and Koopmans, and Stone.[3] Advances related to cross-sectional analysis can be found in the work of Balestra and Nerlove and of Ben-David and Tomek.[4] Advances related to time series analysis stem from the realization that demand behavior is not only static, but that it can be dynamic, the demand response extending over more than one period of time. Koyck in 1954 demonstrated that such dynamic behavior might be explained with a form of distributed lag relationship.[5] Nerlove in 1958 developed a similar form of relationship which is based on expectations theory and introduces the distributed lag implicitly.[6] While this approach relies on the concept of partial adjustment, Houthakker and Taylor in 1966 extended the explanation of dynamic behavior to include differential adjustment.[7]

Other recent contributions to demand analysis have concentrated on methods of transforming the theoretical demand model to one which can be more easily estimated and interpreted. In effect, the realization that the demands for all commodities are interrelated has led to empirical investigation of the complete interdependent nature of demand. Frisch in 1959 proposed that demand relationships could be used to compute all direct and cross-price elasticities for a number of commodities based on the assumption that certain commodities could be separated according to the concept of want independence.[8]

An attempt to estimate these elasticities followed in 1961 with Brandow's study involving 24 food commodities, and in 1964 with Barten's analysis consisting of a much wider market.[9] Strotz in 1959 introduced the notion of the utility tree which led to the possibility that commodities could be divided into separable groups.[10] Further interpretation of this concept in the form of weak, strong, and Pearce separability can be found in a study by Goldman and Uzawa.[11] The problem of empirically identifying separable groups based on marginal utilities was later solved by deJanvry using factor and cluster analysis.[12] The most recent commodity study to empirically investigate the generalized demand model is that of George and King, which enlarges upon and advances the earlier work of Brandow.[13]

Static Relationships

The static relationship used to explain commodity demand derives from consumer demand theory. That theory would explain demand based on the maximization of consumer utility subject to an appropriate budget constraint. Solution of the maximization problem through differentiation leads to a set of demand equations of the form

$$c_{it} = f_i(p_{it}, p_{jt}, \ldots, p_{nt}, y_t) \qquad i = 1, \ldots, n \qquad (2.1)$$

which relate consumption of a commodity c_{it} to its price p_{it}, the prices of other commodities $p_{jt}, \ldots, p_{nt}$, and income y_t. As relevant for the commodity models considered here, demand behavior is assumed to be time variant. There are a number of considerations of importance which surround the demand equations 2.1. The first of these are a set of underlying restrictions known as the Homogeneity condition, Engel aggregation condition, Cournot aggregation condition, Symmetry condition, and the Slutsky condition. While the full implications of these conditions can be found elsewhere, a simplified interpretation is that they provide the properties normally associated with demand equations.[14] There is also some question as to the exact meaning these conditions have for empirical research, and readers should consult a recent paper by Barten.[15] A second consideration is that the above equations are designed to explain individual consumer behavior, and that consistency in aggregation must be assumed if the equations are to explain market demand. Finally, the generalized model implied by equations 2.1 and their restrictions would stipulate that the demands for all commodities are interrelated. Several other assumptions regarding separability as explained elsewhere are necessary in order to explain demand for one or only several commodities.[16]

Fulfillment of these conditions and assumptions is normally assumed in bridging the gap between the above theoretical model and the empirical equations which are estimated in commodity demand studies. The equations that might be estimated for a single commodity would be of the following form, which includes the price of the commodity of interest, prices of only one or two complementary or substitute commodities, income, and possible other explanatory variables, the latter being indicated by z_t.

$$c_t = f(p_t, p_{jt}, \ldots, p_{kt}, y_t, z_t, u_t) \qquad (2.2)$$

A stochastic disturbance term u_t also is added relevant to statistical estimation.[a] The requirements for u_t are that it be independent of the other explanatory variables, be free from autocorrelation, and have constant variance.

While equation 2.2 is linear in form, we occasionally have need to investigate equations of a nonlinear form such as

$$c_t = a_0 p_t^{a_1} y_t^{a_2} u_t \qquad (2.3)$$

The estimation of such an equation would require a nonlinear estimation method, and so it is normally dealt with in its log-linear form.

$$\log c_t = \log a_0 + a_1 \log p_t + a_2 \log y_t + u_t \qquad (2.4)$$

---

[a] To simplify notation, no differentiation is made among the disturbance terms u_t introduced in different equations except where necessary.

Burrows in estimating a number of cobalt demand equations based on this form stresses its several conveniences.[17] The log-linear form provides for a multiplicative effect in p_t and y_t and implies that a given percentage change in p_t or y_t will have a constant percentage effect on consumption for all values of p_t and y_t. This latter property has the advantage that consumption will not become negative for low values of p_t and high values of y_t. Other forms of logarithmic transformations considered useful are the semilogarithmic

$$c_t = a_0 + a_1 \log p_t + a_2 \log y_t + u_t \tag{2.5}$$

and the inverse semilogarithmic

$$\log c_t = a_0 + a_1 p_t + a_2 y_t + u_t \tag{2.6}$$

A more complete discussion of these and other forms of demand equations can be found in Klein and in Parks.[18] Relevant to that discussion are the deficiencies that static relationships suffer such as the failure to make a distinction of differences in demand response between the short run and the long run, the omission of possible links with inventory adjustment, and the exclusion of the influence of past levels of demand. For these reasons, we turn to the consideration of dynamic relationships.

Dynamic Adjustment Relationships

As a greater variety of commodity demand relationships are formulated and empirically tested, the increasing experience is that commodity demand behavior in many situations is more appropriately described dynamically. When income or prices change, commodity consumers do not respond immediately, nor do they delay their response. Rather, they spread their response over some period of time. Of course the nature of such response would vary from commodity to commodity, a major differentiating factor being the durability or perishability of the commodity of interest.

Consider the case of commodities which serve as an input to manufacturing or food processing industries. Various institutional and technological rigidities often prevent demand for these commodities from adjusting immediately to changes in their determining factors. The demand for lauric oils, for example, is not met by substitute oils as soon as the price of coconut oil increases. Technological methods have to be changed before these other oils impart similar qualities to the final product, be it in the soap or food category. Changes in the prices of coconut oil, therefore, influence consumption not only in the short run but also over the long run.

Of the different theories which have been proposed to explain such behavior, the most well known are those of Koyck and of Nerlove. Koyck would assume that a direct form of distributed lag exists between any dependent variable and one or more of its explanatory variables.[19] Such a relationship represents one type of the general class of distributed lag functions, in which the distributed lag weights can in principle take on any value. The exact distribution of the lag need not be known in advance but can be assumed, and later it can be refined on the basis of the results of estimation. An example of a demand function of the Koyck type is as follows, assuming that the lag weights decline geometrically

$$c_t = a_0 + a_1 \sum_{i=0}^{n} \lambda^i y_{t-i} + a_2 \sum_{i=0}^{n} \lambda^i p_{t-i} \tag{2.7}$$

where λ is defined as the reaction coefficient and takes on values $0 \leq \lambda < 1$. Estimated values of λ are normally obtained through the use of a transformed equation. This requires multiplying the above equation lagged one period by λ,

$$\lambda c_{t-1} = \lambda a_0 + a_1 \sum_{i=1}^{n} \lambda^i y_{t-i} + a_2 \sum_{i=1}^{n} \lambda^i p_{t-i}$$

and subtracting it from the original equation to obtain

$$c_t = a_0(1 - \lambda) + a_1 y_t + a_2 p_t + \lambda c_{t-1} \tag{2.8}$$

Equation 2.8 can be stated in terms of a set of composite coefficients that would result from estimation and a stochastic disturbance term.

$$c_t = b_0 + b_1 y_t + b_2 p_t + b_3 c_{t-1} + u_t \tag{2.9}$$

Since the parameters λ, a_0, a_1 and a_2 can be determined uniquely from b_0, b_1, b_2 and b_3, equation 2.8 is appropriately identified.

$$\lambda = b_3 \qquad a_1 = b_1$$
$$a_0 = b_0/(1 - \lambda) \qquad a_2 = b_2$$

Other forms of lag structures which might be useful in describing demand behavior can be found in a paper by Almon and more recently by Grilliches.[20] One useful aspect of the Koyck lag function is that it permits a distinction to be drawn between the short run and long run adjustments mentioned above. The estimates of b_1 and b_2 are the short run income and price coefficients and the values of $b_1/(1 - \lambda)$ and $b_2/(1 - \lambda)$ are the respective long run coefficients.

A similar form of explanation can be obtained following the dynamic theory of Nerlove.[21] Only now a more marked distinction is made between short run and long run demand, and demand in any period is assumed to adjust only partially towards desired or equilibrium demand. Nerlove would begin by considering the long run demand for a commodity which would exist if no demand rigidities were present

$$c_t^* = a_0 + a_1 y_t - a_2 p_t \qquad (2.10)$$

where c_t^* represents long run or equilibrium demand and the other variables are as previously defined. Since the actual values of equilibrium demand cannot be observed, equation 2.10 cannot be estimated directly. Thus it is necessary to introduce the postulate that the change in current consumption will vary in proportion to the difference between long run equilibrium consumption and past consumption

$$c_t - c_{t-1} = \delta(c_t^* - c_{t-1}) \qquad (2.11)$$

where δ is a coefficient describing the rate or speed of adjustment. This would imply that actual demand in a single period adjusts partially or only a fraction δ of the distance towards equilibrium demand. Equation 2.11 also implies that actual consumption is a distributed lag function of past desired or equilibrium consumption.

$$c_t = \sum_{i=0}^{t} \delta(1 - \delta)^i c_{t-i}^*$$

A dynamic equation suitable for estimation can be obtained by substituting the adjustment relationship 2.11 into the long run demand equation, and by eliminating the unobservable variable c_t^*. Witherell suggests a modification to the long run equation which would make it more appropriate in explaining the demand for commodities that are semidurable.[22] That is, a change in income variable Δy_t can be added to test the possibility that purchases of certain commodities might be deferred if income temporarily declines or they might be speeded up if income temporarily increases. To such an equation also should be added a price or other variable z_t to reflect competitive or complementary adjustment to another commodity or possibly to a group of commodities. Equation 2.10 now becomes

$$c_t^* = a_0 + a_1 y_t + a_2 \Delta y_t - a_3 p_t + a_4 z_t \qquad (2.12)$$

The final dynamic relationship is obtained upon performing the desired substitution

$$c_t - c_{t-1} = \delta a_0 + \delta a_1 y_t + \delta a_2 \Delta y_t - \delta a_3 p_t + \delta a_4 z_t - \delta c_{t-1}$$

which becomes

$$c_t = \delta a_0 + (1 - \delta)c_{t-1} + \delta a_1 y_t + \delta a_2 \Delta y_t - \delta a_3 p_t + \delta a_4 z_t$$

or

$$c_t = b_0 + b_1 c_{t-1} + b_2 y_t + b_3 \Delta y_t - b_4 p_t + b_5 z_t + u_t \qquad (2.13)$$

where u_t is the required stochastic disturbance term.

Values of the coefficient of adjustment and the short and long run elasticities of price and income can be easily obtained from this relationship, although one must be careful in interpreting the elasticity estimates. The coefficient of adjustment δ is obtained from $(1 - b_1)$, its value ranging between 0 and 1; it is interpreted such that the adjustment of consumption within a single period becomes more complete as the value of δ approaches 1. Confirmation of δ near 1 would refute the hypothesis that changes in the determining variables influence demand in future periods as well as the present period. Values of δ greater than 1 are not generally easy to interpret and imply overreaction by market participants.[23] The adjustment coefficient determines the relationship which should exist between the short run and long run elasticities of price and income. The short run elasticity of price is obtained by multiplying the coefficient of price b_4 by the ratio of the mean value of price and demand. A similar definition is used for the elasticity of income.

$$E_{ps} = b_4(\bar{p}/\bar{c}) \qquad E_{ys} = b_2(\bar{y}/\bar{c}) \qquad (2.14)$$

The long run elasticity in both cases results from dividing the right-hand side by the coefficient of adjustment.

$$E_{pl} = E_{ps}/\delta \qquad E_{yl} = E_{ys}/\delta \qquad (2.15)$$

There is some question as to the interpretation of these elasticities where δ may be biased either because of specification error or because of autocorrelation in the disturbances. The latter situation leads to an inconsistent estimate of the coefficient of the dependent lagged variable. Nerlove has suggested that in some cases the bias in δ need not influence values of the elasticities while in more critical cases the bias can be reduced through the use of an appropriate estimating procedure.[24]

Dynamic Differential Relationships

Houthakker and Taylor have developed a dynamic theory of demand which differs from the above in two respects.[25] To begin with, they recognize that the decision process underlying demand is actually undertaken more frequently than the typical quarterly or annual period of observation. Thus, they formulate their theory not only in terms of continuous time but also in terms of functional relationships expressed in the form of differential equations. Demand equations that formerly expressed behavior in terms of discrete time series now are stated in terms of the underlying continuous process.

A second difference is that the concept of demand adjustment is replaced by that of stock adjustment. Stock adjustment is used to explain the behavior of durable goods, and it can be extended to nondurable goods where habit formation is considered as an equivalent form of adjustment. It seems appropriate consequently that this theory can be used to explain the behavior of a wide class of commodities.

Formulation of the theory begins by distinguishing between the concepts of *state adjustment* relevant to the stock adjustment process, and *flow adjustment*.[26] The former implies that current consumption is influenced by past consumption as is reflected in the current value of "state variables" of which inventories are a prime example. The latter suggests that current consumption represents an attempt to adjust actual consumption closer to some desired level. The present discussion is concerned only with the theory of *state* adjustment; the notion of *flow* adjustment is taken up in regard to the specification of import functions.

The adjustment of consumption to a "state" variable such as stocks is expressed as follows

$$c(t) = a_0 + a_1 s(t) + a_2 y(t) \qquad (2.16)$$

where $c(t)$ and $y(t)$ are rates of demand and of income at time t respectively and $s(t)$ is the corresponding level of stocks. The notation now used refers to demand behavior as a continuous process. Equation 2.16 can be applied to either durable or nondurable commodities depending on the sign of the coefficient a_1. For durable goods, the rate of demand should decline as stock levels become larger and $a_1 < 0$. For nondurable goods, stock adjustment is replaced with the notion of habit formation, and $a_1 > 0$.

To develop this approach more completely, one must consider the rate of demand for stocks as being the sum of the rate of change in the physical or psychological stocks and of the depreciation of those stocks

$$c(t) = \frac{ds}{dt}(t) + \alpha s(t) \qquad (2.17)$$

where α represents a constant depreciation rate. It should be observed that a relationship exists between the value of a_1 given above and α. For durable goods, the rate of depreciation would be lower and this would correspond to $a_1 < 0$. For nondurable goods, the rate of depreciation is relatively higher and $a_1 > 0$. Thus, greater or less durability results in slower or more rapid depreciation as is reflected in the changing value of a_1.

While it might be desirable to expand our original expression for demand (2.16) to include this dual purpose of stock holding, the stocks of which we are speaking are difficult to observe. This applies either to the case of durables or to nondurables where they represent a form of psychological stock. Consequently, Houthakker and Taylor have derived an expression for demand that eliminates the stocks variable. This derivation is accomplished by differentiating equation 2.16 with respect to t

$$\frac{dc}{dt}(t) = a_1 \frac{ds}{dt}(t) + a_2 \frac{dy}{dt}(t)$$

and adding it to the original equation multiplied by α

$$\alpha c(t) = \alpha a_0 + \alpha a_1 s(t) + \alpha a_2 y(t)$$

such that

$$\frac{dc}{dt}(t) + \alpha c(t) = \alpha a_0 + a_1 \left[\frac{ds}{dt}(t) + \alpha s(t) \right] + a_2 \left[\frac{dy}{dt}(t) + \alpha y(t) \right]$$

The stock variable can be removed from this equation by combining it with expression 2.17.

$$\frac{dc}{dt}(t) = \alpha a_0 + a_1 c(t) - \alpha c(t) + a_2 \frac{dy}{dt}(t) + a_2 \alpha y(t)$$

$$= \alpha a_0 + (a_1 - \alpha)c(t) + a_2 \frac{dy}{dt}(t) + a_2 \alpha y(t) \qquad (2.18)$$

Since such an equation must be estimated in terms of discrete economic series, it must be converted to its discrete analog

$$\Delta c_t = a_0 + (a_1 - \alpha)c_t + a_2 \Delta y_t + a_2 \alpha y_t$$

which becomes

$$c_t = a_0 + (a_1 - \alpha)c_t + c_{t-1} + a_2 \Delta y_2 + a_2 \alpha y_t$$

or introducing the composite coefficients and the disturbance term

$$c_t = b_0 + b_1 c_{t-1} + b_2 \Delta y_t + b_3 y_t + u_t \qquad (2.19)$$

One disadvantage of this equation is that it does not include the price effect relevant to explaining demand behavior. By adding the price term $a_3 p(t)$ to equation 2.16, a final expression is reached similar to that proposed for the dynamic adjustment process in equation 2.13.

$$c_t = b_0 - b_1 c_{t-1} + b_2 \Delta y_t + b_3 y_t + b_4 \Delta p_t + b_5 p_t + u_t \qquad (2.20)$$

Elasticities of price and income comparable to those also reached in equation 2.13 can be derived from equation 2.18. The interpretation of the coefficients which Houthakker and Taylor apply to the latter equation is simply that of multipliers. If a_2 represents the short term multiplier of income on demand, then the long term multiplier would be given by

$$\frac{a_2 \alpha}{\alpha - a_1} \quad \text{where} \quad \frac{dc}{dt}(t) = \frac{dy}{dt}(t) = 0$$

For durable goods $a_1 < 0$, and

$$a_2 > \frac{a_2 \alpha}{\alpha - a_1} \qquad (2.21)$$

This would imply that the short run income effect is much greater than the long run effect. For the case of nondurable goods, $a_1 > 0$, and

$$a_2 < \frac{a_2 \alpha}{\alpha - a_1} \qquad (2.22)$$

Thus, the short and long run multiplier effects would be reversed.

Substitution Effects

The static and dynamic equations 2.2 and 2.13 called for the inclusion of prices and other variables which could account for any interdependence arising between a commodity of interest and complementary or substitute commodities. The inclusion of these variables can occur at the final demand level or at the level of derived demand where two or more commodities serve as interdependent in the production of a secondary good. Examples of substitutes at the final demand level are cocoa and coffee; possible substitutes at the derived demand level are aluminum and copper. As a first step to determining how best to specify demand equations to incorporate this interdependence, approaches to measuring complementarity and substitution must be investigated. The conventional approach is to determine the cross-elasticity of demand between related commodities and to evaluate the magnitude and sign of the elasticity. This measure indicates the effect on the commodity being demanded of a change in the price of some alternative commodity

$$\eta_{ij} = \frac{\Delta c_i}{c_i} \bigg/ \frac{\Delta p_j}{p_j} \tag{2.23}$$

where $\Delta p_j/p_j$ is the relative change in the price of some commodity j and $\Delta c_i/c_i$ is the resulting relative change in the demand for commodity i. When the commodities are substitutes, the sign of η_{ij} will be positive; and when the commodities are complements, the sign will be negative.

Another approach is to consider two commodities as inputs to a production process and to utilize the elasticity of substitution η_{ij}^* defined in terms of movements along an indifference curve.

$$\eta_{ij}^* = \left(\frac{\dfrac{\Delta c_i}{c_i} \quad \dfrac{\Delta p_i}{p_i}}{\dfrac{\Delta c_j}{c_j} \quad \dfrac{\Delta p_j}{p_j}} \right) = \left(\frac{\Delta c_i/\Delta c_j}{c_i/c_j} \bigg/ \frac{\Delta p_i/\Delta p_j}{p_i/p_j} \right) \tag{2.24}$$

Again, if the elasticity is positive, the related commodities are substitutes; if it is negative, the commodities are complements. This measure appears to be similar to that of 2.23 except for the inclusion of both relative price and relative quantity movements, but a number of other factors have to be considered in order that the elasticity of substitution may be interpreted correctly. In fact, it is difficult to reconcile theoretical and empirical interpretations of either measure, and readers are referred to the discussion of this problem in Leamer and Stern and elsewhere.[27]

A more thorough approach, where adequate data are available, is that of examining the interdependent nature of commodity demand within a full commodity system as implied by the generalized demand model 2.1. Attempts at empirical demand analysis utilizing this approach mentioned earlier include the work of Brandow, Barten, and George and King.[28] Its principal advantage is that it can provide uniform estimates of all direct and cross-price elasticities among a large group of commodities so as to minimize problems of isolating substitutes and complements.

Consider the approach of George and King, which relates the consumption of each commodity in a consumer budget system to its own price and to prices of each of the other commodities, and income[29]

$$c_{1t} = b_{10} + b_{11}p_{1t} + \cdots + b_{1j}p_{jt} + \cdots + b_{1n}p_{nt} + b_{1y}y_t$$

$$c_{2t} = b_{20} + b_{21}p_{1t} + \cdots + b_{2j}p_{jt} + \cdots + b_{2n}p_{nt} + b_{2y}y_t$$

$$\vdots$$

$$c_{it} = b_{i0} + b_{i1}p_{1t} + \cdots + b_{ij}p_{jt} + \cdots + b_{in}p_{nt} + b_{iy}y_t$$

$$\vdots \tag{2.25}$$

$$c_{nt} = b_{n0} + b_{n1}p_{1t} + \cdots + b_{nj}p_{jt} + \cdots + b_{nn}p_{nt} + b_{ny}y_t$$

$$c_{kt}^f = b_{k0} + b_{k1}p_{1t} + \cdots + b_{kj}p_{jt} + \cdots + b_{kn}p_{nt} + b_{ky}y_t$$

$$c_{mt}^{nf} = b_{m0} + b_{m1}p_{1t} + \cdots + b_{mj}p_{jt} + \cdots + b_{mn}p_{nt} + b_{my}y_t$$

where $p_{1t}, \ldots, p_{nt}$ = the complete set of prices, y_t = income, c_{kt}^f = total food consumption, and c_{mt}^{nf} = total nonfood consumption. Direct and cross-price elasticities corresponding to the coefficients of the above equations are obtained by transforming the data into logarithms and first differences of logarithms, and incorporating a number of restrictions. In general, the restrictions are those implied for the general demand model 2.1, excepting the addition of what has been termed the Frisch condition. If we consider the data transformation as providing the elasticity estimates (e_{ij}) directly from the regression coefficients (b_{ij}), the restrictions would be of the form

Homogeneity Condition:

$$e_{i1} + e_{i2} + \cdots + e_{if} + e_{inf} + e_{iy} = 0$$

Symmetry Condition:

$$e_{ij} = w_{ij}e_{ji} - w_j(e_{ij} - e_{iy})$$

Cournot Aggregation Condition:

$$w_1 e_{1j} + w_2 e_{2j} + \cdots + w_f e_{fj} + w_{nf} e_{nfj} = -w_j \tag{2.26}$$

Engel Aggregation Condition:

$$w_1 e_{1y} + w_2 e_{2y} + \cdots + w_f e_{fy} + w_{nf} e_{nfy} = 1$$

Frisch Condition:

$$e_{ij} = -\frac{1}{\phi} e_{iy} e_{jy} w_j - e_{iy} w_j \quad \text{for } i \neq j, \qquad \text{and}$$

$$e_{ii} = -e_{iy} w_i - \frac{1 - w_i e_{iy}}{\phi}$$

where w_i refers to the expenditure proportion weights for particular commodities, and ϕ designates separable groupings.[30] Interpretable are the direct price elasticity (e_{ii}), cross-price elasticity (e_{ij}), income elasticity (e_{iy}), total food elasticity (e_{if}), and total nonfood elasticity (e_{inf}).

The value of the George and King study can be seen in the favorable comparisons of the elasticities found using system 2.26 relative to those found in other studies. In terms of methodology they also introduced a two-stage maximization procedure, which yielded all direct and cross-price elasticities with respect to all commodities in the same separable group from a given demand equation. The implication of their results for empirical demand analysis are many as can be consulted in that study. Certainly the approach can be used to better specify substitution patterns in commodity models related to consumer items. Having examined several ways of measuring substitution elasticities, at the next stage we consider how the discovered substitution effects might be specified in individual demand equations.

System Specification

An attempt to incorporate the above system approach directly as a means of specifying substitution patterns within a commodity model can be found in the work of Wickens, Greenfield, and Marshall.[31] They have constructed a coffee model which explains the import demand for each type of coffee bean for each country where country imports vary according to the prices of four substitutable bean varieties. The methodology employed resembles the above except for the estimation procedure which stems from the work of Court and of Byron.[32] That procedure is based on Aitkens method of generalized least squares as featured in Zellner's work concerning the estimation of "seemingly unrelated regressions".[33] While the results achieved from the coffee import equations are interesting, the signs obtained for both the direct and the cross-price elasticities often diverge from *a priori* expectations. The authors have attributed this either to the possibility that consumers do not behave according to the tenets of classical demand theory or that demand reflects a rather complex adjustment process also involving the interaction of coffee processors.

Price Specification

Because of the prevalence of such difficulties and the extent of the work involved, several simpler approaches are advised as providing a useful alternative to specifying commodity interdependence within a commodity model. The incorporation of only several price variables into a single demand relationship represents the approach followed most frequently. These variables may be introduced in a variety of ways. Normally, one or two prices may be entered to reflect interdependence with one or two alternative commodities. Where the intention is to measure the relative change in demand between commodities, the variable to be introduced would be a price ratio containing the price of the commodity of interest and the price of the alternative commodity. Occasionally it is necessary to measure changes in demand relative to the influence of an entire class of commodities. The appropriate variable to introduce would then be a weighted price index reflecting the collective influence of those commodities. This practice has been found necessary, for example, in working with demand relationships for oils and fats markets where a large number of substitutes are normally available.[34]

Where the practice of commodity substitution is a less frequent occurrence, it might be preferable to introduce a dummy variable which normally equals zero, but which equals one for periods in which the price differential between two or more commodities is sufficient to encourage substitution. Should the substitution process reflect a cumulative one-way effect, the dummy variable could be compiled cumulatively. It should be added that although dummy variables have a clear interpretation in terms of representing shifts in demand, they suffer the disadvantage of describing substitution between commodities to be perhaps more abrupt than it really is.

Quantity Specification

Some concern has been expressed over the use of a quantity variable to represent the substitution effect of an alternative commodity in the demand equation of interest. However, it has been found that the introduction of a quantity variable is meaningful where it represents the consumption of a single commodity or a synthetic substitute.[35] One popular variation has been to formulate the quantity variable in the form of an index representing changes in market penetration. Where the evidence suggests that the substitution effect assumes the form of a shift in demand, it might prove useful to introduce a dummy variable such that the new variable represents the product of a quantity variable and the dummy variable. An example would be the case where the quantity of the substitute commodity influences demand once total market supply has exceeded a certain level. This situation is sometimes found in the oils and fats markets where commodity substitution might change substantially, once the world supply of oils and fats reaches a certain level. A problem with either the price or quantity approach is that they often do not identify any underlying causal relationships.

Technological Specification

Where the change in the quantity demanded appears to be a result of technological changes rather than economic factors, the substitution effect might be more appropriately explained by a variable representing time, such as trend, or a variable whose value depends on some function of time. This situation is apt to occur where the substitution effects are attributable to the growth of synthetic products. Such is the case, for example, of wool and noncellulosic fibers, lauric oils and synthetic alcohols, or natural rubber and synthetic rubber. While a time trend represents constant growth of technology for an industry, the more likely situation is that the change has been logistic or exponential.

The logistic approach has received increased attention in explaining the growth of synthetics and in measuring their diffusion or impact with respect to the market of a nonsynthetic commodity. Polasek and Powell, for example, have defined a variable representing the synthetic share of the wool market by fitting a logistic curve to the ratio of synthetic fibers consumption to total wool and synthetic consumption.[36] Similarly, Grilliches has used a logistic growth function to explain the rates at which hybrid seed corn was adopted in the United States.[37] Behrman has also found such a technological variable useful in explaining the impact of the supply of synthetic rubber on the demand for natural rubber.[38] Finally, the work of Mansfield should be emphasized because it represents the most thorough examination of technological change and of rates of diffusion and of adoption.[39] He would explain typical substitution effects involving logistic growth as an S-shaped curve in which the new technology is adopted initially at increasing rates throughout the industry, and then at decreasing rates once the technology becomes more common.

An appropriate method for introducing the impact of substitution through technological change into a consumption equation would be to specify a new variable that represents market share or market growth. As suggested above, simple trend variables or variables representing complex time functions could be used. For example, where the substitution effect occurs initially at an increasing rate and later at a decreasing rate, the substitution variable could be derived from a logistic function of the following form[40]

$$z_t = e^{a_0 - a_1(1/T)} \qquad (2.27)$$

or

$$\log z_t = a_0 - a_1 \frac{1}{T}$$

For the case where change occurs at a decreasing rate until some asymptotic limit or saturation level is reached, one can use a simple reciprocal transformation.

$$z_t = a_0 - a_1 \frac{1}{T} \qquad (2.28)$$

It would be worthwhile to experiment with different functional forms until a substitution effect is suitably described.

Demand as Imports

In the specifications developed for the demand equations thus far, demand has been viewed primarily as domestic consumption. Many commodity models, particularly those designed to explain international markets, require that a distinction be made between the demand for imports and current domestic consumption. The demand for imports, accordingly, should be divided into the quantity consumed currently, and the quantity used to replenish inventories. This can be better illustrated using a total market identity, which would equate consumption during period t to net imports and production during that period $+$ or $-$ the corresponding change in stocks.

$$c_t = m_t + q_t \pm \Delta s_t \qquad (2.29)$$

Since variations in both import demand and consumption demand are related to variations in income or output and prices, it would seem redundant to include both import and consumption equations in the same model. Deciding which set of equations to include normally can be solved by economic considerations. Consumption behavior might be the more important aspect of a model; consumption equations would then be included, with imports determined subsequently through an identity such as 2.29. Alternatively, a trade oriented model would require import equations, with consumption now being determined through an identity.

The theoretical basis for specifying import relationships does not differ significantly from that of specifying consumption equations except where it is necessary to include an explicit stock adjustment variable. A good discussion of these basic considerations can be found in Leamer and Stern or in Adams, et al.[41] The functional form to be adopted would be static or dynamic depending on the temporal response of imports to the explanatory variables or past values of imports. Confirmation of dynamic response would suggest a model similar to that of equation 2.13

$$m_t = b_0 + b_1 m_{t-1} + b_2 y_t + b_3 \Delta y_t - b_4 p_t + b_5 z_t + u_t \qquad (2.30)$$

where m_t is the quantity of imports in a given year and the other variables are as previously defined. Some changes in the definition of these variables may be necessary. The price variable, for example, may no longer be defined as the commodity wholesale price taken relative to a general price index but rather as the commodity import price divided by the corresponding domestic wholesale price.

Additional variables that might be included refer to foreign exchange reserves, financial assets, or to business cycle influences. The latter might be represented by a ratio reflecting the relation of current to normal inventories or by deviations from trend of industrial production. One could also introduce dummy variables to reflect sudden changes in international political conditions or changes in policy regarding tariff structures.

Import equations also can be formulated using the dynamic differential method. An example of the use of the latter is restricted to the flow adjustment process mentioned earlier.[42] The corresponding flow adjustment relationship defined in terms of imports would require the use of two separate expressions as described in continuous time

$$\frac{dm}{dt} = a_0 + (m^* - m) \qquad (2.31)$$

and

$$m^* = a_1 + a_2 y \qquad (2.32)$$

where dm/dt reflects the rate of import and m^* is desired imports. Combining these two expressions and transforming them to discrete time produces an equation suitable for estimation.

$$m_t = b_0 + b_1 m_{t-1} + m_2(y_t + y_{t-1}) \qquad (2.33)$$

An application of this relationship developed also to include a price term can be found in a study by Houthakker and Magee that estimates demand elasticities for both imports and exports with respect to income in the United States.[43]

The actual equation estimated is of the form

$$\log m_t = b_0 + b_1 \log m_{t-1} + b_2 \log(y_t + y_{t-1}) + b_3 \log(p_t + p_{t-1}) + u_t$$

(2.34)

where price and income appear as a two-year moving average, and the short run price and income elasticities can be determined directly from b_2 and b_3.[44] Also of interest is the application of Turnovsky, which explains total import demand for New Zealand.[45]

Highly related to the structuring of import and consumption relationships are the difficulties of measuring elasticities of demand as derived from the log-linear relationship

$$\log c_t = b_0 + b_1 \log p_t + b_2 \log y_t + u_t$$

(2.35)

where b_1 is the elasticity of demand with respect to price, which also has the interpretation $\dfrac{\Delta c_t/c_t}{\Delta p_t/p_t}$, and b_2 is the elasticity with respect to income also given by $\dfrac{\Delta c_t/c_t}{\Delta y_t/y_t}$. Unfortunately, these difficulties have been discussed extensively with so many controversies still remaining that a thorough evaluation of them is beyond the scope of this study.[46] We summarize instead only four major difficulties as originally pointed out by Orcutt.[47]

1. *Shifts in Commodity Demand and Supply Curves.* Shifts in these curves over time may cause the observed price-related observation points to be scattered such that fitting a line between these points would result in a greater slope than that associated with the true demand curve, understating the demand elasticity. Once this bias is discovered, however, Leamer and Stern suggest that meaningful elasticity estimates may be obtained where shifts in the supply curve are substantial relative to those of the demand curve, and/or the supply curve is highly elastic.[48]

2. *Errors of Observation.* Values of demand, price, and income used for estimation may contain errors of sampling and measurement; these errors can lead to different forms of bias in the demand elasticities depending on the proportional distribution of the errors among the variables. No simple restrictions can be applied here as for (1) that would compensate for the resulting bias, although some progress has been made concerning this difficulty by Kemp and by Heien.[49]

3. *Data Aggregation.* Commodities with relatively low price elasticities may also have substantial price variation; this condition will tend to influence the elasticities where the relevant prices are aggregated in the form of index

numbers. Orcutt observes that the exact nature of the influence will be to understate the corresponding true elasticity. Houthakker and Magee, however, come to opposite conclusions when using the same data over a longer time period.[50] This is a difficult problem to deal with and elasticity measurements under such conditions should be restricted to single commodities or to a small group of commodities, each possessing a low price variance.

4. *Short versus Long Run Elasticities.* The measurement of elasticities such as those given by 2.14 and 2.15 will normally result in the short run values being less than the long run values. Where this difference fails to appear consistently in empirical work, Nerlove and Heien suggest approaches for obtaining useful estimates at least for the long run values.[51] Interested readers are advised also to consult a number of other sources.[52]

Estimation of Demand Equations

A detailed discussion of the estimation of demand and other structural equations present in commodity models takes place in Chapter 6. It would be useful from the start, however, to point out some of the problems that arise in estimating demand functions and to suggest how these problems might be reduced through the use of appropriate estimation methods. There are two problems in particular which occur when estimating demand equations.[53] Both these violate one or more assumptions of Ordinary Least Squares (OLS) estimation. The first problem termed " simultaneous equation bias " appears when the demand variable c_t and the price variable p_t are simultaneously determined. The immediate result is that the price variable p_t and the disturbance terms u_t are likely to be correlated, leading to biased and inconsistent values of the estimated coefficients when using OLS. The second problem arises when a lagged value of the dependent variable appears as an independent variable in the regression. Even if the disturbance terms of such an equation are independent, the coefficients if estimated by OLS will be biased, although asymptotically efficient and consistent. How can demand equations be estimated given the likelihood of either problem?

Before suggesting more sophisticated approaches, it would be valuable to consider what merits still exist in using OLS. With respect to simultaneous equation problems, Fox has suggested that the nature of demand for certain agricultural commodities is such that the estimation of small models using OSL may still provide meaningful results.[54] Klein has also proposed that OLS may be suitable for international trade models where a country's imports may be small relative to the total world trade.[55] Since the trade of the country is relatively minor, world price may be taken as given. With respect to the lagged dependent variable problem, OLS can still provide meaningful results when the corresponding errors are not correlated. Rao and Miller indicate this to be particularly true for the case of small samples since no other estimation procedure has been shown to be better (in the sense of being "best").[56]

The methods of simultaneous equation estimation become useful for estimating demand functions where the total demand relationship includes a supply equation and possibly a stock adjustment equation. Not only are demand and prices intercorrelated but this interdependence extends to supply. Even here, however, estimation of individual equations by OLS may be appropriate. Reaching such a conclusion (as is explained in Chapter 6) results from performing tests regarding the causal ordering of the system variables. The decision to use OLS becomes crucial where the goal is to estimate demand elasticities of price and income as mentioned previously. Should OLS not represent a valid approach, then the "simultaneous equation bias" mentioned earlier can be reduced utilizing a number of possible methods such as Two-Stage Least-Squares, Limited-Information Maximum-Likelihood, or Three-Stage Least-Squares.

The methods of estimating dynamic equations become useful where the disturbance terms are not only correlated with the lagged dependent variable, but where they may also be autocorrelated. While the first condition results in bias of OLS estimates, the second condition causes the estimated coefficients also to be inconsistent. The estimation methods that can be recommended to cope with this problem will restore only consistency, although for large samples a portion of the bias may be reduced. In selecting a method the assumption which is made regarding the autoregressive nature of the disturbances is critical, and the discussion by Johnston is very helpful in this respect.[57]

The simplest assumption is that the disturbances follow a first order autoregressive scheme, $u_t = \rho u_{t-1} + e_t$. One can then utilize the Cochrane-Orcutt iterative technique or the scanning technique, both of which select the value of ρ designed to maximize the explained sums of squares in the equations and to restore the desired properties to the disturbance terms.[58] Other estimation methods of interest related specifically to demand equations are those of Zellner and Geisel and of Dhrymes and Mitchell.[59] Also see the papers of Wallis and of Sargen.[60]

Commodity Experience

Cobalt

The results presented by Burrows concern a special application of the dynamic relationship to explain end uses for cobalt in the United States.[61] The approach taken has been to consider a partial demand structure of the form suggested in equation 2.9.

$$c_t = b_0 + b_1 p_t + b_2 y_t + b_3 c_{t-1} + u_t \qquad (2.36)$$

Rather than estimate this equation directly, it is converted to the following form to permit the use of an independent price variable as a weighted average of present and past prices, the weights being selected according to the assumed shape of the lag distribution

$$c_t = b_0 + b_1 p_t + b_1 \lambda p_{t-1} + \cdots + b_1 \lambda^k p_{t-k} + b_2 y_t + v_t \qquad (2.37)$$

where $v_t = u_t + \lambda u_{t-1} + \cdots + \lambda^k u_{t-k}$. Burrows in experimenting with a variety of distributed lag structures found that an inverted V structure worked best. In fact, he has indicated that lag structures other than the Koyck lag are to be preferred in dealing with mineral commodities.[62] Most of his equations are estimated in log-linear form.

$$\log c_t = b_0 + b_1 \log p_t + b_2 \log y_t + b_3 \log c_{t-1} + u_t \qquad (2.38)$$

The distributed lag version of this equation would be

$$\log c_t = b_0 + b_1 \log p_t + b_1 \lambda \log p_{t-1} + \cdots + b_1 \lambda^k \log p_{t-k} + b_2 \log y_t + v_t \qquad (2.39)$$

where $v_t = u_t + \lambda u_{t-1} + \cdots + \lambda^k u_{t-k}$.

The exact way in which the equations are estimated to determine both short and long run elasticities b_1 and $b_1(1 - \lambda)$ follows from a procedure suggested by Grilliches and earlier by Sargan.[63] This procedure, which accounts for the fact that the presence of autocorrelated errors in equations with lagged endogenous variables can bias the estimates of the regression coefficients, operates in two stages. The first stage requires estimating an equation of the following form, which is simply a restatement of the unconstrained or distributed lag equations specified in 2.37 and 2.39.

$$c_t = a \sum_{i=0}^{m} \gamma^i p_{t-i} + \sum_{i=0}^{m} \gamma^i u_{t-i} \qquad (2.40)$$

Values of c_{t-1} predicted from this equation can then be used to estimate coefficients in the original dynamic function containing only one lag.

$$c_t = a p_t + \gamma \hat{c}_{t-1} + u_t \qquad (2.41)$$

It is believed that this procedure will yield a consistent estimate of the adjustment coefficient γ.

Burrows has estimated both linear and log-linear versions of the unconstrained equation where the distributed lag appears in prices but not in income. These results, together with the estimated short and long run elasticities for a sample of the demand equations estimated in that study, appear in Table 2-1. Note that the reported coefficient on the price variables appears

Table 2-1. Results Obtained for Dynamic Demand Equations: Cobalt

$$c_t = b_0 + b_1 \sum_{i=0}^{m} k_i p_{t-i} + b_2 y_t + b_3 z_t + u_t \text{[a]}$$

	Coefficients and t values for regressions				
Explanatory variables	Consumption in high speed steel	Consumption in super- alloys	Consumption in other alloys	Consumption in high temperature alloys[b]	Consumption in cemented carbides[b]
Intercept	0.401	0.371	4.98	−3.57	−2.00
	(2.56)	(2.71)	(2.79)	(−2.35)	(−5.20)
$\sum_{i=0}^{m} k_i p_{t-i}$	−0.103	−0.083	−1.50	−0.374	−0.466
	(−2.47)	(−2.47)	(−2.81)	(−1.94)	(−1.85)
y_t	0.178	0.158	0.007	0.547	0.881
	(1.08)	(1.17)	(2.34)	(5.38)	(4.93)
z_t	—	—	−0.145	0.422	—
			(−2.10)	(−3.05)	
Descriptive statistics					
R^2	0.66	0.66	0.82	0.89	0.90
DW	2.14	1.61	3.44	2.03	2.05
E_{ps}	−0.06	−0.04	−0.20	−0.02	−0.46
E_{pl}	−0.86	−0.69	−3.10	−0.37	−0.88

[a] $\sum_{i=0}^{m} k_i p_{t-i} =$

$0.063p_t + 0.126p_{t-1} + 0.189p_{t-2} + 0.252p_{t-3} + 0.189p_{t-4} + 0.126p_{t-5} + 0.063p_{t-6}$ for all equations except cemented carbides where the lag structure is $0.17p_t + 0.34p_{t-1} + 0.34p_{t-2} + 0.17p_{t-3}$.
[b] Equations estimate in log-linear form.
Source: James C. Burrows, *Cobalt: An Industry Analysis* (Lexington, Mass.: D. C. Heath & Co., 1971), pp. 191–192.

only in terms of the summation of the lag. All equations are estimated on the basis of annual data covering the period 1943–1967. These results show relatively high levels of goodness of fit as was true for most of the linear and log-linear demand functions estimated in the study. Realistic values were found for the short and long run price elasticities, although the long run elasticities were considered to represent an underestimate of the total elasticity which would also include technological change.

Wool

The model of the international wool market constructed by Witherell features dynamic relationships for both demand and production variables.[64] The demand sector contains eight country equations and a "rest of the world" equation that explains mill consumption of raw wool for each country plus net imports of semifinished and finished wool products. The dynamic equation that provided the basis for explaining net imports is similar to that of equation 2.13.

$$m_t = b_0 + b_1 m_{t-1} - b_2 p_t + b_3 y_t + b_4 \Delta y_t + b_5 z_t + u_t \qquad (2.42)$$

Results of estimating this equation are reported in Table 2-2 for the countries where the dynamic adjustment process was verified. Estimated coefficients have been obtained using 2SLS with annual data covering the years 1943 to 1964.

Table 2-2. Results Obtained for Dynamic Demand Equations: Wool
$$m_t = b_0 + b_1 m_{t-1} - b_2 p_t + b_3 y_t + b_4 \Delta y_t + b_5 z_t + u_t$$

	Coefficients and t values for regressions			
Explanatory variables	United States	Italy	Netherlands	Rest of World
Intercept	419.93	—	38.55	—
m_{t-1}	0.987	0.793	0.742	0.882
	(3.90)	(7.93)	(3.22)	(5.47)
p_t	−4.250	0.403	−0.122	−1.294
	(3.59)	(3.37)	(1.22)	(2.71)
y_t	0.167	0.696	−1.237	4.290
	(0.61)	(1.74)	(1.28)	(1.65)
Δy_t	9.298	—	—	−3.016
	(5.41)			(1.01)
z_t [a]	0.210	—	—	0.446
	(1.39)			(2.23)
z_t [b]	266.33	—	−38.058	—
	(2.81)		(3.80)	
Descriptive statistics				
R^2	0.85	0.57	0.64	0.96
DW	2.12	1.84	2.11	1.79
δ	0.121	0.207	0.258	0.118

[a] Substitution Effect Variable: Net consumption of noncellulosic fibres.
[b] Korean War Dummy Variable.
Source: William H. Witherell, *Dynamics of the International Wool Market: An Econometric Analysis*, Econometric Research Program Memorandum No. 91, Princeton University, 1967, pp. 151–163.

The adjustment process reported for the equations is slow, with the coefficient of adjustment possessing an average value of $\delta = 1 - b_1$ equal to 0.2. The significance of the various price and income variables is not particularly high, but many of the signs agree with what would be expected from theory. The substitution effect found to be significant in the United States and the rest of the world equations implies that an increase in the consumption of synthetics would lead to a decrease in natural wool consumption, as might be expected.

Zinc

Results are available regarding the application of the dynamic adjustment process to refined zinc demand from what appears to be a preliminary version of a world model. Banks has presented a series of demand relationships incorporating adaptive expectations in prices for the United States, United

Table 2-3. Results Obtained For Dynamic Demand Equations: Zinc

$$c_t = b_0 + b_1 c_{t-1} - b_2 p_t + b_3 y_t + b_4 \Delta_{y_t} + b_5 z_t + u_t$$

Explanatory Variables	Coefficients and t Values for Regressions		
	United States	F.R. Germany	United Kingdom
Intercept	242.17	119.85	122.7
c_{t-1}	0.489	0.334	0.439
	(2.49)	(1.15)	(4.78)
p_t	—	−0.254[a]	−0.180[a]
		(1.21)	(3.68)
y_t	2.171	1.170[a]	0.342
	(1.31)	(1.74)	(1.98)
Δy_t	12.736	—	4.12
	(3.46)		(7.15)
z_t	44.66	—	—
	(1.14)		
Descriptive Statistics			
R^2	0.91	0.88	0.96
DW	1.84	1.89	2.34
δ	0.510	0.666	0.561
E_{ps}	—	0.118	0.090
E_{pl}	—	0.178	0.160

[a] Variables lagged one period.

Source: F. E. Banks, "An Econometric Note on the World Zinc Market," Mimeographed, University of Uppsala, 1971.

Kingdom and the Federal Republic of Germany.[65] The form of equation estimated also follows that of 2.13. Equation results together with estimated elasticities and adjustment constraints are reported in Table 2-3. These are based on the OLS method using annual data for the period 1953–1968.

Analysis of the results indicate that the adjustment process is significant in two out of three equations with the coefficient of adjustment near 0.5. A reasonable degree of goodness of fit is found in each case, although a price response is lacking in the U.S. equation and no variable is significant in the F.R.G. equation.

Lauric Oils Demand

The previous example given regarding the adjustment process of the demand for lauric oils indicates that it would be useful to specify country demand relationships in the form of equation 2.13.[66] The output variable selected for each country consists of an index of edible and inedible product output of industries utilizing lauric oils. The substitution variable employed could not easily be specified because of the complex relationship existing between lauric oils and their likely substitutes.

This complexity can be attributed to three different factors. First, the nature of the substitution process appears to be a combination of economic, technical, and consumer preference effects. Second, lauric oils are used in a number of end uses such that any description of substitution effects would require detailed data regarding relative amounts of lauric and other oils consumed in the more important of these end uses. Finally, substitution effects previously experienced by the industry have not been substantial, since lauric oils have certain technical properties distinct from other oils and fats. These properties, however, are being duplicated to an increasingly greater extent.

After much experimentation it appeared that possible substitution effects might be detected by examining the price differentials which have existed between lauric oils and more closely related oils and fats such as palm oil or marine oils. Such an examination suggested that some substitution away from lauric oils has taken place when the differentials were particularly wide. For example, the relatively low prices of fish oil in 1962 encouraged technological transformations that would permit its adoption to some lauric uses. Consequently, the low fish oil prices of 1967 and 1968 saw it being introduced in even greater quantities.

A logical response to this situation, therefore, has been to introduce a substitution variable composed of price differentials or price ratios between lauric oils and such oils. In several cases, a dummy variable was used with values of 0 in years where the price differential indicated no substitution and

1 in years of likely substitution. For most of the consumption equations the different substitution variables proved significant, although the signs of the respective coefficients did not always agree with *a priori* reasoning.

Results of estimating consumption equations for the United States, United Kingdom, the E.E.C., Japan, and a "rest of the world" residual are reported below. The method of estimation used for the equations is OLS with annual observations covering the period 1953 to 1967. While the results obtained following simultaneous equation methods is presented in Chapter 6, the OLS method was considered practical for two reasons: (1) the sample size is small suggesting that no great improvements in consistency will be obtained using more sophisticated techniques, and (2) actual comparisons of parameters with those from more sophisticated methods do not reveal noticeable differences. The elasticities reported are obtained by adjusting the price coefficient.[a]

$$c_t^{us} = 89.77 + 0.379c_{t-1}^{us} + 0.100y_t^{us} - 165.87p_t^w$$
$$(2.37) \quad . \quad (3.80) \quad (-2.25)$$
$$\bar{R}^2 = 0.97,^b \quad D.W. = 2.85,$$
$$\delta = 0.621, \quad E_{ps} = -0.155, \quad E_{pl} = -0.249$$

$$c_t^{uk} = 76.73 + 0.588c_{t-1}^{uk} + 0.307y_t^{uk} - 259.25p_t^w - 36.42z_t^{uk}$$
$$(4.32) \quad (2.78) \quad (-2.57) \quad (-2.52)$$
$$\bar{R}^2 = 0.89, \quad D.W. = 1.88$$
$$\delta = 0.412, \quad E_{ps} = -0.411, \quad E_{pl} = -1.00$$

$$c_t^{ec} = 658.33 + 0.028y_t^{ec} - 0.196\,\Delta y_t^{ec} - 507.22p_t^w + 22.73z_t^{ec}$$
$$(11.19) \quad (-3.07) \quad (-4.11) \quad (2.11)$$
$$\bar{R}^2 = 0.73, \quad D.W. = 2.16,$$
$$\delta = 1.0, \quad E_{ps} = E_{pl} = -0.306$$

$$m_t^{jp} = 13.75 + 0.587m_{t-1}^{jp} + 0.24y_t^{jp} - 118.66p_t^w + 35.83z_t^{jp}$$
$$(3.76) \quad (1.67) \quad (-1.39) \quad (2.09)$$
$$\bar{R}^2 = 0.84, \quad D.W. = 2.67,$$
$$\delta = 0.413, \quad E_{ps} = -0.656, \quad E_{pl} = -1.590$$

$$m_t^{rw} = -537.86 + 5.438RT + 222.04p_t^w + 0.528x_t^w$$
$$(2.00) \quad (0.71) \quad (5.17)$$
$$\bar{R}^2 = 0.77, \quad D.W. = 1.46,$$
$$\delta = 1.00, \quad E_{ps} = E_{pl} = 0.144 \tag{2.43}$$

---

[a] A complete list of variables and their notations appears on page 156.

[b] R^2 is the coefficient of determination adjusted for degrees of freedom.

where $c_t =$ country consumption, $m_t =$ net imports for consumption[c], $y_t =$ output index, $RT =$ reverse trend, $p_t^w =$ world coconut oil price, $z_t^{uk} =$ ratio of coconut oil prices to palm and fish prices, $z_t^{ec} =$ coconut oil and fish oil dummy variable, and $z_t^{jp} =$ ratio of coconut oil to all other edible oil prices.

The dynamic equations provide an adequate explanation of demand for most countries. For the E.E.C. and Rest of World equations, the lagged dependent variable was not significant and a static explanation is used. Most of the predetermined variables are significant in the explanation with values of t above 1.79 or 1.81 required for significance at the 95 percent level with 11 or 12 degrees of freedom respectively. The values of the Durbin-Watson statistic found are less useful where equations contain lagged dependent variables but as a rough measure the values observed do not suggest strong autocorrelation in any of the equation disturbances.[d] The substitution variables are significant for two country explanations although the sign of the coefficient is negative, which was anticipated only for the United Kingdom. The change in output variable describing short term cyclical effects was removed from the United States, United Kingdom, and Japan equations where it was clearly insignificant. A significant but negative coefficient is obtained for this variable in the E.E.C. equation implying that manufacturers have adjusted to short run changes in output by consuming oils other than lauric oils. Values obtained for the short run and long run elasticities in the United States are almost identical to those obtained by Nyberg in an earlier study, -0.19 and -0.25 respectively.[67]

Conclusions

This chapter has attempted to review and to analyze a number of theories and approaches that can be used to improve the specification of commodity demand relationships. One principal outcome has been a confirming of the applicability of dynamic relationships in explaining changes in demand over time. Whereas this form of relationship had formerly been developed in terms of partial adjustment or distributed lags, Houthakker and Taylor have shown its usefulness when formulated in continuous time as state adjustment or flow adjustment. While the flow adjustment approach has been applied to aggregative commodity categories, the state adjustment approach has been utilized

---

[c] Japanese and Rest of World demand data could not be disaggregated beyond the import level.

[d] Values of the Durbin-Watson statistic relevant for determining the presence of autocorrelation in the lauric oils equation are those presented for $n = 15$ with the following possible parameters: $k = 1$, $d_u = 1.23$, $d_l = 0.95$; $k = 2$, $d_u = 1.40$, and $d_l = 0.83$; $k = 3$, $d_u = 1.61$, $d_l = 0.71$; $k = 4$, $d_u = 1.84$ and $d_l = 0.59$; $k = 5$, $d_u = 2.09$, $d_l = 0.48$. These values are taken at the 5 % level for significance points in two-tailed tests.

only with goods of personal consumption. Both these approaches offer potential for explaining commodity demand.

One major problem requiring further work is that of developing a methodology for specifying substitution patterns among commodities. Recent progress which would be of most use in future work involves that of analyzing interdependent demand systems and that of quantifying patterns of technological change. In either case, considerable preliminary analysis appears to be necessary, and this task becomes more difficult where a number of substitutes exist or where a commodity is employed in a large number of end uses.

A number of other problems also can be identified. The first of these relates to the fact that shifts in demand may result from factors other than economic ones, and it is difficult to adjust demand parameters to correspond to such changes. There is also the possibility of commodity demand functions being irreversible; Goodwin has proposed a solution for beef demand by incorporating lagged response coefficients that vary with phases of the business cycle.[68]

Another problem relates to the need to aggregate the demand for individual commodities or different forms or varieties of a commodity, and one should look to the theory of index numbers for a solution. Consumption data should refer to quantities purchased; where this is not possible, production data may be used only after it has been adequately adjusted for exports, imports, and changes in stocks. Finally, the demand for commodities is often simultaneously related to production and inventories, and methods of dealing with this interdependence will be taken up later in the discussion of complete models.

3 Supply

The nature of commodity supply is much more diverse than the nature of commodity demand. As shown in Table 3-1, commodities can be classified into four categories that reflect the different conditions surrounding production: (1) commodities of regular supply such as those which are mined or forested; (2) commodities whose supply fluctuates annually such as vegetables or cereals; (3) commodities whose supply originates from perennial crops such as cocoa or coffee; and (4) commodities whose supply fluctuates cyclically such as hogs and cattle. This diversity in the underlying conditions provides the starting point for presenting the economic and statistical theory relevant to explaining commodity supply. Supply relationships explaining both static and dynamic behavior are considered, the latter being divided to include annual supply, perennial supply, and cyclical supply. Also considered are export relationships as they refer to supply in the country of origin and to demand in the countries of destination. Empirical examples pertain to wheat, feedgrains, tungsten, and lauric oils.

Table 3-1. Commodities Classified According to Production Conditions

Regular Supply				Annual Supply		
Aluminum	Lead	Silver		Barley	Onions	Soybeans
Beer	Lumber	Steel		Corn	Peanuts	Sugar
Cadmium	Magnesium	Sulfur		Cotton	Potatoes	Tobacco
Chrome	Mercury	Tallow		Flaxseed	Rapeseeds	Wheat
Chromite	Milk	Tin		Jute	Rice	Wool
Coal	Molybdenum	Titanium		Oats	Rye	
Cobalt	Natural Gas	Tungsten			Sorghums	
Copper	Nickel	Uranium				
Gold	Petroleum	Vanadium		Perennial Supply		
Iron	Platinum	Zinc				
	Propane			Apples	Coffee	Oranges
				Asparagus	Dates	Peaches
Cyclical Supply				Bananas	Grapefruit	Pears
Broilers	Fish	Olives		Cherries	Grapes	Pepper
Cattle	Hides	Turkeys		Cocoa	Lemons	Rubber
	Hogs			Coconuts	Nuts	Tea

Supply Relationships

The theoretical and statistical development of commodity supply relationships has been described by Nerlove.[1] His review concentrates on the explanation of supply response for agricultural crops, beginning with the studies of Smith and of Bean published in 1928 and 1929. These works deal principally with the recognition of lagged response in describing the reaction between production and prices. Shortly afterwards, Block extended the study of the dynamic character of production processes, and Walsh concentrated on the refinement of price series to be used. By 1950 Kohl and Paarlberg developed some of those earlier theories and applied them to a wide range of agricultural commodities, stressing that farmers respond only partially to prices when planting. Beyond this period, the many advances that took place are best explained according to the different forms of supply relationships to be examined. But first, some background is necessary concerning the various factors known to influence commodity supply.

Background

Since the theory of supply expresses a general response of producers to a number of causal determinants, we can best begin by examining the major classes of those determinants: (1) economic, (2) ecological, (3) technological, (4) institutional, and (5) uncertainty. Each of these is discussed independently before being integrated within the static and dynamic relationships that follow.

Economic. Determinants of supply normally classified as economic relate to the process of acquiring inputs and selling products in the market. Most obvious are the market prices of a commodity and the prices of the inputs used in the related production process. One might also want to include the investment in the fixed or quasi-fixed factors associated with that process. Nerlove has provided a thorough explanation of investment factors and indicated how varying these factors over time might be used to draw the traditional distinction between short and long run supply response to price.[2] Examples of investments with different time horizons include buildings and machinery used immediately; trees which require a number of years before they begin to yield, or seeds consumed in production of the same.

Ecological. A number of different determinants can be listed as ecological. Most often they relate to yield levels and can include crop rotation and land use patterns as well as climatic conditions such as rainfall, humidity, or temperature. Geographical conditions might include fertility of soil or richness of ore deposits, and, most recently, minimization of environmental damage. A general characteristic of many of these factors is that they are often unpredictable. For example, some areas are subject to drought or typhoons, and it is not possible to determine when these events will occur.

Technological. In the past it was often assumed that technology does not produce any noticeable effect on supply in the short run; rather, it produces a more gradual effect detected only in the long run. Today there is reason to believe that the effect is otherwise, extending from the short to the long run according to the process of diffusion, mentioned in Chapter 2.[3] Once a supply innovation is introduced, it is utilized by more and more production units until all adopt it.

The impact of innovations on supply also would vary depending on the nature of the related industry involved. For example, innovations in mining may require substantial capital outlays such as purchases of labor saving machinery, while innovations in agriculture may necessitate only a smaller investment in new fertilization techniques. Oury, in addition, points out that evaluating the influence of technology necessitates choosing among several dominant technologies and combining their effects in view of their complementary nature.[4] Fertilization, for example, is only effective when a number of conditions are present, consequently one must measure its impact by integrating processes related to hydrology and biochemistry.

Institutional. Determinants normally classified as institutional relate to the nature of commodity policies, restrictions on international trade, or perhaps the social structure under which production is organized. While the effect of the more general institutional factors can be analyzed within the context of a complete commodity model, information that can be expressed in the form of continuous or dummy variables could be incorporated directly into supply relationships.

Uncertainty. Determinants influencing supply that reflect uncertainty in a commodity market or its surrounding environment are often expressed in the form of expectations. For example, when a producer decides what to put on the market, he must form a set of expectations about what he expects prices to be in the future. As the time horizon increases, the attempt to form expectations becomes even more difficult; such is the case of investing in a tree crop, which may not become productive for a number of years. Nerlove suggests a number of certainty equivalents that might transform expectational variables into ones which are measurable.[5] Among these are the extrapolative equivalent, which assumes that future values of a variable will relate to its past value; the adaptive equivalent, which suggests that previously perceived errors must also be taken into account; and the rational equivalent, which implies that predictions made will be consistent with the economic model or assumptions followed. More will be said later regarding the introduction of certainty equivalents.

Static Relationships

Just as the demand function derives from a set of maximization conditions under constraint, the supply relationship stems from the maximization of profits for a producing unit subject to the production function constraint.[6]

The satisfaction of these conditions requires that each producing unit be in competitive equilibrium with the real cost of a factor equalling its marginal productivity. Defined in terms of the underlying cost relationships, the supply curve of a market or industry represents the summation of that portion of the marginal cost curve lying above the average variable cost curve for individual producers. As distinguished from a production function, which describes the relationship between output and various inputs, a supply function is more concerned with the response of output to one or more prices. Static supply relationships which might be formulated to describe commodity behavior are normally of the following form

$$q_t = f(p_{1t}, p_{2t}, w_{1t}, \ldots, w_{kt}, u_t) \qquad (3.1)$$

where p_{1t} is the price of the commodity of interest; p_{2t} refers to the prices of inputs to the production process or to prices of other commodities closely related in production; $w_{1t}, \ldots, w_{kt}$ normally represent noneconomic determinants such as technological or institutional factors; and u_t is a stochastic disturbance term.

A special form of static supply relationship sometimes employed derives from the class of Cobb-Douglas production functions. Such a relationship would be multiplicative or nonlinear in the following form

$$q_t = b_0 \, z_{1t}^{b_1} \, z_{2t}^{b_2} \, u_t \qquad (3.2)$$

where z_{1t} and z_{2t} refer to levels of inputs, prices, or to appropriate exogenous variables. Some form of cost or price variable is necessary in order for the equation to describe conventional supply response. Equation 3.2 normally is transformed to log–linear form to facilitate estimation.

$$\log q_t = \log b_0 + b_1 \log z_{1t} + b_2 \log z_{2t} + u_t \qquad (3.3)$$

Other possible transformations are the semilog or square root forms

$$q_t = \log b_0 + b_1 \log z_{1t} + b_2 \log z_{2t} + u_t \qquad (3.4)$$

or

$$q_t = b_0 + b_1 z_{1t}^{1/2} + b_2 z_{2t}^{1/2} + u_t \qquad (3.5)$$

The extension of these equations to polynomials or more complex forms of transformation is thoroughly discussed in Heady and Dillon.[7] An econometric interpretation of the equations can be found in Johnston.[8]

A final form of static supply relationship would link output to changes in the number of producing units and/or changes in output per producing unit. Oury discusses the general relationship proposed for this purpose based on the identity

$$q_t = d_t \cdot y_t \qquad (3.6)$$

where d_t = number of trees, acres or other producing units and y_t = average yield per tree, per acre or other producing unit.[9] Because of the general tendency of crop yield data to exhibit an inverse semilog trend when plotted over time, the yield component of the identity can be represented by an equation of the form

$$\log y_t = b_0 + \sum_{i=1}^{n} b_i z_{it} + u_t \qquad (3.7)$$

The number of producing units corresponding to this yield could then be taken as given or explained by means of a linear or inverse semilog trend.

$$\log d_t = b_0 + \sum_{i=1}^{n} b_i z_{it} + u_t \qquad (3.8)$$

Where both yield and numbers are determined nonlinearly, it might prove more efficient to estimate the supply function directly in inverse semilog form.

$$\log q_t = b_0 + \sum_{i=1}^{n} b_i z_{it} + u_t \qquad (3.9)$$

Both of these variations have been used in practice.[10]

Dynamic Relationships—Annual Supply

Dynamic relationships of the adjustment and general distributed lag form discussed in Chapter 2 can be used to explain the supply response of all the classes of commodities featured in Table 3-1 (see above). The history of development of this approach begins with applications to crops planted and harvested annually, and Nerlove is largely responsible for advances made in this area.[11] More recent confirmations of the usefulness of this approach can be found in studies by the U.S.D.A. and in works by Behrman, and by Fisher and Temin.[12]

Describing annual supply response in adjustment form begins with the stipulation that producers anticipate what they expect to be the planned long run or equilibrium level of supply. Planned or desired supply can be explained as follows

$$q_t^* = a_0 + a_1 p_t^* + a_2 z_t \qquad (3.10)$$

where $q_t^* =$ desired supply, $p_t^* =$ expected future price of the commodity of interest, and z_t is as previously defined. Dynamic adjustment is introduced through the assumption that supply cannot change immediately in response to new economic conditions so as to reach levels planned for the same period. The actual change in supply in season t is only a fraction δ of the planned or equilibrium change in supply.

$$q_t - q_{t-1} = \delta(q_t^* - q_{t-1}) \tag{3.11}$$

The fraction δ also known as the coefficient of adjustment can be said to measure the speed with which actual supply adjusts in response to the factors influencing planned supply. Sometimes these factors are also included explicitly in the above equation by including a variable such as w_t reflecting ecological, technological, or other noneconomic influences.

$$q_t - q_{t-1} = \delta(q_t^* - q_{t-1}) + a_3 w_t \tag{3.12}$$

Combining equation 3.12 with 3.10 yields an equation in which the supply variables are represented only in terms of their actual or statistically observable quantities.

$$q_t = \delta a_0 + \delta a_1 p_t^* + \delta a_2 z_2 + a_3 w_t + (1 - \delta)q_{t-1} \tag{3.13}$$

The price variable is now the only variable left in expectations form. Nerlove indicates that it can be removed by making certain assumptions regarding the manner in which producers form their price expectations.[13] These assumptions are expressed in terms of expectations models or certainty equivalents as given below, the more important being the extrapolative model of Goodwin, the adaptive model of Cagan, and the rational model of Muth.[14] The most simple model is that of *naive expectations*, where the current expected price equals the previous actual price.

$$p_t^* = p_{t-1} \tag{3.14}$$

Simple weighted expectations relates expected price to a weighted combination of the two previously observed prices.

$$p_t^* = \beta p_{t-1} + (1 - \beta)p_{t-2} \tag{3.15}$$

Only slightly more complex is the model of *extrapolative expectations*, where expected price is a function of previous actual price plus or minus a fraction of the previous price change.

$$p_t^* = p_{t-1} + \beta(p_{t-1} - p_{t-2}) \qquad -1 < \beta < 1 \tag{3.16}$$

Adaptive expectations introduces the influence of previous forecast error implying that current expected price differs from the past expected price by an amount proportional to the previous forecast error.

$$p_t^* - p_{t-1}^* = \beta(p_{t-1} - p_{t-1}^*) \qquad 0 < \beta < 1$$

or

$$p_t^* = p_{t-1}^* + \beta(p_{t-1} - p_{t-1}^*) \tag{3.17}$$

The *rational expectations* model is not summarized here because of the complexities of translating this model into observable variables. Equation 3.13 can now be stated in terms of observable variables by adopting one of those models such as that of naive expectations.

$$q_t = \delta a_0 + \delta a_1 p_{t-1} + \delta a_2 z_2 + a_3 w_t + (1 - \delta)q_{t-1}$$

With the coefficients expressed in composite form, the equation to be estimated would be

$$q_t = b_0 + b_1 p_{t-1} + b_2 z_t + b_3 w_t + b_4 q_{t-1} + u_t \tag{3.18}$$

Since the difference between the q_t and q_t^* can be interpreted as the difference between short run and long run supply adjustment, the results obtained from estimating equation 3.18 or similar versions can be interpreted in terms of both short run and long run elasticities on price and other variables. Why this should be so has been explained in relation to the dynamic demand equations of the previous chapter. The short and long run price elasticities of producers' response, for example, are given by

$$E_{ps} = b_1(\bar{p}_{t-1}/\bar{q}_t) \qquad \text{and} \qquad E_{pl} = E_{ps}/\delta \tag{3.19}$$

Similar to the demand model, the coefficient of adjustment δ provides the link between the short and long run elasticities.

Dynamic Relationships—Perennial Supply

Development of the dynamic relationship in explaining the output from perennial crops can be traced to the works of Ady, Bateman, Behrman, Chan, French and Bressler, French and Matthews, and Stern.[15] The production process associated with perennial crops differs considerably from that of annual crops. There is a long gestation period between planting and first output; output from a single planting period continues for some time; and yields of the crop eventually decline. Relationships designed to explain this behavior, therefore, must account for the planting and removal of crops as well as for lags between planting and output.

French and Matthews recently have presented a rather broad analytical framework for constructing such relationships. This framework would stipulate that perennial supply response can best be described by incorporating five possible components:

(1) a pair of functions that explain the quantity of production and bearing acreage desired by growers, (2) a new plantings function defined by the adjustments that would shift acreage toward the desired level, (3) an equation to explain acreage removed each year, (4) relationships between unobservable expectation variables and observable variables, and (5) an equation that explains year-to-year variations in the values of average yields.[16]

The net acreage existing in any year would be determined by a combination of components (2) and (3), and total production is obtained by multiplying the resulting equation by the yield equation.

Perhaps the greatest difficulty in applying this framework is the frequent lack of planting and removal data. Thus the authors suggest a shortcut in which the acreage adjustment component is estimated directly after substituting appropriate expectations relationships. This simpler approach is elaborated further here, following the method of Bateman that consists of only two components: (1) a *planting relationship*, which describes the forces which motivate farmers to plant, and (2) an *output relationship*, which links the output harvested to the acreage planted.[17] The only drawback is that for most applications of this approach one must follow the crude assumption that the plants or trees of interest have an infinite life. However, this is not too serious a problem for the case of tree crops where the yield of the trees is maintained over a substantial number of years.

The Planting Relationship. Bateman considers four planting response models that relate to the economic forces that motivate farmers to plant.[18] Any of these can be combined with the general output relationship to be presented later. The first of these, known as the *gross investment* model, relates crop investment as acreage planted to two different sets of expected prices

$$d_t = a_0 + a_1 p_t^* + a_2 z_t^* \tag{3.20}$$

where

$$p_t^* = \sum_{i=0}^{n} \tilde{p}_{t+i}/n + 1$$

$$z_t^* = \sum_{i=0}^{n} \tilde{z}_{t+i}/n + 1$$

and d_t = number of acres planted in year t, $\tilde{p}_{t+i}$ = the expected real producer price in year $t = i$ of the commodity of interest, $\tilde{z}_{t+i}$ = the expected real producer price of an alternative commodity and, n = expected age after which crops or trees planted in t cease to bear. It is also assumed that producers form their expectations on the basis of previous actual prices as follows

$$p_t^* - p_{t-1}^* = \beta(p_t - p_{t-1}^*) \tag{3.21}$$

$$z_t^* - z_{t-1}^* = \beta(z_t - z_{t-1}^*) \tag{3.22}$$

The expectation variables can be removed from the first equation by substitution to obtain the following

$$d_t = a_0 \beta + a_1 \beta p_t + a_2 \beta z_t + (1 - \beta)d_{t-1} \tag{3.23}$$

This model does provide the required functional relationship between planting and prices, but Bateman is concerned that it may not be correctly price responsive.

As an alternative, he offers two forms of *stock adjustment* models, both phrased in terms of tree crops. The first is concerned with the *actual stock* of trees as they relate to the previously given price variables

$$s_t = a_0 + a_1 p_t^* + a_2 z_t^* \tag{3.24}$$

where s_t = the total stock of trees in year t. This expression can be combined with 3.21 and 3.22 to obtain an equation suitable for estimation.

$$s_t = a_0 \beta + a_1 \beta p_t + a_2 \beta z_t - \beta s_{t-1} \tag{3.25}$$

The second form is concerned with the *desired stock* of trees, also as a function of prices.

$$s_t^* = a_0 + a_1 p_t^* + a_2 z_t^* \tag{3.26}$$

This equation is then combined with a relationship that implies partial adjustment in the planting process

$$s_t - s_{t-1} = \delta(s_t^* - s_{t-1}) \tag{3.27}$$

such that

$$s_t = a_0 \beta \delta + a_1 \beta \delta p_t + a_2 \beta \delta z_t + (1 - \beta - \delta)z_{t-1} - \beta \delta s_{t-2} \tag{3.28}$$

This model normally is preferred to the first two because it recognizes the constraints the farmer faces in attempting to adjust his stock of trees and also includes a suitable price response variable. Its deficiency rests in its assumption of infinite tree life.

The fourth model posed is a *liquidity* model, which includes the influence of the income received by the producer in the previous year, v_{t-1}.

$$d_t = a_0 + a_1 p_t^* + a_2 z_t^* + a_3 v_{t-1} \qquad (3.29)$$

It is believed that the price effects produced in this model when combined with equation 3.21 and 3.22 would be sufficiently strong to prevent output adjustments from being overwhelmed by the income effect.

The Output Relationship. The model that most ably represents the relationship existing between output and planting is based on the mathematical identity existing between these two variables and can also include certain economic and ecological factors. This model begins by defining the potential output $\bar{q}_t$ of a crop in terms of yields and acreage planted

$$\bar{q}_t = \sum_{i=k}^{\infty} (y_i \cdot d_{t-i}) \qquad (3.30)$$

where y_i = the potential average yield of the crop in year t of acres d planted in $t - i$, and k = the age at which the planted trees become productive. Actual output q_t then relates to potential output plus the above related factors

$$q_t = a_0 + a_1 \bar{q}_t + a_2 p_t + a_3 w_t \qquad (3.31)$$

where p_t and w_t are as previously defined. Actual output can now be stated in terms of past prices by inserting into equation 3.30 one of the previously derived equations describing the acres planted d_{t-i} or the stock of trees s_{t-i}.

Alternatively, Bateman suggests that equation 3.30 may be transformed into a first order difference equation that eliminates all past plantings. This would permit the supply relationship to be estimated based on variables that relate to a crop's or tree's period of growth and decline. Further differencing or substitution will simplify the final relationship even further.

Dynamic Relationships—Cyclical Supply

The early development of supply relationships to be used with commodities where production fluctuates cyclically is based on Ezekiel's work with the cobweb model.[19] By now, the usefulness of this approach has been confirmed in the works of Waugh, of Nerlove, and of Harlow.[20] Another approach which can be taken to explain cyclical supply behavior is a deterministic one based on different forms of harmonic models. Examples of commodities to which either approach is appropriate include hogs,[21] cattle,[22] broilers,[23] and fish.[24]

Cobweb Models. The simplest model for describing cyclical commodity behavior is that of the cobweb. This model normally generates supply cycles of a two-year variety; supply begins in one period and is realized only in the next. The supply relationship featured in the model is a recursive one with supply in the current period determined by price in the previous period, where that price is based on the previous level of demand which also equals supply.

$$q_t = (p_{t-1}, z_{1t}, \ldots, z_{kt}, u_t) \tag{3.32}$$

Chapter 7 shows that the solution of the model containing this equation results in an expression capable of explaining cyclical behavior

$$q_t = b_2 + b_3 \bar{p} + b_3 \left(\frac{b_3}{b_1}\right)^{t-1} (p_0 - \bar{p}) \tag{3.33}$$

where p_0 is the initial price at which the system is in steady state and $\bar{p}$ is the equilibrium level of price given by $\bar{p} = \dfrac{b_2 - b_0}{b_1 - b_3}$. Supply would oscillate continuously for values of $b_3/b_1 = -1$, the period of oscillation being determined from the modulus of the latent roots of the system solution.[a]

Harmonic Models. These represent a special case of supply relationships where production is explained purely deterministically rather than on the basis of economic factors. Since it is rare for economic variables to exhibit purely deterministic behavior, this model has not been widely used to the present. However, several studies such as those of Abel and of Waugh and Miller have shown it to work reasonably well in explaining the supply of hogs and of fish.[25]

We define the basic harmonic model as

$$q_t = a_0 + a_1 \cos \omega t + a_2 \sin \omega t \tag{3.34}$$

where a_1 and a_2 refer to amplitudes of the cyclical components and ω is the frequency of the harmonic. The latter sometimes is written in terms of the period of occurrence, the period being the inverse of the frequency, i.e., $\omega = 2\pi f = 2\pi/P$. A slightly more sophisticated version would permit us to test

---

[a] A complete description of the solution of the system together with definitions of the parameters and conditions of oscillation appears in Chapter 7, pp. 170–172.

whether the amplitudes of the cycle have been changing over time or whether there has been a shift in the cyclical pattern[26]

$$q_t = a_0 + (a_1 + a_1't)\sin\left(\frac{2\pi t}{12} + \phi\right) + (a_2 + a_2't)\cos\left(\frac{2\pi t}{12} + \phi\right) \quad (3.35)$$

where $a't$ is a linear trend term used to determine the rate of change in amplitude over time and ϕ is a phase-angle used to reveal movements in cyclical patterns such as a shifting seasonal.

Estimating a model of this form suitable for explaining commodity supply requires careful interpretation of the time-series graph of the data. Once an appropriate period is selected, the equation in its simpler form can be estimated using regression methods to determine the amplitudes of the cyclical components, a_1 and a_2. If the possibility exists of a trend in amplitude, equation 3.35 can be estimated where the coefficients are expanded. If a phase shift seems possible, different values of ϕ can be substituted into the equation until the goodness of fit is optimal or an alternative procedure followed. This entire process becomes more complicated where it appears that the time series reflects a complex cyclical pattern generated by several different frequency components. In this case, graphical analysis must be used to decompose the complex cycle, and the resulting more elaborate equation can be estimated only where a substantial number of observations exist.

Supply as Exports.

So far, the different forms of supply equations discussed relate to supply as emanating from actual sources of production. Certain commodity models, especially those constructed on an international basis, require that a distinction be made between country supply and country exports. These variables are usually linked through the identity that exports during period t = production during that period $-$ consumption during that period $+$ or $-$ the change in stocks.

$$x_t = q_t - c_t \pm \Delta s_t \quad (3.36)$$

Similar to the discussion of demand as imports in Chapter 2, strong economic reasons normally exist as to whether both supply equations and export equations will be estimated as behavioral in a single model, or whether one set of equations will be estimated and the other determined through identities. Where the model builder prefers to concentrate on export behavior, export equations can be included following the different theories of supply behavior presented above, and supply can be determined subsequently through an identity such as 3.36. Where the desire is to incorporate both supply and export behavioral equations, it is possible instead to base the latter equations on the demand and market situation in the corresponding countries of destination. Specifying such equations would obviously require that the explanatory variables be demand oriented, including factors such as export price variables measured relatively to prices of competing countries, pressure of demand in importing countries, business cycle indicators, policy variables, or certain dummy variables describing strikes, devaluations, etc.[27] The export demand approach to specification has been used infrequently in the construction of commodity models, but its application is likely to increase as more models become trade oriented.

Estimation of Supply Equations

The problems dealt with in estimating supply equations are similar to those related to demand equations as discussed on pages 25 to 26, but in some sense they are more intractable because long production or adjustment periods often lead to serious autocorrelation difficulties in the equation disturbances. Most of the discussion of the estimation of dynamic equations presented in Chapter 2 including simultaneity is relevant here, and there is no need to repeat it. With respect to the possibility of serious autocorrelation, Fisher and Temin recommend that a form of the Cochrane-Orcutt or iterative scanning techniques be used in estimating supply equations.[28] Certainly the more recent of the estimation procedures designed for the same purpose also would be appropriate.

Commodity Experience

Static Supply

Examples of earlier applications of static theory to explain commodity supply are well summarized in a study by Knight.[29] Of particular importance are: (1) Foote's description of the supply of livestock and livestock products within his model of the feed-livestock economy; (2) Cromarty's formulation of supply equations for milk, eggs, and wheat in his aggregate model of U.S. agriculture; and (3) Cochrane's study of the supply of potatoes. More recent applications relate to countries where data may be of insufficient quantity and quality to permit the construction of more sophisticated models or to particular commodities where the static model well describes actual supply behavior.

As an example of the latter, Oury shows that where supply is known to depend strongly on acreage and yield factors, optimal predictions of supply can be obtained by combining estimates based on separate acreage and yield equations.[30] In his study explaining the supply of wheat and feed grains in France, he reports results of estimating such equations. Factors found to be most influential in explaining yield are environmental or seasonal effects, aridity, prices, and fertilizer applications. Factors used to explain acreage planted are principally climate and prices. The original study contains a large number of yield and acreage equations, many of equally good quality, but only a sampling of those results can be reported here. The method of estimation employed throughout is OLS, and results are based on annual data covering the years 1946 to 1961.

Equations representing wheat yield and acreage variables are

$$y_t^w = 656.52 - 28.259z_{1t} - 9.163z_{2t} + 1066.3p_t^w + 2.945c_t$$
$$\quad\quad\quad (-1.60) \quad\quad (-4.52) \quad\quad (2.99) \quad\quad (8.98)$$
$$R^2 = 0.91, \quad D.W. = 2.54$$

$$d_t^w = 1893.4 - 1.719z_{3t} - 199.04z_{1t} + 2160.5p_t^w - 0.0083q_{t-1}$$
$$\quad\quad\quad (-1.28) \quad\quad (-11.44) \quad\quad (5.92) \quad\quad (-0.513)$$
$$R^2 = 0.93, \quad D.W. = 2.18$$

where z_{1t} = winter effect, z_{2t} = aridity index, z_{3t} = fall aridity index, p_t^w = deflated wheat price, c_t = nitrogen fertilizer consumption, and q_{t-1} = lagged annual wheat production. Similarly, the expressions for feedgrain are

$$y_t^f = -746.3 + 49.638z_{1t} + 2.3266z_{2t} + 1221.9p_t^f + 3.297c_t$$
$$\quad\quad\quad (3.08) \quad\quad (1.93) \quad\quad (2.30) \quad\quad (11.52)$$
$$R^2 = 0.94, \quad D.W. = 2.15$$

$$d_t^f = 4115.5 + 1.5101z_{3t} + 136.75z_{1t} + 0.198z_{4,\,t-1} - 2245.7p_t^{wb} - 1105.9p_{t-1}^{wc}$$
$$\quad\quad\quad (1.13) \quad\quad (8.76) \quad\quad (5.98) \quad\quad (-4.26) \quad\quad (-2.58)$$
$$R^2 = 0.95, \quad D.W. = 2.13$$

where $z_{4,\,t-1}$ = lagged number of livestock units on farms, p_t^f = deflated average price of feedgrains, p_t^{wb} = wheat-barley price ratio, and p_{t-1}^{wc} = lagged wheat-corn price ratio.

The quality of these and other equations constructed can be reviewed in Oury's study with respect to the results obtained in predicting the impact upon French agriculture of varying grain adjustment policies within the European Economic Community.

Dynamic Supply

There has been extensive application of the dynamic adjustment relationship in explaining commodity supply. We have cited a number of studies earlier; others appear in the bibliography. While it would be interesting to analyze more traditional applications in agriculture, we examine instead the work of Burrows dealing with applications to a commodity of regular supply—tungsten.[31] The particular value of his work is the expansion of the dynamic relationship to include a number of different shapes in the pattern of the distributed lags. He begins with a Koyck lag which specifies that output must be a distributed lag of past prices

$$q_t = a_0 + a_1 \sum_{i=1}^{\infty} \lambda^i p_{t-i} \qquad 0 \leq \lambda < 1 \qquad (3.37)$$

where successive values of the lag coefficient λ decline geometrically. This expression is simplified by first lagging it one period and by multiplying it by λ

$$\lambda q_{t-1} = \lambda a_0 + \lambda a_1 \sum_{i=1}^{\infty} \lambda^i p_{t-i}$$

and then subtracting this equation from the original

$$q_t = [(1 - \lambda)a_0 + \lambda a_2] + a_1 p_t + \lambda q_{t-1}$$

The final equation to be estimated is of the form

$$q_t = b_0 + b_1 p_t + b_2 q_{t-1} + b_3 z_t + u_t \qquad (3.38)$$

where z_t is an exogenous factor as previously given and where the original parameters can be uniquely determined from the estimated parameters. A second set of equations is then estimated in which the distributed lag on prices is of the inverted V form previously explained in Chapter 2.[32] Each of these equations directly incorporates the lag structure on prices as follows.

$$q_t = b_0 + b_1 \sum_{i=0}^{m} \lambda_i p_{t-i} + b_2 z_t + u_t \qquad (3.39)$$

Results of applying equations 3.38 and 3.39 to explain the supply of tungsten appear in Table 3-2. The period of estimation is 1947 through 1968.

Table 3-2. Results Obtained for Dynamic Supply Equations: Tungsten

$$q_t = b_0 + b_1 p_{1t} + b_3 p_{2t} + b_2 q_{t-1} + b_4 z_t + u_t \quad \text{and}$$

$$q_t = b_0 + b_1 \sum_{i=0}^{m} \lambda_i p_{1,t-i} + b_2 \sum_{i=0}^{m} \lambda_i p_{2,t-i} + b_3 q_{t-1} + b_4 z_t + u_t$$

Explanatory Variables	Coefficients and t Values for Regressions			
	Brazil	Portugal	Burma	Spain
Intercept	0.788	2.087	4.18	15.23
	(0.55)	(1.46)	(0.96)	(2.41)
p_{1t}	0.280	0.858	—	—
	(3.68)	(4.14)		
p_{2t}	−0.0072	−0.0124	—	—
	(−0.86)	(−1.31)		
$\sum_{i=0}^{m} \lambda_i p_{1,t-i}$	—	—	1.24	2.61
			(4.63)	(5.59)
$\sum_{i=0}^{m} \lambda_i p_{2,t-i}$	—	—	−0.97	−3.43
			(−1.03)	(−2.57)
q_{t-1}	0.661	0.393	—	—
	(2.06)	(2.04)		
z_{1t}	—	—	−0.85	−1.62
			(−2.55)	(−2.53)
z_{2t}	—	—	—	−1.47
				(2.59)
Descriptive Statistics				
R^2	0.79	0.89	0.81	0.76
$D.W.$	—	—	1.80	1.02
E_{ps}	0.41	0.48	0.13	0.65
E_{pl}	1.21	0.79	1.24	2.01

Source: James C. Burrows, *Tungsten: An Industry Analysis* (Lexington, Mass.: D. C. Heath & Co., 1971), pp. 149–51.

Koyck equations are shown for Brazil and Portugal and inverted V equations for Burma and Spain. The former two equations contain current price variables for tungsten p_{1t} and tin p_{2t}, while the latter feature a lag distribution on each of the price variables taken separately. Burrows found the Koyck lag distribution preferable in only several cases, whereas the inverted V distribution worked well for countries with mines of similar size and for countries with mines of a smaller size and a greater geographical distribution.

Lauric Oils Supply

The dynamic relationship also has been applied extensively to explain perennial supply. Table 3–3 summarizes a variety of applications pertaining to different tree crops. Also of interest is the work of Bateman and of French and

Table 3-3. Results Obtained For Dynamic Supply Equations: Cocoa, Coffee, Lemons, and Rubber

Crop and country or region	Period	Elasticity[a] Harvest	Short run	Long run	Source
Cocoa					
Ghana	1930–40		0.43		Ady, 1949
Ghana	1920–39	0.17			Stern, 1965
Ghana	1920–46	0.15			Stern, 1965
Nigeria	1920–45		1.29		Stern, 1965
Ghana (Model No. 1)					
Ashanti	1949–62		0.42		Bateman, 1965
Brong-Ahafo	1949–62		0.87		Bateman, 1965
Central	1946–62		0.44		Bateman, 1965
Eastern	1946–62		0.32		Bateman, 1965
Volta	1946–62		0.61		Bateman, 1965
Western	1946–62		0.71		Bateman, 1965
Ghana (Model No. 3)					
Central	1946–62		0.51	1.28	Bateman, 1968
Eastern	1946–62		0.39	0.77	Bateman, 1968
Volta	1946–62		0.53	1.06	Bateman, 1968
Western	1946–62		0.31[e]	0.68[e]	Bateman, 1968
Ghana (Model No. 3)	1947–64			0.71	Behrman, 1966
Nigeria (Model No. 3)	1947–64			0.45	Behrman, 1966
Ivory Coast (Model No. 3)	1947–64			0.80	Behrman, 1966
Cameroun Republic (Model 3)	1947–64	0.68		1.81	Behrman, 1966
Brazil (Model No. 3)	1947–64	0.53		0.95	Behrman, 1966
Ecuador (Model No. 3)	1947–64			0.28	Behrman, 1966
Dominican Republic (Model 3)	1947–64	0.03		0.15	Behrman, 1966
Venezuela (Model No. 3)	1947–64	0.12		0.38	Behrman, 1966
Coffee					
Brazil					
São Paulo[b]	1930–55		2.02		Arak, 1967
São Paulo[b]	1930–55		2.28		Arak, 1967
Espirito Santo	1927–55		0.08	0.54	Arak, 1967
Minas Gerais	1927–55		0.20	0.28	Arak, 1967
Parana	1945–62			0.96	
Colombia[c]	1947–65		0.47		Bateman, 1968
Colombia[d]	1952–65		0.84		Bateman, 1968
Lemons					
California	1947–60	No Estimates			French and Bressler, 1962
Rubber					
Malaysia					
Estates	1953–60	0.0			Stern, 1965
Smallholders	1953–60	0.02			Stern, 1965
Estates	1951–61	−.02[e,f]			Chan[h]
Smallholders	1948–61	0.12[f]			Chan
Estates	1954–61	0.03[e,g]			Chan
Smallholders	1953–60	0.34[g]			Chan

Footnotes on page 52

Matthews mentioned earlier.[33] Our concern in this section is with the usefulness of this approach for explaining the supplies of lauric oils emanating from the major exporting countries.[34] Following the previous structuring of the perennial relationship, the planting component or relationship is formulated first and the output relationship second.

The Planting Relationship

The number of trees or acres to be planted in coconut trees is assumed to be a function of expected prices and the existing stock of trees

$$d_t = a_0 + a_1 p_t^* + a_2 s_{t-1} \qquad (3.40)$$

where d_t = trees or acres newly planted, s_t = trees or acreage at time t, p_t^* = mean value of an expected stream of future prices, and $d_t = s_t - s_{t-1}$. It would be preferable to adjust tree or acreage figures for tree mortality, but little useful data are available regarding the age structure of existing trees. To replace the expected price variable with an actual price variable, an additional assumption must be made regarding price expectations. Normally introduced at this point is the assumption that changes in producers' prices from one year to the next will be the most important factor influencing planters' expectations. More particularly, the difference between expected price in two successive periods is

---

Footnotes for Table 3–3

a Three different price elasticities are distinguished for perennials. The first is the farmer response at harvest time to the current price. This response occurs over a time period too short for new plantings to come into bearing. The second is the response of planting or output to lagged prices without taking into account a Nerlovian adjustment mechanism. The long-run estimate allows for adjustment lags, provided they are real.

b Different models were used by Arak for São Paulo. The first utilized new acres planted as the dependent variable, while the second utilized new acres as a proportion of the total stock of trees.

c Output data are from the Colombian National Accounts and the price series is the producer price, deflated by a cost-of-living index for Manizales.

d The output data are from FAO publications, and the price series is the minimum producer price guaranteed by the government, which is deflated by a cost-of-living index for Colombia.

e Not significant at 10 per cent level.

f Based on annual data.

g Based on monthly data.

h Reported in C. R. Wharton, "Rubber Supply Conditions," *Studies in the Malayan Economy*, T. H. Silcock (Ed.) (Canberra: Australian National Press, 1963).

Source: Reprinted from Clifton R. Wharton, Jr., editor: *Subsistence Agriculture and Economic Development* (Chicago: Aldine Publishing Company, 1969), p. 251; copyright © 1969 by Aldine Publishing Company. Reprinted by permission of Aldine Publishing Company.

proportional to the difference between actual and expected prices in the previous period.

$$p_t^* - p_{t=1}^* = \beta(p_{t-1} - p_{t-1}^*) \qquad 0 < \beta < 1 \tag{3.41}$$

This expression can be written in terms of expected prices

$$p_t^* = p_{t-1}^* + \beta(p_{t-1} - p_{t-1}^*)$$

and the plantings equation 3.40 becomes

$$d_t = a_0 + a_1[p_{t-1}^* + \beta(p_{t-1} - p_{t-1}^*)] + a_2 s_{t-1} \tag{3.42}$$

The expected price variable can be removed from the planting relationship by lagging equation 3.40 and performing the following transformation

$$d_{t-1} = a_0 + a_1 p_{t-1}^* + a_2 s_{t-2}$$

or

$$a_1 p_{t-1}^* = d_{t-1} - a_0 - a_2 s_{t-2}$$

Upon substitution

$$d_t = a_0 + [d_{t-1} - a_0 - a_2 s_{t-2}] - \beta[d_{t-1} - a_0 - a_2 s_{t-2}] + a_1 \beta p_{t-1} + a_2 s_{t-1}$$

which becomes

$$d_t - (1 - \beta)d_{t-1} = a_0 \beta + a_1 \beta p_{t-1} + a_2 s_{t-1} - a_2(1 - \beta)s_{t-2} \tag{3.43}$$

The Output Relationship

The potential output of coconuts is assumed to be the result of plantings in recent years. Potential output $\bar{q}_t$, therefore, is related to all past tree numbers or acreage planted weighted by the average per unit yield in any year i, y_i

$$\bar{q}_t = \sum_{i=k}^{\infty} (y_i \cdot d_{t-i}) \tag{3.44}$$

where k is the number of years after planting at which the tree becomes productive. This expression can be given a more specific form because of the particular yield pattern known to exist for tree crops such as coconuts. This

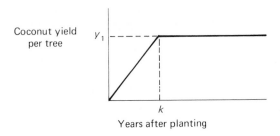

Figure 3–1. Coconut Tree Yield Profile.

pattern is illustrated in Figure 3-1 where output is low for the first $k - 1$ years of a tree's life, but then suddenly reaches a plateau which can be considered the effective yield of the tree. For coconut trees, the effective yield is reached after approximately eight years and continues for approximately 50 to 60 years. There is some evidence that the yield peaks again after approximately 12 years, but the increase is not sufficiently dramatic to warrant a more complex yield pattern. As indicated earlier, data regarding the age of existing trees are not available, and one, unfortunately, must disregard tree mortality. This necessitates the crude assumption that the effective yield is maintained indefinitely. The relationship for potential output can now be restated as

$$\bar{q}_t = y_1 \sum_{i=k}^{\infty} d_{t-i} \tag{3.45}$$

where y_1 is the per unit yield at the first year of full production with production remaining at a plateau afterwards. A further simplification can be made by substituting $d_t = s_t - s_{t-1}$ to obtain potential output in terms of the total number of trees of acreage planted.

$$\bar{q}_t = y_1 s_{t-k} \tag{3.46}$$

The relationship describing actual output can be formulated in terms of potential output together with climatic and economic factors. Climatic factors influencing coconut production include rainfall and humidity, particularly during the formative "dry season" of coconut growth. Although no useful humidity data were available for this study, data could be found describing rainfall over the year and during the "dry season." Abeywardena notes that the harvest of coconuts for a year is influenced by the rainfall of at least one year previously.[35] The effect of rainfall is thus considered in terms of a lagged rainfall variable, r_{t-1}. The choice of economic factors to be used also was limited; it has seemed most useful to introduce only a current producer price variable p_t, which could be said to reflect the current costs of gathering and marketing nuts. Combining these factors, actual output can be expressed as

$$q_t = \bar{q}_t + e_1 r_{t-1} + e_2 p_t$$

or

$$q_t = y_1 s_{t-k} + e_1 r_{t-1} + e_2 p_t \tag{3.47}$$

Other variables, which have not been included here but which might be contained in future work, are those reflecting the influence of government policies and randomly occurring events such as typhoons or crop disease.

Some Empirical Results

The planting and output equations can be combined to obtain an expression suitable for estimation. One can easily transform equation 3.47 to obtain an expression for q_t by forming a first order difference equation.

$$\Delta q_t = y_1 d_{t-k} + e_1 \Delta r_{t-1} + e_2 \Delta p_t \tag{3.48}$$

It is then a matter of performing certain transformations and substitutions to reach a final expression for exports. Begin by stating equation 3.48 in terms of d_{t-k} and lagging the same one period.

$$y_1 d_{t-k} = \Delta q_t - e_1 \Delta r_{t-1} - e_2 \Delta p_t \tag{3.49}$$

$$y_1 d_{t-k-1} = \Delta q_{t-1} - e_1 \Delta r_{t-2} - e_2 \Delta p_{t-1}$$

Also lag equation 3.43 by k periods

$$d_{t-k} - (1 - \beta)d_{t-k-1} = a_0 \beta + a_1 \beta p_{t-k-1} + a_2 s_{t-k-1} - a_2(1 - \beta)s_{t-k-2}$$

Replace the expression in d_t by equations 3.49

$$[\Delta q_t - e_1 \Delta r_{t-1} - e_2 \Delta p_t] - (1 - \beta)[\Delta q_{t-1} - e_1 \Delta r_{t-2} - e_2 \Delta p_{t-1}]$$
$$= y_1 a_0 \beta + y_1 a_2 s_{t-k-1} - y_1 a_2(1 - \beta)s_{t-k-2} + y_1 a_1 \beta p_{t-k-1}$$

Rearrange

$$\Delta q_t - (1 - \beta)\Delta q_{t-1} = y_1 a_0 \beta + y_1 a_1 \beta p_{t-k-1} + y_1 a_2 s_{t-k-1}$$
$$- y_1 a_2(1 - \beta)s_{t-k-2} + e_1 \Delta r_{t-1} + e_2 \Delta p_t$$
$$- [(1 - \beta)(e_1 \Delta r_{t-2} + e_2 \Delta p_{t-1})]$$

Substitute from 3.47 lagged one and two periods

$$y_1 s_{t-k-1} = q_{t-1} - e_1 r_{t-2} - e_2 p_{t-1}$$

$$y_1 s_{t-k-2} = q_{t-2} - e_1 r_{t-3} - e_2 p_{t-2}$$

such that

$$
\begin{aligned}
\Delta q_t - (1 - \beta)\Delta q_{t-1} = {}& y_1 a_0 \beta + y_1 a_1 \beta p_{t-k-1} + a_2[q_{t-1} - e_1 r_{t-2} - e_2 p_{t-1}] \\
& - a_2(1 - \beta)[q_{t-2} - e_1 r_{t-3} - e_2 p_{t-2}] + e_1 \Delta r_{t-1} \\
& + e_2 \Delta p_t - [(1 - \beta)(e_1 \Delta r_{t-2} + e_2 \Delta p_{t-1})] \quad (3.50)
\end{aligned}
$$

This produces an equation in twelve variables counting the autoregressive term, Δq_{t-1}. With the data available for the exporting countries covering only the years 1953 to 1967, the number of available degrees of freedom relevant to least squares estimation becomes very small. To help overcome this difficulty, both Ady and Bateman have made the assumption regarding the adjustment coefficient that coconut farmers form their expectations naively, i.e., $p_t^* = p_{t-1}$.[36] This assumption is adopted here; the coefficient β as defined in equation 3.41 equals 1 and equation 3.50 becomes

$$
\Delta q_t = y_1 a_0 + y_1 a_1 p_{t-k-1} + a_2 q_{t-1} - a_2 e_1 r_{t-2}
$$
$$
- a_2 e_2 p_{t-1} + e_1 \Delta r_{t-1} + e_2 \Delta p_t + u_t \quad (3.51)
$$

now including a stochastic disturbance term.[b]

Several adjustments are necessary in selecting data to estimate this equation for the three major exporting countries: the Philippines, Ceylon, and Indonesia. The best rainfall data selected would be that describing the months of "dry season," but such data could be compiled only for the Philippines. That data, as well as the annual rainfall data employed for Ceylon and Indonesia, are appropriately weighted according to the output of individual producing regions within each country. Exports data had to be used in preference to inadequate supply data, with adjustments made to account for smuggling. Finally, the price data selected for the producers' price variable suffered two limitations: First, only prices describing exports rather than production proved to be adequate for the Philippines and Indonesia; and second, the available series proved to be sufficiently long to test the hypothesis that coconut farmers plant in response to expected prices only for the Philippines and Ceylon.

---

[b] It is hoped that the assumption $\beta = 1$ may be verified in future work. Bateman in later work was able to provide a better estimate for β.

The preliminary tests of equation 3.51 which took place have been based on the above data and also included a variation whereby the price variable corresponding to the gestation lag is replaced by one reflecting the relative influence of the world coconut oil price. The results of these tests showed, first, that no form of supply response to prices could be observed when the price variable was lagged successively from six to twelve years and, second, that no improvement in explanation could be obtained when world prices or a differential between world and country export prices replaced the given price variable. To a great extent, the first result agrees with the opinions of experts who find no particular expectations patterns being followed on a long run basis, although improved data may produce a different outcome.

As a consequence of these tests, we discuss further only the results of estimating a modified version of equation 3.51 in the following form

$$\Delta x_t = y_1 a_0 + a_2 x_{t-1} - a_2 e_1 r_{t-2} - a_2 e_2 p_{t-1} + e_1 \Delta r_{t-1} + e_2 \Delta p_t + u_t$$

or

$$\Delta x_t = b_0 + b_1 x_{t-1} - b_3 r_{t-2} - b_4 p_{t-1} + b_5 \Delta r_{t-1} + b_6 \Delta p_t + u_t \quad (3.52)$$

This equation has been estimated utilizing the OLS and Cochrane-Orcutt techniques, with the results of the latter presented here. The estimated coefficients and the descriptive statistics obtained are as follows.

$$\Delta x_t^{ph} = 131.26 - 0.914 x_{t-1}^{ph} + 0.132 r_{t-2}^{ph} + 3.86 p_{t-1}^{ph} + 0.179 \Delta r_{t-1}^{ph} + 4.61 \Delta p_t^{ph}$$
$$(-3.42) \qquad (1.35) \qquad (303) \qquad (4.25) \qquad (1.90)$$

$$\bar{R}^2 = 0.85, \qquad E_{p_{t-1}} = 0.11, \qquad \rho = 0.40$$

$$\Delta x_t^{cy} = 1.38 - 1.34 x_{t-1}^{cy} + 0.103 r_{t-2}^{cy} - 574.52 p_{t-1}^{cy} + 0.066 \Delta r_{t-1}^{cy} - 306.17 \Delta p_t^{cy}$$
$$(-8.05) \qquad (7.72) \qquad (-3.25) \qquad (7.55) \qquad (-2.54)$$

$$\bar{R}^2 = 0.94, \qquad E_{p_{t-1}} = -0.25, \qquad \rho = 0.40$$

$$\Delta x_t^{in} = -386.94 - 1.40 x_{t-1}^{in} + 0.154 r_{t-2}^{in} + 12.34 p_{t-1}^{in}$$
$$(-6.32) \qquad (2.28) \qquad (3.53)$$

$$+ 0.029 \Delta r_{t-1}^{in} - 19.15 \Delta p_t^{in}$$
$$(0.57) \qquad (-2.90)$$

$$\bar{R}^2 = 0.72, \qquad E_{p_{t-1}} = 0.56, \qquad \rho = 0.20$$

The levels of adjusted $\bar{R}^2$ discovered are moderately high for the three equations, and most of the coefficients on the predetermined variables are significant. The most noticeable deficiency appears to be the negative sign and the greater than one value of the lagged dependent variable, but a similar outcome can be found in the published results regarding cocoa and coffee. The negative price coefficients found in the Ceylon equation also differ from our initial expectation. As was true for the coffee equations, the negative sign could imply that producers increase output when prices fall so as to maintain their income; they also may not be able to harvest additional amounts when prices rise.[37] This same situation is reflected in the change in price variable for Indonesia.

The most positive results concerning the equations are in terms of the variables describing rainfall and prices. The rainfall coefficients are, for the most part, highly significant; rainfall exerts a strong influence on coconut production, as has been stressed both here and in other studies. Furthermore, coconut production is shown to be influenced by rainfall not only during the entire year but particularly during the "dry season"; the effect of both variables extends up to two years prior to the year of harvest. The elasticities of price computed by adjusting the coefficient for p_{t-1} at the sample mean indicate that the flexibility of adjusting exports of copra or oil to prices is not high. Although no other published information is available for directly comparing these elasticities, Nyberg reports an elasticity of 0.29 close to the 0.11 found for the Philippines, based on an equation linking tree numbers and current prices.[38]

Conclusions

In this chapter we have shown how the demand side of a commodity model can be complemented through specification of the supply side. From a theoretical point of view, the forms of specification which can be best used relate to the nature of commodity supply: regular, annual, perennial, or cyclical. The econometric relationships selected as applicable to these different forms include the static, dynamic, perennial, and harmonic models. The dynamic adjustment model is recommended for explaining annual or regular supply. Perennial supply is best described by combining the dynamic adjustment model with one that determines the optimum capital stock so as to solve the stock formation and adjustment problems at the same time. The most important need in adapting these models to particular commodities appears to be correctly identifying the nature of response lags and gestation lags. Other tasks include correct specification of yield curves over time as well as accounting for removals or replacements in tree crops. However, simpler perennial models can be formulated which disregard the more difficult to obtain yield and tree numbers data.

A considerable number of practical problems remain to be solved in constructing supply equations, no matter which of the above methods is used.

For many commodities data are inadequate, not only for yields and numbers and age distribution of trees, but also for production, fertilizer applications, weather indexes, etc. Also, not much evidence has been accumulated to help estimate and interpret elasticities of response. The need exists to determine elasticities for a number of commodities in many countries so as to provide useful benchmarks for comparison. Explaining supply behavior based on aggregate data becomes a problem where individual producing units respond quite differently. Finally, it is necessary to expand explanations of supply to include the noneconomic factors mentioned in the first part of this chapter. No approach has yet been devised to introduce the impact of technological change in the form of a diffusion process, as for the case of the demand equations.

Factors of investment and uncertainty are just beginning to be explored in greater depth. The prospects are for developing a theory of supply which would combine them as well as technological factors according to the theory of optimal capital accumulation under uncertainty.

4 Inventories

Developing a sound theory of commodity inventory behavior is most essential to describing the workings of commodity markets. Inventory adjustment represents an important mechanism whereby short run price equilibrium is reached for commodities where consumption or production or both are price inelastic within a given time period (the likelihood of such inelasticity increasing as the time period of interest becomes shorter). If, for example, a time period is so short that consumption and production cannot be varied, then a high price would normally cause some stockholders to sell inventories, driving prices downwards until sales and purchases are in equilibrium. At any point in time, we would like to explain the level of inventories held. Our interest is with the transactions, precautionary and speculative motives for holding commodities, and their appearance in modern inventory theories including the modified flexible accelerator, buffer stocks, and the supply of storage. These theories will be considered at the level of disaggregation of consumers' and producers' inventories, with empirical examples provided from studies related to coffee, linseed oil, wool, and lauric oils.

Nature of Commodity Inventories

A major problem in defining and explaining commodity inventory behavior is that inventories have been recorded as being held by one or two groups of market participants, whereas each of these groups contains participants who accumulate inventories for different purposes, with one or more of these purposes overlapping between groups. Typical inventory holders include consumers, processors, producers, and a combination of dealers, brokers, wholesalers, and others vaguely classified as speculators. Yet a consumer as well as a producer may possess inventories for transaction, precautionary, or speculative reasons. This would not impose a serious problem, for example, if the data regarding producers' inventories are divided to reflect transactions motives and speculative motives separately, but accounting systems seldom report inventory data even at the level of disaggregation of producers and consumers.

For commodities where better data are available, the published groupings include: (1) commercial stocks held in consuming countries, (2) supply or carryover stocks held in producing countries, (3) warehouse stocks, (4) stocks in bond, and (5) buffer stocks or government stockpiles. Where surveys have been taken or data obtained directly from manufacturers or processors, the groupings are raw materials, goods in process, or finished goods.

Because data at the national level can only crudely reflect the motives of major groups of stockholders, it is no wonder that theoretical and empirical studies in this area have been so few. In discussing inventory behavior further, it would be best to think that the data might be arranged at least according to the following classes, where the major participants are listed in order of importance.

1. Consumers
   a. Manufacturers
   b. Processors
   c. Importers, wholesalers, or dealers
2. Producers
   a. Source suppliers
   b. Exporters, wholesalers, or dealers
   c. Processors
3. Speculators
   a. Dealers or brokers
   b. Holders of stocks in transport or in ships afloat

Our approach in examining the various theories of inventory behavior is to concentrate on the first two classes.

Consumer Inventory Relationships

The Accelerator

The simplest known explanation of inventory behavior is the accelerator, according to which inventories vary directly and proportionately with output. Although normally applied in cases of manufacturers who are final consumers of certain commodities, it might also be applied to processors classified as producers. Clark is one of the first to present this theory and Abramovitz developed it more thoroughly, stressing its relevance to commodity behavior.[1] The accelerator can be stated in two different forms: first that commodity inventories should rise or fall with sales or manufacturing activity, and second that the rate of change of stock holding should vary directly with the rate of change of this activity

$$s_t = \alpha y_t \tag{4.1}$$

and

$$\frac{ds_t}{dt} = \alpha \frac{dy_t}{dt} \tag{4.2}$$

where s_t and y_t represent appropriate stock and output variables respectively.

Abramovitz offers a number of reasons as to why such a proportionality should exist. Basically, they relate to the need to hold stocks for pipeline or reserve purposes. Manufacturers need stocks to meet production goals efficiently; they also need stocks to avoid delays, providing for continuity in production. To some extent, stocks are also accumulated as protection against loss from price fluctuations. The only drawback to the accelerator appears to be in the time lag likely to take place between inventory buildup and sales of output. Abramovitz suggests that a minimum lag must exist in a given industry between a peak in manufacturing activity and a peak in commodity stocks. The lag would vary from two to four months should stocks be obtained domestically, or from four to six months should stocks be obtained from abroad. Domestic sources would include manufacturers or processors, farms, forests, mining industries, or importers. The length of either lag would vary depending on the extent to which the stocks are influenced by the size of a harvest or crop.

Testing this theory has yielded some results for a number of commodities based on pre-World War II data, including cotton, silk, hides, newsprint, lead, petroleum, sugar, and rubber. Table 4-1 summarizes these results where the conformity and timing of stock and manufacturing activity cycles are measured by NBER chronology. Abramovitz found that his results could neither strongly confirm nor reject the hypothesis that manufacturers keep a constant ratio between stocks and output. Though a significant positive conformity between the cycles could be found for the first five commodities in that table, this conclusion appears to be restricted to commodities where rates of supply can be controlled. More crucially, however, timing was not noticeably coincidental for any of these commodities and the hint of a lag in stocks behind manufacturing activity is confirmed.

The Flexible Accelerator

Using the simple accelerator as a means of explaining commodity stocks brings up several problems. To begin with, the presence of a lag as suggested by Abramovitz does not controvert the theory, but it certainly makes the theory less applicable to more than manufacturers' inventories where the lag can be closely measured. When the data utilized in testing the theory are highly aggregated over space or over time, this problem becomes more severe. Among other criticisms of the accelerator, Goodwin found that it did not account for business firms attempting to adjust inventories only partially to what their equilibrium level should be during a particular period.[2] Lundberg and Metzler have criticized that it does not consider that errors made by firms in forecasting future sales can cause discrepancies to arise between the actual

Table 4-1. Commodity Inventories. Conformity to Manufacturing Activity Cycles, and Timing at Turns in Manufacturing Activity

Commodity Inventories	At Peaks in Activity				Over Full Cycle
		Number of		Av. lead (−) lag(+) months	Index of conformity to activity
	leads	lags	coin.		
Raw cotton at mills	3	5	0	+1.5	+62
Raw silk at mfr.	1	3	0	+0.5	+100
Raw cattle hides at tanners	2	2	0	+1.2	+71
Newspring at and in transit to pub.	0	4	0	+9.8	+100
Lead at warehouses	2	2	1	+3.0	+100
Refinable petroleum in pipelines and at tank farms and refineries	0	2	1	+3.7	+14
Raw Sugar at refineries	4	3	0	−4.4	−20
Crude rubber in and afloat for U.S.[a]	1	1	0	+1.0	−71
Sum of first five series with significant positive conformity	8	16	2		
	At Troughs in Activity				
Raw Cotton at mills	0	6	1	+5.1	
Raw silk at mfr.	1	2	0	+1.0	
Raw cattle hides at tanners	1	3	0	+6.2	
Newsprint at and in transit to pub.	0	4	0	+9.2	
Lead at warehouses	1	3	0	+3.0	
Refinable petroleum in pipelines and at tank farms and refineries	0	3	0	+10.7	
Raw sugar at refineries	1	6	0	+5.4	
Crude Rubber and afloat for U.S.[a]	0	2	0	+1.5	
Sum of first five series with significant positive conformity	3	18	1		

[a] Timing measured unvertedly.
[b] Measured synchronously, except in the case of newsprint stocks, which were assumed to lag 10 months behind newsprint consumption at both peaks and troughs.
Source: Moses Abramovitz, *Inventories and Business Cycles* (New York: National Bureau of Economic Research, 1950), pp. 189–190.

and the equilibrium level of inventories.[3] Finally, Mack argues that the theory fails to include other important factors such as expectations about prices and market conditions and the cost of funds with which to buy stocks.[4]

In an attempt to overcome some of these problems, Goodwin has developed what is known as the flexible accelerator.[5] To examine this theory, one must first restate the simple accelerator in the form of a linear equation such that the desired or equilibrium stocks existing at the *beginning* of a production period, s_t^*, are proportional to the output occurring *during* that period, y_t

$$s_t^* = a_0 + a_1 y_t \qquad (4.3)$$

where a_1 can be considered as the marginal desired inventory coefficient. Goodwin subsequently introduces the assumption that firms attempt to adjust inventories only partially toward their desired or equilibrium level in each period. There are a number of reasons as to why this occurs. For example, the costs of acquiring stocks quickly may be prohibitively high. Or the composition of the stocks held may be so varied that all cannot be adjusted at the same time. Finally, commodities may also be ordered only infrequently or under some long term contractual arrangement. This may require holding large stocks at one time and small stocks at another time, regardless of the level of productive activity.

One can assert, therefore, that firms adjust actual stocks in a certain period only a fraction δ of the distance required to reach desired or equilibrium stocks.

$$s_t - s_{t-1} = \delta(s_t^* - s_{t-1}) \qquad (4.4)$$

Introducing the relationship for desired stocks from equation 4.3, the final expression for the flexible accelerator can be reached

$$s_t - s_{t-1} = \delta(a_0 + a_1 y_t) - s_{t-1}$$

such that

$$s_t = \delta a_0 + \delta a_1 y_t + (1 - \delta)s_{t-1}$$

or

$$s_t = b_0 + b_1 y_t + b_2 s_{t-1} + u_t \qquad (4.5)$$

which includes a random disturbance term, u_t.

Lundberg and Metzler have taken an alternative approach to developing the basic accelerator whereby inventories are defined as being a "buffer" between changes in sales and production. Since this approach is directed primarily towards the adjustment of finished goods inventories, it would be most useful when explaining the stocks of finished goods or processors. In equation form, the desired *end of period* inventories s_t^{**} are assumed to be linearly related to the volume of sales during that period, $\hat{v}_t$.

$$s_t^{**} = a_o + a_1 \hat{v}_t \tag{4.6}$$

Since the actual volume of sales is not known by a firm in advance, this equation may be redefined showing planned inventories, s_t^p, to be proportional to the expected volume of sales, $\hat{v}_t$

$$s_t^p = a_o + a_1 \hat{v}_t \tag{4.7}$$

A final expression for actual inventories can be reached by assuming that actual end of period inventories will differ from this planned level if the expected sales volume exceeds the actual volume, and conversely.

$$s_t - s_t^p = \hat{v}_t - v_t \tag{4.8}$$

Substituting for s_t^p from equation 4.7, actual inventories are

$$s_t = a_o + (1 + a_1)\hat{v}_t - v_t \tag{4.9}$$

Consequently, one can explain deviations in actual inventories from their equilibrium levels by examining the errors experienced in anticipating the future volume of sales.

Two other versions of buffer stock theory have recently been developed. Mills attempts to extend the operation of the buffer stock model under conditions of uncertainty.[6] His optimal or expected inventory is then seen as the difference between optimum supply and the mathematical expectation for the volume of sales. Lovell's alternative version attempts to combine the buffer stock model with the flexible accelerator.[7] Planned inventories are assumed to be adjusted only a fraction δ of the distance to desired or equilibrium inventories

$$s_t^p - s_{t-1} = \delta(s_t^{**} - s_{t-1}) \tag{4.10}$$

where δ represents the coefficient of adjustment. When the deviation of planned from actual inventories is expressed in terms of the difference between expected and actual sales, an expression can be reached corresponding to equation 4.9

$$s_t = s_t^p + \hat{v}_t - v_t = s_t^{**} + (1 - \delta)s_{t-1} + \hat{v}_t - v_t$$

or

$$s_t = \delta(a_0 + a_1 \hat{v}_t) + (1 - \delta)s_{t-1} + \hat{v}_t - v_t \tag{4.11}$$

This reduces to the conventional buffer stock model for the case of $\delta = 1$. It will be shown later how Witherell found this combination of the buffer stock and flexible accelerator model applicable to explaining mill stocks for raw wool.[8]

The Modified Flexible Accelerator

One version of the accelerator appropriate to examine as a separate development is Lovell's modified flexible accelerator.[9] Though not a "pure" theory of commodity inventory behaviour in as far as the data studied have contained some goods in process, the modified accelerator has value in its judicious selection of the following explanatory factors.

Changes in Output. A first way of extending the flexible accelerator is to include the additional pressure exerted on stocks when output is sharply changing. Lovell notes that when output is increasing rapidly, orders may be submitted by consumers to suppliers in an attempt to build up stocks, but serious delays may occur in delivery. As a result, there may be a tendency for commodity inventories to fall below the desired level when output is increasing, $\Delta y_t > o$. Conversely, the same inflexibility could cause inventories to cumulate above desired levels when output is falling, $\Delta y_t < o$.

Price Speculation. Also to be included is the speculative motive for adjusting inventories. Speculative behavior on the part of manufacturers implies a tendency to insure themselves against increasing prices by purchasing additional stocks as price rises are expected and by reducing stock levels when price falls are expected. While a price expectations variable would best reflect that behavior, the scarcity of such data leads us to other forms of price variables. Where a commodity also possesses futures or forward trading, it might be of use to substitute a future price variable, although Labys and Granger have shown this normally to be inadequate.[10] Rather Lovell indicates that price expectations be stated in the form of percentage increase of actual prices in the next period. Although such a variable does reasonably describe the hypothesis that manufacturers speculate successfully by accumulating stocks in advance of price increases, Abramovitz would argue that price speculation as an influence in manufacturers adjustments is not easy to detect.[11] Not only do inventory records lack the detail necessary for interpreting speculative holdings but prices during the business cycle tend to move at rates normally different from those associated with business activity.

Unfilled Orders. Also to be considered is that manufacturers begin building inventories to insure against possible shortages and price changes as unfilled orders for finished goods become large. Except in the case of certain industry surveys, it is extremely difficult to compile order data that might relate to individual commodities.

Lovell includes all of these influences in the equation 4.3 for desired stocks

$$s_t^* = a_o + a_1 y_t + a_2 \Delta y_t + a_3 \frac{(p_t - p_{t-1})}{p_t} + a_4 o_t \qquad (4.12)$$

where o_t represents unfilled orders.

This equation is then combined with the expressions for partial adjustment

$$s_t - s_{t-1} = \delta(s_t^* - s_{t-1})$$

such that

$$s_t = \delta a_o + \delta a_1 y_t + \delta a_2 \Delta y_t + \delta a_3 \frac{(p_t - p_{t-1})}{p_t} + \delta a_4 o_t + (1 - \delta)s_{t-1}$$

or

$$s_t = b_0 + b_1 y_t + b_2 \Delta y_2 + b_3 \frac{(p_t - p_{t-1})}{p_t} + b_4 o_t + b_5 s_{t-1} + u_t \qquad (4.13)$$

Results obtained by his estimating this model using quarterly data for aggregate manufacturers stocks are reported in Table 4-2. The values obtained for the various coefficients and their variances confirm the existence of partial adjustment as well as the importance of the unfilled orders variable. The factor proving to be the least explanatory was that of price speculation, confirming the tentative conclusion reached by Abramovitz.

Producer Inventory Relationships

The role played by producers' inventories in market adjustment has not received the attention it deserves. Producers' inventories or a form of buffer stock, for example, could possibly be used to stabilize export quantities and prices around their equilibrium levels. Desai shows this in his study of the tin market, and Stern investigates the possibility in his investigation of the price of inventories for rubber.[12] While there has been much discussion about the theoretical relationships necessary between inventories and prices to achieve stabilization, the scope of this topic and the complexities involved do not permit its analysis here.

Among the theories which have been proposed to explain producers' inventory behavior, the various forms of the accelerator model have received

Table 4-2. Inventories of Purchased Materials and Goods in Process. Explanation Provided by the Modified Flexible Accelerator

$$s_t = \delta a_0 + \delta a_1 y_t + \delta a_2 \triangle y_t + \delta a_3 \frac{(p_t - p_{t-1})}{p_t} + \delta a_4 o_t + (1 - \delta)s_{t-1} + u_t$$

Coefficients	Total Manufacturing	Total Durables	Total Nondurables
Number of Observations	29	29	29
δa_0	4004	1412	−356.0
δa_1	0.0620 (0.0160)	0.0528 (0.0187)	0.0230 (0.0209)
δa_2	−0.0997 (0.0303)	−0.0803 (0.0296)	−0.0366 (0.0559)
δa_3	−0.3204 (0.2061)	0.0385 (0.1732)	0.1481 (0.1208)
δa_4	0.0609 (0.0053)	0.0384 (0.0041)	0.2207 (0.0514)
δ	0.4576 (0.0455)	0.3628 (0.0338)	0.0974 (0.0665)
R^2	0.993	0.994	0.970
$D.W.$	2.273	1.822	2.019
a_1	0.1355	0.1455	0.2361
a_4	0.1332	0.1055	2.266

Source: M. Lovell, "Manufacturers' Inventories, Sales Expectations, and the Accelerator Principle," *Econometrica* 29 (July 1961): 300.

attention for manufacturers or processors who act as suppliers. Where inventories are held by exporters or dealers in the form of unsold carryover, an alternative approach that describes the primary motive of stock holders to be price speculation is desirable. Such an approach has been followed by Witherell in relating actual stocks held to current and expected future prices

$$s_t = a_o + a_1 p_t + a_2 p_t^* \tag{4.14}$$

where s_t now represents carryover stocks and p_t^* expected prices.[13] The major assumption underlying this model is that the major holders of speculative stocks are usually fairly sophisticated and possess sufficient capital to manipulate these inventories without difficulty, i.e., actual stock levels can be adjusted easily to that of desired levels. The above model also assumes that the effects of the other economic and noneconomic variables are included in the stated price behavior.

To replace the expectations variable, Witherell prefers the *adaptive* expectations certainty equivalent introduced previously to that of Lovell's price rate of change variable. That is, expectations are revised each period according to the difference between the actual price and the expected price obtained in the previous period

$$p_t^* = p_{t-1}^* + \beta(p_{t-1} - p_{t-1}^*) \tag{4.15}$$

where β is the constant of revision. Combining this equation with equation 4.14 and performing the necessary transformations results in

$$s_t = \beta a_o + (1 - \beta)s_{t-1} + (a_1 + a_2 \beta)p_t - (1 - \beta)a_1 p_{t-1} \tag{4.16}$$

A similarly useful expression can be obtained if the assumption of partial adjustment replaces that of perfect adjustment, suggesting that producers no longer have complete control over their stock holdings. Begin by expressing desired stocks as a function of current and expected prices.

$$s_t^* = a_0 + a_1 p_t + a_2 p_t^*$$

To simplify the expression for expected prices, assume that stockholders follow extrapolative expectations. That is, the expected price is a function of previous actual price plus or minus a fraction of the previous price change.

$$p_t^* = p_{t-1} + \beta(p_{t-1} - p_{t-2}) \tag{4.17}$$

The concept of partial adjustment in stocks is introduced following the previous specification by Goodwin.

$$s_t - s_{t-1} = \delta(s_t^* - s_{t-1}) \tag{4.18}$$

Combining this expression with equations 4.17 and 4.18

$$s_t = \delta[a_o + (a_1 + a_2)p_t + a_2 \beta \Delta p_t] + (1 - \delta)s_{t-1}$$
$$= \delta a_o + \delta(a_1 + a_2)p_t + \delta a_2 \Delta p_t + (1 - \delta)s_{t-1}$$

or

$$s_t = b_o + b_1 p_t + b_2 \Delta p_t + b_3 s_{t-1} + u_t \tag{4.19}$$

The worth of the perfect and the partial adjustment model for explaining producer inventories is considered on pages 80–81.

Supply of Storage Relationship

All the theories of inventory behavior discussed so far attempt to explain stock holding in terms of adjustment to the transactions or speculative motives for keeping commodities. Yet some manufacturers and dealers are willing to hold certain minimum stock levels even though they expect an inverted relationship between the spot and the forward or nearest futures price, because of the "convenience yield" that stocks provide to them. This theory known as the "supply of storage" is based on the premise that each firm will adjust its inventory levels until the marginal revenue of holding stocks equals the marginal cost of holding stocks. This theory has its origins in the works of Keynes, Kaldor, Working, Telser, and Brennan; and more recently has been extended and applied by Weymar.[14] Its potential rests in its simplicity of interpretation and its applicability to consumers' or producers' inventory behavior.[15]

Our explanation begins with a commodity which has no futures trading; at least some portion of the total existing inventory provides "a yield or return to the holders of the inventory just in the process of being held."[16] Kaldor termed this return the "marginal convenience yield" and justified its existence on two grounds.[17] First, the processing of a commodity in many cases requires substantial capital investment and the possibility of that capital lying idle decreases as increased inventories are held. This is referred to as "stockout yield." Second, a processor may want the price of his finished product to remain relatively stable despite fluctuations in raw materials prices. By increasing his normal level of inventory coverage, he would reduce the frequency of changes in finished product prices. The extent of actual coverage maintained depends generally on the coverage of competitors so that the processor can move his prices in line with the rest of the industry. The service provided by these inventories is termed "coverage yield."

These different forms of yields can now be considered together to determine the marginal inventory holding cost for a commodity. This cost is defined as equal to the marginal storage cost CS minus the insurance against stockout (or stockout yield) IS and the insurance against over or under coverage (or coverage yield) IC.

$$C = CS - IS - IC \qquad (4.20)$$

The marginal cost of storage refers to the overall costs of warehousing.

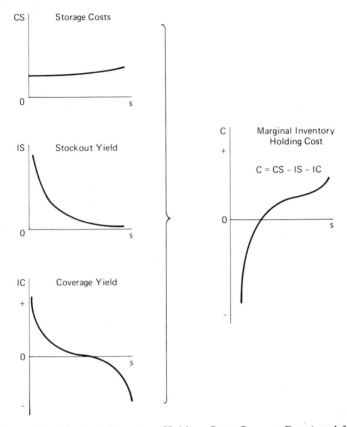

Figure 4-1. Marginal Inventory Holding Cost. Source: Reprinted from *Dynamics of the World Cocoa Market* by F.H. Weymar by permission of the MIT Press, Cambridge, Mass. 1968, pp. 35–36.

Each of these factors can be further explained by inspecting Figure 4-1. Marginal storage costs are shown to increase slightly as total inventories increase. Both stockout and coverage forms of marginal convenience yield are high at low inventory levels because of the convenience obtained from holding an additional unit of inventory. Both yields decline as more inventories are held and coverage yield may even become negative as warehouse facilities become saturated and coverage is excessive. When these factors are summed according to equation 4.20, marginal inventory holding costs are shown to be negative at low inventory levels because of the high convenience yields and become positive as the storage costs overwhelm the yields to be gained from holding additional inventories.

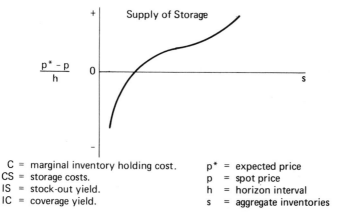

C = marginal inventory holding cost.   p* = expected price
CS = storage costs.   p = spot price
IS = stock-out yield.   h = horizon interval
IC = coverage yield.   s = aggregate inventories

Figure 4-2. Supply of Storage Function. Source: See Figure 4-1.

The key to determining what levels of inventories manufacturers of processors will hold in the aggregate is to assume that "they will increase or decrease their inventory levels to the point where their marginal inventory holding cost equals the rate at which they expect the commodity price to appreciate."[18] The loci of equilibrium points between marginal holding costs and marginal revenue can be illustrated by tipping the marginal cost diagram on its side and interpreting the aggregate demand for inventories as a function of the expected price rate of change. Retitling the cost axis to reflect the rate of price change as shown in Figure 4-2 produces the familiar supply of storage function

$$s_t = f\left(\frac{p^* - p_t}{h}\right) \tag{4.21}$$

where the expected price p^* refers to a particular horizon point in the near future, with the interval between the current (spot) price and the expected price equalling the horizon time, h. Inventories are held as a function of expected price changes, and desired inventory holding increases as the expected price difference widens.

The equation normally utilized to solve this relationship empirically is of the following form.

$$\log \frac{s_t}{c_t} = b_o + b_1 \log\left(\frac{p^* - p_t}{p_t}\right) + u_t \tag{4.22}$$

The adoption of a logarithmic equation permits a reasonable approximation of the nonlinear shape of the function given in Figure 4-2. Both of the variable terms also are expressed in the form of a ratio for definite reasons. Inventories are expressed in a ratio with consumption because convenience yields are interpreted in terms of inventory coverage. Proportional price spread is used since the magnitude of any speculative holdings as well as much of the carrying cost varies in proportion with price. Weymar has applied this theory to cocoa by inverting it as a spot price function, while Burrows has utilized it directly to explain movements in tungsten stocks.[19]

Other Approaches

With the exception of the promising work of Weymar, theories of inventory behavior have not been developed to deal specifically with commodity markets. Possibilities do exist, however, for the application of inventory or investment theories developed in other areas. One example is Yver's study of investment behavior in the Argentinian cattle industry.[20] The maximization of net returns for cattle farmers or any firm in that industry is seen as the maximization of the net present discounted values of each animal at birth or for its remaining lifetime. Borrowing from an early study on optimal portfolio arrangement, Yver assumes that the firm at any point in time holds a mixed portfolio of cattle of different sex and age.[21] Thus, the inventory behavior of firms can be explained assuming such firms to be profit maximizers, equalizing rates of return to investment in their mixed portfolio of cattle. Another possibility for application is a fuller system approach envisioned in the "ecological price-timed buying" model of Mack, which examines the basic structural characteristics of the market, behavioral characteristics of the participants, and the correct sequence of market action.[22]

Commodity Experience

Among the theories of inventory behavior examined, empirical applications at most extend to one or two commodities. In fact, the relatively inadequate nature and scarcity of inventory data has prevented many commodity models from including a thorough explanation of inventory-price adjustments. Most applications of theory have led to relatively simple empirical relationships, although most of them are of a dynamic nature including partial adjustment or expectational variables. Results presented below derive from studies of coffee, linseed oil, and wool.

Coffee

Stock equations appearing in the Wickens, Greenfield, and Marshall coffee model are based on the specification that total stock holding in a country can be linked to the principal motives for holding stocks—transactions, precautionary, and speculative.[23] This requires formulating the desired stock relationship as

$$s_t^* = a_0 + a_1 c_t + a_2(p_t^* - p_t) - a_3 p_t \qquad (4.23)$$

where s_t^* = desired stocks, c_t = commodity demand, p_t^* = expected price, and p_t = actual price. Variables in the relationship received the following interpretation: precautionary demand is given in the form of a_o implying that such demand is approximately constant over time (alternatively, one might assume precautionary demand to be proportional to the variance of production); transactions demand is characterized by the consumption variable; and speculative demand is represented by the combined price expectations variable. The authors of that study also offer two other possibilities in their specification. One is that the actual price variable represents the demand for buffer stocks. Another is that a stochastic variable might be used to explain undesired or unwanted stocks. That variable has not been included in the results presented here.

The desired stocks equation is then combined with a partial adjustment mechanism in the form given by equation 4-4 to reflect that fluctuations in harvests as well as operations of the International Coffee Agreement prevent the actual level of stocks from adjusting rapidly to the desired level. The outcome is an equation in actual stocks of the following form

$$s_t = \delta a_o + \delta a_1 c_t + \delta a_2 (p_t^* - p_t) - \delta a_3 p_t - \delta s_{t-1} \qquad (4.24)$$

which after introduction of a certainty equivalent and appropriate transformation becomes

$$\Delta s_t = b_o + b_1 c_t + b_2 p_{t-1} + b_3 p_t + b_4 s_{t-1} + u_t \qquad (4.25)$$

This equation was estimated utilizing stocks and related data for the United States and Brazil. The method used is OLS, based on ten annual observations extending from 1957 to 1967

$$\Delta s_t^{us} = 3.655 + 0.46 \, \Delta p_t^b - 0.975 s_{t-1}^{us}$$
$$\qquad\qquad (15.20) \qquad (2.07)$$
$$R^2 = 0.63, \; D.W. = 2.46$$
$$\Delta s_t^b = -4268 - 220 \, \Delta p_t^b + 0.517 q_t - 0.101 s_{t-1}^b$$
$$\qquad\qquad (1.01) \qquad (2.00) \qquad (0.71)$$
$$R^2 = 0.65, \; D.W. = 1.47$$

where s_t^{us} = closing stocks—all four coffee varieties combined, p_t^b = Brazilian prices, s_t^b = closing stocks—Brazil variety, and q_t = Brazilian coffee output.

Only limited results were obtained, two variables being retained in the regressions with p_t^* and p_{t-1} combined into a single variable. In addition, the coefficient on the lagged variable in the U.S. equation is close to one which suggests near-perfect adjustment; the price variable is of incorrect sign in the Brazil equation. Why the consumption variable or an appropriate surrogate could not be retained in either model remains a question, but such results typify the many problems encountered in estimating commodity inventory equations.

Linseed Oil

An early study of commodity stocks by S. G. Allen is worth examining.[24] Linseed oil and flaxseed stocks are described within a model explaining the supply of and demand for these commodities over the period 1926–1939. The demand for linseed oil stocks is explained dynamically through a variable defining unintended inventory accumulation; including this variable accounts for the fact that oil consumers often defaulted on orders, leaving producers with undelivered inventories. Also introduced is a consumption expectations variable, which reflects the tendency of consumers not only to form anticipations about final demand but also of producers to form anticipations regarding deliveries. The final model with the timing of variables expressed in terms of quarterly stock movements is as follows:

$$s_t^1 = b_0 + b_1(s_{t-1}^1 - c_t) + b_2 c_{t,i}^* + b_3 T + u_t \qquad (4.26)$$

where s_t^1 = closing stocks, $(s_{t-1}^1 - c_t)$ = unintended inventories, T = trend, and u_t = a stochastic disturbance term. The expectations variable c_{ti}^* is designed such that "the next period's consumption will be greater or less than the last year's consumption in the corresponding period depending on whether current building activity is greater or less than that during the same time last year."[25] The subscript i refers to the quarter of activity and y_t and y_{t-4} are the current and lagged levels of building activity.

$$c_{t,i}^* = \frac{y_t}{y_{t-4}} (c_{t-3} + c_{t-2}) \qquad i = 1, 4 \qquad (4.27)$$

$$= \frac{y_t}{y_{t-4}} c_{t-3} \qquad (4.28)$$

The demand for stocks of flaxseed is specified somewhat differently; production and price variables now enter the equation. The price variable is in the form of a ratio reflecting the importance of domestic prices relative to import prices

$$s_t^f = b_0 + b_1 \frac{p_t}{p_t^b} + b_2 s_t^1 + b_3 c_{t,i}^{**} + b_4(s_{t-1}^f + q_{t,i}) + b_5 T + u_t \quad (4.29)$$

where s_t^f = closing flaxseed stocks, p_t/p_t^b = ratio of Minneapolis to Buenos Aires prices, and $q_{t,i}$ = annual domestic flaxseed production ($=0$ for $i = 1, 2, 4$). The compound production and lagged stocks variable reflects the assumption that existing flaxseed stocks include the domestic harvest of flaxseed. The consumption expectations variable is now defined as

$$c_{t,i}^{**} = \frac{y_t}{y_{t-4}} c_{t-3} \qquad i = 1, 3 \tag{4.30}$$

$$= \frac{y_t}{y_{t-4}} (c_{t-3} + c_{t-2} + c_{t-1}) \qquad i = 2 \tag{4.31}$$

$$= \frac{y_t}{y_{t-4}} (c_{t-3} + c_{t-2}) \qquad i = 4 \tag{4.32}$$

Results of estimating the equation are given below following a limited information least-squares procedure:

$$s_t^1 = 97800 + 0.122(s_{t-1}^1 - c_t) + 0.182c_t^* - 312T$$
$$\quad\quad\quad (0.92) \quad\quad\quad\quad\quad (7.01) \quad\quad (1.27)$$

and

$$s_t^f = -67800 + 93500 \frac{p_t}{p_t^b} - 0.711s_t^1 + 0.116c_t^{**} + 0.800(s_{t-1}^f + q_{t,i}) + 457T$$
$$\quad\quad\quad\quad (0.24) \quad\quad (0.28) \quad\quad (0.76) \quad\quad (4.86) \quad\quad\quad\quad\quad\quad (0.95)$$

Values of R^2 for the linseed oil and flaxseed equations are 0.79 and 0.97 respectively. In the linseed oil equation, only the consumption expectations variable is significant, reflecting the importance of that variable in explaining stock adjustments. In the flaxseed equation, however, the consumption variable is no longer significant and stock adjustment appears to respond to production.

Wool

A fairly sophisticated application of inventory theory to commodities can be found in the wool model developed by Witherell.[26] He employs dynamic formulations to explain both commercial wool stocks in consuming countries and carryover wool stocks in producing countries.

Consumer Stocks. Commercial stocks of wool are held primarily for expected and future mill consumption and secondarily for speculation or price hedging. To explain these stocks, Witherall utilizes a version of the combined flexible accelerator and buffer stock model as proposed by Lovell and described earlier.

$$s_t^p - s_{t-1} = \delta(s_t^* - s_{t-1})$$

or

$$s_t^p = \delta s_t^* + (1 - \delta)s_{t-1} \tag{4.33}$$

But the buffer stock mechanism is stated such that errors in desired or equilibrium stocks depend on errors in anticipated mill consumption rather than in anticipated sales volume.

$$s_t^* = s_t^p + (mc_t^* - mc_t) \tag{4.34}$$

The expected consumption variable can be removed by adopting the assumption that the dealers forecast of consumption is somewhere between a naive and a perfect forecast.

$$mc_t^* = \theta\, mc_{t-1} + (1 - \theta)\, mc_t \tag{4.35}$$

This can be interpreted more clearly if mc_{t-1} is subtracted from both sides of the equation.

$$mc_t^* - mc_{t-1} = (\theta - 1)\, mc_{t-1} + (1 - \theta)\, mc_t$$

or

$$mc_t^* - mc_{t-1} = (1 - \theta)\, (mc_t - mc_{t-1}) \tag{4.36}$$

Forecast ability would be perfect if $\theta = 1$. For the case of $\theta < 1$, there would be a tendency to overestimate the change in consumption; for $\theta > 1$, the sign of the change is forecast incorrectly.

A final expression for wool stocks is obtained by introducing expectations regarding both consumption and prices into the flexible accelerator.

$$s_t^* = a_0 + a_1 mc_t^* + p_t^* \tag{4.37}$$

The expression for expected consumption is replaced by equation 4.35 and current prices are taken as a proxy for expected prices.

$$s_t^* = a_o + a_1\theta mc_{t-1} + a_1(1 - \theta)mc_t + a_2 p_t \qquad (4.38)$$

This equation can now be combined with the three previous equations (4.33, 4.34, and 4.35) to obtain

$$s_t = a_o + (1 - \delta)s_{t-1} + \delta\, a_1 mc_t - (\delta a_1 + 1)\,\theta\Delta mc_t + \delta a_2 p_t$$

or

$$s_t = b_o + b_1 s_{t-1} + b_2 mc_t + b_3\,\Delta mc_t + b_4 p_t + u_t \qquad (4.39)$$

Witherell has estimated this equation for the United States, United Kingdom, and Japan employing annual data over the period 1948–1964. He observes that the use of annual data probably results in an upward bias in the adjustment coefficients and that the importance of the short run stock fluctuations and related price effects is reduced. Among the different equations tested and presented in the study utilizing 2SLS methods, the following are representative.

$$s_t^{us} = 0.064 s_{t-1}^{us} + 0.311 mc_t^{us} - 0.132\Delta mc_t^{us}$$
$$(0.34) \qquad (4.51) \qquad (1.59)$$
$$R^2 = 0.64,\ D.W. = 1.87$$

$$s_t^{uk} = 0.186 s_{t-1}^{uk} + 0.300 mc_t^{uk} + 0.074\Delta mc_t^{uk}$$
$$(1.09) \qquad (4.61) \qquad (0.12)$$
$$R^2 = 0.59,\ D.W. = 1.93$$

$$s_t^{jp} = 0.812 s_{t-1}^{jp} + 0.176\Delta mc_t^{jp} + 0.034 p_t$$
$$(8.46) \qquad (1.96) \qquad (1.10)$$
$$R^2 = 0.73,\ D.W. = 1.93$$

The levels of multiple correlation reached are only moderate, although the explanation provided by mill consumption is noticeably significant. The flexible version of the accelerator appears to be least applicable to the United States, where the adjustment coefficient equal to $1 - 0.064$ indicates that adjustment takes less than one year. The accelerator coefficient a_1 defining the ratio of stocks to output is 0.332 and 0.368 for the U.S. and the U.K., but rises to 0.936 for Japan.

Producer Stocks. Two separate inventory models have been used to explain producer carryover stocks. The first is identical to that described earlier in equation 4.19.

$$s_t = b_o + b_1 p_t + b_2 \Delta p_t + b_3 s_{t-1} + u_t \qquad (4.40)$$

This equation implies that price speculation is the most important reason why inventories are carried over into the next period. Such an assumption is applied to inventories held in Australia, New Zealand, and South Africa. Results obtained in describing inventories in these countries are given below, based on data and method of estimation similar to that of the consumer inventory equations.

$$s_t^{au} = 0.978 s_{t-1}^{au} + 0.075 p_t - 0.054 p_{t-1}$$
$$(7.41) \qquad (1.59) \qquad (1.13)$$
$$R^2 = 0.72, \ D.W. = 1.92$$

$$s_t^{nz} = -19.856 + 0.631 s_{t-1}^{nz} + 0.662 p_t - 0.402 p_{t-1}$$
$$(2.57) \qquad (8.07) \qquad (0.35)$$
$$R^2 = 0.85, \ D.W. = 1.82$$

$$s_t^{sa} = 0.594 s_{t-1}^{sa} + 0.029 p_t - 0.023 p_{t-1}$$
$$(2.27) \qquad (7.25) \qquad (3.29)$$
$$R^2 = 0.77, \ D.W. = 1.46$$

The levels of multiple correlation achieved are better than moderate with a considerable number of the variables being significant.

The speculative motive was also shown to provide an adequate explanation of stocks in Argentina and Uruguay. A slightly different model is used, however, in which the lagged stocks variable is removed, current price is replaced by current price changes, and a "policy" dummy variable is included.

$$s_t^{ag} = -53.70 + 0.927 p_t - 0.475 \Delta p_t + 98.48 D_t^{ag}$$
$$(4.73) \qquad (2.75) \qquad (8.84)$$
$$R^2 = 0.95, \ D.W. = 2.10$$

$$s_t^{up} = 0.131 p_t - 0.206 \Delta p_t + 22.34 D_t^{ur}$$
$$(4.68) \qquad (2.48) \qquad (3.98)$$
$$R^2 = 0.73, \ D.W. = 1.95$$

Values of multiple correlation reached here are also better than moderate. The negative sign accompanying the change in price variable is not easy to interpret except that producers may believe that the most recent change in price will be reversed.

Lauric Oils Inventories

A number of different theoretical approaches have been taken in specifying the inventory equations for the lauric oils model.[27] The applicability of these approaches for the most part has been limited by the quality and quantity of the available data. Reasonably accurate data could be compiled for the three major importing countries and for one of the producing countries accounting for the majority of inventories held. Since the composition of the data from the importing countries relates principally to holdings of manufacturers and dealers, a modified form of the flexible accelerator seemed the most appropriate for explaining consumer inventory behavior. Specifying that form of relationship requires beginning with an expression for desired stocks

$$s_t^* = a_0 + a_1 y_t + a_2 \Delta y_t + a_3 p_t^* \tag{4.41}$$

where y_t represents an index of manufacturing output for industries utilizing lauric oils. After deliberating on the nature of price expectations followed by decision makers in the market, it appeared best to introduce the assumption of extrapolative expectations.

$$p_t^* = p_{t-1} + \beta(p_{t-1} - p_{t-2})$$

Combining this expression with that of the partial adjustment mechanism, one obtains

$$s_t = \delta a_0 + \delta a_1 y_t + \delta a_2 \Delta y_t + \delta a_3 p_{t-1} + \delta a_4 \beta \Delta p_{t-1} + (1 - \delta)s_{t-1} \tag{4.42}$$

Because data are reported in the form of closing stocks, the variables have to be adjusted to reflect activity in the following period.

$$s_t = \delta a_0 + \delta a_1 y_{t+1} + \delta a_2 \Delta y_{t+1} + \delta a_3 p_t + \delta a_4 \beta \Delta p_t + (1 - \delta)s_{t-1}$$

or

$$s_t = b_0 + b_1 y_{t+1} + b_2 \Delta y_{t+1} + b_3 p_t + b_4 \Delta p_t + b_5 s_{t-1} + u_t \tag{4.43}$$

Two other modifications also have been found necessary in moving from this theoretical formulation to the empirical equations. First, it appears best to consider the equation also in the form of a flow relationship. Though equation 4.43 worked well for the U.S. and U.K., a change in inventory equation seemed most appropriate for the E.E.C. Second, it was necessary to include a dummy variable to account for the unusual fluctuations in stock holdings which occurred at several different periods in each of the above. The equations reported below have been estimated using OLS.

$$s_t^{us} = 13.73 + 0.464\,\Delta y_{t+1} + 115.50 p_t - 314.38\,\Delta p_t + 68.171\,D_t^{us}$$
$$\quad\quad\quad\quad (2.55)\quad\quad\quad (1.22)\quad (-3.50)\quad\quad (7.52)$$

$$\bar{R}^2 = 0.91,\ D.W. = 2.36$$

$$s_t^{uk} = -9.16 + 0.574 s_{t-1}^{uk} + 0.160\,\Delta y_t + 81.29 p_t - 52.81\,\Delta p_t - 18.05 D_t^{uk}$$
$$\quad\quad\quad (8.26)\quad\quad (2.87)\quad\quad\quad (3.07)\quad (-2.50)\quad\quad (-7.63)$$

$$\bar{R}^2 = 0.94,\ D.W. = 1.80$$

$$\Delta s_t^{ec} = 18.47 - 0.099 s_{t-1}^{ec} - 0.060\,\Delta y_t^{ec} - 26.78\,\Delta p_t^{w} - 49.87 D_t^{ec}$$
$$\quad\quad\quad\quad\quad (-0.37)\quad\quad (-0.49)\quad\quad (-2.54)$$

$$\bar{R}^2 = 0.51,\ D.W. = 2.38$$

These results differ from the theoretical specification mainly in that the output level variable, insignificant for all three equations, was removed. This was done with some hesitancy since eliminating output upsets the normal definition of the accelerator. Before removal, an attempt was made to determine whether the accelerator adjustment occurs with respect to supply rather than sales or output, but this produced less useful results. That the major output variable is in change form, however, need not negate our interpretation of the accelerator entirely. Perhaps the adjustment process should be considered as cyclically proportional rather than linearly proportional.

For the U.S. equation, adjustment was found to be complete within a year, and the lagged inventories variable removed. Price variables are significant in both the U.S. and U.K. equations, which suggests some strength in the influence of price speculation. The negative sign accompanying the change in price variable in all equations is difficult to explain. One possibility is that stockholders react as if the most recent change in price will be reversed Examination of the price change variable over the period of estimation indicates that price reversals did occur in seven of fourteen possible years. For lauric oil producers, results of estimating equations are available only for Ceylon, and a conventional distributed lag of stocks on past prices appeared to provide an adequate explanation of inventory movements.

Conclusions

Our examination of results of a number of different studies of commodity inventory behavior has shown the many difficulties encountered in specifying and estimating inventory relationships. Drastic improvements are needed in compiling commodity inventory data before available theories of inventory behavior can be fully evaluated and tested. Inventory data relative to consumers' holdings or producers' carry-over should be compiled and published in the manner suggested earlier, on a monthly, quarterly, and annual basis. When possible, this data should be disaggregated to reflect the attitudes of subclasses of owners. Records should also be kept of inventories in moving along the pipeline from supplier to ultimate consumer as well as of critical market phenomena such as stocks in ships afloat.

Another need would be not only to investigate further the supply of storage approach but also to develop inventory theories specific to commodity markets. One possibility would be to conduct a behavioral study of the motives of commodity holders. This would require an interview survey or at least the use of questionnaires. Another possibility would be to examine the influence of the availability of funds for financing inventories as well as for placing orders.[28] Regarding behavioral factors that influence inventory holding such as transactions, precautionary, speculative, or other motives, it would be useful to explain their influence separately or in a way different from the conventional method of combining them in a single regression equation.

The need also exists to include "feedback" from the environment in explaining inventory formation, and this might involve control theory, for example, where one wants to directly manipulate inventories as in the case of a buffer stock scheme. The manner in which inventory behavior interacts with total market adjustment is shown in Chapter 6.

5 Prices

Commodity price theory as an area separate from demand or equilibrium theory has received only scant attention. Several factors are responsible for this predicament. First, where commodity price forecasting has been the goal, more reliance has been placed on statistical or pragmatic price relationships requiring no sophisticated price theory. Second, where price explanation based on demand or market studies has been sought, price relationships have been derived simply by inverting or normalizing an appropriate demand or inventory relationship. Finally, even where complete commodity models have been constructed it has not always been necessary to incorporate an explicit price relationship, since an expression for prices can often be derived from the reduced form.

This chapter begins by discussing the basic characteristics or patterns of price behavior. Next the various theories or studies which have appeared thus far to explain price behavior are reviewed. To show how several of these theories can be used to specify individual price relationships, a general framework is presented capable of dealing with competitive as well as noncompetitive price adjustments. Specific forms of price relationships are examined within this context, and price equations estimated for different commodities appear as examples. Several of the specifications are compared in as far as they can be of use in explaining lauric oils price behavior.

Price Behavior

Price Characteristics

Deciphering the patterns or cycles that commodity prices follow over time is a first step to discovering the economic and social determinants that underlie price behavior. The types of patterns that we search for often vary with the time period of interest. Depending on whether the time period is a long run, short run, or market period, the nature of the patterns can be secular or cyclical, annual or seasonal, or irregular, respectively. Irregular fluctuations are also called random when they arise from no known causes, or episodic when they result from causes which are known but not predictable. Most price behavior represents a combination of these different patterns, as for example, in the case of a shorter run seasonal fluctuating around a longer run cycle.

Techniques used for discovering the underlying patterns in price fluctuations have been trend or regression fitting and subtraction, computation of seasonal indexes, or application of moving averages. Yet recently advances in time series methods such as spectral analysis or autoregressive integrated moving averages have greatly improved our ability to decipher these patterns.[1] In particular, spectral analysis can be applied to decompose complex waveforms generated by prices into basic frequency components, which can be interpreted in terms of the cyclical, seasonal, or random patterns mentioned above. This is normally accomplished through the estimation of a spectrum that transforms a time series into a set of frequency bands and indicates the relative importance of these bands in terms of their contribution to the total variance of the series.[a] A frequency band which contributes a larger proportion of the total variance is considered more important in describing the fluctuations of a series than one which contributes less, with the important frequencies or cycles appearing as a peak or jump in the spectrum. The general shape of the spectrum also provides information regarding the behavior of the series.

The actual nature of the frequency components discovered for a large number of commodity price series can be reviewed in a recent study by Labys and Granger; commodities analyzed are principally those classified as oils and fats, foods, and grains.[2] Also important are several studies dealing with individual commodities. e.g., copper, cocoa, and broilers.[3] Figures 5-1, 5-2, and 5-3 contain examples of commodity price spectra estimated from monthly series of broilers, wheat, and coconut oil prices extending from 1956 through

---

[a] The spectral estimate is defined as follows: Consider a sample time series to be draw on the basis of some variable X_t; $t = 1, 2, \ldots, T$ where the sample can be said to be generated from a stationary stochastic process. Stationarity implies that there is no trend in mean or variance. If the sample does contain a trend in mean, for example, this can be removed by estimating and subtracting an appropriate regression or by differencing the data. The effect of either will be to filter the true series such that the resulting time series is stationary. This resulting process can then be characterized in terms of its autocovariance function, which is given by

$$R(v) = \frac{1}{T} \sum_{t=1}^{t-v} (X_t - \overline{X})(X_{t+v} - \overline{X})$$

for $v = 0, 1, 2, \ldots, T - 1$, where $X = \frac{1}{T} \sum_{t=1}^{T} X_t$ and $R(-v) = R(v)$

This process provides the basis for the definition of the spectral estimate which is given as

$$S_x(\omega) = \frac{1}{2\pi} \sum_{v=-T+1}^{T-1} k(v)R(v)\cos v\omega, \quad -\pi \leq \omega \geq \pi$$

where $k(v)$ is a weighting function that declines as v increases such that $k(v) = 0$ for $v > \eta$ where $\eta < T$. The value of η is chosen to allow for the fact that with a sample of fixed length T, the estimate of the autocovariance function becomes steadily more unreliable as v increases.

Further details can be found in C. W. J. Granger and M. Hatanaka, *Spectral Analysis of Economic Time Series* (Princeton: Princeton University Press, 1964).

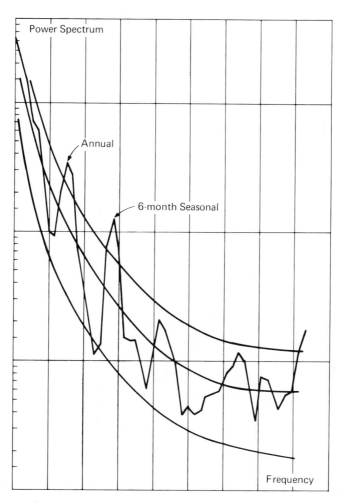

Figure 5-1. Typical Spectrum of Broiler Prices, Monthly: 1956-1971.

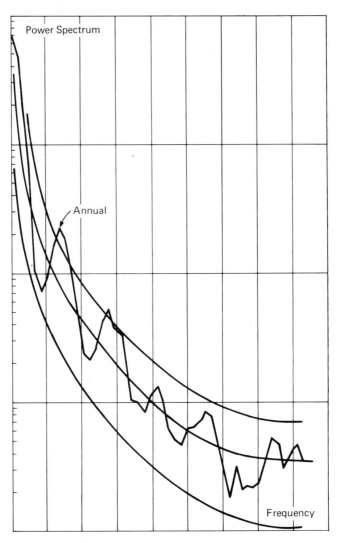

Figure 5-2. Typical Spectrum of Wheat Prices, Monthly: 1956-1971.

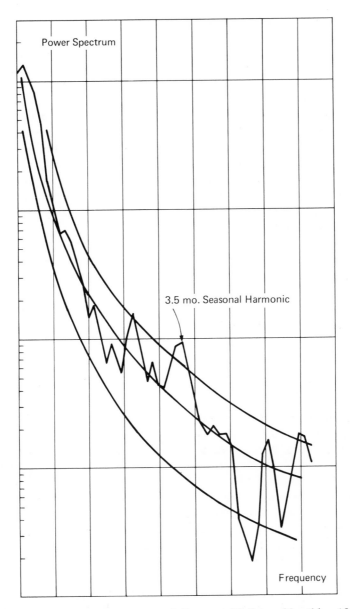

Figure 5-3. Typical Spectrum of Coconut Oil Prices Monthly: 1956–1971.

1971. The spectral power or variance appears on the ordinate of those figures and the frequencies are defined on the abcissa, the frequencies being of a shorter run nature in moving from left to right. All of the spectral diagrams show prices to have some conformity to long run business cycles as witnessed by the prevalence of spectral power in the long run frequencies. The broiler price spectrum suggests the presence of an annual and a six month component while the wheat price spectrum displays only the annual component. A shorter run component of 3.5 months appears in the coconut oil price spectrum.

How the interpretation of these components can help specify individual price equations is also discussed in Labys and Granger, although the equations analyzed relate to shorter run price movements of monthly timing or less. The method followed is a pragmatic one; the discovery of certain time patterns in the price series would suggest that the corresponding price relationships include causal variables also exhibiting those patterns. For example, if the price behavior appears as some combination of cyclical and seasonal patterns, one of the causal variables selected should reflect the underlying cyclical pattern and another variable should reflect the seasonal pattern. Where the dependent price variable tends to autoregressive behavior it would be appropriate to insert a lagged value of that variable. More complex patterns are less easy to explain and, of course, the pragmatic method is less comprehensive than one based on the theory of market equilibrium.

Price Data

Selecting price data to be used for spectral or econometric analysis can involve problems, particularly when using prices that have been aggregated over time or space. With respect to aggregation over time, it has been shown that where daily commodity price behavior suggests a random walk, working with the differences of the monthly averages of that data is likely to lead to an autoregressive sequence of prices.[4] Aggregation in the form of a weighted price index also can be troublesome. Take the example of a monthly price series obtained by multiplying daily prices by the weights of the carlots sold and dividing the aggregate by the total number of carlots. Such price series have been shown to exhibit behavior noticeably different from that which could be expected on the basis of underlying market factors.[5]

When dealing with aggregation over space, one may confront a similar difficulty in attempting to form a weighted price index based on a commodity produced or traded in different regions. One approach to solving this problem has been to derive the unit value of a commodity based on the total value and volume of trade for a country, but this approach has been shown to be inadequate.[6] Using actual or offer prices is usually preferable when working at the import or export level. Another approach has been to form a single international price index based on a weighted average of prices at which the commodity is traded in different parts of the world. Such a price index will be inadequate where the individual price series display cycles which are significantly out of phase, and one might do better to select the price series from a single major market for that commodity.

Price Relationships

From the historical background of commodity price theory we can formulate a general market framework suitable for specifying individual price relationships. The framework is first considered as it relates to competitive commodity markets. Particular theories of price behavior which can be applied within this context are classified according to whether or not they also involve adjustments in inventories. Also discussed is the influence that speculative activity will have on price behavior. The framework then shifts to include noncompetitive markets.

Background

The development of commodity price behavior ranges from the early work on deciphering patterns of price behavior to recent studies embodying expectations and uncertainty. The earliest work of note is that of Holbrook Working, who sought to determine the nature of the regular and irregular patterns found in commodity price fluctuations.[7] He also pointed out some of the weaknesses in conventional demand theory of the time for explaining price fluctuations, especially those of a short run nature. Two studies which attempted to advance from a technical explanation of price behavior to a fundamental or behaviorial one based on the theory of market equilibrium are those of Thomsen and Foote in 1936 and Shepherd in 1941.[8] These studies continually updated still provide a useful overview.

Both the technical and the behaviorial interpretations of commodity prices continued to receive attention following World War II. Working's technical study of price behavior extended to future markets and stimulated a variety of studies concerned with the possibility of a random walk in shorter run price movements.[9] Kendall in 1953 and Samuelson in 1965 developed new theoretical approaches and these and others have been evaluated empirically for several important commodities.[10] Larson in 1960 analyzed corn prices; Houthakker in 1961 examined cotton prices; and Cootner, Gray, and Smidt in 1965 evaluated soybean prices.[11] A more complete examination of the various theories incorporating the experience of a large number of commodities can be found in Labys and Granger.[12]

Advances in the behaviorial theory of commodity prices following World War II are associated with the U.S.D.A. Of principal interest are the studies of Meinken in 1955, Foote in 1958, Breimyer in 1961, and Houck in 1963.[13] Later developments have sought to include the influence of future market activity for certain commodities, either directly with causal mechanisms or indirectly through market expectations. The former would explain spot price behavior using variables that describe futures activity such as the volume of speculation and hedging.[14] The latter would extend the supply of storage theory mentioned in the previous chapter to a theory of spot price behavior; prices are explained by long run price expectations and expectations regarding inventory coverage.[15]

Other developments of commodity price theory are less relevant to constructing explicit price relationships. One theory attempts to establish a causal relationship between speculation, profits, and possible price instability. A number of studies have been published analyzing this theory and are reviewed and compared by Venkataramanan.[16] Another area which has been explored is that of deterministic price expectations models. As described in Chapter 3, the more important of these models have been developed by Goodwin, Nerlove, Mills, Fishman, and others.[17]

General Framework

The major problem in specifying price relationships is that the theories to be applied depend on a wide range of assumptions. These assumptions relate not only to the general competitive or noncompetitive nature of a market, but also to the structures underlying price determination and explaining consumption, production, and inventories. One method for simplifying the specification problem is to establish a framework within which individual price relationships can be formulated. Such a framework is developed here by considering, in sequence, (1) the nature of market organization, (2) a general model which can be used to describe that organization, and (3) the relationships to be included in the model.

A competitive market organization has been traditionally assumed in formulating commodity price relationships. That is, prices are determined in a market composed of freely competing buyers and sellers where the buyers are identical and the sellers deal in a reasonably homogeneous commodity. The commodity or commodities also must be reasonably mobile and information regarding market variables must be freely available. This form of market organization becomes less relevant for explaining price behavior where one or several buyers or sellers dominate the market or where severe price constraints exist. Our attention must then turn to utilizing monopolistic, oligopolistic, or other noncompetitive market structures.

The general model that we present as capable of explaining different forms of market organization is formulated first to reflect competitive behavior. It features the following structural relationships which describe the underlying consumption, production, and price-inventory conditions as well as a market-clearing identity

$$c_t = f(p_t, p_{t-1}, y_t, z_t, u_t) \tag{5.1}$$

$$q_t = f(p_t, p_{t-1}, z_t, u_t) \tag{5.2}$$

$$p_t = f(\Delta s_t, z_t, u_t) \tag{5.3}$$

$$\Delta s_t = s_t - s_{t-1} = q_t - c_t \tag{5.4}$$

where p_{t-1} is lagged price, z_t represents appropriate exogenous variables, and u_t is a stochastic disturbance term.

The nature of the model is such that we can postulate different forms of price relationships which would be theoretically valid, given different assumptions regarding the price elasticity of response of consumption and production or the length of the data interval used relative to the important lags in the market.[18]

1. If the data interval is quite long relative to the consumption and/or production lags, and if inventories vary considerably, price behavior can be explained by the simultaneous interaction of the relationships in the model.

2. If the data interval is again relatively long but inventories do not vary, price behavior can be explained according to adjustments in consumption or production. When both consumption and production are highly price responsive, then we must revert to a simultaneous explanation.

3. If the data interval is short relative to the lags and inventories vary considerably, price behavior can be explained in terms of adjustments in inventories.

Our present concern is with the specification of a single price relationship as suggested in cases 2 and 3. Whereas the specification of such relationships might also be appropriate for simultaneous models, we concentrate in this chapter on single equations for which the estimation methods of Chapters 2 and 3 are valid. Simultaneous price determination is examined in Chapter 6.

Competitive Markets Without Inventories

The simplest form of price relationship which can be specified stems from case 2 which assumes that either consumption or production may be price responsive but that inventories do not vary or do not exist. This is a typical situation for highly perishable commodities not suitable for storage. These particular conditions suggest that the preceding model be modified as

$$c_t = f(p_t, y_t, z_t, u_t) \tag{5.5}$$

$$q_t = f(p_{t-1}, z_t, u_t) \tag{5.6}$$

$$c_t = q_t \tag{5.7}$$

where production is determined by past prices and consumption equals production in the same period. In the absence of inventories, price behavior can be explained using a single consumption equation or its inversion.

$$p_t = f^{-1}(c_t, y_t, z_t, u_t) \tag{5.8}$$

An example of the use of an inverted consumption relationship to explain prices can be found in Breimyer's study of the demand and prices for meat.[19] Since the assumptions which he makes regarding the consumption and production relationships are identical to the above, the price relationship specified also is similar.

$$p_t = f^{-1}(q_t, y_t, q_t^0, i_t, u_t) \tag{5.9}$$

Only now the supply variable is used in place of demand where q_t^0 = supply of other meats, and i_t = consumer price index. Examples of equations estimated for beef, pork, and lamb are given below based on OLS estimation with annual data extending from 1948 to 1960.

$$\log p_t^b = -1.435 - 1.565 \log q_t^b - 0.389 \log z_t^p + 1.641 \log y_t + 0.836 \, i_t$$
$$ (-10.1) (-1.87) (4.10) (2.76)$$

$$R^2 = 0.972$$

$$\log p_t^p = 5.462 - 1.084 \log q_t^p - 0.361 \log z_t^b - 1.026 \log y_t + 1.061 \log i_t$$
$$ (-4.46) (-2.01) (-2.20) (3.03)$$

$$R^2 = 0.88$$

$$\log p_t^l = 0.100 - 2.262 \log q_t^l - 0.763 \log z_t^{b,p} + 0.389 \log y_t + 1.339 \log i_t$$
$$ (-2.71) (-2.70) (0.76) (3.71)$$
$$ - 0.012 \, T$$
$$ (-2.40)$$

$$R^2 = 0.92$$

Although these equations show a reasonable degree of explanation, this approach has the disadvantage of excluding the possible influence of market expectations.

Competitive Markets with Inventories

Several different theories of specification can be offered for case 3 where the data interval is reasonably short relative to the consumption and production lags, and inventories fluctuate considerably. The general model relevant under these conditions is

$$c_t = f(p_{t-1}, y_t, z_t, u_t) \tag{5.10}$$

$$q_t = f(p_{t-1}, z_t, u_t) \tag{5.11}$$

$$p_t = f(\Delta s_t, z_t, u_t) \tag{5.12}$$

$$\Delta s_t = q_t - c_t \tag{5.13}$$

Although the price relationship shows prices to be a function of changes in inventories, any final specification adopted would depend on whether the underlying price structure reflects a flow adjustment or a stock adjustment process. The problem of whether the price determination can best be represented as a stock or flow process has received some attention in the literature, principally as it relates to market stability.[20] Our present concern is only with the practical consequences of either approach for specifying price relationships within the given model.

Flow Adjustment.   The above model suggests that prices can be explained using equation 5.12, where the change in inventories variable reflects a flow adjustment process. Prices could also be expressed within this context as a function of the difference between consumption and production.

$$p_t = f(c_t - q_t, z_t, u_t) \tag{5.14}$$

Such a relationship embodies conventional equilibrium theory that excess demand or excess supply leads to an increase or decrease in prices and that the respective price difference will be reduced as consumers and producers react to the new market situation, prices eventually returning to their equilibrium level.

Stock Adjustment. The price relationship 5.12 could also be specified as a stock adjustment process by replacing the change in inventories variable with one describing inventory levels.

$$p_t = f(s_t, z_t, u_t) \tag{5.15}$$

The identity 5.13 also should be rewritten

$$s_t = s_{t-1} + q_t - c_t \tag{5.16}$$

The potential usefulness of this specification has been realized only recently. Previously, one usually obtained a suitable price relationship by inverting an inventory relationship as, for example, in the study of McKenzie, Philpott, and Woods.[21] They begin with an inventory relationship similar to the buffer stock variant of the flexible accelerator given in Chapter 4. The demand for inventories is a function of demand for transactions purposes to meet future consumption and demand for speculative purposes to profit from price changes

$$s_t = f(c_t^*, p_t^*) \tag{5.17}$$

where c_t^* reflects expectations regarding future consumption and p_t^* reflects expectations regarding future prices. The inventory variable s_t is expressed as actual inventories, although it would be more appropriately defined as desired inventories. Also assumed is that the adjustment of actual to desired inventories within a single period is fairly complete.

Using this approach, the price relationships specified depend on the assumptions made regarding the nature of expectations for consumption and prices. The simplest model is obtained by assuming naive expectations for both variables. Thus

$$c_t^* = c_t \quad \text{and} \quad p_t^* = p_t$$

such that

$$s_t = f(c_t, p_t) \tag{5.18}$$

Inversion of this equation yields prices in terms of consumption and stocks, both in observable values.

$$p_t = f^{-1}(c_t, s_t) \tag{5.19}$$

McKenzie, Philpott, and Woods estimate an equation of this form for raw wool prices based on world demand and stocks recorded quarterly from

1952 to 1966. The results obtained are given below where several dummy variables are also included to account for seasonal effects.

$$p_t = 97.40 + 0.196c_t - 0.127s_t - 11.17D_1 - 10.31D_2 - 1.32D_3$$
$$(4.91)\ (-6.40)\quad (-3.34)\quad (-3.27)\ (-0.44)$$

$$R^2 = 0.54;\ D.W. = 0.56$$

Because the quality of this equation is limited, they also present a version which assumes that price expectations follow a distributed lag of past prices and that consumption expectations fall somewhere between a perfect and a naive forecast. The assumption of a distributed lag in prices

$$p_{t+1} = \beta \sum_{i=0}^{\infty} (1 - \beta)^i p_{t-1} \tag{5.20}$$

is equivalent to that of adaptive expectations given in Chapter 3.

$$p_{t+1}^* = \beta p_t + (1 - \beta)p_t^* \tag{5.21}$$

The assumption regarding demand expectations leads to

$$c_{t+1}^* = \theta c_{t+1} + (1 - \theta)c_t \tag{5.22}$$

Inserting both of these assumptions into an equation where prices are expressed as changes yields

$$\Delta p_t = f(c_{t+1}, c_t, s_t, s_{t-1}) \tag{5.23}$$

The equation estimated is

$$\Delta p_t = -39.55 + 0.118c_{t+1} + 0.152c_t - 0.104c_{t-1} - 0.008s_t - 0.031s_{t-1}$$
$$(2.94)\qquad (3.01)\ (-3.47)\qquad (-0.40)\ (-0.15)$$
$$-4.54D_1 - 17.48D_2 - 8.95D_3$$
$$(-0.96)\quad (-6.04)\quad (-3.57)$$

$$R^2 = 0.61;\ D.W. = 2.20$$

Though several of the variables are significant, they are likely to be highly multicollinear.

A more recent formulation of the stock adjustment approach as well as one which is more theoretically sound is that proposed by Weymar.[22] Utilizing the concept of supply of storage presented in Chapter 4, he begins with the same model given by equations 5.10, 5.11, 5.15, and 5.16 but replaces the price equation with one based on the supply of storage function.

$$\frac{p^* - p_t}{h} = f^{-1}(s_t) \qquad (5.24)$$

where the expected price p^* refers to a particular point in the near future with the interval between the current price and the expected price equalling the horizon time h. The actual price relationship finally adopted is based on the supply of storage function expressed in the following form and subsequently combined with Muth's rational expectations hypothesis and the concept of the long run equilibrium price.[23]

$$\frac{dp_t^*}{dh} = f^*(Y_t) \qquad (5.25)$$

where $\dfrac{dp_t^*}{dh}$ = the price rate of change expectation for the time increment from t to $t + dh$, and Y_t = the current inventory level required for coverage measured in time units, i.e., coverage required to meet current consumption. Weymar shows this relationship to be modified as follows with the imposition of Muth's hypothesis

$$\frac{dp_t^{*h}}{dh} = f^*(Y_t^{*h}) \qquad (5.26)$$

where $\dfrac{dp_t^{*h}}{dh}$ = price rate of change expectation for the time increment from $t + h$ to $t + h + dh$ and Y_t^{*h} = current inventory ratio expectation for time $t + h$. The final step requires transforming the left-hand side variable to include the expected long run price $p_t^{*\infty}$.

$$p_t^{*\infty} - p_t = \int_0^\infty f^*(Y_t^{*h}) \, dh \qquad (5.27)$$

or

$$p_t = p_t^{*\infty} - \int_0^\infty f^*(Y_t^{*h}) \, dh \qquad (5.28)$$

The current price level is given as a function of long run equilibrium price expectations and the expected future behavior of the inventory coverage.

An empirical application of this relationship can be found in his study of the cocoa price mechanism. With the price variables now defined as ratios, the following equation best represents those estimated in the study

$$\log\left(\frac{\bar{p}_t}{p_t}\right) = 0.265 + \underset{(1.84)}{0.0092h_t} + \underset{(2.62)}{0.0209z_t} + \underset{(8.60)}{0.524\log Y_t^{*h_1}} - \underset{(-8.57)}{25.7\sum a_i^*\left(\frac{\Delta\bar{p}_t}{p_t}\right)}$$

$$R^2 = 0.85, \ D.W = 2.19$$

where $\bar{p}_t$ = postwar average real spot price of Accra cocoa in New York, p_t = monthly average real spot price of Accra cocoa in New York, h_t = horizon interval, z_t = summary figure of monthly coefficients for inventory ratio expectations, $Y_t^{*h_1}$ = expected inventory ratio at the horizon time, and $\sum a_i^*\left(\frac{\Delta\bar{p}_t}{p_t}\right)$ is the price expectation multiplier expressed as an exponential function of the past cocoa price trend.

Stock-Flow Adjustment. A final form of price relationship appropriate to case 3 represents a combination of stock and flow adjustments. Flow adjustment is present to the extent that it describes the pressure placed by consumption on production. However, the pressure mechanism is stock formulated since it reflects the pressure of consumption or of production on available inventories. Since the consumption to inventory ratio when inverted reflects inventory coverage, the approach resembles that of supply of storage. A price relationship containing both consumption and production ratios, for example, would appear as follows.

$$p_t = f(s_t/c_t, s_t/q_t, z_t, u_t) \tag{5.29}$$

Where the previous period's consumption or production is important relative to current stocks, either of these variables could be lagged. Alternatively, one could introduce changes in one or both of these variables or in the ratio itself.

Desai has used this approach in specifying the price relationship in his tin model where the assumptions correspond to that of case 3.[24] Three separate equations are reported prior to selecting one to be included in the model. These equations vary according to the specification of the stock/flow ratio: (1) inventories at the beginning of the year relative to demand during that year, (2) inventories at the end of the year relative to demand during that year, and (3) inventories at the end of the year and demand during the previous year. Results of estimating the respective equations based on annual data extending from 1940 to 1961 and including a dummy variable reflecting the Korean War period are as follows:

$$p_t = 130.91 - 0.300 \frac{s_t}{c_t} + 29.20 D_t^k \qquad \bar{R}^2 = 0.48$$
$$(-2.16) \qquad (3.51)$$

$$p_t = 137.34 - 0.355 \frac{s_{t-1}}{c_t} + 28.26 D_t^k \qquad \bar{R}^2 = 0.53$$
$$(-2.61) \qquad (3.64)$$

$$p_t = 139.36 - 0.354 \frac{s_{t-1}}{c_{t-1}} + 30.73 D_t^k \qquad \bar{R}^2 = 0.76$$
$$(-7.01) \qquad (5.43)$$

The third equation was selected for use in his model.

Competitive Markets with Speculation

A unique feature of a number of commodity markets is that in addition to trading in the physical commodity, they also feature speculative trading using forward contracts, or futures trading using futures contracts. The principal difference between forward and futures trading is that the latter can more readily include hedging as well as speculation and that the liability of the contract can be shifted more easily. The influence that futures trading has on spot commodity price behavior has been the subject of extensive investigation.[25] Although several approaches to explaining this relationship have been suggested, no comprehensive price theory has resulted from this effort. One approach would imply that the influence of futures market activity may be included in any explanation of spot price behavior by introducing a price variable that reflects futures expectations. For example, the price expectations variable contained in the supply of storage relationship could be specified as the current value of some distant futures contract, pf_t^*:

$$p_t = b_0 + b_1 pf_t^* + b_2 s_t/c_t + u_t \qquad (5.30)$$

Labys and Granger, however, have shown that futures market expectations are likely to influence spot and futures prices simultaneously so that pf_t^* provides little forecast information in the short run.[26] Instead, they take the approach that the influence of futures market activity can best be demonstrated by relating prices to variables reflecting the state of futures market activity such as the volume of short hedging or long speculation commitments. The influence of these variables might best be shown by arranging them as a pressure ratio that reflects the demand for futures contracts relative to the supply of those contracts

$$p_t = b_0 + b_1 p_t^* + b_2 s_t/c_t + b_3 v_t^s/v_t^h + u_t \tag{5.31}$$

where v_t^s = long speculation and v_t^h = short hedging commitments. Including such variables becomes more important where the volume of futures trading for a commodity greatly exceeds the volume of supply or demand; in some cases this may represent a factor of 5 to 20 times. A more detailed explanation of how futures market activity and futures expectations relate to spot price behavior can be found in Weymar, as well as in Labys and Granger.[27]

Noncompetitive Markets

Not all commodity markets possess a competitive structure leading to price adjustments of the forms presented above. As mentioned previously, commodity markets can be dominated by one or a few buyers and sellers with market structures such as monopoly, duopoly, or oligopoly. The principal transformation that must come about in describing price adjustments in noncompetitive markets is to consider prices from the point of view of the actions of individual market participants rather than of the workings of the total market. Such a transformation is described here for the simplest noncompetitive market, that of monopoly. In particular, we illustrate how a general form of price relationship can be derived for a commodity market with one dominant (monopolist) producer and many (perfectly competitive) consumers. The single producer thus maximizes his own profits given the aggregate demand function for the commodity of interest and the supply response of the other firms in the industry.

Our general commodity model presented earlier can be modified to accommodate noncompetitive behavior by replacing the production relationship with an arbitrary cost function.[28]

$$c_t = b_0 + b_1 p_t + b_2 y_t + u_t \tag{5.32}$$

$$\Psi(q)_t = f(q_t) \qquad f'(q_t) > 0 \tag{5.33}$$

$$c_t = q_t \tag{5.34}$$

There is an assumed equivalence between consumption and production and $f'(q_t) > 0$ implies that total cost increases as production increases. Since the monopolist sets his prices to maximize profits, the model framework must also contain a profit relationship.

$$\pi_t = p_t . q_t - \Psi(q)_t \tag{5.35}$$

Equations 5.32 and 5.33 can now be substituted into 5.35.

$$\pi_t = b_0 p_t + b_1 p_t^2 + b_2 y_t p_t - f(q_t) \tag{5.36}$$

To solve for the quantities and prices at which the monopolist maximizes profits, first differentiate equation 5.36 with respect to q_t and set the result equal to zero.

$$\frac{\partial p_t}{\partial q_t} = b_0 \frac{\partial p_t}{\partial q_t} + 2b_1 p_t \frac{\partial p_t}{\partial q_t} + b_2 y_t \frac{\partial p_t}{\partial q_t} - f'(q_t) = 0 \tag{5.37}$$

or introducing $\dfrac{\partial p_t}{\partial q_t} = -\dfrac{1}{b_1}$ from 5.32

$$b_0 + 2b_1 p_t + b_2 y_t - b_1 f'(q_t) = 0 \tag{5.38}$$

Then combine this expression with the consumption equation 5.32 such that

$$p_t = f'(q_t) - \frac{1}{b_1} q_t \tag{5.39}$$

A final relationship suitable for estimation is reached assuming that the cost curve is linear or $f'(q_t)$ is constant.

$$p_t = b_0' - \frac{1}{b_1} q_t \tag{5.40}$$

An example of the use of a price equation of this form can be found in Burrow's model of the cobalt market where prices are set by a dominant producer who maximizes profits.[29] Burrow's basic consumption relationship also contains net exogenous consumption c_t^x which is unaffected by prices

$$c_t = b_0 + b_1 p_t + b_2 y_t + b_3 c_t^x + u_t \tag{5.41}$$

such that the price equation specified is of the form

$$p_t = b_0' - \frac{1}{b_1} c_t - \frac{1}{b_1} c_t^x + v_t \tag{5.42}$$

where c_t is defined as industrial demand and v_t is a stochastic term including variation due to errors in variables. Both linear and nonlinear versions of this equation have been estimated using an instrumental variables technique based on annual data for the years 1947–1966. An example of the results obtained is given below where the equation also contains a U.S. government stockpile variable and a dummy variable reflecting the years of the Congo insurrection.

$$p_t = 1.44 + 0.0661c_t + 0.0457c_t^x - 0.00715s_t^g + 0.650D_t^c$$
$$(3.16) \quad (5.89) \quad (-2.51) \quad (3.18)$$

$$R^2 = 0.96, \ D.W. = 2.38$$

The signs of the variables are as expected since b_1 in equation 5.42 is negative and the coefficients are significant at well over the 5 percent level.

Some research has already taken place regarding the derivation of price relationships for other noncompetitive markets such as duopoly and oligopoly, and this should lead to greater realism in dealing with commodity markets of this nature.[30]

Lauric Oils Prices

The behavior of lauric oils prices is best explained by recalling that both imports and exports of lauric oils tend to be relatively price inelastic in the short run.[31] The annual data interval being short relative to the lags whereby consumers and producers adjust their behavior, market equilibrium follows from the interplay of inventories and prices. However, it should be recognized that prices are more related to inventory changes during years of "normal" export conditions. Given years of extreme export fluctuations such as those of 1962 or 1966, price swings tend to follow inversely the swings in exports, with inventories being less important.

As for other variables to be incorporated into the price relationship, it should be observed that the high prices reached in 1959 and 1960 had been mitigated to some extent by the release of lauric oil stockpiles held in the U.S. by the General Services Administration. This would warrant also introducing an appropriate dummy variable. Finally, while the spectrum of coconut oil prices given in Figure 5-3 (above) contains no cycles, the presence of a low degree of positive autocorrelation indicates that it might be useful to also include a lagged term based on the dependent price variable.

The first equation presented specifies inventory adjustment as a flow process, using changes in total inventories, exports, and lagged prices as explanatory variables. Prices are defined as deflated New York coconut oil prices, and inventories include estimates of year-end inventories for the U.S., U.K., and the E.E.C. among the importing countries and for the Philippines and Ceylon among the exporting countries. The equation is estimated using OLS with annual data covering the period 1953 through 1967.

$$p_t = 0.85 - 0.105p_{t-1} + 0.00056\Delta s_t^w - 0.00029x_t^w$$
$$(-0.47) \qquad (2.71) \qquad (-4.47)$$
$$\bar{R}^2 = 0.63, \ D.W. = 1.10$$

Two of the variables are significant although lagged prices has the wrong sign. When the G.S.A. dummy variable is added to this equation, the lagged price variable has the correct sign but the change in inventories variable becomes insignificant.

$$p_t = 0.60 + 0.398 \ p_{t-1} - 0.00045 \ \Delta s_t^w - 0.00024 \ x_t^w - 0.045 \ D_t^{gsa}$$
$$(2.21) \qquad (-1.15) \qquad (-3.46) \qquad (-2.32)$$
$$\bar{R}^2 = 0.58, \ D.W. = 2.06$$

The next equations examine the price determination process as one of stock adjustment. Of these, the first includes the influence of the total oils and fats market in the form of a general oils and fats price index as well as that of consumption using a variable reflecting demand in the major importing countries. The G.S.A. dummy variable is excluded from the remaining equations since it was best included in the U.S. inventory equation.

$$p_t = 0.63 - 0.00006s_t^w - 0.00040c_t^m + 0.00237p_t^o - 0.00010x_t^w$$
$$(-0.31) \qquad (-2.57) \qquad (1.83) \qquad (-1.16)$$
$$\bar{R}^2 = 0.57, \ D.W. = 2.10$$

Only the total consumption variable is significant. The following relationship, which includes a lagged inventory variable, provides a generally better explanation.

$$p_t = 0.52 + 0.371p_{t-1} - 0.00035s_t^w - 0.00022s_{t-1}^w - 0.00011x_t^w$$
$$(1.68) \qquad (-1.58) \qquad (-1.14) \qquad (-1.32)$$
$$\bar{R}^2 = 0.64, \ D.W. = 1.45$$

Although none of the variables in the equation are highly significant, it did explain turning points reasonably well and is included in the linear version of the lauric oils model presented in Chapters 6, 7, and 8.

Finally, price adjustment has been considered as a combined stock-flow process. This particular specification reflected the attitude of a number of market experts as to the nature of price determination, and the inventory variable is probably more meaningful when normalized relative to consumption. The inventory variable now relates only to the major importing countries.

$$p_t = 0.42 + 0.603p_{t-1} - 0.521 \frac{s_t^m}{c_t^m} - 0.00019x_t^w$$
$$(3.37) \qquad (-2.37) \qquad (-1.87)$$

$$R^2 = 0.59, \ D.W. = 1.57$$

While this equation is superior to the others with two out of three variables being highly significant, the presence of nonlinearity in the form of the inventory/consumption ratio makes it less useful for analyzing the dynamic properties of the model as will be explained in later chapters. It did, nonetheless, prove successful when used in the model for the simulation exercises of Chapter 9.

One major criticism of the above equations, aside from displaying only a moderate degree of explanation, is that they do not include the possibility that price response may differ as world export levels of lauric oils exceed 1.6 million tons. At this level the market is said to move from a condition of supply scarcity to that of supply abundance. Beyond this level prices are said to react more readily to changes in market variables as well as to changes in the market for substitutes. Preliminary tests of this hypothesis have not shown this to be true, although better tests can be devised once improved data are accumulated.

Conclusions

In this chapter we have pointed out some of the problems encountered in specifying commodity price relationships. Many of the problems originate from the fact that a single price relationship cannot describe the price mechanism correctly without considering the assumptions followed in other equations within the same model. The best approach which might be taken to solving these problems would be to develop a general theory that considers actual rather than ideal market structure, relates to speculation and hedging as well as physical trading, and includes factors such as expectations or information which reflect market psychology.[32]

In the absence of such an approach, we have concentrated instead on a framework that considers separately stock and flow relationships within a competitive market, the modification of these relationships in the presence of speculative activity, and a profit maximizing relationship within a noncompetitive market. Any of these relationships can be formulated dynamically and can include expectations, although the more complex aspects of market psychology are neglected.

Of the theories of price behavior examined, the most promising are those of stock adjustment or supply of storage. These come the closest to being relevant for markets containing both physical and speculative trading, and are being applied empirically to a greater number of commodities. Where price making behavior reflects flow adjustment conditions, one of the simpler models presented would be appropriate. The question still remains of how to explain price behavior of a very short run nature; statistical time series methods can be used, but any general price theory must also include this special aspect of commodity price behavior.

Part II
Complete Commodity Models

6 Model Specification and Estimation

This chapter introduces the theory and method of constructing dynamic commodity models. The approach taken involves two separate yet integral considerations. The first concerns incorporating the component behavioral relationships presented earlier into complete and unified models. The second pertains to the econometric techniques of specifying, identifying, and estimating such models. After an introduction to the historical background relevant to commodity models, the chapter begins with a general discussion of the different model types. Our principal concern is with equilibrium econometric models, but some attention is also given to process, trade, industrial dynamics, and systems models. The specification of equilibrium models is considered next, together with procedures for determining causality and for model identification. Methods of estimation are presented emphasizing those which would be the most practical for dealing with commodity models. As an example of model specification and estimation, the lauric oils behavioral relationships presented thus far are assembled into a complete model. The conclusions summarize the difficulties encountered in moving from abstract model construction to practical model use.

Nature of Commodity Models

Background

A commodity model can be defined as a formal representation of a commodity market or industry where the behavioral relationships selected reflect the underlying economic laws. The attributes of commodity models resemble those of other economic models. They can be static or dynamic, linear or nonlinear, stochastic or nonstochastic, open or closed, recursive or simultaneous. Their performance can be stable or unstable, or transient or steady state. The commodity models of most interest in this study are those which are dynamic, nonlinear, closed systems of a simultaneous or recursive nature with stable performance.

The historical development of commodity models can be traced to the early studies regarding the demand for agricultural commodities. The concept of a microeconomic model appears earlier in the writings of economists, but one of the first attempts to formulate it on an empirical basis can be found in a study published by Moore in 1919.[1] This development also appears to coincide with beginnings of commodity model research within the U.S.D.A.[2]

The next publications that mark an advance in model development begin with the works of Schultz, the first one appearing in 1928, and his important *Theory and Measurement of Demand* appearing in 1938.[3] Ezekiel also published a paper in 1938, which summarizes and advances the theory of the cobweb; this is often considered the first dynamic commodity model.[4] Particular attention to obtaining an equilibrium solution from solving sets of equations can be found in a 1939 study by Tinbergen.[5] Research concerning the difficult problems of identification and simultaneity also began during this period. Most of the advances made in this respect are associated with the work of the Cowles Commission. Related publications are a paper by Haavelmo in 1943 and the well known *Statistical Inference in Dynamic Economic Models*, edited by Koopmans, which appeared in 1950.[6]

These advances, together with the publication of *Demand Analysis* by Wold and Jureen in 1953, are largely responsible for the active commodity model building that characterized the 1950s.[7] As in earlier periods, much of this activity took place within the U.S.D.A. Meinken published several models related to the demand and price structure of oats, barley, soybeans, grain, and wheat.[8] Fox published a detailed study of the supply and demand for farm products,[9] and Rojko is known for his model of dairy products.[10] A study of special interest is that of Foote, which provided a general approach to building models for different commodities.[11] Outside the U.S.D.A., Hildreth and Jarrett published an elaborate model of the livestock-feed economy, Wallace and Judge produced a model of the beef and pork economy, and Cohen produced one of the first evolutionary simulation models in his study of the shoe, leather, and hide sequence.[12] With respect to the problem of determining the stability or internal consistency of models, Suits provided a useful method of solution in his dynamic analysis of the watermelon market.[13] Selecting one publication which seems to best describe the model building that took place in that period, Fox's *Econometric Analysis for Public Policy* is the most appropriate.[14]

The 1960s brought a substantial change in the levels of sophistication of commodity models. Not only did emphasis shift to constructing models that could be dynamic and nonlinear, but advances took place both in methods of estimation and of simulation. Some of this progress stems from the work of economists such as Klein, Goldberger, Fromm, Fisher, and Evans, whose studies dealt with the development of macroeconometric models of the U.S. economy.[15] Other progress relates directly to the development of micro-econometric commodity models, and the extent of the model building which has taken place since then can be viewed in Appendix C. Of particular interest among models advancing useful techniques are the potato model of Zusman, the livestock-feed model of Egbert and Reutlinger, the hog model of Harlow, the cocoa model of Weymar, and the tin model of Desai.[16] The latter model is the first of many which have been constructed at the Wharton School; others include the rubber model of Behrman, the tea model of Murti, the petroleum model of Adams and Griffin, and the steel model of Higgins.[17] Recent agricultural models of interest are Witherell's wool model, Mo's wheat model, Labys' lauric oils model, Matthews and Womack's soybean and tung oil models, the Houck and Subotnik model of soybeans and soybean products, and Hayenga and Hacklander's model of the hog sector.[18] A number of nonferrous metal models have been built by Burrows and his colleagues at Charles River Associates.[19] Finally, some research has concentrated on designing models to explain the behavior of all agricultural commodities combined. Of particular interest here are the works of Cromarty appearing in 1959, and of Evans and of Egbert appearing in 1969.[20]

To provide further detail as to the different types of models recently constructed, it is necessary to discuss the major types separately. We first consider the theoretical structure of equilibrium econometric models, contrast this structure to that of other model types, and then develop the equilibrium approach more fully.

Equilibrium Econometric Models

The form of commodity model most commonly considered is one whose solution is reached through the equilibrium of a set of demand and supply conditions—for example, as shown in Figure 6–1. Expressed more formally, let c_t and q_t represent the quantities of a commodity demanded and supplied to a particular market where p_t is the price at which transactions take place.[21] Both c_t and q_t are known to depend on p_t, although they may also depend on its lagged values, p_{t-j}. Under these conditions the equilibrium model would consist of two parts: (1) a set of two equations $c_t = f(p_t)$ and $q_t = g(p_t)$ composed of three real nonnegative endogenous variables c_t, q_t, and p_t where f and g are the given functions; and (2) an identity $c_t = q_t$ which assures that the market is in equilibrium. This can be written more generally as

$$c_t = f(p_t, p_{t-j}, y_t, z_{1t}, \ldots, z_{kt})$$
$$q_t = g(p_t, p_{t-j}, z_{1t}, \ldots, z_{kt}) \tag{6.1}$$
$$c_t = q_t$$

where $z_{1t}, \ldots, z_{kt}$ represent appropriate exogenous variables required to complete the equations. Econometric methods are normally followed in translating this theoretical model into its more useful empirical or statistical counterpart. The procedure followed requires that each of the behavioral equations in model 6.1 include a disturbance term and that the variables and parameters in the equations follow the assumptions of classic regression theory. Stated more formally, the model must be specified, estimated, and

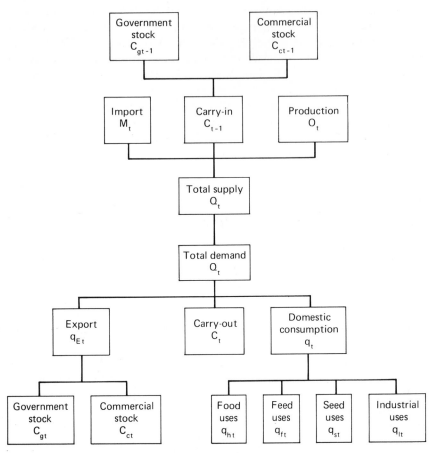

Figure 6-1. Flow–Diagram of U.S. Wheat Supply and Utilization. Source: William Y. Mo, *An Economic Analysis of the Dynamics of the United States Wheat Sector*, Tech. Bull. No. 1395, Economic Research Service, U.S.D.A., April 1968.

tested in a specific manner that includes the following steps: (1) selecting variables, (2) applying economic theory to hypothesize relationships between the variables, (3) combining the equations into the model structure, (4) identification, (5) refining some a priori model based on statistical inference and a particular set of data, (6) validating the final model, (7) and applying it to historical explanation, prediction or decision making.

To select variables for the model, one must first classify the variables as being endogenous, exogenous, or predetermined, depending on the economic system to be described. Variables whose values are determined within the model are *endogenous*; variables whose values are not determined within the model but are taken as given from outside of the model are *exogenous*. The latter variables, together with any lagged endogenous variables, are defined as *predetermined* variables. A number of relationships are then formed which represent the interaction between the endogenous and the predetermined variables. The actual selection of variables to be included in the relationships follows from one or more hypotheses that reflect various aspects of microeconomic theory as, for example, featured in the previous chapters.

The assembling of the equations to form the a priori *model* or *structure* should follow the equilibrium or other characteristics of the commodity market of interest. The total number of behavioral or structural equations should equal the total number of endogenous variables, including as many identities as required. The completed model describes the distribution of endogenous variables corresponding to every set of values of the exogenous variables. The nature of the interdependence found among the endogenous variables will be either recursive, extending from one period to the next, or simultaneous, occurring within the same period. Finally the model must be identified and an appropriate estimation technique selected.

The transformation from an a priori model to some final model requires statistical inference based on the observed values of the endogenous and the exogenous variables. One assumes that one of several alternative model structures represents the actual process which has determined the values of the variables. Through statistical inference the choice of alternative structures is narrowed to obtain a final structure that agrees with the empirical facts. One can also determine the validity of the structure adopted using stability analysis.

Assuming that the phenomena to be studied entail random determination of certain quantities or prices where the values of the exogenous variables are assumed to be fixed and known, the final structure selected defines a probability distribution of the endogenous variables on the sample space. The model would represent the true one only if it defines the probability distribution that would be found if numerous samples were taken with the same set of exogenous variables. Given the complexity of the phenomena that we attempt to measure in commodity markets, as well as the lack of opportunity to conduct controlled experiments, one must work with the found or estimated structure as if it were the true structure.

The model can then be used to analyze policy questions through historical explanation or prediction. Naylor has suggested three approaches, which can be used to evaluate the impact of alternative policies on a commodity economy.[22] The first of these entails Theil's method of maximizing a welfare function, which contains a set of policy goals ranked by the decision maker and is subject to the constraints imposed by the model. The second is the

Tinbergen method, which requires setting policy goals or targets for selected endogenous variables and then solves for values of the other variables which are consistent with the goals and the model. The third and most practical approach is the policy simulation method, which determines values of the endogenous variables from the reduced form or structural form of the model based on given values of the policy variables. Policy simulation is particularly useful for forecasting because the predicted endogenous variables can be one-period ahead or evolutionary, depending on whether the model generates its own values for the lagged endogenous variables.

Process Econometric Models

Commodity models of the process econometric type differ from equilibrium models in several respects.[23] Most commonly, process models deal with supply and demand as inputs and outputs of an industry rather than as equilibrating factors in a market. The particular industry of interest also may have product markets displaying varying degrees of monopoly. Under these circumstances it would follow that the functional relationships required for explaining the behavior of the endogenous variables involve transforming one or more of the finished product demands into commodity inputs. This flow of action suggests that the form of the model be recursive with lines of causality extending from demand to supply. Price determination, of course, would not result from market equilibrium but rather from a system of cost plus markup; alternatively prices may be administered.

The best known of these models are the petroleum model of Adams and Griffin and the steel model of Higgins, both mentioned above. Taking the steel model as an example, the concept of a process model can be further explained. That model is constructed to reflect lines of economic causality emanating from product demand and running recursively backwards toward production and input demands. As shown in Figure 6–2, the principal relationships contained in the model describe domestic and import demand, production and input demand, and investment in inventories and plant and equipment.

Beginning with the determination of domestic and import demand, Figure 6–2 implies that detailed demand projections could be obtained based on general economic conditions as in *B* or that aggregate demand could be generated from a macroeconometric model as in *A*. Product prices, rather than being determined endogenously, are administered. Demand for these products subsequently induces finished product output, which becomes transferred to input requirements. These requirements are finally reflected in the demand for commodity inputs such as pig iron and coke. The important characteristic of input demand is that it reflects the technical qualities of the

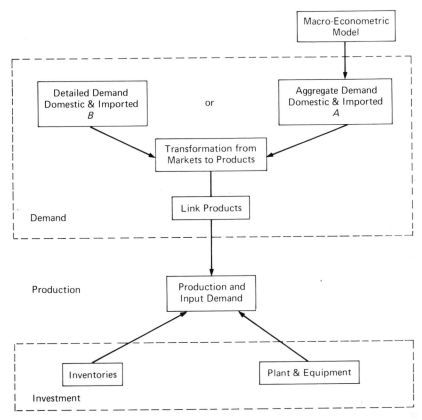

Figure 6-2. Causal Flows in a Commodity Process Model. Source: C.I. Higgins, "An Econometric Description of the U.S. Steel Industry," in *Essays in Industrial Econometrics*, Vol. II, L.R. Klein (Ed.) (Philadelphia: Wharton School of Finance and Commerce, 1969), p. 5.

production process more so than input prices, the relative degree depending on the nature of the vertical structure of the industry. The determination of investment in inventories and plant and equipment follows from lagged production, indicating that investment precedes current production in filling the gap between anticipated output and efficient capacity utilization. Predictions from the model based on conditional forecasts can be provided for important variables such as total domestic shipments of steel, value of finished goods inventories, pig iron consumption, coal consumption, and so forth.

Process models have an important advantage in that they can be readily combined with other types of models to provide a more complete description of both competitive and noncompetitive market and industry behavior. On the one hand, forecasts from a macroeconomic model can be used to determine general economic conditions and, consequently, aggregate demand for final products. On the other hand, engineering information such as that contained in a linear programming model can serve as a link describing the transformation between input demands and the final products. This latter approach has been taken by Adams and Griffin in their redesigning of the petroleum model.

Customarily used for refinery scheduling, the linear programming framework provides a useful method for determining input demands or supply in an industry characterized by joint products and many processes. The econometric approach is retained in the model for estimating the demand relationships based on influences exogenous to the petroleum industry, and for approximating price determination within the industry. One can still surround such a combination of models with simulation analysis, and this improves the effectiveness of process models in forecasting and in analyzing policy decisions.

Trade Econometric Models

Only very recently have trade models received attention or application in describing individual commodity flows. Definitions of trade models vary, depending on whether one is considering flow models or spatial equilibrium models. Traditional flow models pertain to a system of import and export equations that together with a trade flow matrix explain the effects of changes in economic conditions upon trade between two or more countries. Interregional or spatial equilibrium models are a special form of trade model. They also contain a system of import and export equations, but trade flows are determined by using an objective function which, for example, minimizes transfer costs between regions. While both these approaches are amenable to determining trade flows for individual commodities, the latter approach has been more fully examined in empirical studies.

The major forms of flow models are summarized in a recent paper by Taplin.[24] These forms vary depending on the selection of trade flows to be studied and the way the selected flows are approached. One form of model may have separate functions for total imports and exports of each country, but does not necessarily attempt to estimate individual flows between countries. Another form may attempt to determine individual import-export flows directly, and obtains total imports and exports only as a summation of appropriate flows. The first of these forms can also be classified as a *transmissions* approach, which traces the transmissions of short run fluctuations in domestic economic activities between countries; the second can be classified as a *structure of trade* approach, which analyzes the actual structure of trade based on income, population, geographical distances, and related factors.

Rhomberg further analyzes these approaches as they might relate to explaining commodity trade between countries.[25] He first observes that a modification of the transmissions approach is useful with models where the goal is to produce forecasts of imports and exports based on domestic conditions and certain exogenous variables. When the forecasts of the world totals of imports are inconsistent with respect to forecasts of total exports, an iterative procedure can be used to generate a new set of forecasts based on different assumptions regarding the domestic and exogenous conditions. The world totals are compared again, and the process of iteration continues until the forecasts of world exports and imports are consistent.

Adams et al. have taken this approach in constructing a flow model designed to explain the imports and exports of OECD countries.[26] Rhomberg points out that such a model could be used to explain trade for individual commodity groupings. He also suggested that one could incorporate into the model a procedure for estimating commodity prices, utilizing a set of demand and supply estimates made by the respective countries.[27]

To adapt the structure of trade approach to explaining individual or group commodity flows, a more complex procedure is necessary. First, import functions and a fixed coefficient trade-share matrix must be estimated; and second, exports must be determined based on the matrix transformation of the import estimates. It is difficult to obtain useful results with such a procedure because of problems in estimating the trade-share matrix and in computing exports given differences in valuation bases (c.i.f. and f.o.b.). As these difficulties are overcome, Rhomberg claims that such a model could be extended to forecast trade by commodity class. Substantial progress has already taken place as is witnessed by Armington's work on the market shares problem and by Taplin's commodity trade version of the "Expanded World Trade Model" being built for project LINK.[28]

The interregional or spatial equilibrium model provides a more practical approach to forecasting levels of commodity imports and exports. Fox and Bawden had previously suggested this approach, and, more recently, Takayama and Judge have developed and refined it.[29] A spatial equilibrium model generally describes an economic system of a competitive nature, utilizing a set of equations that include the aggregate demand and supply for one or more commodities, the distribution of activities over space, and the equilibrium conditions.[a] When applied to explaining commodity trade, it can assign flows directly in addition to determining equilibrium quantities and prices. Further-

[a] Although the spatial equilibrium model is discussed here within the context of trade models, Takayama and Judge show that it represents an approach to commodity modeling which can also be applied to domestic spatial or regional equilibrium analysis.

more, the solution is obtained by a programming algorithm that attempts to optimize the flow allocation according to some objective function. Where the objective function is in the form of a linear program, the model builder can now incorporate additional constraints into the model, which provides a more flexible tool for evaluating policy decisions. The only immediate disadvantage of this approach is that certain variables such as income or export earnings cannot be readjusted within the model to accommodate sharp changes in the size and direction of trade.

A recently constructed combination equilibrium-flow trade model following the spatial equilibrium form is that of Rojko, Urban, and Naive.[30] Their model determines world demand prospects for wheat, rice, and coarse grains in 1980 based on given levels of exogenous factors such as population, income, changing tastes, and technology. This is accomplished by utilizing a linear programming transportation matrix, which determines trade flows among 22 regions based on the objective of minimizing transfer costs. The econometric portions of the model consist of a set of import and export relationships, a set of price relationships distinguished according to farm and consumer wholesale prices and import and export wholesale prices, and a set of transportation constraints. One added feature of the model is that trade prices are partly determined by the dual shadow prices reflecting price differentials among shipping points. Projections to 1980 are then made based on perceived changes in agricultural productivity and development policies. Variables forecast include consumption, production, and net trade, as well as import costs and export values.

It seems that this approach could be useful in further commodity analysis where the number of commodities and major regions of interest are also of a small number. It would also be useful to endogenize the earnings and income or population variables, allowing for suitable feedback of these factors on trade.[31]

Industrial Dynamics Models

The industrial dynamics approach to constructing commodity models differs considerably from those mentioned above. Although the approach is applicable to market equilibrium or industrial process, it requires an integrated methodology similar to systems models and data compiled as rates or flows rather than as static observations. Industrial dynamics can be defined as the study of the information characteristics of industrial activity to show how organizational structure and amplifications and time delays within a system interact to influence its final performance.[32] These interactions are considered in terms of the flow of commodities, capital, money, orders, personnel, and information.

In addition to economic factors, flows of information can relate to biological, technological, or psychological considerations. The principal characteristic of the approach is that it analyses time-linked decision making processes that contain information feedback loops. When considering commodity markets these loops can be described in terms of consumption and production variables that constantly adjust to maintain inventory coverage at some desired level. When inventories decline below this level, price increases cause rates of consumption to decrease or rates of production to increase until inventories return to the desired level. Thus industrial dynamics can be described as a feedback process that shows how an environment leads to a decision that results in an action that influences the environment and, consequently, any future decisions.

In practice, the application of this approach has been facilitated through the development of a special computer language known as DYNAMO.[33] Examples of applications include Ballmer's study of the copper industry, Schlager's study of the aluminum industry, and Raulerson and Langham's study of the concentrated frozen orange juice industry.[34] One should observe that there are certain similarities among these commodities that lend themselves to the industrial dynamics approach.

First, differences between supply and demand normally have resulted in proportionally greater swings in prices. Second, other changes in the system often have led to amplified swings in production as well as prices. Third, these commodity systems typically are influenced by noneconomic factors such as biological, physical, or psychological conditions. Finally, all the systems are characterized by definite time lags between production, actual and desired inventories, and consumption.

A most recent extension of the industrial dynamics approach has been Meadow's development of a unique form of a model directly applicable to commodity markets featuring the above characteristics.[35] His *Dynamic Commodity Cycle Model* concentrates on the formulation of the important production–price response mechanism. In particular, it features the following characteristics: (1) producers may employ any function of current and past prices to form expectations about future prices; (2) flows are included in the form of inventories of processed commodities and other information; (3) rate analysis is used implying that production and consumption adjust continuously rather than abruptly to price changes; and (4) prices, consumption, inventories, and production are interrelated through two negative feedback loops.

Commodity markets which have been simulated utilizing the DCCM include hogs, broilers, and cattle. Results of the studies suggest that factors such as the desired coverage decision may be more important than price elasticities in determining long run production policies. There is some question concerning additional commodities which might be adapted to the DCCM framework without requiring major changes, but the method should prove effective where commodities possess the attributes mentioned earlier and are highly sensitive to expectations and other information flows.

Systems Models

Commodity systems models explain commodity activity in terms of a broader range of objectives and information flows than do econometric, equilibrium, process, or trade models, taken by themselves. One of the advantages of the systems approach is that it can be more easily adapted to explain noncompetitive commodity markets such as those characterized by oligopoly or duopoly.[36] It also permits models to be operated on a reasonably large scale, enabling all major economic and noneconomic relationships to be contained within a single structure. These relationships can also be specified on the basis of a number of different techniques, utilizing almost any kind of information; the resulting model often represents a multiplicity of models. Finally, the systems approach allows models to be operated sequentially, and this feature, when based on feedback or adaptive control mechanisms, should permit models to cope with problems of stuctural change. Below we examine systems models as classified according to three types.

Structural Models. Perhaps the least complex of the approaches in a mathematical sense is that of Arthur. His systems model would be a "complex of numerous interrelated variables and dimensions relating to a definable set of objectives."[37] The components that would be assembled to form such a model include system objectives, functions to be performed in fufilling the objectives, and a management control structure. A commodity model assembled according to this approach can be found in his study of the banana industry, though not in the form of a computer simulation.[38]

Econometric Models. A typical procedure in constructing a systems model involves integrating an equilibrium econometric model with a number of operating or decision rules, with other forms of engineering, biological, or least-cost programming models such as linear or nonlinear programming, or with a number of specialized techniques such as cost-benefit analysis or program budgeting. For example, if one wishes to determine the values of certain control or policy variables that would optimize some welfare function for a particular commodity market, the econometric model could be combined with a dynamic programming model according to the theory of feedback control.[39]

Among models of this type, a distinction can be drawn between industry models and agricultural market models.

Examples of industry models would be those often referred to as computer simulation models: (1) Cohen's model of the shoe, leather, and hide sequence; (2) the Naylor, Sasser, and Wallace model of the textile industry; (3) the Balderston and Hoggatt model of the lumber industry; and (4) the Vernon, Rives, and Naylor model of the tobacco industry.[40] The common properties of these models include the selection of variables that describe the basic flow characteristics of the industry rather than conventional market behavior as well as the adoption of a fully recursive structure that permits an evolutionary description of the industry variables extending over a large number of future periods. The models are also of a form that would permit individual firms within the industry to evaluate the impact of their policy decisions and the reactions of the other firms to these decisions over the past historical period as well as over some future period.

The agricultural market models which are being developed as systems simulations relate to the livestock industries and include beef, hogs, pork, broilers, dairy products, eggs, and turkeys. This work is being carried out principally by the Animal Products Branch of the Economic Research Service of the U.S.D.A. Among those currently in operation are the price-output model of the beef and pork sector developed by Crom, the forecast model of the broiler industry developed by O'Mara, and the hog-pork model of Sullivan and Liu.[41]

All these models have the major characteristic of not only providing estimates of an evolutionary nature for the basic variables but also of being strongly systems oriented. Each model normally contains three different subsystems: the physical flows of product; pricing points together with flows of prices between markets; and a coordinative system described by the nature of contractual arrangements, lines of integration, or other linkages. This form of model lends itself well to the analysis of some of the policy issues common to livestock industries, which include questions of vertical integration and coordination, regulatory and antitrust policy, capital requirements, substitutes and synthetics, and environmental balance.

Maximization Models. This class of models, although only vaguely of the systems type, can be distinguished according to the nature of the programming or maximization algorithm followed. Of most recent interest is the systems model of the U.S. rice industry designed by Holders, Shaw, and Snyder.[42] This model is built around a nonlinear programming algorithm so as to evaluate policies regarding the optimum location of rice mills and flows of rice from producers to consumers. Other models can be identified as being built around the spatial equilibrium algorithm mentioned previously. Worthy of mention also are the Lee and Seaver model of the U.S. broiler market and the Bawden, Carter, and Dean model of interregional competition in the U.S. turkey industry.[43]

Related to this type of model is that of reactive programming. Tramel and Seale have used this algorithm to describe the behavior of the markets for fresh vegetables; and more recently Dhillon has applied it to markets for milk, and King and Ho have constructed a simple beef and pork simulation.[44] A final form of model to be mentioned is that developed by Gulbrandsen *et al.*, based on a price equilibrium algorithm, which determines world market prices for agricultural commodities utilizing alternative assumptions about national price policies.[45] This approach has found application in the recent projections to 1980 of equilibrium commodity quantities and prices made by the F.A.O.[46]

In conclusion, although systems models would appear to be extremely flexible in their ability to deal with surrounding market institutions and changing market structures, they do not necessarily provide advantages over ordinary econometric models. The excessive concern that a systems model should simulate the actual observations perfectly leads to "data fitting" and may result in neglect of the behavioral theory underlying the model. Also, systems models at present cannot cope any better with problems of excessive fluctuations in variables or what Arthur has termed "episodic events."[47]

Structure of Commodity Models

In the following section the discussion of the structure of the equilibrium econometric model considered above will be expanded, although the theories and methods examined here are relevant also for other forms of commodity models. We will be concerned in particular with the first three of the steps of model specification and use mentioned earlier.

The first step includes examining the basic economic and institutional structure of the market or industry of interest, selecting which variables, both endogenous and predetermined, best describe that structure, and applying economic theory to hypothesize the relationship that should exist in combining the variables and equations into a complete model. The second step requires examining the lines of causality in the model and verifying the nature of the relationship between the endogenous variables to be recursive or simultaneous. Finally, one must determine whether the model finally reached is identified. Obviously, one cannot structure a model without considering these steps simultaneously, but our distinction provides an appropriate departure for discussion.

Specification

The general specification of any linear dynamic commodity model can be written in the following form

$$\Gamma Y_t + \beta_1 Y_{t-j} + \beta_2 X_t = U_t \tag{6.2}$$

where $Y_t = a\ G \times n$ matrix of current endogenous variables, $Y_{t-j} = a\ G \times n$ matrix of lagged endogenous variables, $X_t = a\ M \times n$ matrix of exogenous variables, $U_t = a\ G \times n$ matrix of stochastic disturbance terms. Γ and $\beta_1 = G \times G$ matrices of coefficients on the endogenous variables and their lagged values, and $\beta_2 = a\ G \times M$ matrix of the coefficients on the exogenous variables. Intercepts can be obtained by letting $X_t = 1$ for all t where desirable.

This model, quite general in structure, can include any number of commodities and equations or relationships. Among the types of equations considered for commodity models are behavioral relationships based on economic theory, such as those previously given explaining demand, supply, inventories, and prices: identities that reflect market clearing conditions or market aggregations; definitional or technical equations, etc.

The a priori structure adopted for commodity models of this form depends on the assumptions made regarding the relationships between the endogenous variables in the market as well as the behavioral equations that explain the endogenous variables. These relationships can be illustrated using charts which show the flow of commodities from producer to consumer and generally describe the economic forces that underlie a commodity market. Figures 6–1 to 6–3 feature examples of typical commodity flow charts. Each of these charts is based on certain perceptions regarding the flow of commodities and the process of price determination as well as the nature of institutional arrangements and information flows. A number of possible specifications exist for translating these charts to some a priori structure, as the diversity of existing commodity models shows. We begin by demonstrating several elementary specifications that could be extended to develop more sophisticated models. Though this approach tends towards oversimplification, it avoids the difficulties of attempting to generalize from a number of elaborate model structures.

The simple equilibrium model given earlier represents the most elementary form in which the general model 6.2 would appear. Demand and supply for a commodity are explained in terms of two equations composed of three endogenous variables and an indentity describing the market clearing condition[a]

$$c_t = f(c_{t-1}, p_t, p_{t-j}, y_t, z_t, u_t)$$
$$q_t = g(q_{t-1}, p_t, p_{t-j}, z_t, u_t) \tag{6.3}$$
$$c_t = q_t$$

---

[a] Each of the behavioral equations presented in this section is based on an arbitrary selection of explanatory variables. No causality is implied in the selection but could very well exist through reorganization of the variables. Specifications are also presented independently of any normalization arguments which would justify including equations only for certain endogenous variables.

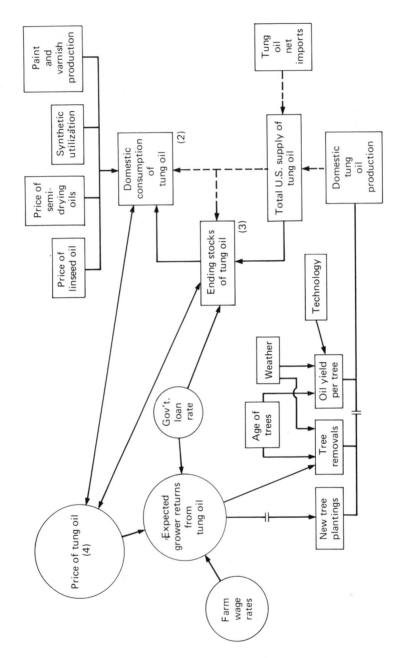

Figure 6-3. Flow-Diagram of the United States Tung Oil Economy. Source: J.L. Matthews and A.B. Womack, "An Appraisal of the U.S. Tung Oil Economy", *Southern Journal of Agricultural Economics*, (December 1970), p. 163.

where more than one exogenous variable z_t may be included in each equation as considered necessary. Recall that for such a model to be complete, it must contain the same number of equations as endogenous variables. In this case there are two stochastic equations plus one nonstochastic equation equal in number to the three endogenous variables.

The first level of sophistication normally brought to this model requires introducing the assumption that inventories exist and that they explicitly influence price determination.

$$c_t = f(c_{t-1}, p_t, p_{t-j}, y_t, z_t, u_t)$$

$$q_t = g(q_{t-1}, p_t, p_{t-j}, z_t, u_t)$$

$$p_t = h(p_{t-1}, s_t - s_{t-1}, z_t, u_t) \tag{6.4}$$

$$s_t - s_{t-1} = q_t - c_t .$$

A practical example of how inventories might be integrated into a model can be found in the tung oil model of Matthews and Womack or the tungsten model of Burrows.[48] The importance of selecting an identity that correctly closes a model should be obvious in an example such as this. A major factor in completing any commodity model is the judicious selection of identities, which will aid not only in explaining an endogenous variable difficult to interpret otherwise, but also in closing the model in the sense of making it self-contained or capable of evolutionary behavior. Where data for a commodity market are incomplete it may not be possible to accomplish closure, and one must search for other means to make the model as self-contained as possible.

It frequently happens that the total quantity of a commodity demanded or supplied is not resolved within the domestic market and a portion of this quantity must be imported from or exported to foreign markets. In adapting the above model to include foreign trade, the question arises as to whether separate import or export behavioral equations should be added to the model or whether imports or exports should be determined on the basis of identities. As to which of these alternatives is preferable, some guidelines are given in Chapters 2 and 3. If import or export fluctuations are determined by factors other than those explaining demand or supply, it might be useful to introduce one or more new behavioral equations in to the model. Also, if imports or exports are more relevant to explaining market behavior, a behavioral equation representing either of these variables might replace either a consumption or production equation. The model given below represents a third alternative, namely that imports or exports constitute a residual reflected in the domestic stock adjustment

$$c_t = f(c_{t-1}, p_t, p_{t-j}, y_t, z_t, u_t)$$

$$q_t = g(q_{t-1}, p_t, p_{t-j}, z_t, u_t)$$

$$p_t = h(p_{t-1}, s_t - s_{t-1}, z_t, u_t) \qquad (6.5)$$

$$s_t = v(s_{t-1}, p_t, p_{t-j}, z_t, u_t)$$

$$xm_t = s_t - s_{t-1} + q_t - c_t$$

where xm_t represents levels of exports or imports. In some cases, it may be desirable to replace the identity with a net trade behavioral relationship. The inclusion of export equations in an otherwise domestic model can be seen in the Houck and Manne soybean study.[49]

The discussion of inventory behavior in Chapter 4 has revealed the possibility that the process of market adjustment can be expanded to include separate behavioral equations for inventories held by consumers and inventories held by producers. An equation for speculative inventories could also be of importance. The change brought to model 6.3 by introducing the first possibility is as follows

$$c_t = f(c_{t-1}, p_t, p_{t-j}, y_t, z_t, u_t)$$

$$q_t = g(q_{t-1}, p_t, p_{t-j}, z_t, u_t)$$

$$s_t^c = v(s_{t-1}^c, p_t, p_{t-j}, z_t, u_t) \qquad (6.6)$$

$$s_t^q = w(s_{t-1}^q, p_t, p_{t-j}, z_t, u_t)$$

$$c_t + s_t^c - s_{t-1}^c = q_t + s_t^q - s_{t-1}^q$$

where s_t^c and s_t^q represent consumer and producer inventory levels respectively. An example of including both consumer and producer inventory equations can be found in Witherell's wool model.[50]

Another modification consists of expanding any of the above systems to include disaggregation of one or more endogenous variables. One may wish to consider demand from the point of view of joint products and examine the demand for a commodity such as oilseeds in terms of both meal and oil. Alternatively, the demand for a commodity may be considered in terms of the derived demand in final or consumer products. Some further examples are separating the demand for tin according to tinplate or non-tinplate uses, or making a distinction between primary and secondary sources of the supply of copper.[51] A simple demand disaggregation of model 6.4 would be

$$c_t^1 = f^1(c_{t-1}^1, p_t, p_{t-j}, y_t^1, z_t, u_t)$$
$$c_1^2 = f^2(c_{t-1}^2, p_t, p_{t-j}, y_t^2, z_t, u_t)$$
$$q_t = g(q_{t-1}, p_t, p_{t-j}, z_t, u_t) \qquad\qquad (6.7)$$
$$p_t = h(p_{t-1}, s_t - s_{t-1}, z_t, u_t)$$
$$s_t = s_{t-1} + q_t - c_t^1 - c_t^2$$

where c_t^1 and c_t^2 represent alternative uses of a commodity and y_t^1 and y_t^2 are corresponding activity indexes. This same approach could also be used to provide separate equations for commodities which are close substitutes or complements. This is true for the Wickens, Greenfield, and Marshall coffee model where total import demand for each country is disaggregated using four separate coffee variety equations, one each for extra milds, other milds, Brazils, and robustas.[52]

Although the relationships included in models 6.3 through 6.7 are dynamic, they lack variables reflecting expectations about some future state of the market or the economy. Expectation variables can be introduced, for example, through the use of dynamic partial adjustment equations reflecting demand or supply, or various forms of the accelerator explaining inventories. One could also replace the price function with one based on the supply of storage theory, where prices depend on long run or future price expectations and expectations regarding inventory coverage. Yet another possibility would be to explain dynamic behavior using differential equations based on continuous time and to introduce expectations using explicit relationships. Wymer has proposed that a commodity model based on this approach could be formulated as follows:[53]

$$Dc(t) = f[c^*(t) - c(t)]$$
$$Dq(t) = g[q^*(t) - q(t)]$$
$$Dp(t) = h[q^*(t) - q(t); c^*(t) - c(t)] \qquad\qquad (6.8)$$
$$Ds(t) = q(t) - c(t)$$

where

$$c^*(t) = f'[p(t), \tilde{p}(t), s(t), z(t)]$$
$$q^*(t) = g'[p(t), \tilde{p}(t), z(t)]$$

Notation for continuous time is used with D representing an appropriate differential operator; desired values of consumption and production are given by $c^*(t)$ and $q^*(t)$ respectively, and $\tilde{p}(t)$ defines the expected value of price in some future period. Consumption and production are shown to adjust to their own excess demand and excess supply while prices adjust directly to the combined excess of desired over actual flows.

Up to now, variations in model specification have included only stock adjustment, trade flows, disaggregation, and expectations. Of the remining possible variations we can sample only a few.[54] One of the most important is that price formation may be of a noncompetitive nature. This was shown in Chapter 5, for example, where the Burrows' cobalt model is adjusted by replacing the conventional price equation with one that reflects the behavior of a dominant producer who maximizes profits.[55] Another important variation is found in Behrman's rubber model, where an elaborate set of technological change relationships are used to describe the demand for natural rubber relative to synthetic rubber.[56] He also disaggregates prices in the model, adding equations which link individual country prices to a world rubber price. Finally, Quirk and Smith present a theoretical model of a fish market where they introduce adaptive control to explain feedback between the size of the fish stock and the growth of the market.[57]

Causality

It has been explained that the relationship between endogenous variables within a model can be recursive, implying a causal dependence from one period to the next; or simultaneous, indicating interdependence within a single period. Determining the causality or interdependence among the endogenous variables is essential to constructing a commodity model, otherwise the model will contain considerable specification error and the parameters will lack optimal properties.[58]

To discover causality we examine two factors in particular: (1) the chain of response existing in a market—most often supply is determined by prices existing in a previous period with consumption equalling supply in the current period; (2) the length of the data interval relative to the time lags existing between variables—data often are available in quarterly or annual intervals, and if this interval is long relative to the actual lags, some form of simultaneity is inevitable.

A system of equations is described as recursive when the endogenous variables enter the system one at a time. The impact of one variable on the other is successive in time, the final result being a causal chain. An example of recursive behavior can be drawn from the cobweb version of the elementary model 6.3 as transformed below.

$$p_t = f^{-1}(c_t) + u_t^p$$

$$q_t = g(p_{t-1}) + u_t^q \qquad (6.9)$$

$$c_t = q_t$$

The causality reflected in these equations implies that current supply is determined by price in the previous period and that current price is determined from current consumption, which always must equal supply. A flow diagram is sometimes used for interpreting this sequence of action.

p_{t-1}	p_t	p_{t+1}	p_{t+n}
↑	↑	↑	↑
c_{t-1}	c_t	c_{t+1}	c_{t+n}
↑	↑	↑	↑
q_{t-1}	q_t	q_{t+1}	q_{t+n}

To verify that a model is recursive the following conditions should exist, based on the nature of the endogenous coefficients and the related disturbances of the general model 6.2:

1. The matrix of endogenous coefficients Γ is triangular.
2. The variance-covariance matrix Σ of the current disturbances U_t is diagonal
3. No current disturbance is correlated with any past disturbance.

The discovery that a system satisfies these conditions is important because it greatly simplifies the task of estimating the model, permitting the use of Ordinary Least Squares.

A number of economists would suggest that all models are recursive in the sense that only recursive systems describe the true influence of both endogenous and predetermined variables on the endogenous variable to be explained. Normally this is illustrated by making a distinction between a "basic model" and a "derived model." The former is described as a complete model which attempts to incorporate the causal response of all economic factors by pushing the disaggregation process to its ultimate limit.[59] That there is some value in considering all models of this form is confirmed by Strotz and Wold, and Bentzel and Hansen.[60]

Yet this approach also involves a major difficulty; basic models must be described at such a high level of abstraction that they are generally unfit for empirical testing. The alternative is to work with "derived models," representing simplification of basic models whose variables can now be defined in terms of available statistics. In fact the availability of data often determines the unit of time selected for a commodity model as well as the degree of aggregation. For example, if only annual data are available, the actual time lags existing between the variables are likely to be less than the period of observation. The dependency that can be observed between such variables, therefore, is a simultaneous one, and the likelihood of observing only simultaneous behavior increases as the time unit of observation becomes longer.

The theory of simultaneous models has been applied extensively to econometric commodity models. With respect to the diagrammatical interpretation of model 6.3, price, demand, and supply are now considered to be jointly determined within a single time period. It is now difficult to arrange the corresponding flow diagram such that all arrows within a period have the same direction, and the dual–directionality of the arrows implies that the variables are interdependent.

$$
\begin{array}{cccc}
c_{t-1} & c_t & c_{t+1} & \quad c_{t+n} \\
\updownarrow & \updownarrow & \updownarrow & \quad \updownarrow \\
p_{t-1} & p_t & p_{t+1} & \quad p_{t+n} \\
\updownarrow & \updownarrow & \updownarrow & \quad \updownarrow \\
q_{t-1} & q_t & q_{t+1} & \quad q_{t+n}
\end{array}
$$

The general statistical criteria for verifying that a commodity model is simultaneous cannot be stated as definitively as in the case of a recursive model. It is apparent, nontheless, that a model is simultaneous if the following conditions exist:

1. The matrix of endogenous coefficients Γ has entries above and below the major diagonal, i.e., the test for triangularity fails.

2. The variance-covariance matrix Σ of the current disturbances is other than diagonal.

3. The disturbance terms of individual equations are correlated with one or more of the explanatory endogenous variables in the corresponding equation.

4. No current disturbance is correlated with any past disturbance.

The consequence of simultaneity in a system is that more elaborate methods of estimation must be introduced to break the dependency between the disturbances and the explanatory endogenous variables. Prior to examining appropriate estimation methods, we discuss problems of system identification and of selecting and using commodity data.

Identification

The problem of identification received its first attention in attempts to estimate parameters of commodity models. The works of Schultz, Haavelmo, Wold and Jureen, and members of the Cowles Commission are notable in this respect.[61]

More recent studies include that of Liu and particularly of Fisher.[62] Identification at an elementary level can be described using an approach that appears frequently in the literature. Assume the commodity model 6.3 to be of the following form:

$$c_t = b_0 + b_1 p_t + u_t^c$$

$$q_t = b_2 + b_3 p_t + u_t^q \qquad (6.10)$$

$$c_t = q_t$$

One notes that the first two equations in the model are not statistically distinguishable. Given that demand and supply are always equal, the two equations are simply linear combinations of the same variables. In fact, to identify which is the demand equation or which the supply equation is not possible even after estimation.

The steps usually taken to identify either equation consist of adding as many additional exogenous variables to the system as are considered necessary. If our model refers to the market for an agricultural commodity, for example, the inclusion of a rainfall variable r_t in the supply equation helps to identify the demand equation because changes in rainfall can now explain shifts in the supply curve as it may move along the demand curve. But both the demand and supply curves are identifiable only if an exogenous variable z_t not present in the supply equation is included in the demand equation. The above model becomes

$$c_t = b_0 + b_1 p_t + b_4 z_t + u_t^c$$

$$q_t = b_2 + b_3 p_t + b_5 r_t + u_t^q \qquad (6.11)$$

$$c_t = q_t$$

That the equations in this model are exactly identified can be verified by using the normal method of computing the reduced form of the model. The reduced form represents a transformation of the structural equations such that a new set of equations is obtained in which each endogenous variable is expressed only in terms of the predetermined variables of the system. The reduced form of model 6.11 is given by

$$p_t = \frac{b_2 - b_0}{(b_1 - b_3)} + \frac{b_5}{(b_1 - b_3)} r_t - \frac{b_4}{(b_1 - b_3)} z_t + v_t^p$$

$$q_t = \frac{(-b_0 b_3 + b_2 b_1)}{(b_1 - b_3)} + \frac{b_1 b_5}{(b_1 - b_3)} r_t - \frac{b_3 b_4}{(b_1 - b_3)} z_t + v_t^q \qquad (6.12)$$

or

$$p_t = \pi_0 + \pi_1 r_t + \pi_2 z_t + v_t^p$$
$$q_t = \pi_3 + \pi_4 r_t + \pi_5 z_t + v_t^q$$

where π represents the parameters of the reduced form. Inspection of equations 6.12 reveals that the model is exactly identified; all of the structural parameters can be obtained uniquely from the parameters of the reduced form. Over-identification exists when the reduced form parameters yield two or more values for a single structural parameter. Underidentification occurs when the reduced form parameters cannot be solved to yield the structural parameters.

Commodity models normally are larger and more complex than the example just given, and they must be identified not only to assure existence of separate demand and supply equations but also to determine which form of estimation is most appropriate for a given model.

General statistical criteria for identifying an economic model consist of an order condition and a rank condition.[63] Consider the general economic model 6.2, which contains a total of G current endogenous variables and $K = M + G$ predetermined variables. Also let g be the number of endogenous variables and k be the number of predetermined variables included in a particular equation respectively. The order condition for identification is defined as follows:

1. The number of endogenous and predetermined variables excluded from the equation must be at least as great as the number of equations in the model less one.

$$G - g + K \geq G - 1 \tag{6.13}$$

or

$$K - k \geq g - 1$$

2. Or, alternatively, the number of predetermined variables excluded from the equation must be at least as great as the number of endogenous variables included less one.

$$K - k \geq g - 1 \tag{6 14}$$

Underidentification occurs when the equality or inequality are not met; exact identification requires that the equality be met; and overidentification results when the inequality is met. While the order condition is described as a necessary condition for identification, the rank condition is referred to as a sufficient one. The rank condition requires that the rank of the submatrix of the reduced form coefficients given by the number of included endogenous variables and excluded predetermined variables equal the number of included endogenous variables less one.

$$\rho(\pi_g, K - k) = g - 1 \tag{6.15}$$

Identification generally is not a serious problem with commodity models because most systems contain a large number of predetermined variables resulting in overidentification. Readers should consult Fisher for further discussion of the above conditions, methods of introducing other information to achieve identification, and other matters such as coping with problems of nonlinearities.[64]

Data Selection

A consideration that normally occurs earlier in formulating a commodity model is that of determining the time interval of observation which corresponds to the commodity behavior to be investigated. Commodity models based on monthly data, for example, can explain within the year seasonal patterns or short term cycles. Such models can also explain behavior relevant to speculative phenomena such as the price movements or trading patterns occurring in commodity future markets. Since monthly commodity models tend to be unstable in testing and in operation, quarterly models are often more useful. These models can explain seasonals and other within the year patterns as well as provide slightly longer range forecasts.

Unfortunately, neither monthly nor quarterly data are plentiful for many commodities, and the majority of commodity models have been constructed using annual data. One can consider an annual model as restrictive since it does not pertain to the short run phenomena mentioned above; nor does it provide suitable estimates of short run elasticities of supply or demand. Nonetheless an annual model permits analysis of long run policy decisions such as those related to support prices, tariffs, or crop acreage.

Among the problems associated with obtaining commodity data, a number of these are sufficiently severe to seriously restrict model building activities. Some of the problems have been mentioned in earlier chapters. Of particular interest, for example, is the fact that industry and commodity market accounting systems seldom provide the information necessary to close a model completely. First, identities between data series are seldom maintained, i.e., principally that net imports must equal production less domestic consumption plus or minus stock changes. And second, inventories are rarely disaggregated according to producer versus consumer holdings, or according to finished goods versus goods in process or the raw commodity. In this respect, conversion ratios between the raw material and the finished product are also often unavailable. Data are also improperly deflated or the deflators not given.

With respect to agricultural commodities, much of the data is recorded on a seasonal basis while related economic series are compiled on a calendar basis. The agricultural data can be adjusted only where monthly data is available for shifting the series to a calendar base. Irregularities in data also arise because of severe political disturbances. When using data extending from World War II, for example, model response may have to be adjusted for the impact of the Korean War, the war in Vietnam, or intervening recessions.

Finally, commodity records rarely document important changes in surrounding institutional structures or cataclysms such as typhoons or droughts. Where such data are available, they can often be included as system information in a very valuable way through the use of "dummy" variables.

Estimation of Commodity Models

Some of the problems and methods of estimating commodity equations and models have already been discussed. For example, Chapters 2 and 3 suggested several estimating procedures that might be appropriate where an equation contains lagged endogenous variables or where an equation is embedded in a more complete set of simultaneous equations. We will now evaluate these and other methods of estimation more thoroughly. Our general goal is to offer criteria deemed practical for selecting among these methods, although any final choice of method must depend on the economic and econometric characteristics of the model. Altogether, the following estimating procedures are considered:

1. Ordinary Least Squares
2. Generalized Least Squares
3. Two Stage Principal Components
4. Structurally Ordered Instrumental Variables
5. Least Variance Ratio
6. Three Stage Least Squares
7. Full Information Maximum Llikelihood

Criteria

The choice as to which estimation method to use for a particular econometric commodity model is not an easy one. In fact, most textbooks and studies have concentrated on comparing the properties of estimators to the neglect of practical criteria for selecting among them.[65] Some of the criteria available are clear enough; they depend on sample size, causality, and degree of identification. Other criteria not as clear hinge upon the degree of multicollinearity between the predetermined variables, the degree of correlation between the endogenous explanatory variables and the disturbance terms, and the serial correlation among successive disturbances. Our choice of criteria, which stems from the practical consideration of estimating and using commodity models, includes the following: (1) theoretical and computational complexity, (2) necessary sample size, (3) equation or system approach, (4) nature of consistency, and (5) sensitivity to specification errors, identification, and multicollinearity. A comparison of both methods and criteria appears on Table 6-1. While the comparison is by no means exhaustive, it should provide help in making the trade-off between computational ease and desirable properties of estimates.

Ordinary Least Squares

There are several cases in which OLS may provide suitable parameter estimates for equations imbedded in commodity models. OLS can provide estimates which are unbiased, consistent, and efficient, as well as maximum likelihood for a recursive system of equations. Although this is convenient in that some commodity markets display a natural recursiveness in the way in which production and consumption decisions are reached, the appropriateness of OLS depends on the three conditions presented earlier. Fisher has warned that the first condition for recursivity—triangularity in the matrix of the endogenous coefficients—does not suffice to make OLS consistent: the second and third conditions must also be met.[66]

Satisfying these latter conditions is difficult. Even in well specified models, variables are omitted in a way that influences the disturbance terms, making the variance-covariance matrix of these terms nondiagonal; also, it is rare to find disturbances that are not serially correlated. These difficulties also increase for recursive models when data are subject to larger than normal errors, when one or more variables is affected seriously by errors of aggregation, or when omitted variables such as climatic conditions are known to influence two or more equations. In a practical sense, at least if the first and third conditions can be met, an argument can still be made for using OLS since the resultant loss of efficiency may be tolerated in dealing with small samples.

OLS can also provide parameters for a system of equations which are simultaneous, but the system also must be exactly identified. This approach, known as Indirect Least Squares, requires that the reduced form of a model first be estimated by OLS, and that the structural parameters be obtained by transformation from the reduced form. As long as the structural disturbances are uncorrelated and independent of the predetermined variables, the struc-

Table 6-1. Comparison of Estimation

Criteria for Comparison	Ordinary Least Squares	Generalized Least Squares	Two Stage Principal Components
Theoretical and Computational Complexity	Simplest	Greater than OLS	Greater than OLS
Necessary Sample Size	Small	Medium	Small with incorporation of principal components
Equation or System Approach	Equation	Equation	Equation
Nature of Consistency	Normally consistent unless simultaneity and/or serial correlation in errors present	Normally consistent unless simultaneity present	Normally consistent
Sensitivity to Specification Errors, Multicollinearity, and Identification	Use in models thought to be simultaneous requires careful specification of right hand variables as predetermined	—	Less sensitive to specification error than OLS, SOIV, or FIML
Advantages	Parameters are generally robust. Consistency not superior to other methods, but small variance is favorable. Optimal properties obtained when Indirect Least Squares possible. Directly applicable to certain recursive models	Parameters consistent in presence of lagged dependent variables and serially correlated errors	Parameters are generally robust even where sample size is small relative to the number of predetermined variables in the system
Disadvantages	Parameters biased as well as inconsistent when simultaneity is present. Serial correlation in errors increases inconsistency. Not designed to cope with simultaneous systems	Not designed to cope with simultaneous systems	Parameters are biased in same direction as OLS

a This comparison of properties does not purport to be exhaustive. For further information see: Carl F. Christ, *Econometric Models and Methods* (New York: John Wiley & Sons, 1966); J. Johnston,

Methods Relevant to Commodity Models

Structurally Ordered Instrumental Variables	Limited Information Least Variance Ratio	Three Stage Least Squares	Full Information Maximum Liklihood
Greater than 2SPC	Greater than 2SPC	Greater than LI–LVR	Greater than 3SLS
Small with Incorporation of Principal Components	Large	Large	Large
Equation	Equation	System	System
Normally consistent	Normally consistent	Normally consistent	Normally consistent
More sensitive to specification error than 2SPC	More sensitive to multicollinearity and weak identification than 2SPC	More sensitive to specification error than 2SPC	More sensitive to specification errors, weak identification, and multicollinearity than other methods
Instruments chosen on the basis of economic rather than statistical criteria. Provides clear lines of economic causation	Parameters are maximum liklihood	Takes account of covariance between errors of included equations. Estimates all parameters simultaneously	Estimates all parameters simultaneously including restrictions on some parameters. Uses full information
Method used for final selection of instruments not optimal	Parameters can be unstable with small samples or changing sample size	Superior to 2SLS SOLV or LI–LVR only when covariance matrix is not diagonal	Errors in specification transmitted to parameters throughout the model

Econometric Methods (New York: McGraw-Hill Book Co., 1972); or H. Theil *Principles of Econometrics* (New York: John Wiley & Sons, 1971).

tural parameters will be consistent although unbiased only asymptotically.

Applications of OLS to other situations where simultaneity may be present are not as straightforward. Consider a single equation taken from the system 6.2

$$y_t = \delta_1 X_{1t} + u_t \tag{6.16}$$

where X_{1t} is a subset of the matrix X_t, and u_t is a vector of disturbances. Desirable properties for estimates can be obtained when the explanatory variables in the above equation are either nonstochastic or distributed independently of all past, present, and future values of the disturbances and when successive disturbance terms are serially uncorrelated and homoscedastic. The first of these conditions typically is not satisfied in simultaneous models and the estimates are biased and inconsistent. There are a number of situations, however, where the correlation between the explanatory variables and the disturbances is small, where the intercorrelation between disturbance terms of different equations is limited, and where any remaining simultaneity can be lessened by one or more simplifying assumptions. Examples of these can be found in studies comparing single equation and simultaneous methods such as those of Fox, Foote, or Klein.[67]

Even without these exceptional circumstances, however, a number of commodity model builders use OLS as a means for obtaining final model parameters. This is probably most true where sample size is small, and there would be no differences regarding the choice of variables, selecting of functional forms, or interpreting results even if more sophisticated methods are used. Similarly, no need exists for sophisticated methods where the parameters of a model are mechanically adjusted, as sometimes is the case in simulation models. It should be kept in mind that OLS results in biased parameter estimates where simultaneity is present, but the same is true of estimates from other methods unless the given sample is relatively large and the model specification is fairly exact. Thus, one must weigh resulting bias against the fact that OLS estimates typically have lower variance than estimates obtained from other methods.

Generalized Least Squares

The major problem other than simultaneity which arises in estimating commodity models stems from estimating equations that contain lagged dependent variables.[68] Consider a single dynamic equation taken from the general model 6.2

$$y_t = \delta_0 y_{t-j} + \delta_1 X_{1t} + u_t \tag{6.17}$$

If the disturbances u_t are normally and independently distributed with zero mean and constant variance, then using OLS will result in parameter estimates which are biased although consistant and asymptotically efficient. The bias arises because of the correlation between the lagged dependent variable and the disturbances. If the disturbances should become serially correlated, then the estimates will be inconsistent as well as biased. It can also be shown that where the first of these circumstances produces a small negative bias using OLS, the second circumstance normally causes a larger positive bias.

There are two aspects of the dynamic equation that should be kept in mind before examining estimation methods which can restore the properties of the parameter estimates. First, the Durbin Watson test of serial correlation in the disturbances is generally not applicable to an equation of this form. Taylor and Wilson, however, show that in certain situations the test may still be effective; more recently, Durbin has produced a revised test applicable to dynamic models, although meaningful only with large samples.[69] Second, Grilliches points out that if the true relationship contains only current variables but the disturbances are serially correlated, estimating a dynamic equation will result in a statistically significant coefficient for the lagged dependent variable.[70] Consequently, one may end up with a statistically meaningful though false model, at least from the point of view of theory. To overcome this difficulty, Grilliches interprets the dynamic relation as one having the simultaneous equation problem of correlation between an explanatory variable and the disturbance term; he then proceeds to estimate the parameters by considering the lagged dependent variable as endogenous and replacing it with an instrumental variable.

The approach prescribed here for estimating dynamic equations involves the iterative and the search methods of Generalized Least Squares mentioned in Chapter 2. In following this approach, one begins with a model of the form given in 6.17 where the disturbances u_t are assumed to follow some form of an autoregressive scheme

$$u_t = \rho u_{t-1} + \varepsilon_t \qquad 0 < \rho < 1 \tag{6.18}$$

and the errors ε_t are normally and independently distributed with zero mean and variance. If the value of ρ is known, then an appropriate transformation matrix Ω can be described in terms of the variance-covariance matrix of the disturbances u_t.

$$\sigma^2 \Omega = \sigma^2 \begin{bmatrix} 1 & \rho & \rho^2 & \cdots & \rho^{n-1} \\ \rho & 1 & & \cdots & \rho^{n-2} \\ \vdots & \vdots & \vdots & & \vdots \\ \rho^{n-1} & \rho^{n-2} & \rho^{n-3} & \cdots & 1 \end{bmatrix} \tag{6.19}$$

This transformation matrix also provides the basis for obtaining estimates of the coefficients b in the GLS estimator.

$$b = (X'\Omega^{-1}X)^{-1}X'\Omega^{-1}Y \qquad (6.20)$$

One can show that this is equivalent to applying OLS to a set of transformed data based on a regression of the form 6.17. Assuming that the disturbance terms are defined as in 6.18, the coefficient ρ provides the basis for transforming the original data according to

$$(y_t - \rho y_{t-1}) = b_0(1 - \rho) + b_1(y_{t-1} - \rho y_{t-2}) + b_2(x_t - \rho x_{t-1}) + v_t$$
$$(6.21)$$

The manner in which this equation can be solved utilizing OLS depends on the method of determining the value of ρ.

The iterative procedure would require obtaining a preliminary estimate of ρ based on the residuals from OLS estimates of the original equation. The data are transformed according to some ρ as in equation 6.21 and parameter estimates $\hat{b}_0$, $\hat{b}_1$, $\hat{b}_2$ are obtained. The residuals from the newly estimated equations provide the basis for a recomputation of $\hat{\rho}$, namely $\hat{\hat{\rho}}$. One can then obtain parameter estimates $\hat{\hat{b}}_0$, $\hat{\hat{b}}_1$, and $\hat{\hat{b}}_2$ and continue in this way until the values of ρ achieve a given degree of convergence. Alternatively, the search technique requires that one select a range of values for ρ_1 and an equation of the form 6.21 be estimated for each ρ. The estimates of the parameter finally adopted conform to the value of ρ which minimizes the sum of squared errors of the transformed equation. Through this transformation, the errors v_t in equation 6.21 become random and the resultant estimators are consistent and asymptotically efficient.

A problem with applying iterative and search techniques of this variety to dynamic commodity equations is that the final value of ρ may not be obtained sufficiently quickly, making the techniques computationally expensive. Several recent techniques are perhaps more efficient alternatives. For example, Zellner and Geisel's methods might be applied if the assumptions surrounding the autoregressive scheme conform to those specifically followed by the Koyck and Nerlove formulations.[71] Or one might consider the technique proposed by Wallis.[72] In any case, however, the estimates will still be biased. In fact, where autocorrelation is present, only larger samples will yield consistency. Although OLS provides a helpful shortcut to obtaining estimates under these circumstances, GLS is often preferred for models where there is a greater likelihood of autocorrelation in the disturbances.

Two Stage Principal Components

Where there is strong simultaneity in a commodity model, one must turn to estimation methods specifically designed for use with simultaneous systems. These methods can apply to one equation at a time or to the system as a whole.

Two Stage Least Squares, an example of the former, needs little introduction. Whereas OLS applied to single equations containing significant correlation between an explanatory endogenous variable and the disturbance terms leads to a positive bias, 2SLS purges the equation of this intercorrelation and reduces the amount of the bias, unless a substantial degree of multicollinearity is present between the independent variables. It also leads to consistent parameter estimates with large samples, is the simplest of the simultaneous equation methods, and can be combined with an instrumental variables approach to make up for degrees of freedom lost with short time series. Because commodity model builders often must deal with short data series, it is this latter aspect of 2SLS which we explore further.

Consider a single equation embedded in the general model 6.2 where the lagged endogenous variables are contained in X_1 and the time subscript is removed for simplification. Usually that equation must be normalized in coefficients such that we deal with an expression of the form

$$y = Y_1\beta_1 + X_1\beta_2 + u \qquad (6.22)$$

The relevant dimensions are $y = n \times 1$ vector of observations on the dependent variables, $Y_1 = n \times g$ matrix of observations on the g other current endogenous variables in the equation, $X_1 = n \times k$ matrix of observations on the k predetermined variables in the equation, $\beta_1 = g \times 1$ vector of coefficients related to the endogenous variables, $\beta_2 = k \times 1$ vector of coefficients related to the endogenous variables, and $u = n \times 1$ vector of disturbances. Because one or more variables in Y_1 are correlated with u, OLS cannot be used and a two-stage procedure is preferred. The first stage requires breaking up this correlation, by replacing Y_1 with a computed matrix $\hat{Y}_1$ (based on instruments), which is purged of its relation to u. Estimates of β_1 and β_2 are then obtained at the second stage, which consists of the OLS regression of y on $\hat{Y}_1$ and X_1. The success of this method depends on the use of instruments or variables which are not related to previously included variables and thus uncorrelated with u; the predetermined variables make a logical choice for the instruments because they bear some causal relation to the endogenous variable being replaced.

The normal method for computing $\hat{Y}_1$ utilizes the $n \times k$ matrix of observations on all the predetermined variables in the complete model

$$X = [X_1 \; X_2] \qquad (6.23)$$

such that

$$\hat{Y}_1 = X(X'X)^{-1}X'Y_1 \qquad (6.24)$$

X_2 is interpreted as the matrix of observations on the predetermined variables excluded from the equation of interest. Unfortunately, this method fails where the total number of predetermined variables K is greater than the number of observations n. It may also be inappropriate even if K is less than n, if the number of degrees of freedom $n - K$ is very small.[73] Consequently, we turn for help to other methods of forming the first stage instrumental variable, namely principal components. A principal component represents a linear combination of a set of variables such that the covariance of the linear combination is a maximum. Since a small number of components might account for a large proportion of the total variance of X, one can replace the X matrix with one of smaller dimension containing only several principal components based on X. Applications of this method have been proposed by Kloek and Mannes, Taylor, Dhrymes, Fisher, and others.[74]

The method of constructing the principal components requires deriving a new set of variables Z of dimension $r < K$ such that Z be formed as a linear function of the predetermined variables with maximum variance. This is given by

$$Z = \tilde{X}A \tag{6.25}$$

where $Z = n \times K - 1$ matrix of principal components, $\tilde{X} = n \times K - 1$ standardized matrix of X, and $A = K - 1 \times K - 1$ matrix transforming $\tilde{X}$ into Z. Premultiply 6.25 by Z to obtain

$$Z'Z = A'\tilde{X}'\tilde{X}A \tag{6.26}$$

Define $\tilde{X}'\tilde{X}/n$ as the sample covariance matrix of X and $Z'Z/n$ as a diagonal matrix. The maximization problem can be solved by extracting roots from the characteristic equation

$$|\tilde{X}\tilde{X}/n - (Z'Z/n)I| = 0 \tag{6.27}$$

The corresponding characteristic vectors can be found from solving a series of equations

$$(\tilde{X}\tilde{X}/n - \lambda_i I)a_i = 0 \tag{6.28}$$

where the vectors are defined in terms of a_i, $i = 1, \ldots, K - 1$ as taken from A; the associated characteristic roots are given by λ_i, $i = 1, \ldots, K - 1$ denoted in order of decreasing magnitude. The normalization of the characteristic vector is chosen such that

$$\begin{aligned} a_i' a_j = 1 \quad & i = j \\ a_i' a_j = 0 \quad & i \neq j \end{aligned} \tag{6.29}$$

The characteristic vector a_1 associated with the largest root λ_1 will be used to form the first principal component Z_1. If we are interested in up to r principal components, then the rth component will be given by

$$Z_r = \tilde{X}a_r \tag{6.30}$$

Each successive component $Z_1, \ldots, Z_r$ will decline in importance.

Choosing how many principal components to use begins with a definition of the variance of X accounted for by successive principal components. The variance of X accounted for by the first principal component is given by

$$\frac{\lambda_1}{T_r X'X/n} \tag{6.31}$$

Since the principal components are orthogonal, the total variance accounted for by the r principal components would cumulate to

$$\frac{\lambda_1 + \lambda_2 + , \ldots, + \lambda_r}{TrX'X/n} \tag{6.32}$$

No definite conclusions have been reached as to the number of principal components to include, although Kloek and Mennes indicate lower and upper limits.[75] The number r should exceed the number of endogenous variables g but r taken together with the number of included predetermined variables k should be less than one-third of the observations, $(r + k)/n < \frac{1}{3}$. The author's experience suggests that a sufficient number of components should be taken such that the variance accounted for in 6.32 is 90 percent; one normally finds that $(r + k)/n$ is greater than $\frac{1}{3}$ but less than $\frac{1}{2}$. One also can apply additional criteria in selecting principal components such that they have least correlation with the included predetermined variables X_1, as is suggested by Kloek and Mennes.[76]. A further possibility proposed by Fisher is discussed in the next section.

Once the desired principal components are selected, the estimation of the parameters of the original model 6.22 can take place at the second stage. This solution normally is given by

$$\begin{bmatrix} b_1 \\ b_2 \end{bmatrix} = \begin{bmatrix} Y_1'Y_1 - V_1'V_1 & Y'X_1 \\ X_1'Y_1 & X_1'X_1 \end{bmatrix}^{-1} \begin{bmatrix} (Y_1 - V_1)'y \\ X_1'y \end{bmatrix} \tag{6.33}$$

where

$$V_1 = Y_1 - \hat{Y}_1 = Y_1 - X(X'X)^{-1}X'Y_1 \tag{6.34}$$

Since the endogenous variable $\hat{Y}_1$ is now obtained from a regression on the principal components Z, the two-stage principal component solution requires that V_1 now be computed according to

$$V_1 = Y_1 - Z(Z'Z)^{-1}Z'Y_1 \tag{6.35}$$

The parameter estimates derived from the original 2SLS procedure are known to be consistent. It cannot be expected that the 2SPC estimates will be as efficient. However, Dhrymes has shown that for larger samples where the number of components selected increases, the 2SPC estimates are consistent with the same asymptotic efficiency as 2SLS.[77] Obviously, as the sample becomes so large that the problem of $K > n$ vanishes, the solution would revert to 2SLS. An example of the application of 2SPC to a commodity model can be found in Witherell's wool study.[78]

Structurally Ordered Instrumental Variables

That the instrumental variables based on principal components or other methods can be possibly selected by a more sophisticated procedure has been advocated by Fisher, whose method of Structurally Ordered Instrumental Variables makes use of a priori exclusion and normalization restrictions to select a set of instruments for each endogenous variable. With this procedure the behavioral equations are treated as causal relations where the complete model is normalized with a different left-hand endogenous variable for each equation. One can consult the original study for the exact way in which the restrictions are used in selecting the instrumental or predetermined variables.[79] In brief, one begins by causally ordering the variables in the system: right-hand endogenous variables in the equation to be estimated are of zero causal order; variables in other equations explaining the zero order endogenous variables will be of first causal order; variables in other equations explaining the first order variables will be of second causal order (except for those variables already assigned as zero or first order); variables explaining the second order variables given the lower order exception rule will be third order; and so on. A complete ordering is this provided for the instrumental variables and adjustments are made by using the posterior information from a set of sample correlations. The instrumental variables finally used to explain the right-hand endogenous variables are obtained by successively dropping instruments or the ordered predetermined variables from the lower end of the preference ordering and observing significant changes in the overall regression R^2. At this stage, the appropriate set of estimators may even be obtained by either 2SPC or a reasonable alternative.

If this method is to be applied to commodity models, several qualifications must be made. First of all, the method requires that the underlying endogenous variables have some degree of causal dependence. Though appearing in macroeconomic models, such causality is less prevalent in commodity models. Second, the use of extensive a priori information is not an easy matter and the accompanying computational time is substantial. Thirdly, as Grilliches has suggested, the reliance on maximizing the regression R^2 in the end may not reduce inconsistency by as much as is desirable.[80]

This last difficulty returns us to the original question of providing an appropriate estimator to reduce the inconsistency generated by the dependency between the explanatory endogenous variables and the disturbance terms. It has been shown that the use of 2SLS with exactly or overidentified models under normal conditions leads to consistent estimates, although the estimates still are biased. When 2SLS is combined with principal components as instrumental variables, the 2SPC approach also can be regarded as consistent, especially since this reverts to the 2SLS approach as the sample size increases.

McCarthy questions whether this property will always be maintained, and suggests that this can be assured only when the predetermined variables in the equation under estimation are included in the set of first stage regressors.[81] Dhrymes has confirmed this conclusion.[82] Mitchell and Fisher in extending this discussion compare the consistency properties of the estimates obtained from SOIV to that of 2SPC.[83] The SOIV method was found to produce at least equally good estimates by selectively incorporating fewer instruments at the first stage. Yet the relative simplicity of 2SPC makes it preferable to SOIV except where the model may have a strongly recursive structure or where it may prove beneficial to introduce additional economic insight.

Of the newer instrumental variable approaches which may be added as potentially useful for estimating commodity models, the works of Brundy and Jorgenson and of Mosback and Wold are of value.[84] While none of the methods mentioned so far has been designed specifically to accommodate the problem of certain equations in the model possessing lagged dependent variables and serially correlated disturbances, this problem can be solved without great difficulty as shown in the recent work of Fair.[85]

Least Variance Ratio

The remaining estimation methods to be discussed are less frequently used in constructing commodity models. The first is a variant of LISE known as the Least Variance Ratio. Other single equation methods which might be of interest include those known as k-class or h-class estimators. The method of least variance ratio originally was devised by Anderson and Ruben.[86] It begins with the stipulation that any equation of a model should be described using two specifications: one in which some original set of variables accounts for the variance in the dependent variable, and another in which an additional variable has been added to help increase the explained variance. The least variance ratio principle would assert that the parameters of the original regression should be chosen to minimize the ratio of the disturbance variance in that regression relative to the disturbance variance of the regression containing the additional explanatory variable. As shown above in Table 6-1, the estimates obtained under normal conditions will have the properties of consistency and asymptotic efficiency. For the case of an exactly identified model, the methods of ILS, 2SLS, and LVR yield identical results.

The criteria for adopting the LVR method are not at all obvious. Where there are a sufficient number of observations available, the method provides estimates that are maximum likelihood and that possess other desirable properties. Nonetheless, this advantage must be weighed against the disadvantage that the LVR estimates are less stable than those obtained from OLS or 2SLS. Instability in estimates can arise from shifts in the sample over time, changes in sample size, or multicollinearity between the predetermined variables. One would use this method, therefore, principally when the data is of sufficient quantity and quality to minimize instability, and when the gains in the properties of the estimates are clearly superior to those of 2SLS.[87]

Three Stage Least Squares

The first of the two popular methods of systems estimation is known as Three Stage Least Squares. Originally developed by Zellner and Theil, this method is designed to estimate the unknown parameters of all the equations in a simultaneous commodity model at the same time.[88] Generally speaking, it is termed a three stage procedure because it represents a one stage extension of the Two Stage Least Squares method. One begins by casting the latter method within the context of Generalized Least Squares. This results in a situation where all the coefficients or parameters of the system can be solved at once utilizing the variance-covariance matrix of the disturbance terms from the included equations. Of course, the values of the covariances between the equation disturbances must be known in advance, and this requires applying 2SLS to each of the equations separately. Among the advantages attributed to 3SLS, it can provide greater asymptotic efficiency than 2SLS, and it can include information about the covariance of disturbances between equations. An essential criterion for adopting 3SLS is that a contemporaneous correlation should exist between equation disturbances; otherwise, the method reduces simply to that of 2SLS. An additional criterion is that the equations of the system be overidentified. The improvements in estimation to be gained here, of course, depend on the use of large samples, and it is difficult to determine on a practical basis why 3SLS might be preferred over 2SLS where the sample size is small.

Full Information Maximum Likelihood

The second of the system methods known as Full Information Maximum Likelihood estimates all of the parameters of a commodity model at the same time without reverting to stage-wise estimation—that is, it exploits the structure of all equations at once. Obviously, the method requires a greater computational burden and a larger sample size than any of the methods considered so far. The latter problem is sometimes handled by subdividing the entire model into blocks and estimating parameters one block at a time. A number of recent developments also suggest that the computational problems can be simplified. Klein reports positive results in using a nonlinear FIML procedure developed by Eisenpress.[89] The Brundy and Jorgenson approach mentioned above can also be extended to produce FIML estimators.[90] Finally, Chow and Fair offer an FIML procedure which can be expanded to the case where the disturbances are also serially correlated.[91] The actual procedure to be followed in carrying out estimation by FIML can be found in Klein and elsewhere.

As above, criteria available for applying the method are only general. Where data samples are of reasonable size, FIML could be used when one wishes to obtain individual equation estimates while incoporating a priori information such as restrictions on the parameters of the full model. Using such additional information also improves the asymptotic efficiency of the parameters. Against this should be weighed two disadvantages in particular. First, if there is a specification error in even a single equation, this error is transmitted throughout the whole model; and second, the stability of the estimates is highly sensitive to any multicollinearity that could occur between the predetermined variables.

Finite sample properties of FIML and the other methods presented here are compared in a number of Monte Carlo studies which have been carried out in this respect. Among the more notable studies, are the recent works of Fair and of Lyttkens, Dutta, and Bergstrom related to fixed point and iterative methods and the comparative survey of Johnston.[92] In general, none of the Monte Carlo studies reveals that the more complex methods yield superior estimates to that obtained by 2SLS or 2SPC—at least where small samples are concerned. As for the problems of specification error and multicollinearity associated with the more complex methods, it seems that 2SLS or 2SPC are preferable to LVR, 3SLS, or FIML when commodity models of relatively small sample size are estimated.

Lauric Oils Model

Thus far we have mentioned a number of commodities for which models of a variety of forms exist. Some of the characteristics of those models which are of equilibrium form are summarized in Table 6-2. This table suggests that a

Table 6-2. Summary of Selected Commodity Equilibrium Models: Size, Interdependency, and Methods of Estimation

Models	Number of Endogenous variables and equations	Sample size	Observation unit and period	Interdependence	Methods of estimation
Cattle and Calves—Kulreshtha	9	20	Annual 1949–1969	Simultaneous	2SLS
Cocoa—Goreux	12	17	Annual 1950–1967	Simultaneous and Recursive	OLS
Coffee—Epps	15	40	Quarterly 1955–1965	Simultaneous	2SLS
Copper—Fisher	17	19	Annual 1947–1966	Simultaneous and Recursive	GLS
Dairy—Wilson[a]	13	17	Annual 1947–1963	Simultaneous	2SLS
Fed Cattle and Hogs—Hayenga	5	62	Monthly 1963–1968	Simultaneous	2SLS
Lauric Oils—Labys	23	14	Annual 1953–1967	Simultaneous and Recursive	OLS, GLS 2SPC
Lumber—McKillop	20	31	Annual 1929–1960	Simultaneous	2SLS
Meat—Yandle	17	48	Quarterly 1953–1965	Simultaneous	2SLS
Oranges—Matthews	13	12	Annual 1957–1969	Simultaneous and Recursive	OLS, 2SLS
Potatoes—Zusman	14	20	Annual 1930–1942 1950–1958	Simultaneous	2SLS
Rubber—Behrman	25R[b] 46S	18	Annual 1947–1965	Simultaneous and Recursive	OLS, GLS
Shrimp—Gillespie	20	17	Annual 1957–1967	Simultaneous	2SLS
Soybeans—Houck	13	21	Annual 1946–1967	Simultaneous	OLS, 2SLS 3SLS
Tea—Murti	17	13	Annual 1948–1961	Recursive	OLS
Tin—Desai	18	13	Annual 1948–1961	Simultaneous and Recursive	OLS
Tung Oil—Matthews	6	18	Annual 1950–1968	Simultaneous	2SLS
Tungsten—Burrows	27	28	Annual 1940–1968	Simultaneous	2SLS
Wheat—Mo	6	36	Annual 1928–1964	Simultaneous	OLS, 2RLS
Wool—Witherell	28	15	Annual 1949–1964	Simultaneous and Recursive	GLS, 2SPC

[a] Only first authors have been included for identification of models.
[b] Rubber model contains 25 recursive and 46 simultaneous variables.
Source: See Appendix C.

substantial portion of these models are of only moderate size, possess a simultaneous character, and are estimated by methods no more complex than 2SLS. While further discussion and comparison of these models would be interesting, we will concern ourselves with this matter in a later study. Our present interest is to concentrate on a practical example of specifying and estimating commodity models through a discussion of the formulation of the lauric oils model. This discussion takes place in two parts: first, the structure of the complete model is presented relying on the behavioral equations presented in Chapters 2 through 5; and second, the problems of estimating the model are discussed utilizing the methodology of this chapter.

Structure

A simplified or hypothetical structure of the lauric oils market is presented in Figure 6-4, where the basic market components are described in terms of flows between production, exports, stocks, prices, imports, and consumption.[93] That structure is typical of many primary commodities. Supply originates mostly in developing countries and consumption takes place mostly in developed countries. As shown in Table 6-3, the Philippines, Ceylon, Indonesia, and Oceania account for 72 percent of all exports with the remainder produced in Africa. The U.S., U.K., and Japan, and the E.E.C. countries also represent 72 percent of world imports. The total lauric oil flows can be further divided according to whether they represent coconut oil, copra, palm kernel oil, or palm kernels. The principal characteristic of these flows is that they pass through a number of dealers or export firms in the Philippines and other producing countries whose market strength is roughly the same as that of the major dealers, crushers, and import firms in the U.S., the E.E.C., and other consuming countries. Thus one can begin with the assumption that the lauric oil market is reasonably competitive implying that the commodity equilibrium model will furnish a reasonable approximation to actual market behavior.

A number of other assumptions can also be made to further justify the model structure which will be proposed. These include the following:

1. Coconut oil and palm kernel oil are considered near-perfect substitutes and all quantity variables are measured by data reflecting combined totals. The New York coconut oil price is preferred to a palm kernel oil price for use as the general world price because (a) trade in coconut oil represents 80 percent of total lauric oils exports and (b) palm kernel prices are influenced more by quantities of coconut oil than by quantities of palm kernel oil.

2. Although the role of other coconut products in the total coconut economy such as dessicated coconut, meal, and cakes is important, they have been omitted as not reflecting a substantial influence on the copra and oil market.

150

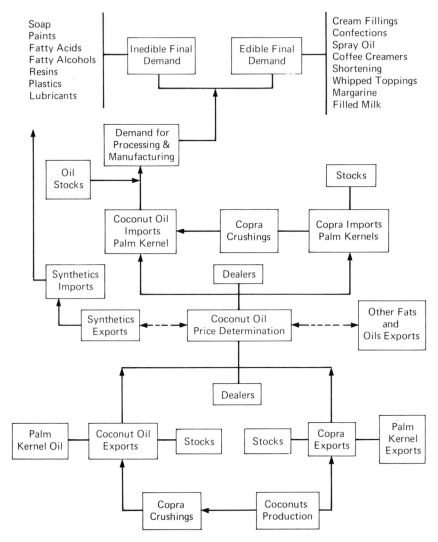

Figure 6–4. Hypothetical Structure of the World Lauric Oils Market.
Source: W.C. Labys, *An Econometric Model of the International Lauric Oils Market: Statistical Considerations and Results*, UNCTAD/CD/Misc. 43/Rev. 1, Geneva, June 1971.

Table 6-3. Distribution of Net Lauric Oil Exports and Imports (Quantities in 000 metric tons represent total for period considered)

	1951–60		1961–70		1951–70	
	Q	%	Q	%	Q	%
Distribution of Exports						
Coconut oil and copra						
Philippines	6054	51.2	7262	58.4	13316	54.9
Ceylon	1048	8.9	1063	8.5	2111	8.7
Indonesia	1977	16.7	1219	9.8	3196	13.2
Oceania	1569	13.3	1732	13.9	3301	13.6
ROW[a]	1174	9.9	1170	9.4	2344	9.7
Total	11822	100.0	12445	100.0	24267	100.0
Palm Kernel and Palm Kernel oil						
Nigeria	1972	49.6	1683	47.8	3655	48.8
Sierra Leone	290	7.3	256	7.3	546	7.3
Congo (Kins)	628	15.8	452	12.8	1080	14.4
French W. and Eq. Africa	560	14.1	560	15.9	1120	14.9
ROW[a]	529	13.3	567	16.1	1096	14.6
Total	3979	100.0	3518	100.0	7497	100.0
Total Exports	15801		15963		31764	
Distribution of Imports						
Combined Lauric Oils						
U.S.	2953	18.7	3957	24.8	6910	21.0
E.E.C.	5338	33.8	5268	33.0	10606	33.4
U.K.	2503	15.8	1593	10.0	4096	12.9
Japan	373	2.4	771	4.8	1144	3.6
ROW[a]	4634	29.3	4374	27.4	9008	28.4
Total Imports	15801	100.0	15963	100.0	31764	100.0

[a] Rest of World Residual

Source: World Oils and Fats Statistics, Prepared by Economics and Statistics Department, Unilever Limited, for the Congress of the International Association of Seed Crushers, various issues.

3. The crushing aspect of the market has been temporarily excluded, mainly because of its rapidly changing structure, but also because it has not been found to represent a major influence on price making. At present, less than one-half of the oil available in the U.S. is obtained by domestic crushing of copra. In the U.K. crushing has ceased for all practical purposes, while in the E.E.C. the crushing industry is undergoing certain changes. Thus, net import data has been adjusted such that volumes of all copra and kernels imported within a year are converted into oil equivalent and included in the oil total.

4. Impact that effects of substitution of other oils and fats have on lauric oils will be considered in terms of the impact that sustained price differentials

between lauric oils and other oils could have on the consumption and imports of lauric oils into a particular country.

The simplest model which can be proposed to describe the lauric oils market is similar to that specified in system 6.4

$$
\begin{aligned}
c_t &= f(c_{t-1}, p_t, y_t, z_t, u_t) \\
q_t &= g(q_{t-1}, p_t, p_{t-j}, z_t, u_t \\
p_t &= h(p_{t-1}, s_t - s_{t-1}, z_t, u_t) \\
s_t - s_{t-1}, &= q_t - c_t
\end{aligned}
\tag{6.36}
$$

This model incorporates the dynamic specifications suggested for the individual behavioral relationships in the previous chapters. The interdependency proposed to exist between the relationships is a simultaneous one. Normally, price is determined by the interaction between supply and demand in a competitive market and the values of price can be obtained by solving the final model. The explanation of price, however, is sufficiently important to the policy applications of the model that it is necessary to specify an explicit price equation.

A number of modifications of the above model are necessary. Some occur because the number of variables required to describe market behavior more completely must be expanded. Others result because of the practical difficulties of obtaining data to describe all of the variables adequately in all of the included countries. The first of these changes requires that commodity demand be distinguished according to imports and domestic consumption. Since consumption and imports both depend on the same set of explanatory variables, imports are explained by the identity which equates them to consumption and stock changes.

$$
m_t^1 = c_t \pm \Delta s_t^m
\tag{6.37}
$$

Of the total possible consumption equations, final end use and corresponding stock data are available only for the U.S., U.K., and the E.E.C., dictating that a behavioral equation be used for Japan.

$$
m_t^2 = m(m_{t-1}, p_t, y_t, z_t, u_t)
\tag{6.38}
$$

The impact of the release of the U.S. General Services Administration stockpile also necessitates adjusting the corresponding U.S. import identity

$$
m_t^3 = c_t \pm \Delta s_t^m - s_t^{gsa}
$$

The lack of adequate supply data in the exporting countries prevented the specification of separate production and export relationships. Only export data are available and exports are explained following the dynamic theory of perennial supply.

$$x_t^1 = s(x_{t-1}^1, p_{t-j}, r_{t-j}, z_t, u_t) \tag{6.40}$$

For the aggregate export sectors of the model, supporting information on supply conditions is lacking, and exports are explained using a distributed lag on prices.

$$x_t^2 = x(p_{t-1}, p_{t-2}, p_{t-3}, u_t) \tag{6.41}$$

The stock or inventory data that was available permitted that total stocks be divided according to holdings of importers and exporters as suggested in Figure 6–4. Behavioral equations for the importing countries are of the dynamic form.

$$s_t^m = v(s_{t-1}^m, p_t, y_t, z_t, u_t) \tag{6.42}$$

For the exporting countries, only a simpler version could be postulated based on distributed lags.

$$s_t^{x1} = w(s_{t-1}^{x1}, p_{t-1}, p_{t-2}, p_{t-3}, u_t) \tag{6.43}$$

A technical relationship approximating the actual stock holding is used for the Philippines

$$s_t^{x2} = \alpha x_t^{ph} \tag{6.44}$$

where α represents the proportion of exports generally held as carryover.

Two price equations are hypothesized as describing price behavior; each is used separately in a different version of the model. The first equation is of a linear form providing the basis for multiplier analysis and reduced form simulation.

$$p_t = h(p_{t-1}, s_t - s_{t-1}, x_t, u_t) \tag{6.45}$$

The second equation more realistically is nonlinear and is used for structural form simulation.

$$p_t = h[p_{t-1}, (s_t/c_t), x_t, y_t] \tag{6.46}$$

As previously explained, including both stocks and export flows appeared to provide the best description of price adjustments.

The most difficult aspect of completing the a priori form of the model is selecting identities with which to close it. The exporters' and importers' stock data, though it represented 70 percent of the world total, could not be defined by an identity which equated stock changes to differences between demand and supply. Consequently, the stock equations are retained solely to explain fluctuations in price. If a residual stock could be computed on the basis of differences between total imports and exports, an identity of the following form could close the model.

$$\Delta s_t^{est} = \Delta s_t^m + \Delta s_t^x + x_t - m_t \qquad (6.47)$$

The price equation could then include a total stock figure computed from

$$\Delta s_t^t = \Delta s_t^{est} + \Delta s_t^m + \Delta s_t^x \qquad (6.48)$$

Otherwise, the identity that had to be used to close the model is

$$m_t^1 + m_t^2 + m_t^3 = x_t^1 + x_t^2 \qquad (6.49)$$

which implies that total world imports equal total world exports within a single period.

The above equations can now be summarized to represent the conceptual model to be estimated. However, it would help to perform a recursive ordering of these equations, forming them into blocks of subsystems of equations which follow the lines of causality thought to exist in the model. Three strategic assumptions are necessary: first, exports primarily depend on climatic conditions, thus being determined prior to price, inventory, and demand; second, market equilibrium represents a simultaneous adjustment between prices and inventories; and third, demand being price inelastic takes place at a subsequent stage. This would suggest that the conceptual model be ordered with respect to a recursive block I, a simultaneous block, and a recursive block II as follows.

Recursive Block I:

$$x_t^1 = x(x_{t-1}^1, p_{t-j}, r_{t-j}, z_t, u_t) \qquad (6.40)$$

$$x_t^2 = x(x_{t-1}^2, p_{t-1}, p_{t-2}, p_{t-3}, u_t) \qquad (6.41)$$

Simultaneous Block:

$$s_t^m = v(s_{t-1}^m, p_t, y_t, z_t, u_t) \tag{6.42}$$

$$s_t^{x1} = w(s_{t-1}^{x1}, p_{t-1}, p_{t-2}, p_{t-3}, u_t) \tag{6.43}$$

$$s_t^{x2} = \alpha x_t^{ph} \tag{6.44}$$

$$p_t = h(p_{t-1}, s_t^{m+x} - s_{t-1}^{m+x}, x_t, u_t) \tag{6.45}$$

Recursive Block II:

$$c_t = f(c_{t-1}, p_t, y_t, z_t, u_t) \tag{6.36}$$

$$m_t^1 = c_t \pm \Delta s_t^{m+x} \tag{6.37}$$

$$m_t^2 = (m_{t-1}^2, p_t, y_t, z_t, u_t) \tag{6.38}$$

$$m_t^3 = c_t \pm \Delta s_t^{m+x} - s_t^{gsa} \tag{6.39}$$

$$m_t^1 + m_t^2 + m_t^3 = x_t^1 + x_t^2 \tag{6.49}$$

Estimation

The statistical version of the conceptual model to be estimated consists of 15 behavioral relationships, 1 technical relationship and 6 identities arranged as follows:

1. Export Sector—6 relationships
2. Stock Sector—3 relationships for importing countries, 1 technical equation and 1 identity for exporting countries
3. World Prices—1 relationship
4. Consumption Sector—3 relationships
5. Import Sector—1 relationships plus 3 identities
6. World Stocks and World Imports and Exports—3 identities

In number, these equations agree with the 22 variables that are endogenous or determined within the system. The list of the endogenous variables together with the exogenous variables in the system appears in Table 6-4. The breakdown according to country of the endogenous variables is as follows: (1) *Exports*: Philippines, Ceylon, Indonesia, Oceania, and Rest of World.

Table 6-4. Classification and Listing of Variables

No.	Identification	Definition
		Endogenous Variables
1	x_t^{ph}	Philippine Coconut Oil Exports
2	x_t^{in}	Indonesia Coconut Oil Exports
3	x_t^{cy}	Ceylon Coconut Oil Exports
4	x_t^{oc}	Oceania Coconut Oil Exports
5	x_t^{rw}	Rest of World Coconut Oil Exports
6	x_t^{pk}	World Palm Kernel Oil Exports
7	x_t^{w}	World Lauric Oil Exports
8	s_t^{us}	U.S. Lauric Oil Stocks
9	s_t^{uk}	U.K. Lauric Oil Stocks
10	s_t^{ec}	E.E.C. Lauric Oil Stocks
11	s_t^{cy}	Ceylon Coconut Oil Stocks
12	s_t^{ph}	Philippine Coconut Oil Stocks
13	s_t^{w}	World Lauric Oil Stocks
14	p_t^{w}	World (N.Y. Crude) Coconut Oil Price
15	c_t^{us}	U.S. Lauric Oil Consumption
16	c_t^{uk}	U.K. Lauric Oil Consumption
17	c_t^{ec}	E.E.C. Lauric Oil Consumption
18	m_t^{us}	U.S. Lauric Oil Imports
19	m_t^{uk}	U.K. Lauric Oil Imports
20	m_t^{ec}	E.E.C. Lauric Oil Imports
21	m_t^{jp}	Japan Lauric Oil Imports
22	m_t^{rw}	Rest of World Lauric Oil Imports
		Exogenous variables
1	y_t^{jp}	Japan output index
2	z_t^{jp}	Japan substitution effect ratio
3	RT	Reverse Trend
4	y_t^{us}	U.S. Output Index
5	y_t^{uk}	U.K. Output Index
6	z_t^{uk}	U.K. substitution effect ratio
7	y_t^{ec}	E.E.C. Output Index
8	z_t^{ec}	U.S.G.S.A. stockpile release dummy
9	D_t^{us}	U.S.G.S.A. stockpile release dummy
10	D_t^{uk}	U.K. stock adjustment dummy
11	D_t^{ec}	E.E.C. stock adjustment dummy
12	D_t^{cy}	Ceylon export tax dummy
13	p_t^{ph}	Philippines copra export price
14	r_t^{ph}	Philippines dry season rainfall
15	p_t^{cy}	Ceylon coconut oil price
16	r_t^{cy}	Ceylon rainfall
17	p_t^{in}	Indonesia copra export price
18	r_t^{in}	Indonesia rainfall
19	p_t^{x}	Philippine implicit coconut oil price

(2) *Stocks*: Philippines, Ceylon, U.S., U.K., and E.E.C. (3) *Consumption and Imports*: U.S., U.K., J., and E.E.C. The model has been estimated using annual data for the period 1953 through 1967. At the time of the estimation this permitted the two-year period 1968 and 1969 to be used as a basis for evaluating the short run performance of the model.

Quarterly data would have better explained the short run behavior of the market, but annual data did permit both an analysis of the impact of an annually operated export norm scheme on price stabilization and an analysis of expected long term market prospects. All the data are in continuous form except for the "dummy" variables specified in the previous chapters.

The assumptions made regarding the block structure of the model indicated that it contained both recursive and simultaneous behavior. To confirm that this is true prior to final estimation requires examining the matrix of the coefficients of the endogenous variables Γ as well as the variance covariance matrix of the disturbances, Σ, where Γ and Σ are as previously defined. Recursiveness for a block follows if the corresponding Γ matrix is triangular such that elements on one side of the diagonal are zero; in addition, the Σ matrix must be diagonal, implying that the covariances between the disturbances of the structural relationships are zero. Tables 6-5 to 6-7 present the Γ matrix divided according to whether the coefficients belong to the simultaneous block or the recursive blocks I and II. All three tables have been set up such that the coefficients on the predetermined variables appear in the upper part of each table and the coefficients on the endogenous variables constituting a subset of Γ appear in the lower part. The patterns formed by the coefficients confirm the assumptions made regarding the block structure. The coefficients appearing in Table 6-5, which describe recursive block I, are triangular with no elements to the left of the diagonal. The coefficients in Table 6-6 occur above and below the diagonal, confirming the interdependency of simultaneous block I. Finally, the pattern of coefficients in Table 6-7 is again triangular.

These same patterns of interdependency are reflected in the correlation matrix presented in Table 6-8, which describes the variance covariance among the residuals. The degree of confirmation, however, is less substantial. The test used in determining covariance is simply whether the r^2 between any pair of structural disturbances is significantly different from zero. The ordering of the r^2 information in that table follows the ordering of the blocks of the overall model.

None of the disturbances belonging to recursive block I is correlated at the 1 percent level, although several of the r^2 values are in the vicinity of 0.5. One of the correlations in the simultaneous block is significant at the 1 percent level, while most of the other r^2 values average 0.3. Again, none of the disturbances are correlated is recursive block II. That several of the correlations approach 0.5 or significance at the 5 percent level is cause for some concern.

Table 6-5. Structural Form of Coefficients—Recursive Block I

Explained variables	23	24	25	26	27	28	29	30	31	32	33	34	35
Explanatory variables	Δx_t^{ph}	Δx_t^{cy}	Δx_t^{in}	Δx_t^{oc}	Δx_t^{rw}	x_t^{pk}	x_t^{ph}	x_t^{cy}	x_t^{in}	x_t^{oc}	x_t^{rw}	x_t^{w}	s_t^{ph}
Intercept	133.29	1.40	−388.4	147.4	169.04	422.67							
1 p_{t-1}^{ph}	3.62												
2 Δp_t^{ph}	3.85												
3 R_{t-2}^{ph}	0.129												
4 ΔR_{t-1}^{ph}	0.182												
5 p_{t-1}^{cy}		−580											
6 Δp_t^{cy}		−300											
7 R_{t-2}^{cy}		0.113											
8 ΔR_{t-1}^{cy}		0.063											
9 p_t^{in}			11.8										
10 R_{t-2}^{in}			−17.3										
11 ΔR_{t-1}^{in}			0.153										
12 p_t^{x}			0.037										
13 Δp_t^{x}				0.096		−0.769							
14 p_{t-1}^{x}					−0.463	1.04							

15	p^x_{t-2}					−0.012	−0.395	
16	x^{ph}_{t-1}							−1.49
17	x^{cy}_{t-1}	−0.854						1
18	x^{in}_{t-1}				1			
19	x^{oc}_{t-1}		−1.31				1	
20	x^{rw}_{t-1}			−0.846		1		
21	x^{pk}_{t-1}			−1.26			1	
22	Δx^{ph}_t			0.163				1
23	Δx^{cy}_t	−1			1			
24	Δx^{in}_t		−1		1			
25	Δx^{oc}_t			−1		1		
26	Δx^{rw}_t			−1		1		
27	x^{pk}_t						1	
28	x^{ph}_t			−1	−1			
29	x^{cy}_t				−1	1	0.10	
30	x^{in}_t				−1	1		
31	x^{in}_t				−1	1		
32	x^{oc}_t				−1	1		
33	x^{rw}_t				−1	1		
34	x^w_t				−1	−1		
35	x^{ph}_t					−1		

Table 6-6. Structural Form of Coefficients—Simultaneous Block

Explained Variables		49	50	51	52	53	54	55	56	57	58
Explanatory Variables		s_t^{us}	Δs_t^{us}	s_t^{uk}	Δs_t^{uk}	Δs_t^{ec}	s_t^{ec}	s_t^{cy}	s_t^w	p_t^w	Δp_t^w
	Intercept	13.73		−9.16		18.47		−14.3		0.522	
34	x_t^w									−.00011	
35	s_t^{ph}								1		
36	Δy_t^{us}	0.464									
37	D_t^{us}	68.1									
38	Δy_t^{uk}			0.160							
39	D_t^{uk}			−18.0							
40	Δy_t^{ec}					−0.60					
41	D_t^{ec}					−49.9		6.38			
42	D_t^{cy}										
43	s_{t-1}^{us}		−1								
44	s_{t-1}^{uk}			.574	−1						
45	s_{t-1}^{ec}					−0.10	1				
46	s_{t-1}^w									−0.00022	
47	p_{t-1}^w							46.2		0.371	−1
48	p_{t-2}^w							38.1			
49	s_t^{us}	−1	1						1		
50	Δ_t^{us}		−1						1		
51	s_t^{uk}			−1	1						
52	Δs_t^{uk}				−1						
53	Δs_t^{ec}					−1	1				
54	s_t^{ec}						−1		1		
55	s_t^{cy}							−1	1		
56	s_t^w								−1	−0.00035	
57	p_t^w	115		81.2				−17.1		−1	1
58	Δp_t^w	−314		−52.8	−26.8						−1

Table 6-7. Structural Form of Coefficients—Recursive Block II

Explained Variable		73	74	75	76	77	78	79
Explanatory Variable		c_t^{us}	c_t^{uk}	m_t^{ec}	m_t^{us}	m_t^{uk}	m_t^{ec}	m_t^{jp}
	Intercept	89.7	76.7	658.5				13.8
34	x_t^{w}		0.307					
59	y_t^{uk}				1			
50	Δs_t^{us}					1		
52	Δs_t^{uk}						1	
53	Δs_t^{ec}	-165	-259	-507				-118
57	p_t^{w}	0.10						
60	y_t^{us}		-36.4					
61	y_t^{uk}			0.028				
62	y_t^{ec}			-0.196				
63	Δy_t^{ec}			22.7				
64	z_t^{ec}							0.244
65	y_t^{jp}							35.8
66	z_t^{jp}							
67	RT							
68	z_t^{ec}							
69	s_t^{gsa}				-1			
70	c_{t-1}^{us}	0.379						
71	c_{t-1}^{uk}		0.588					
72	m_{t-1}^{jp}							0.587
73	c_t^{us}	-1			1			
74	c_t^{uk}		-1			1		
75	c_t^{ec}			-1			1	
76	m_t^{us}				-1			
77	m_t^{uk}					-1		
78	m_t^{ec}						-1	
79	m_t^{jp}							-1

Table 6-8. Correlation Matrix Describing Covariance-Variance Among Equation Residuals 1953-76

Required Values for Significance:
0.50 at 5%
0.62 at 1%

Equation	Δx_t^{ph}	Δx_t^{cy}	Δx_t^{in}	Δx_t^{oc}	Δx_t^{rw}	x_t^{pk}	s_t^{us}	s_t^{uk}	s_t^{ec}	s_t^{cy}	p_t^{w}	c_t^{us}	c_t^{uk}	c_t^{ec}	m_t^{jp}
Δx_t^{ph}	1	-0.52	-0.34	-0.43	-0.02	-0.11	0.20	0.09	-0.01	0.29	0.04	-0.13	0.52	0.08	0.37
Δx_t^{cy}		1	0.43	0.14	-0.18	-0.45	0.05	-0.27	-0.05	-0.33	-0.21	0.20	-0.27	0.25	-0.06
Δx_t^{in}			1	-0.13	0.04	-0.16	-0.05	-0.12	0.20	0.08	0.06	-0.06	0.12	-0.18	0.10
Δx_t^{oc}				1	0.26	0.29	0.55	0.28	0.18	-0.10	0.21	0.39	-0.08	-0.05	-0.42
Δx_t^{rw}					1	-0.26	-0.11	0.13	0.04	-0.13	-0.15	0.23	0.33	-0.26	-0.23
x_t^{pk}						1	0.25	0.44	0.11	0.43	0.18	-0.18	-0.27	0.08	-0.14
s_t^{us}							1	0.37	0.16	0.11	0.32	0.39	0.34	0.20	-0.22
s_t^{uk}								1	-0.34	0.78	0.40	-0.13	-0.24	0.27	0.17
s_t^{ec}									1	0.32	0.04	-0.15	0.44	0.14	-0.13
s_t^{cy}										1	0.33	-0.40	-0.26	0.04	0.37
p_t^{w}											1	0.31	0.08	-0.04	0.15
c_t^{us}												1	0.25	-0.31	-0.54
c_t^{uk}													1	-0.14	-0.13
c_t^{ec}														1	0.34
m_t^{jp}															1
m_t^{rw}															

However, this test is indeed a stringent one and the results obtained are not adverse to the evidence presented in Tables 6-5 to 6-7.

Methods of estimation used in obtaining coefficients for the final versions of the model conform to the interdependency found in each of the three blocks.[94] Both the methods of OLS and GLS were employed for the equations appearing in recursive blocks I and II of the model. Because the gains in consistency obtained in GLS relative to OLS are marginal, due to the small sample size and the lack of serious autocorrelation in the disturbances, only the OLS results are presented. For the simultaneous block, the availability of only 14 annual observations dictated that 2SPC be used. Results are presented, however, for both the OLS and 2SPC methods. All price and other variables measured in current monetary values are deflated by an appropriate index. A summary of the estimated equations and identities appears in Table 6-9 below.[b]

Table 6-9. Estimated Equations and Identities Contained in the Lauric Oils Models

Recursive Block I

Philippines—Coconut Oil Exports

$$\Delta x_t^{ph} = 133.29 - 0.854 x_{t-1}^{ph} + 3.62 p_{t-1}^{ph} + 3.85 \Delta p_t^{ph} + 0.129 r_{t-2}^{ph} + 0.182 \Delta r_{t-1}^{ph}$$
$$(-3.09) \qquad (2.37) \qquad (1.15) \qquad (1.31) \qquad (4.37)$$
$$\bar{R}^2 = 0.82, \, DW = 3.04 \qquad (6.50)$$

Ceylon—Coconut Oil Exports

$$\Delta x_t^{cy} = 1.40 - 1.296 x_{t-1}^{cy} - 579.64 p_{t-1}^{cy} - 298.98 \Delta p_t^{cy} + 0.113 r_{t-2}^{cy} + 0.63 \Delta r_{t-1}^{cy}$$
$$(-8.50) \qquad (-3.34) \qquad (-2.28) \qquad (7.94) \qquad (7.02)$$
$$\bar{R}^2 = 0.93, \, DW = 3.12 \qquad (6.51)$$

Indonesia—Coconut Oil Exports

$$\Delta x_t^{in} = -388.35 - 1.312 x_{t-1}^{in} + 11.89 p_{t-1}^{in} - 17.31 \Delta p_t^{in} + 0.153 r_{t-2}^{in} + 0.037 \Delta r_{t-1}^{in}$$
$$(-5.41) \qquad (3.50) \qquad (-2.59) \qquad (2.29) \qquad (0.55)$$
$$\bar{R}^2 = 0.69, \, DW = 2.03 \qquad (6.52)$$

Oceania—Coconut Oil Exports

$$\Delta x_t^{oc} = 147.45 - 0.846 x_{t-1} + 0.096 \Delta p_t^x - 0.012 p_{t-1}^x$$
$$(-3.55) \qquad (0.48) \qquad (-0.12)$$
$$\bar{R}^2 = 0.51, \, DW = 2.85 \qquad (6.53)$$

---

[b] Significance levels for the *t* and Durban-Watson statistics are similar to those presented in Chapter 2.

Table 6-9 (*Continued*)

Rest of World—Coconut Oil Exports

$$\Delta x_t^{rw} = 169.04 - 1.261 x_{t-1}^{rw} - 0.463\,\Delta p_t^x - 0.395 p_{t-1}^x$$
$$\phantom{\Delta x_t^{rw} = 169.04}(-4.55)\qquad(-1.78)\qquad(-2.15)$$
$$\bar{R}^2 = 0.66,\ DW = 2.33\qquad(6.54)$$

Total of World—Palm Kernel Oil Exports

$$x_t^{pk} = 422.67 + 0.163 x_{t-1}^{pk} - 0.769 p_t^x + 1.045 p_{t-1}^x - 1.498 p_{t-2}^x$$
$$\phantom{x_t^{pk} = 422.67}(0.47)\qquad(-1.60)\quad(1.81)\qquad(-3.38)$$
$$\bar{R}^2 = 0.70,\ DW = 2.60\qquad(6.55)$$

Simultaneous Block

United States Stocks

OLS
$$s_t^{us} = 13.73 + 0.464\,\Delta y_{t+1}^{us} + 115.50 p_t^w - 314.38\,\Delta p_t^w + 68.18 D_t^{us}$$
$$\phantom{s_t^{us} = 13.73}(2.55)\qquad\quad(1.22)\qquad\quad(-3.50)\qquad\ (7.52)$$
$$\bar{R}^2 = 0.91,\ DW = 2.36\qquad(6.56)$$

2SPC
$$s_t^{us} = -1.28 + 0.142\,\Delta y_{t+1}^{us} + 146.29 p_t^w - 257.88\,\Delta p_t^w + 69.94 D_t^{us}$$
$$\phantom{s_t^{us} = -1.28}(0.80)\qquad\quad(1.01)\qquad\quad(-2.02)\qquad\ (5.87)$$
$$\bar{R}^2 = 0.83,\ DW = 2.10$$

United Kingdom Stocks

OLS
$$s_t^{uk} = -9.16 + 0.574 s_{t-1}^{uk} + 0.160\,\Delta y_t^{uk} + 81.29 p_t^w - 58.21\,\Delta p_t^w - 18.04 D_t^{uk}$$
$$\phantom{s_t^{uk} = -9.16}(8.26)\qquad\quad(2.87)\qquad\quad(3.07)\qquad(-2.50)\qquad(-7.62)$$
$$\bar{R}^2 = 0.94,\ DW = 1.80\qquad(6.57)$$

2SPC
$$s_t^{uk} = -25.06 + 0.550 s_{t-1}^{uk} + 0.087\,\Delta y_t^{uk} + 132.28 p_t^w - 93.88\,\Delta p_t^w - 21.38 D_t^{uk}$$
$$\phantom{s_t^{uk} = -25.06}(5.19)\qquad\quad(1.04)\qquad\quad(2.91)\qquad(-2.46)\qquad(-6.18)$$
$$\bar{R}^2 = 0.89,\ DW = 1.63$$

E.E.C. Stocks

OLS
$$\Delta s_t^{ec} = 18.467 - 0.099 s_{t-1}^{ec} - 0.060\,\Delta y_t^{ec} - 26.78\,\Delta p_t^w - 49.87 D_t^{ec}$$
$$\phantom{\Delta s_t^{ec} = 18.467}(-0.03)\qquad\ (-0.37)\qquad\quad(-0.19)\qquad\ (-2.54)$$
$$\bar{R}^2 = 0.51,\ DW = 2.38\qquad(6.58)$$

2SPC
$$\Delta s_t^{ec} = 29.09 - 0.100 s_{t-1}^{ec} + 0.005\,\Delta y_t^{ec} + 101.39\,\Delta p_t^w - 49.59 D_t^{ec}$$
$$\phantom{\Delta s_t^{ec} = 29.09}(-0.49)\qquad\ (0.40)\qquad\quad(0.50)\qquad\quad(-2.14)$$
$$\bar{R}^2 = 0.42,\ DW = 2.19$$

.Ceylon Stocks

OLS

$$s_t^{cy} = 14.26 - 17.29p_t^w + 46.25p_{t-1}^w + 38.08p_{t-2}^w + 6.38D_t^{cy}$$
$$(-1.04) \quad (3.24) \quad\quad (2.47) \quad\quad (3.47)$$

$$\bar{R}^2 = 0.57, \; DW = 1.93 \qquad (6.59)$$

2SPC

$$s_t^{cy} = -13.57 - 8.44p_t^w + 35.74p_{t-1}^w + 39.27p_{t-2}^w + 5.75D_t^{cy}$$
$$(-0.47) \quad (2.49) \quad\quad (2.11) \quad\quad (2.29)$$

$$\bar{R}^2 = 0.42, \; DW = 1.78$$

Philippines Stocks (Year-end stocks are estimated at 10% of annual exports)
SPH = 0.10 XPH

Prices—Linear Model

OLS

$$p_t^w = 0.522 + 0.371p_{t-1}^w - 0.00035s_t^w - 0.00022s_{t-1}^w - 0.00011x_t^w$$
$$(1.68) \quad\quad (-1.58) \quad\quad (-1.14) \quad\quad (-1.32)$$

$$\bar{R}^2 = 0.64, \; DW = 1.45 \qquad (6.60)$$

2SPC

$$p_t^w = 0.657 + 0.227p_{t-1}^w - 0.0046s_t^w - 0.00028s_{t-1}^w - 0.00014x_t^w$$
$$(2.46) \quad\quad (-1.50) \quad\quad (-1.11) \quad\quad (-1.98)$$

$$\bar{R}^2 = 0.61, \; DW = 1.67$$

Prices—Nonlinear Model

OLS

$$p_t^w = 0.416 + 0.603p_{t-1}^w - 0.521(s_t^m/c_t^m) - 0.00019x_t^w$$
$$(3.37) \quad\quad (-2.37) \quad\quad (-1.87)$$

$$\bar{R}^2 = 0.59, \; DW = 1.57 \qquad (6.61)$$

2SPC

$$p_t^w = 0.575 + 0.535p_{t-1}^w - 0.680(s_t^m/c_t^m) - 0.00019x_t^w$$
$$(2.38) \quad\quad (-12.08) \quad\quad (-2.32)$$

$$\bar{R}^2 = 0.45, \; DW = 1.90$$

Recursive Block II

United States Consumption

$$c_t^{us} = 89.77 + 0.379c_{t-1}^{us} + 0.100y_t^{us} - 165.87p_t^w$$
$$(2.37) \quad\quad (3.80) \quad\quad (-2.25)$$

$$\delta = 0.621, \; E_{ps} = 0.155, \; E_{pl} = 0.249 \qquad \bar{R}^2 = 0.96, \; DW = 2.85 \qquad (6.62)$$

United Kingdon Consumption

$$c_t^{uk} = 76.73 + 0.588c_{t-1}^{uk} + 0.307y_t^{uk} - 259.25p_t^w - 36.42z_t^{uk}$$
$$(4.32) \quad\quad (2.78) \quad\quad (-2.57) \quad (-2.52)$$

$$\delta = 0.412, \; E_{ps} = -0.441, \; E_{pl} = -1.00 \qquad \bar{R}^2 = 0.89, \; DW = 1.88 \qquad (6.63)$$

Table 6-9 (*Continued*)

E.E.C. Consumption

$$c_t^{ec} = 658.33 + 0.028y_t^{ec} - 0.196\,\Delta y_t^{ec} - 507.22p_t^w + 22.73z_t^{ec}$$
$$\phantom{c_t^{ec} = 658.33 + }(11.19)\quad\quad(-3.07)\quad\quad(-4.11)\quad\;(2.11)$$

$$\delta = 1.0,\, E_{ps} = E_{pl} = -0.306 \qquad\qquad\qquad \bar{R}^2 = 0.73,\, DW = 2.16 \qquad (6.64)$$

Japan Imports

$$m_t^{jp} = 13.75 + 0.587m_{t-1}^{jp} + 0.244y_t^{jp} - 118.66p_t^w + 35.83z_t^{jp}$$
$$\phantom{m_t^{jp} = 13.75 + }(3.76)\quad\quad(1.67)\quad\quad(-1.39)\quad\;(2.09)$$

$$\delta = 0.413,\, E_{ps} = 0.656,\, E_{pl} = 1.590 \qquad\qquad \bar{R}^2 = 0.84,\, DW = 2.67 \qquad (6.65)$$

United States Imports

$$m_t^{us} = c_t^{us} \pm \Delta s_t^{us} - s_t^{ysa} \tag{6.66}$$

United Kingdom Imports

$$m_t^{uk} = c_t^{uk} \pm \Delta s_t^{uk} \tag{6.67}$$

E.E.C. Imports

$$m_t^{ec} = c_t^{ec} \pm \Delta s_t^{ec} \tag{6.68}$$

Remaining Identities

$$s_t^w = s_t^{us} + s_t^{uk} + s_t^{ec} + s_t^{cy} + s_t^{ph} \tag{6.69}$$

$$x_t^w = x_t^{ph} + x_t^{cy} + x_t^{in} + x_t^{oc} + x_t^{rw} + x_t^{pk} \tag{6.70}$$

$$m_t^{rw} = x_t^w - m_t^{us} - m_t^{uk} - m_t^{jp} - m_t^{ec} \tag{6.71}$$

Source: W. C. Labys, *An Econometric Model of the International Lauric Oils Market: Considerations for Policy Analysis*, UNCTAD/CD/Misc.43, Rev. 1, United Nations, Geneva, July 1971.

Conclusions

A major concern in this chapter has been the presentation and explanation of recently available econometric methods which can assist us in specifying and estimating commodity models. We are now capable of specifying models to explain commodity behavior dynamically including the use of expectations, to combine stock and flow relationships permitting a better description of movements toward equilibrium, and to modify models such that they reflect noncompetitive market behavior. Causality and simultaneity within a model can also be better explained by decomposing the model into subsystems or blocks, and by determining, where possible, the causal ordering of variables within blocks. The recent development of efficient computer methods involving fixed-point and iterative instrumental variable methods of estimation is also likely to improve our ability to estimate commodity models; for example, it is now possible to estimate at once the parameters of an equation containing lagged endogenous variables where the equation also forms part of a simultaneous system. The application of the Bayesian approach to simultaneous equation systems is also being pursued.

Despite these innovations in methods for constructing commodity models, our optimism has to be tempered with caution. A considerable gap still exists between the theoretical possibilities for model construction and the practical outcome of being able to apply a model with confidence as intended. Among the pitfalls lying between theoretical and useful empirical models are problems of the availability and reliability of data and of the quality and significance of estimated coefficients. Availability of commodity data is limited because much secrecy still shrouds commodity series not openly published and because some information stems from developing countries where adequate data collection is just beginning. Specific problems related to the latter include the shortness of time series, dubious methods of estimating data, and frequent revisions in series.

Concerning the quality and significance or meaning of estimated coefficients, a number of different problems exist. First of all, data lacking in quality can hardly be expected to provide adequate coefficients, especially where the data contain measurement errors known to cause bias. Consequences of using such coefficients are even worsened by the model builder who would attribute a greater degree of causality to the coefficients than they deserve.

Second, if two independent variables in a regression are multicollinear, then the statistical significance of either coefficient is arbitrary and neither coefficient can be interpreted in the conventional sense of a partial derivative of calculus. At best, we can attempt to impose constraints on the coefficients endowing them more realistic values, or to replace the coefficients with values obtained through the use of engineering data.

Third, estimated coefficients can be questioned when specification error is present. If a relatively important variable is left out of an equation, any measured response will not only exclude this factor, but the coefficients of the included variables will be biased. Among the more serious sources of specification error in a commodity model is that we frequently fail to include various institutional aspects of a market simply because it cannot be described by conventional data, whereas an attempt could be made to include such factors by "dummy" variables or other means.

Fourth, there also exists the problem of using estimated coefficients in some future period. Our persistence in using linear rather than nonlinear functional relationships, for example, often prevents us from predicting sharp upturns or downturns in certain variables. The coefficients also become less meaningful over future periods where a market experiences structural changes or what has been termed "episodic events." Coefficients influenced in this way could possibly be made subject to constant adjustment by using a decision rule or feedback control theory or by ultimately respecifying the model to be sensitive to occurrence of such events.

Lastly, methods of validating commodity models have been limited to the mechanical use of conventional goodness of fit measures. At least some indications of a model's validity should be based on other aspects of a model's behavior, including performance in future periods. The question of validation is taken up next with regard to model stability and later with respect to selected parametric and nonparametric tests of estimated and predicted observations.

7   Model Stability[a]

Interpretation of the dynamic properties of a commodity model yields information regarding its stability, the response of endogenous to exogenous variables over time, and the influence of stochastic variations. The first of these is discussed in this chapter. The response characteristics of a model more related to multiplier analysis are examined in Chapter 8, while the impact of stochastic variations is explored within the context of simulation analysis in Chapter 9.

The nature of the stability properties of a commodity model constitutes an important measure of its validity. For most commodity markets, demand, supply, and prices do not increase or decrease without bound but gravitate to what can be considered their equilibrium values. If the market and a corresponding model are to be compatible, then the behavior of the model must conform to this same pattern. Stability thus implies that the endogenous variables of a model approach closely their equilibrium values or the particular solution of the model over time, given the values of the exogenous variables and the stochastic disturbance terms.

In this chapter, the stability properties of commodity models are examined by first comparing the essential differences between static and dynamic models. The susceptibility of different forms of dynamic models to stability analysis is then explored. Since no direct approach is presently available for determining the stability of nonlinear models, emphasis is placed on methods of analyzing the stability of nonstochastic and stochastic linear models. Examples of stability analysis appear for several commodity models, including the lauric oils model. See also Appendix A which reviews methods of solving first and higher order difference equations.

Dynamic Stability Defined

Background

Dynamic analysis of economic systems as distinct from static analysis first appeared in the writings of Marx or Malthus, if not even earlier. In modern economics it emerged in the 1930s with attempts to investigate dynamic properties of mathematical models. Works by Ezekiel, Frisch, Haavelmo, Harrod, Hicks, Kalecki, and Samuelson were among the most prominent.[1] Ezekiel's cobweb theorem, Samuelson's theory of accelerator-multiplier

---

[a] This chapter has been prepared in association with Mr. Ivar Strand, Department of Economics, University of Rhode Island.

169

interaction, and the Harrod-Domar growth models are still used today as classic examples of dynamic analysis.

Two works which appeared at the end of the 1940s are recognized, in particular, as providing the theoretical background to present day dynamic analysis. These include Samuelson's *Foundations of Economic Analysis* and Baumol's *Economic Dynamics*.[2] The recognition that formulation of a model as a set of first or higher order difference equations can lead to an interpretation of its stability soon led to the analysis of dynamic commodity models. Of particular interest are Foote's study of the feed-livestock economy and Suits's study of the watermelon market, both of which appeared in 1953.[3] However, a theory of dynamic analysis which included the multiplier effects of exogenous variables was not formalized until the appearance of Goldberger's study of the dynamic properties of the Klein-Goldberger model in 1959.[4] Also important was the Adelman and Adelman study dealing with the stability and stochastic properties of the same model.[5]

This more complete form of dynamic analysis has also been applied to a number of econometric commodity models.[6] The most comprehensive of these applications is Zusman's analysis of the California potato market appearing in 1962. The same method has been applied by Reutlinger to a dynamic beef model in 1966 and by Witherell to his dynamic wool model in 1968. A slightly different approach can be found in Mo's wheat study based on the Jury stability test.[7] Most recently, the dynamic analysis of commodity models has been expanded to include possible uses of simulation and spectral methods; see papers by Howrey and Witherell as well as by Naylor.[8]

Comparison of Static and Dynamic Models

Static Case. There is a need to make a further distinction between static and dynamic models beyond the explanation given in Chapter 6. In short, a static system will not contain elements of time explicitly. Movements between equilibrium must be explained utilizing comparative static analysis. But when time is explicit in the system, dynamic analysis must replace the latter method. The movement between equilibrium points is a function of time and the "time path" is a matter of interest. The ability of the system to successfully navigate between points of equilibrium is known as dynamic stability.

For illustrative purposes consider a static commodity model containing only supply and demand equations and an identity

$$c = b_0 + b_1 p$$
$$q = b_2 + b_3 p \tag{7.1}$$
$$c = q$$

where c and q are the quantities demanded and supplied, and p is price. Solution of this model yields the equilibrium values

$$(\bar{c}, \bar{p}) = \left(\frac{b_0 b_3 - b_1 b_2}{b_3 - b_1}, \frac{b_0 - b_2}{b_3 - b_1}\right) \tag{7.2}$$

With the application of the comparative static method, one can determine the change in the equilibrium values that will occur if there is, for example, a shift in one of the parameters.

$$d\bar{c} = \left(\frac{b_3}{b_3 - b_1}\right) db_0 \tag{7.3}$$

$$d\bar{p} = \left(\frac{1}{b_3 - b_1}\right) db_0 \tag{7.4}$$

Observe that the equilibrium values specified represent merely the solutions to a set of simultaneous equations. No information is available about the path that the system will take as a result of changes in time. To be able to obtain this from a static system, one must make certain assumptions about the system's equations to make them a function of time. To be sure that our static results are valid, we must examine the dynamic processes of the model. A more detailed explanation of this "correspondence principle" appears in Samuelson.[9]

Dynamic Case. The incorporation of time in the above system, can yield, for example, the conventional cobweb model, as introduced in Chapter 3.

$$c_t = b_0 + b_1 p_t$$
$$q_t = b_2 + b_3 p_{t-1} \tag{7.5}$$
$$c_t = q_t$$

The solution for p_t is

$$p_t = \frac{b_2 - b_0}{b_1} + \left(\frac{b_3}{b_1}\right) p_{t-1} \tag{7.6}$$

which follows from the solution of a first order nonhomogeneous difference equation. Its time-path can be described more appropriately as

$$p_t = (p_0 - \bar{p})\left(\frac{b_3}{b_1}\right)^t + \bar{p} \tag{7.7}$$

where $\bar{p} = \dfrac{b_2 - b_0}{b_1 - b_3}$ is the equilibrium value of price.

The above model will be stable if $p_t \to \bar{p}$ as $t \to \infty$. This result, in turn, depends on the absolute value of the ratio b_3/b_1. If $|b_3/b_1| < 1$, then $(b_3/b_1)^t$ becomes absolutely smaller as time increases and the model is stable. On the other hand, if $|b_3/b_1| > 1$, then $(b_3/b_1)^t$ becomes absolutely larger as time increases and the model is unstable. The presence of negative signs causes the model to be convergent or divergent in oscillations. A value of $0 > (b_3/b_1) > -1$ implies convergent oscillations and $(b_3/b_1) < -1$ implies divergent oscillations. In general, the cobweb model is stable for $-1 < (b_3/b_1) < 1$.

Approaches for Analyzing Dynamic Stability

Analysis of the stability properties of dynamic commodity models requires consideration of models more complex than the cobweb. The latter model assumed that the supply and demand equations are linear and exactly known, containing no stochastic elements. Either of these assumptions may be violated, in which case alternative approaches must be employed to determine stability. These approaches can be classified as they derive from analytical methods or simulation methods. Analytical methods permit stability conditions to be reached from the solution of first or higher order difference equations. Simulation methods permit examination of the response of the endogenous variables to discover whether the latter converge to their equilibrium values after the exogenous variables undergo impact changes. Applications of these methods are discussed below according to whether the form of the model of interest is linear or nonlinear, stochastic or nonstochastic.

Nonstochastic Linear Models. A nonstochastic linear version of a dynamic commodity model can be written in a strucutral form resembling the general model of Chapter 6

$$\Gamma Y_t + \beta_1 Y_{t-1} + \beta_2 X_t = 0 \qquad (7.8)$$

where $Y_t = $ a Gxn matrix of current endogenous variables, $Y_{t-1} = $ a Gxn matrix of lagged endogenous variables, $X_t = $ a Mxn matrix of exogenous variables, Γ and $\beta_1 = GxG$ matrices of coefficients on the endogenous and lagged endogenous variables respectively, and $\beta_2 = $ a GxM matrix of coefficients on the exogenous variables. Its reduced form is given by

$$Y_t = \pi_1 Y_{t-1} + \pi_2 X_t \qquad (7.19)$$

with dimensions as previously indicated. The nonstochastic or deterministic property of the model is defined by the conditions that the estimated parameters of the structural form be constant and the stochastic disturbance terms be zero. As will be shown in the next section, one can determine the stability characteristics of this system by solving the deterministic model as a first order nonhomogeneous system of difference equations. Howrey and Kelejian have shown that simulation of deterministic systems provides no further information regarding their stability or internal consistency.[10]

Stochastic Linear Models. The structural form 7.8 and the reduced form 7.9 become stochastic through the addition of a disturbance term; sometimes a probability distribution on the parameters is also included. The stochastic version of the structural form is

$$Y_t + \beta_1 Y_{t-1} + \beta_2 X_t = U_t \tag{7.8a}$$

where $U_t = $ a $G \times n$ matrix of stochastic disturbance terms. There are presently no analytical solutions based on difference equations which can be used to determine the stability of such a model; in the next section simulation solutions are shown to be of some value in this respect. When the stochastic version of the reduced form is considered,

$$Y_t = \pi_1 Y_{t-1} + \pi_2 X_t + V_t \tag{7.9a}$$

Howrey and Kelejian have shown that stability properties can be determined where V_t represent a $G \times n$ matrix of generated random variates. The method they prescribe is an analytical description of the stochastic processes based on the spectral representation of the random variates. (See Appendix B for further discussion of the general applicability of this approach.)

Nonstochastic Nonlinear Models. The nonlinear structural form of model 7.8 can be expressed conveniently as

$$Y_t = H_1 X_t + H_2 F(Y_t, Y_{t-1}, X_t) + H_3 R(Y_{t-1}, X_t) \tag{7.10}$$

where H_1, H_2, and H_3 are appropriate matrices of parameters, and F and R are vectors whose elements are functions of Y_t, Y_{t-1}, and X_t.[11] These functional terms are such that they depend upon at least one of the endogenous variables and any number of exogenous variables. At least one of the endogenous variables also is assumed to be nonlinear; for example, in the form of ratios or logarithmic dependence. There is little opportunity for directly determining the stability characteristics of such a model based on either simulation or analytical methods. The only possibility that does exist depends on the ability of certain equations of a system to be linearized using a method of polynomial approximation.[12]

Stochastic Nonlinear Models. Determining the dynamic properties of this form of model is indeed most difficult. Analytical methods have not proved helpful and the results of simulation analysis have been inconsistent in quality.

Analysis of Dynamic Stability

Of the above approaches, we consider those two which have been used in analyzing the dynamic properties of commodity models: the analytical approach as applied to nonstochastic linear models and the simulation approach as applied to stochastic linear models.

Nonstochastic Linear Models

Generally it is assumed that the linear first order econometric model is nonstochastic. The reduced form

$$Y_t = \pi_1 Y_{t-1} + \pi_2 X_t \tag{7.11}$$

provides a basis for analyzing stability of two types: (1) stability where in the limit all endogenous values approach their equilibrium level as discussed previously, and (2) stability where the equilibrium values bound the motion but there is no convergence. We will deal only with the former.

Our starting point is with the general solution of the reduced form of the model as a system of difference equations.[b] First, assume that the equilibrium values of the endogenous variables remain the same from period to period: $\overline{Y} = Y_t = Y_{t-1}$. Substitute $\overline{Y}$ for Y_t and Y_{t-1} in equation 7.11 to obtain

$$\overline{Y} = (I - \pi_1)^{-1}\pi_2 X_t \tag{7.12}$$

These values of the endogenous variables are the long run equilibrium values to which the system will converge if it is stable. This is called the particular solution.

The second step is to represent the time path values of the endogenous variables as a sum of the particular solution and a disturbance term

$$Y_t = \overline{Y} + U_t \tag{7.13}$$

Inserting this into 7.10 and using the identity 7.11 we get

$$U_t = \pi_1 U_{t-1} \tag{7.14}$$

---

[b] See Appendix A for a more detailed presentation.

or

$$(Y_t - \bar{Y}) = \pi_1(Y_{t-1} - \bar{Y}) \tag{7.15}$$

We assume a homogenous solution $(Y_t - \bar{Y}) = \lambda^t Im$, where $(Y_t - \bar{Y})$ is a $(G \times 1)$ vector, m is an $(G \times 1)$ vector which equals $Y_0 - \bar{Y}$, and λ is a scaler. This yields

$$\lambda^t Im = \pi_1 \lambda^{t-1} m \tag{7.16}$$

or

$$\lambda^t(\pi_1 - \lambda I)m = 0 \tag{7.17}$$

and the only nontrivial solution to this equation is when $(\pi_1 - \lambda I)^{-1}$ does not exist or

$$|\pi_1 - \lambda I| = 0 \tag{7.18}$$

The λs will be the characteristic or latent roots of the matrix. The condition for stability requires the real roots to lie within the unit circle. If the roots are imaginary or $\lambda = a + bi$, stability requires that the modulus $|Z| = \sqrt{a^2 + b^2} < 1$. If the λs are stable, then the general solution

$$Y_t = \bar{Y} + \lambda^t Im \tag{7.19}$$

will converge to $\bar{Y}$ as $t \to \infty$.

With the computer, the eigen values or latent roots are easily found. If this option is not available, however, a test suggested by Jury may be used. Let us consider first an application of the former approach, as found in Reutlinger's study of the dynamic properties of a simplified beef model.[13] The structural form of his beef model can be transformed as follows

$$Y_{1t} = 0.93\,Y_{1,t-1} + 0.153\,Y_{3,t-1} + 2.80 + 3.32Z_{1,t-1}$$
$$-280\,Y_{1t} + Y_{2t} = 0.49\,Y_{1,t-1} - 0.030\,Y_{3,t-1} + 1.90 + 0.80Z_{1,t-1}$$
$$2.70\,Y_{2t} + Y_{3t} = -70.0 + 0.022Z_{2t} + 0.60Z_{3t}$$

such that the matrices corresponding to those of system 7.8 are given by

$$\Gamma = \begin{bmatrix} 1.00 & 0.00 & 0.00 \\ -2.80 & 1.00 & 0.00 \\ 0.00 & 2.70 & 1.00 \end{bmatrix} \quad \beta_1 = \begin{bmatrix} 0.930 & 0.000 & 0.153 \\ 0.490 & 0.000 & -0.030 \\ 0.000 & 0.000 & 0.000 \end{bmatrix}$$

$$\beta_2 = \begin{bmatrix} 2.80 & 3.32 & 0.00 & 0.00 \\ 1.90 & 0.80 & 0.00 & 0.00 \\ -70.00 & 0.00 & 0.22 & 0.60 \end{bmatrix}$$

After manipulating the matrices, the reduced form would be

$$Y_t = \begin{bmatrix} 0.930 & 0.000 & 0.153 \\ 0.750 & 0.000 & 0.013 \\ 2.026 & 0.000 & -0.035 \end{bmatrix} Y_{t-1} + \begin{bmatrix} 2.800 & -3.320 & 0.000 & 0.000 \\ 2.684 & -0.130 & 0.000 & 0.000 \\ 77.250 & 0.351 & 0.022 & 0.600 \end{bmatrix} X_t$$

The stability condition 7.18 requires that

$$|\pi_1 - \lambda I| = 0 \qquad (7.20)$$

In this case, the characteristic equation is

$$\begin{vmatrix} 0.930 - \lambda & 0.000 & 0.153 \\ 0.750 & 0 - \lambda & 0.013 \\ -2.026 & 0.000 & -0.035 - \lambda \end{vmatrix} = 0$$

Since the rank of the determinant is not full and is two, the second row and column can be deleted resulting in the characteristic equation.

$$\lambda^2 - 0.895\lambda + 0.277$$

The eigen values or latent roots are $0.447 \pm 0.277i$. The dominant of these is $0.477 + 0.277i$ with a modulus $|Z| = [(0.477)^2 + (0.277)^2]^{\frac{1}{2}} = 0.527$. Since the period is defined as the reciprocal of the frequency and the frequency is $\dfrac{\Phi}{2\pi}$ where $\Phi = \dfrac{0.447}{Z}$, the period of oscillation is eleven years. The beef model is seen to be stable, approaching the equilibrium in an oscillatory fashion with an eleven year cycle.

The test proposed by Jury requires principally that the reduced form matrix π_1 be reasonably small.[14] A series of functions of the following form are first derived based on the stability conditions expressed in the determinant 7.18.

$$F_0(\lambda) = P_n \lambda^n + P_{n-1}\lambda^{n-1} + \cdots + P_1\lambda + P_0 = 0 \qquad (7.21)$$

For all λs to be within the unit circle, the following conditions are necessary:

(1): $F_0(\lambda = 1) > 0$

(2): $F_0(\lambda = 1) < 0$, if n is odd $\qquad (7.22)$

$\qquad F_0(\lambda = -1) > 0$, if n is even

(3): $|S_i| < 1$ for $i = 0, 1, \ldots, n - 2$

where the S_i are a series of ingeniously devised quotients. The S_i are obtained on the basis of $\dfrac{F_0^{-1}(\lambda)}{F_0(\lambda)} = S_0 + \dfrac{F_1^{-1}(\lambda)}{F_0(\lambda)}$. Inserting the $F_1^{-1}(\lambda)$ yields the value of S_1 and so on

$$\frac{F_1^{-1}(\lambda)}{F_1(\lambda)} = S_1 + \frac{F_2^{-1}(\lambda)}{F_1(\lambda)} \tag{7 23}$$

where $F^{-1}(\lambda)$ is defined as $P_0\lambda^n + P_1\lambda^{n-1} + \cdots + P_{n-1}\lambda + P_n$. The coefficients of the determinant function are merely reversed; that is if $F_0(\lambda) = 2\lambda^2 + 3\lambda + 6$, then $F_0^{-1}(\lambda) = 6\lambda^2 + 3\lambda + 2$. One follows this procedure until the $(n-2)$nd term is reached. If all $|S_i| < 1$ for $i = 0, 1, \ldots, n-2$, the condition is satisfied. It is strongly suggested that the first approach in which the latent roots are computed be used with matrices of a dimension greater than 3×3.

An illustration of the application of the Jury method can be found in the analysis of Mo's wheat model.[15] It can be shown that the rank (3) of the stability condition 7.18 is such that the determinant of that model reduces to

$$\begin{vmatrix} 0.7446 - \lambda & 0.0000 & 0.0000 \\ -0.0314 & 0.3635 - \lambda & 0.0000 \\ 0.0967 & 0.0967 & 0.6494 - \lambda \end{vmatrix} = 0$$

This yields the function

$$F_0(\lambda) = \lambda^3 - 1.7575\lambda^2 + 0.9903\lambda - 0.1758 = 0$$

from which the appropriate conditions are

(1): $\quad F_0(\lambda = 1) = 0.0570 > 0$

(2): $\quad F_0(\lambda = 1) = -3.9236 < 0$

(3): $\dfrac{F_0^{-1}(\lambda)}{F_0(\lambda)} = -0.1758 + \dfrac{0.6813\lambda^2 - 1.583\lambda + 0.9691}{\lambda^3 - 1.7575\lambda^2 + 0.9903\lambda - 0.1758}$

$\dfrac{F_1^{-1}(\lambda)}{F_1(\lambda)} = 0.7030 + \dfrac{-0.473\lambda + 0.4901}{0.9691\lambda^2 - 1.5834\lambda + 0.6813}$

and thus

$$|S_i| < 1 \text{ for } i = 0, 1 \ldots n - 2.$$

Since the three conditions are satisfied, the system is stable. This method may seem a little roundabout here because the latent roots can be directly obtained by looking at the main diagonal. For the case of a nontriangular 3×3 or 2×2 matrix, however, the roots are not too easily found and the Jury method may offer an advantage.

Stochastic Linear Models

Models of this type resemble the structural form 7.8a or the reduced form 7.9a examined above. Normally the stochastic character of these models is determined through three different ways of applying probability distributions: (1) a probability distribution of the disturbance terms based on the corresponding estimated distribution; (2) a probability distribution of the exogenous variables based on their estimated variances; and (3) a probability distribution of the estimated structural parameters. Applications (1) and (2) are often referred to as shocks of Type I and Type II, respectively.

These were used by Adelman and Adelman in analyzing the stability of the structural form of a linearized version of the Klein-Goldberger model, based on simulation methods.[16] In that study, the emphasis was to determine if the model was stable when subjected to a single exogenous shock, to learn what types of oscillations if any characterized the return to the equilibrium path, and to identify the response of the model to repeated internal and external shocks. Adelman and Adelman concluded that better results of realistic, model behavior are obtained when the stochastic form of the model is used and that simulation analysis in this form provides more information regarding stability than when analytical methods alone are applied to the nonstochastic form. In a sense, the results of nonstochastic analysis provide the necessary conditions for stability and the results of stochastic analysis provide sufficient conditions.

Desai, using a similar approach of simulation analysis based on reduced form analysis and Type I and II shocks, has been able to evaluate successfully the stability of his tin model.[17] However, Howrey and Kelejian point out the shortcomings of simulation studies of stochastic reduced forms in validating a model where the approach taken is to compare simulated and actual values.[18]

Stability of the Lauric Oils Model

Having reviewed the methods for determining the stability of a commodity model, we can now apply them to obtain an analytical solution for the lauric oils model presented in Chapter 6. Our approach will be to consider the simultaneous block of the model as a first order system of linear, nonstochastic equations. The equations comprising that block can be rewritten in a form which facilitates solving for the critical matrix of reduced form parameters, $\pi_1 = \beta_1 \Gamma^{-1}$.

$$s_t^{us} + 198.88 p_t^w = 314.38 p_{t-1}^w + 13.73 + 0.464\,\Delta y_t^{us} + 68.18 D_t^{us} \tag{7.24}$$

$$s_t^{uk} - 23.08 p_t^w = 58.21 p_{t-1}^w - 9.16 + 0.160\,\Delta y_t^{uk} - 18.04 D_t^{uk} - 0.544 s_{t-1}^{uk} \tag{7.25}$$

$$s_t^{ec} + 26.79 p_t^w = 26.79 p_{t-1}^w + 18.47 - 0.06 y_t^{ec} - 49.87 D_t^{ec} + 0.90 s_{t-1}^{ec} \tag{7.26}$$

$$s_t^{cy} + 17.29 p_t^w = 46.25 p_{t-1}^w + 14.26 + 6.38 D_t^{cy} \tag{7.27}$$

$$s_t^w - s_t^{us} - s_t^{uk} - s_t^{ec} - s_t^{cy} = s_t^{ph} \tag{7.28}$$

$$0.00035 s_t^w + p_t^w = 0.0371 p_{t-1}^w + 0.522 - 0.00011 x_t^w - 0.00022 s_{t-1}^w \tag{7.29}$$

It should be noted that equation 7.28 was included in the simultaneous section because it describes the relationship between equation 7.29 and equations 7.24 to 7.27. This identity is necessary to correctly define the nature of the simultaneous reactions. Also, for simplicity, a second order lag was removed in forming equation 7.27. The structuring of the matrices would change and enlarge considerably if this simplification was not made.

Values of the β and Γ matrices and the solved π_1 matrix are as follows:

$$\Gamma = \begin{bmatrix} 1 & 0 & 0 & 0 & 0 & 198.88 \\ 0 & 1 & 0 & 0 & 0 & 23.08 \\ 0 & 0 & 1 & 0 & 0 & 26.79 \\ 0 & 0 & 0 & 1 & 0 & 17.29 \\ -1 & -1 & -1 & -1 & 1 & 0 \\ 0 & 0 & 0 & 0 & 0.00035 & 1 \end{bmatrix}$$

$$\beta_1 = \begin{bmatrix} 0 & 0. & 0 & 0 & 0 & 314.38 \\ 0 & -0.574 & 0 & 0 & 0 & 58.21 \\ 0 & 0 & 0.9 & 0 & 0 & 26.79 \\ 0 & 0 & 0 & 0 & 0 & 46.25 \\ 0 & 0 & 0 & 0 & 0 & 0 \\ 0 & 0 & 0 & 0 & 0.00022 & 0.371 \end{bmatrix}$$

$$\pi_1 = \begin{bmatrix} 0.119 & 0.119 & 0.119 & 0.119 & 0.119 & -340.590 \\ 0.017 & 0.591 & 0.017 & 0.017 & 0.017 & -48.710 \\ 0.019 & 0.019 & 0.919 & 0.019 & 0.019 & -55.144 \\ 0.017 & 0.017 & 0.017 & 0.017 & 0.017 & -50.106 \\ 0.0 & 0.0 & 0.0 & 0.0 & 0.0 & 0.0 \\ 0.00097 & 0.00097 & 0.00097 & 0.00097 & 0.00097 & 0.349 \end{bmatrix}$$

The condition required for the stability of the above system of equations is given by the characteristic equation 7.18.

$$|\pi_1 - \lambda I| = 0 \tag{7.30}$$

Since the rank of the π_1 matrix must be full, the fifth row and fifth column of the solved matrix must be removed. This results in a characteristic equation of the form:

$$
\begin{vmatrix}
0.119 - \lambda & 0.119 & 0.119 & 0.119 & 340.59 \\
0.017 & 0.591 - \lambda & 0.017 & 0.017 & -48.71 \\
0.019 & 0.019 & 0.919 - \lambda & 0.019 & -55.14 \\
0.017 & 0.017 & 0.017 & 0.017 - \lambda & -50.11 \\
0.001 & 0.001 & 0.001 & 0.001 & 0.349 - \lambda
\end{vmatrix} = 0
$$

Solution of the characteristic roots of this equation yields

$$\lambda_1 = 0$$

$$\lambda_2 = 0.85672$$

$$\lambda_3 = 0.31277 + 0.63523i$$

$$\lambda_4 = 0.31277 - 0.63523i$$

$$\lambda_5 = 0.51303$$

From these results we can see that the simultaneous block of the lauric oils model is in fact stable. The conditions that all the λ_i be less than 1 for the real roots and the modulus of the complex roots be less than or equal to 1 are fullfilled. A notion of the time response of the system can be obtained from the dominant characteristic root. In this case, the dominant root is a positive 0.86, implying that the time response will oscillate and approach the equilibrium value from above only. The period of oscillation found from interpreting the given roots is 5.6 years.

While this result pertains to the stability of a nonstochastic version of the lauric oils model in particular, it has been confirmed elsewhere by simulation with a stochastic form of the model over a long run period.[19]

Conclusions

This chapter has presented one approach to validating an econometric commodity model based on its internal consistency. Methodology applied varies according to whether the commodity model is linear or nonlinear, stochastic or nonstochastic. Empirical results have been examined only for the case of linear, nonstochastic models. Because such models or linearized versions of nonlinear models remain the major types for which analytical solution is possible, it is obvious that considerable work remains before analytical solutions can be applied to a wider class of models. Spectral methods of solution as further explained in Appendix B may be of some help. Also, the resolving of the present controversy over the relative qualities of analytical versus simulation solutions for determining stability may yield useful results.

Part III
Applications of Commodity Models

8 Multiplier Analysis

Commodity models are normally constructed for purposes of historical experimentation, decision making, or forecasting. To this end, we employ both methods of multiplier analysis and of simulation analysis. Our present concern is with the former or the change in endogenous variables anticipated because of a unit change in some exogenous variable or policy instrument. The types of multipliers to be considered vary with their function over time. Static multipliers are examined as they explain changes over a single period or over a span of periods; dynamic multipliers define changes occurring from period to period whose total effect can be cumulated over a number of periods. Also explored is the concept of dynamic discrepancy, which explains the extent to which a constant rate of change in an exogenous variable will produce distortions in values of the endogenous variables associated with the long run static multiplier. Examples of multiplier analysis are drawn from several commodity models including that of the lauric oils.

Static and Dynamic Multipliers

Multiplier analysis has developed principally in conjunction with macro-econometric models, the most popular example being the effect of changes in autonomous investment on income. The most thorough study of multiplier analysis in this respect is the work of Goldberger.[1] Also of interest is a paper by Theil and Boot plus the recent works of Evans, and of Fromm and Klein.[2] Commodity studies which have made effective use of multiplier analysis include those of Zusman, Witherell, Reutlinger, Mo, and Vanderborre.[3]

Definitions for both static and dynamic multipliers can be reached using the *final form* of an econometric model as derived by Theil and Boot.[4] We begin with the general commodity model

$$\Gamma Y_t + \beta_1 Y_{t-1} + \beta_2 X_t = U_t \tag{8.1}$$

where Y_t is a $G \times n$ matrix of current endogenous variables; Y_{t-1} is a $G \times n$ matrix of lagged endogenous variables; X_t is a $M \times n$ matrix of exogenous variables; $U_t = $ a $G \times n$ matrix of stochastic disturbance terms; $\Gamma = $ a $G \times G$ matrix of coefficients on the endogenous variables; $\beta_1 = $ a $G \times G$ matrix of coefficients on the lagged endogenous variables; and $\beta_2 = $ a $G \times M$ matrix of coefficients on the exogenous variables. The reduced form of the model is given by

$$Y_t = \pi_1 Y_{t-1} + \pi_2 X_t + V_t \tag{8.2}$$

185

where

$$\pi_1 = -\Gamma^{-1}\beta_1, \ \pi_2 = -\Gamma^{-1}\beta_2, \ V_t = \Gamma^{-1}U_t \tag{8.3}$$

π_1 is a $G \times G$ matrix of reduced form coefficients on the lagged endogenous variables and π_2 is a $G \times M$ reduced form matrix on the exogenous variables. The latter also represents a matrix of multipliers in their simplest form, as will be shown below.

The final form of the model can now be derived from the reduced form 8.2 by first performing a series of substitutions. First, lag 8.2 one period

$$Y_{t-1} = \pi_1 Y_{t-2} + \pi_2 X_{t-1} + V_{t-1}$$

and substitute this expression back into the original equation

$$Y_t = \pi_1(\pi_1 Y_{t-2} + \pi_2 X_{t-1} + V_{t-1}) + \pi_2 X_t + V_t$$
$$= \pi_1^2 Y_{t-2} + \pi_1\pi_2 X_{t-1} + \pi_2 X_t + \pi_1 V_{t-1} + V_t$$

This procedure is repeated s times such that

$$Y_t = \pi_1^{s+1} Y_{t-s-1} + \sum_{\tau=0}^{s} \pi_1^\tau \pi_2 X_{t-\tau} + \sum_{\tau=0}^{s} \pi_1 V_{t-\tau} \tag{8.4}$$

It is then necessary to incorporate the underlying stability conditions as discussed in Chapter 7. Stability conditions are important because long run multiplier analysis will be relevant only if the model is stable. This follows if the matrix π_1^{s+1} approaches a null matrix as s increases to infinity.

$$\lim_{s \to \infty} \pi_1^{s+1} = 0 \tag{8.5}$$

In this case, the diagonal entries of π_1 must be < 1, or, more precisely, the latent roots of the matrix π_1 must be within the interior of the unit circle. Combining equation 8.4 and condition 8.5 yields the final form.

$$Y_t = \sum_{\tau=0}^{\infty} \pi_1^\tau \pi_2 X_{t-\tau} + \sum_{\tau=0}^{\infty} \pi_1 V_{t-\tau} \tag{8.6}$$

Definitions of the various multipliers can be obtained from successive components of the exact part of the final form: π_2, $\pi_1\pi_2$, $\pi_1^2\pi_2$ .. $\pi_1^\tau\pi_2$. These matrices describe the effect of changes in exogenous variables on the endogenous variables in the same or successive periods.[5]

Short Run Static Multipliers

The short run static or impact multipliers reflect the influence that a one unit change in some exogenous variable in X_t will have on the endogenous variables Y_t within the same period while all other predetermined variables are held constant. By taking the partial derivative of Y_t with respect to X_t in the final form 8.2 where $\tau = 0$, the matrix of impact multipliers is

$$\pi^M = \frac{\partial Y_t}{\partial X_t} = \frac{\partial}{\partial X_t}(\pi_1^0 \pi_2 X_t) = \pi_2 \tag{8.7}$$

The impact multiplier between any particular pair of endogenous and exogenous variables identified by i and j respectively would correspond to the $(i,j)^{th}$ element of π_2.

$$\frac{\partial Y_{it}}{\partial X_{jt}} = \pi_{(i,j),2} \tag{8.8}$$

The total number of such elements within π_2 corresponds to the number of endogenous variables times the number of exogenous variables, $G \times M$. As suggested in Figure 8-1, it is important to realize that impact multipliers

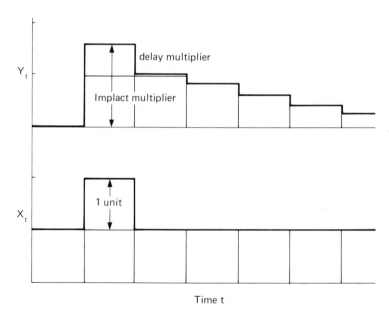

Figure 8-1. Impact and Delay Multipliers.

reflect only the contemporaneous effect of an impulse change in X_t. In the most general case, the multipliers will depend on time and will also be nonconstant for the case of a nonlinear model.

Long Run Static Multipliers

The long run static multiplier is also known as the equilibrium or stationary multiplier. It helps to answer the question as to what the impact of a sustained unit change in an exogenous variable would be on the endogenous variables after a long period of time. One can think of the multiplier as describing the change in an endogenous variable between two stationary states; the differences between the states is caused by a sustained one unit change in some exogenous variable. More precisely, the long run multiplier can be defined by taking the partial derivative of the final form 8.6 where the term X_t^* is introduced to represent a sustained change in some exogenous variable, its value being constant

$$\pi^L = \frac{\partial Y_t}{\partial X_t^*} = \frac{\partial}{\partial X_t^*} (\pi_2 + \pi_1 \pi_2 X_t^* + \cdots + \pi_1^\tau \pi_2 X_t^*)$$

or

$$\pi^L = (I + \pi_1 + \pi_1^2 + \cdots + \pi_1^\tau)\pi_2 \tag{8.9}$$

The latter expression can be simplified by recognizing the series $(I + \pi_1 + \pi^2 + \cdots + \pi_1^\tau)$ as the expansion of $(I - \pi_1)^{-1} (I - \pi_1)^\tau$. Since the final form assumes that π_1 approaches 0 as τ tends to infinity, the second part of the term can be dropped and the multiplier reduces to

$$\pi^L = (I - \pi_1)^{-1}\pi_2 \tag{8.10}$$

A multiplier corresponding to any pair of variables accordingly is defined as $\frac{\partial Y_{it}}{\partial X_{jt}^*}$. Figure 8-2 shows the long run equilibrium value of Y_t obtained from a sustained one unit increase in X_t.

Delay Dynamic Multipliers

One limitation to using static multipliers is that they provide only the first period or a fixed period response of the endogenous variables to a unit change in an exogenous variable. Yet a dynamic model often contains variables that

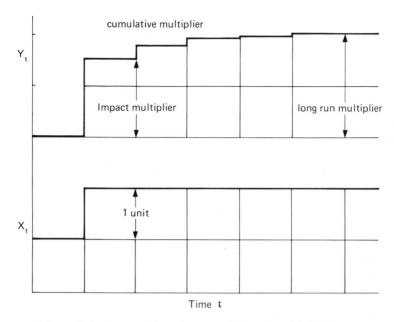

Figure 8–2. Impact, Cumulative, and Long Run Multipliers.

are lagged one or two periods, and the response of the endogenous variables might be different from the response found in the initial period once the lagged feedbacks are taken into account. The effects of cross-temporal feedbacks on the time paths of the endogenous variables can be analyzed by computing dynamic multipliers, the latter differing according to whether the exogenous variables undergo an impulse or a sustained change. The delay multiplier reflects the impact of impulse change; it helps answer the question as to what the current and future values of the endogenous variables would be given an impulse or one period change in an exogenous variable. Since the exogenous variable returns to its original level, its effect on the endogenous variables would decline as time increases, depending on the strength of the feedback and assuming the system to be stable. The delay multiplier is defined by taking the partial derivative of the final form with respect to $X_{t-\tau}$

$$\pi^D = \frac{\partial Y_t}{\partial X_{t-\tau}} = \frac{\partial}{\partial X_{t-\tau}} \left(\sum_{\tau=0}^{\infty} \pi_1 \pi_2 X_{t-\tau} \right) = \pi_1^{\tau} \pi_2 \qquad (8.11)$$

where the elements of $\pi_1 \pi_2$ reflect the impact of an impulse change of an exogenous variable on an endogenous variable after τ periods have elapsed, with all other predetermined variables held constant. The delay multiplier for any pair of variables is given by $\dfrac{\partial Y_{it}}{\partial X_{j,t-\tau}}$. Figure 8-1 describes the decline in the impact of a one unit change in the exogenous variable reflecting the changing value of the delay multiplier over time.

Cumulative Dynamic Multipliers

The cumulative multiplier reflects what will happen to the current and future values of an endogenous variable when the one unit change in the exogenous variable is no longer transient but is maintained over τ periods. Consider the evolutionary expansion of the final form of the model

$$Y_t = \sum_{\tau=0}^{\infty} \pi_1 \pi_2 X_{t-\tau}$$

after some periods $\tau > 0$ to be given by

$$Y_t = \pi_2 X_t + \pi_1 \pi_2 X_{t-1} + \cdots + \pi_1 \pi_2 X_{t-\tau} \tag{8.12}$$

Since the value of the exogenous variables remains constant over the full period, equation 8.12 becomes

$$Y_t = (I + \pi_1 + \pi_1^2 + \cdots + \pi_1^\tau \, \pi_2 X_t^*) \tag{8.13}$$

where $X_t^* = X_{t-1} = \cdots = X_{t-\tau}$. The cumulative or dynamic multiplier is defined by taking the partial derivative of Y_t with respect to X_t^*.

$$\pi^C = \frac{\partial Y_t}{\partial X_t^*} = \frac{\partial}{\partial X_t} (I + \pi_1 + \pi_1^2 + \cdots + \pi_1^\tau) \pi_2 \, X_t^*$$

or

$$\pi^C = (I + \pi_1 + \pi_1^2 + \cdots + \pi_1^\tau) \pi_2 \tag{8.14}$$

The continual change in the endogenous variable results from the sustained change in the exogenous variables with all predetermined variables held constant. Observe that the cumulative multiplier, also referred to as the τ period multiplier, is identical to the short run impact multiplier for the case of $\tau = 0$. Figure 8-2 suggests that the values of the cumulative multipliers increase over time as the endogenous variable Y_t undergoes a sustained change.

A more thorough understanding of the cumulative multiplier can be had using an example from Mo's wheat model. Results summarized in Table 8-1 show the impact of a sustained increase of one dollar per bushel in the wheat support price on government and commercial wheat inventories in successive

Table 8-1. Cumulative Multipliers

The impact of a sustained increase in wheat support price by one dollar per bushel on Government and commercial wheat inventory in successive time periods[1]

	The τ period impact multiplers	
Time period	Government wheat inventory	Commercial wheat inventory
	Mil. bu.	Mil. bu.
1	115.61	−64.06
2	201.69	−90.97
3	265.78	−103.46
4	313.50	−110.01
5	349.04	−113.89
6	375.50	−116.41
7	395.20	−118.15
8	409.87	−119.40
9	420.80	−120.33
10	428.94	−121.00

[1]Ordinary least squares estimates.

Source: Willliam Y. Mo, *An Economic Analysis of the Dynamics of the United States Wheat Sector*, Tech. Bull. No. 1395, Economic Research Service, U.S.D.A., April 1968, p. 20.

time periods.[6] The predicted levels of government inventories suggest an increase of 116 million bushels in period 1, an increase in 202 million bushels at the end of period 2, and a final level of 429 million bushels at the end of period 10. In contrast, the response of the commercial wheat inventories is shown to be a declining one; the magnitudes of the absolute differences of the cumulative multipliers decline in moving from period 1 ot 10. The value of wheat inventories that could be obtained over successive periods is reflected in the multiplier values reached in the limit. Accordingly, the effect of the sustained change in price is substantial in the immediate periods but much less in later periods.[7]

Dynamic Discrepancy

The long run static and the cumulative dynamic multipliers can be used to forecast values of the endogenous variables over a number of periods. One may refer to the next chapter to see how such forecasts are actually generated from the reduced form using simulation. The principal characteristic of a reduced form prediction is that it is most often causal, which leads to a stationary equilibrium.[8] Given an initial change in the exogenous variables of a system, all endogenous variables eventually reach their long run equilibrium values. Yet if the system is subject to continuous changes in the exogenous variables, the predictions are of a historic nature and the resultant values may differ from those describing long run, stationary equilibrium. In effect, the system converges towards an ever-receding equilibrium, but never really arrives there. Dynamic discrepancy refers to this difference between the changed value of an endogenous variable and its long run equilibrium value.

We can derive the dynamic discrepancy for a commodity system by stating more precisely the differences between the forecasts generated by causal as compared to historical systems.[9] A causal system is representative of a dynamic commodity model where stationary state conditions are assumed. The endogenous variables take on values which would be obtained in the long run or in the limit had no continuous variation occurred in any of the exogenous variables. If one assumes that such a model contains lags of only one period, then it can be represented by the reduced form given previously

$$Y_t = \pi_1 Y_{t-1} + \pi_2 X_t + V_t \tag{8.2}$$

where the stochastic term will be neglected to simplify the discussion. The values obtained for the endogenous variables following the conditions of stationary equilibrium are given by

$$Y_t = (I - \pi_1)^{-1} \pi_2 X_t^* \tag{8.15}$$

where $(I - \pi_1)^{-1}\pi_2$ is the long run multiplier previously described in 8.9.

A historical system, in contrast, is based on the much more realistic assumption that the exogenous variables in the underlying model will vary over time. Interpreting a system's response to changes in the exogenous variables can be most simply done by representing the latter as a linear function of time

$$X_t = E_0 + E_1 t \tag{8.16}$$

where E_0 and E_1 are $m \times 1$ vectors of constant coefficients. This functional relationship can be introduced into the above reduced form such that

$$Y_t = \pi_1 Y_{t-1} + \pi_2(E_0 + E_1 t) \tag{8.17}$$

Our interest is with the equilibrium conditions of such a system, which can be obtained from the equivalent final form, assuming the system to be stable.

$$Y_t = \sum_{\tau=0}^{\infty} \pi_1^{\tau} \pi_2 [E_0 + E_1(t - \tau)] \tag{8.18}$$

Expand that final form by factoring out the $E_0 + E_1 t$ such that

$$Y_t = (I + \pi_1 + \pi_1^2 + \cdots)\pi_2(E_0 + E_1 t) - (\pi_1 + 2\pi_1^2 + 3\pi_1^3 + \cdots)\pi_2 E_1$$

The expansionary series in each term can be replaced using definitions similar to those applied in 8.10.

$$Y_t = (I - \pi_1)^{-1}\pi_2 X_t - (I - \pi_1)^{-2}\pi_1\pi_2 E_1 \tag{8.20}$$

The resulting equation describes the equilibrium conditions for systems that are dynamic and historical.[10] Should changes in the exogenous variables cause the endogenous variables to depart from this limiting path, a return to equilibrium is assured.

The concepts of receding equilibrium and dynamic discrepancy can now be defined using equation 8.20. The first term of that equation, which corresponds to receding equilibrium, describes the path obtained when sufficient time is allowed for a system to stabilize given an initial change in some exogenous variable. In other words, if any historic changes are suspended after some point in time, this path would describe the conditions of stationary equilibrium similarly to those given by the static multiplier in 8.15. The second term, which corresponds to dynamic discrepancy, refers to the persistent rather than temporary displacement from equilibrium that occurs when the historic changes continue at a constant rate. If the historic changes cease, this second term would vanish and the equation would yield only the condition of stationary equilibrium. The second term would also vanish if the original model is static in nature since in that case, $\pi_1 = 0$.

A better understanding of these terms follows from a glance at Figure 8-3, which, gives an example of the projected equilibrium path computed by the components of equation 8.20: the receding equilibrium, and the dynamic discrepancy. After suspension of further changes in the exogenous variables in period t_k, the endogenous variables would gradually return to the stationary state level denoted by Y_k.[11]

Several different multipliers based on the receding and the projected equilibrium conditions can be derived as useful in analyzing a historical system.[12] The first of these can be represented in matrix form following partial differentiation of equation 8.20 with respect to E_1.

$$\frac{\partial Y_t}{\partial E_1} = (I - \pi_1)^{-1}\pi_2 t - (I - \pi_1)^{-2}\pi_1\pi_2 \tag{8.21}$$

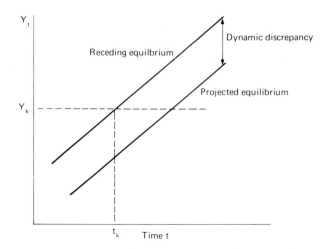

Figure 8-3. Receding and Projected Equilibrium Paths and Dynamic Discrepancy. Source: Shlomo Reutlinger, "Analysis of a Dynamic Model, with Particular Emphasis on Long Run Projections," *Journal of Farm Economics* 48 (1966): 99.

This multiplier explains the impact on the endogenous variables of varying the rates at which certain exogenous variables change over a period of time. A second matrix of multipliers results from partial differentiation of equation 8.20 with respect to time.

$$\frac{\partial Y_t}{\partial t} = (I - \pi_1)^{-1} \pi_2 E_1 \tag{8.22}$$

It suggests the impact that time itself will have on the endogenous variables. An alternative use of the multiplier is that of providing estimates of relative changes in the endogenous variables over time. Consider the relative change in any endogenous variable along the projected equilibrium path to be given by $(y_t^* - y_0^*)/y_0^*$ where t and 0 denote the final and initial periods respectively, and where * refers to values along that path. Given the definition that

$$y_t^* = y_0^* + (I - \pi_1)^{-1} \pi_2 E_1 t \tag{8.23}$$

where $(I - \pi_1)^{-1} \pi_2$ is in vector form, the corresponding relative change in any endogenous variable follows from

$$\frac{y_t^* - y_0^*}{y_0^*} = \frac{(I - \pi_1)^{-1} \pi_2 E_1 t}{y_0^*} \tag{8.24}$$

This measure is useful only if the system converges fairly rapidly to the long run equilibrium path given the period under consideration. Otherwise, it is necessary to use the following measure where y_0 denotes the short run predicted changes of the endogenous variable.[13]

$$\frac{y_t^* - y_0}{y_0} = \left[\frac{y_0^* + (I - \pi)^{-1} \pi_2 E_1 t}{y_0} \right] - 1 \tag{8.25}$$

An example of the use and interpretation of dynamic descrepancy appears in Reutlinger's analysis of a set of stationary equilibrium projections obtained from a simplified beef model.[14] The projected equilibrium values computed are based on constant rates of change in two exogenous variables in the system; population is assumed to increase by 3 million annually and per capita income is assumed to increase at $60 per year. The values found for each year of a ten-year period are reported in Table 8-2 for three of the endogenous variables: beef-cow inventory, beef slaughter, and steer prices. Those results suggest how rapidly the system converges to dynamic equilibrium; the stationary or receding equilibrium values found from the long run static multipliers could be estimated adequately after just five years by calculating the stationary values at time $t + 5$ and adjusting them for the dynamic discrepancy. The latter value can be obtained simply by premultiplying the vector of slope coefficients E_1 based on regression analysis by the matrix $(I - \pi_1)^{-2} \pi_1 \pi_2$. Since the values of the dynamic discrepancies are relatively small for the inventory and slaughter variables, one could also conclude that the estimates of the endogenous variables obtained by neglecting rates of change in the two exogenous variables would be only slightly overestimated. The underestimation of prices resulting from this oversight would be more serious.

Lauric Oils Multipliers

Matrices of static and dynamic multipliers have been computed for the linearized version of the lauric oils model as presented in Chapter 6.[15] Table 8-3 contains the short run static multipliers for only a small number of exogenous variables. Concerning the response of the endogenous variables, the most useful information comes from examining changes in exogenous variables regarded as controllable such as the G.S.A. lauric oil stockpile, or the country activity indexes of production and output. Philippine coconut oil exports and stocks are also considered controllable for this particular analysis because they are determined prior to the simultaneous estimation of world stock and price levels. Interpreting the latter in terms of Table 8-3, the impact of increasing exports of 1000,000 metric tons from the Philippines would be to reduce world lauric oil prices about 1.2 U.S. cents per kilogram.

Table 8-2. Computation of the Projected Equilibrium, the Receding Equilibrium, and the Dynamic Discrepancy for the Beef Model[a]

Time	Beef-Cow inventory			Beef slaughter			Steer slaughter		
	Receding equilibrium values	Projected equilibrium values	Dynamic discrepancy	Receding equilibrium values	Projected equilibrium values	Dynamic discrepancy	Receding equilibrium values	Projected equilibrium values	Dynamic discrepancy
0		30.0						25.00	
1	31.912	31.205	0.707	26.743	25.387	1.356	18.02	21.66	-3.64
2	33.160	31.801	1.359	27.687	26.247	1.440	18.59	22.45	-3.86
3	34.408	32.497	1.911	28.632	26.713	1.919	19.16	24.32	-5.16
4	35.657	33.422	2.235	29.576	27.252	2.324	19.73	25.98	-6.23
5	36.905	34.536	2.369	30.520	27.967	2.553	20.31	27.17	-6.86
6	38.153	35.754	2.399	31.464	28.818	2.646	20.88	27.99	-7.11
7	39.401	37.013	2.388	32.409	29.743	2.666	21.45	28.61	-7.16
8	40.649	38.279	2.370	33.353	30.695	2.658	22.02	29.16	-7.14
9	41.897	39.540	2.357	34.297	31.653	2.644	22.59	29.73	-7.14
10	43.145	40.796	2.349	35.241	32.607	2.634	23.16	30.27	-7.11
Dynamic discrepancy			2.357			2.622			-7.08

[a] No change in price of corn ($1)
Income = $2040 + 60T
Population = 187 + 3T

Source: Shlomo Reutlinger, "Analysis of a Dynamic Model, with Particular Emphasis on Long Run Projections," *Journal of Farm Economics* 48(1966), p. 101.

Table 8-3. Short Run Multipliers for Selected Exogenous Variables: Lauric Oils Model

Endogenous Variables	Exogenous Variables				
	Philippine Stocks s_t^{ph}	World Exports x_t^w	Output U.S. y_t^{us}	Output U.K. y_t^{uk}	Output E.E.C. y_t^{ec}
p_t^w	−0.040	−0.0120	0.0	0.0	0.0
s_t^{us}	0.0753	0.0237	0.0	0.0	0.0
s_t^{uk}	−0.0108	−0.0034	0.0	0.0	0.0
s_t^{ec}	0.010	0.0032	0.0	0.0	0.0
s_t^w	1.0812	0.0255	0.0	0.0	0.0
c_t^{us}	0.0628	0.0197	0.1000	0.0	0.0
c_t^{uk}	0.0981	0.0308	0.0	0.3071	0.0
c_t^{ec}	0.1919	0.0603	0.0	0.0	0.0279
m_t^{jp}	0.0449	0.0141	0.0	0.0	0.0

The impacts that changes in exports and other exogenous variables would have on the lauric oils market when time is a variable can be analyzed in the form of delay and cumulative multipliers. Continuing the above example, Table 8-4 describes the impact of an impulse and sustained change of lauric oil exports over a five-year period. The delay multiplier suggests that an increase in lauric oils exports of 100,000 tons will similarly cause a decline in price of about 1.2 cents per kilogram in the initial period, but this decline will extend only over the next two periods until it becomes much less significant and finally positive. The cumulative multiplier indicates that the price decrease will reach 1.6 cents per kilogram after two periods and then will remain at roughly the same level over the succeeding periods. The price response relative to exports suggested by the linearized version of the lauric oils model is not as substantial as might be expected. A slightly better response is obtained in the simulation analysis of the nonlinear version of the model, as shown in Chapter 9, but the behavior of the model must still be improved in this respect.

Conclusions

Multiplier analysis has been presented as a means to examining policy alternatives in commodity markets where forecast intentions are limited to partial equilibrium analysis. One can thus answer the question concerning

Table 8-4. Delay Multipliers: Philippine Exports: x_t^{ph}

Endogenous Variable	Time Period				
	0	1	2	3	4
p_t^w	−0.011900	−0.003700	−0.000300	0.000400	0.000500
s_t^w	0.025510	−0.037808	−0.023978	−0.006234	0.000159
c_t^{us}	0.019727	0.013531	0.004602	0.000312	−0.000631
c_t^{uk}	0.030832	0.027595	0.015405	0.006819	0.002837
c_t^{ec}	0.060323	0.018533	−0.001594	−0.004374	−0.002292
m_t^{jp}	0.014112	0.012618	0.007033	0.003104	0.001286

Cumulative Multipliers: Philippine Exports: x_t^{ph}

Endogenous Variable	Time Period				
	0	1	2	3	4
p_t^w	−0.011900	−0.015600	−0.015900	−0.015400	−0.014900
s_t^w	0.025510	−0.012297	−0.036275	−0.042509	−0.042550
c_t^{us}	0.019727	0.033258	0.037860	0.038172	0.037541
c_t^{uk}	0.030832	0.058427	0.073832	0.080651	0.083488
c_t^{ec}	0.060323	0.078856	0.077261	0.072887	0.070595
m_t^{jp}	0.014112	0.026730	0.033763	0.036867	0.038152

the impact of a change in an exogenous variable on the endogenous variables while all other variables are held constant. This type of analysis can be performed to evaluate short run and long run effects as well as those involving cross-temporal feedback.

There are other useful aspects of multiplier analysis; for example, multipliers can provide information regarding the functioning or realism of a commodity model. If the multiplier impact suggested by a model does not agree with expert opinion or market experience, the behaviorial relationships underlying a particular multiplier can be adjusted until the model response appears more realistic. One can also check the adequacy of the values of certain parameters by using specialized multipliers. An example is the multiplier associated with the dynamic discrepancy, which can suggest the impact of adjusting actual rates of change in the exogenous variables. Another possibility, as suggested by Zusman, is a multiplier that measures the effects of changes in parameters, such as those associated with structural market adjustments.[16]

Finally, one should be aware of the limitations that exist in multiplier analysis, especially where the exogenous variables undergo constant or varying rates of change or the underlying model is nonlinear. Also because multipliers represent more of a theoretical than a practical method, we devote our remaining attention to simulation analysis.

9 Simulation Analysis

Simulation analysis as a means of applying commodity models offers several advantages over multiplier analysis. It enables the impact of dynamic multipliers to be directly observed in terms of the simulated time paths of the related endogenous variables. It also permits more complex effects to be analyzed as, for example, varying rates of change in an exogenous variable or varying levels of several exogenous variables at once. In this chapter we commence with a brief summary of the background, theory, and problems relevant to the simulation approach. Methods of simulation analysis are then presented for use with either the reduced form or the structural form of a model. Recommendations for dealing with problems of nonconvergence are given, and the validation of models utilizing simulation results is also discussed. (See Appendix B for further information regarding the spectral approach to validation.) Both parametric and non-parametric validation criteria are presented as useful for either the sample or the post-sample period of estimation. Examples of simulation analysis are drawn from studies of the tungsten, coffee, rubber, tin, and lauric oils markets.

Nature of Simulation Analysis

Background

There is a wide and varied background to commodity simulation analysis. Many of the known simulation techniques have been developed for use with macroeconometric models as is witnessed in the works of Klein and Evans, Fromm and Klein, Fromm and Taubman, and Naylor.[1] Some of the techniques have also been developed for use with microeconometric and commodity models; of particular interest are those discussed in Naylor's *The Design of Computer Simulation Experiments*, and his *Computer Simulation Experiments with Models of Economic Systems*.[2] Finally, applications of simulation analysis have been facilitated through the development of specialized computer programs. As mentioned in Chapter 6, the DYNAMO program has provided the basis for Meadows's Dynamic Commodity Cycle Model.[3] Also of interest are Holt's PROGRAM SIMULATE II, Eisner's TROLL/1 system,[4] and Norman's PROGRAM SIM.[5]

With respect to past commodity simulation studies, one of the first was Cohen's simulation of the shoe, leather, and hide sequence which appeared in 1959[6]. Some more recent simulation studies dealing specifically with process models are the Naylor, Wallace, and Sassor model of the textile industry; the Vernon, Rives, and Naylor model of the tobacco industry; the Adams and Griffin model of the petroleum refining industry; and the Adams and Blackwell model of the lumber industry.[7] Applications to equilibrium models have not been as extensive, although they are now rapidly increasing. Early studies in this area include Desai's simulation of the tin market and Behrman's simulation of the rubber market.[8] More recent applications involve Epp's coffee model, Burrow's tungsten model, Crom's model of the U.S. beef and pork sector, and Labys' lauric oils model.[9] Simulation analysis can also be employed as a method of validating commodity models. See, for example, Howrey and Witherell's wool model analysis and the Naylor, Wertz, and Wonnacott textile model study.[10]

Simulation Theory

The "policy simulation" approach has been presented in Chapter 6 along with the Theil "welfare criterion" approach and the Tinbergen "target value" approach as a means of performing policy analysis with a commodity model. Our major concern is with the policy simulation approach because it does provide policy makers with the type of information necessary for decision making, and does not require knowledge about the policy maker's welfare preferences or his particular targets.[11] This approach is able to analyze the impact of policy decisions on a commodity economy where the underlying model is of econometric form and contains structural equations which can be linear or nonlinear in the endogenous variables. While nonlinearities and the presence of dynamic lags influence the actual nature of a simulation solution, most simulations represent a solution sequence generated by a dynamic model under a set of conditions in which the exogenous variables are taken as given and the endogenous variables are generated sequentially.[12]

Consider the structural form of the dynamic commodity model given previously

$$\Gamma Y_t + \beta_1 Y_{t-1} + B_2 X_t = U_t \qquad (9.1)$$

where Y_t = a $G \times n$ matrix of current endogenous variables, Y_{t-1} = a $G \times n$ matrix of lagged endogenous variables; X_t = a $M \times n$ matrix of exogenous and policy controllable variables; U_t = a $G \times n$ matrix of current disturbance terms; Γ and $B_1 = G \times G$ matrices of coefficients on the current and lagged endogenous variables respectively; and B_2 = a $G \times M$ matrix of coefficients on the exogenous and policy variables. This model can be transformed to its reduced form

$$Y_t = \pi_1 Y_{t-1} + \pi_2 X_t + V_t \qquad (9.2)$$

where $\pi_1 = $ a $G \times G$ matrix of reduced form coefficients on the lagged endogenous variables, and $\pi_2 = $ a $G \times M$ matrix of reduced form coefficients or multipliers on the exogenous and policy variables X_t.

Simulation methods enable us to solve for Y_t in terms of Y_{t-1}, X_t and U_t or V_t. Three different methods of generating simulated values of Y_t are associated with model solution: partial, total, and final.[13] According to the partial method, data for the exogenous and policy variables X_t, the lagged endogenous variables Y_{t-1}, and the endogenous variables appearing on the right hand of the equations are fed into the computer, and one obtains a set of partial predictions for each of the endogenous variables, Y_t. The total method requires greater dependence on the model's ability to generate the Y_t, and only data for the exogenous variables X_t and the lagged endogenous variables Y_{t-1} are required. With the final method, values of the lagged endogenous variables Y_{t-1} as well as the current values of Y_t are generated by the model, and only values for the exogenous variables X_t are needed. This latter method of solution is that most often associated with policy simulation analysis. It implies evolutionary behavior in which a model generates its own values for the endogenous variables Y_t over a large number of future periods.

Policy simulation analysis is normally performed by manipulating the values of the exogenous or policy controllable variables X_t, and by observing the resulting changes in Y_t. The disturbances U_t or V_t may be suppressed or generated following a random or autoregressive process to obtain greater realism.[14] The analysis can be carried out over the period corresponding to that of the sample used to estimate the model parameters or over some short run or long run post-sample period. In the former case, one's goal can be explaining how a commodity market would have behaved if other policies had been followed; in the latter case, the goal becomes one of determining the future impact of such policies. Simulation analysis can also produce forecasts of key market variables based on conditional predictions of the exogenous variables.

Related Problems

A number of methodological problems are encountered in conducting policy simulation analysis based on an econometric model.[15] The more important of these relate to nonlinearities, lagged variables, nonconvergent solutions, stochastic variations, structural changes, and validation.

Nonlinearities. The presence of nonlinearities in variables or coefficients often prevents one from simulating directly from the reduced form of a model. Nonlinearities can arise, for example, from a logarithmic form of supply equation, relative prices in the consumption equations, or a consumption-stock ratio in the price equation. A reduced form solution still may be obtained if the model can be linearized; otherwise, a structural form solution is advisable.

Lagged Variables. The appearance of lagged endogenous variables in a model also may prevent simulation from the reduced form. As pointed out by Klein and Evans, this may not completely disrupt a solution, but it will make it less efficient.[16] This difficulty also can be better handled through a structural form solution.

Nonconvergent Solutions. Yet another difficulty found in policy simulation is obtaining meaningful and convergent solutions. Even when the structural form of the model has been soundly estimated, for example, transformation of these estimates into a reduced form suitable for simulation may produce changes in the magnitude or sign of a coefficient leading to a meaningless solution. On the other hand, simulation from a structural form may not lead to convergence in the endogenous variables. While the first problem requires respecifying one or more equations, the second might also necessitate that the equations be reordered, perhaps reflecting lines of causality in time or space.

Stochastic Variations. Nonstochastic or exact simulation requires that the path of the endogenous variables Y_t be sequentially generated by supressing the stochastic variation in U_t. Stochastic or inexact simulation demands that U_t no longer be suppressed; in fact, it may be generated randomly or according to some autoregressive function of time. One would also like to add stochastic variation to individual exogenous variables within the model or even to the model parameters, although it becomes more difficult to reach a solution in the latter case.[17] Experience has shown that stochastic shocks sometimes lead to values of the endogenous variables which are outside the realm of possibility; and it would be necessary to introduce equilibrating constraints similar to those found in the real world when unforseen events cause market relationships to be out of line.

Structural Changes. A similar problem is that the structure of a market may change or evolve over time, but the simulation must be conducted with parameters estimated over the sample period. When this occurs, it has been found useful to introduce mechanical adjustments for less critical parameters such as constants or intercepts. Not much research has taken place as to ways of introducing these adjustments. The parameters could be made time-variant or they could be multiplied by "dummy" variables, which could be 0 or 1 in certain periods or which could possibly even take on numerical values.

Validation. Although simulation analysis has received increased attention as a means of verifying commodity models, this approach does not always provide additional information over that available from an analytical solution, nor is it equally valid for all test situations.[18] The decision as to when it should be applied is sometimes complex, and together with a discussion of the above problems is considered in further detail below.

Reduced Form Solution

Simulation of a commodity model can follow directly from its estimated reduced form as previously given by

$$Y_t = \pi_1 Y_{t-1} + \pi_2 X_t + V_t \qquad (9.2)$$

Obtaining a sequential set of values for the endogenous variables requires solving the model based on the actual or predicted values of all lagged endogenous variables and the exogenous variables. The nature of the computational process involved is depicted in the flow diagram of Figure 9-1, which shows that the sequential values of Y_t are obtained through iterating over the G endogenous variables and over n time periods. That diagram also suggests that the disturbance terms V_t can be suppressed or generated, making the solution nonstochastic or stochastic.[19] The stochastic solution consists of generating the disturbances according to Type I or Type II shocks, as described in Chapter 7.[20] Type III shocks represent a combination of Type I and II shocks.

One would hope that with its convenience and ease of interpretation, the reduced form solution could be applied to almost any appropriate commodity model. Unfortunately, this method becomes less applicable as the commodity model becomes more complex. Referring to the problems mentioned earlier, solution of the reduced form becomes difficult when nonlinearities exist in variables or coefficients, or when equations are dynamic, containing lagged endogenous variables.

Difficulties encountered when nonlinearities are present can be shown using as an example a simplified version of model 9.1

$$c_t = b_1 p_t + b_2 y_t + u_t^c \qquad (9.3)$$

$$q_t = b_3 p_t + b_4 z_t + u_t^q$$

$$c_t = q_t$$

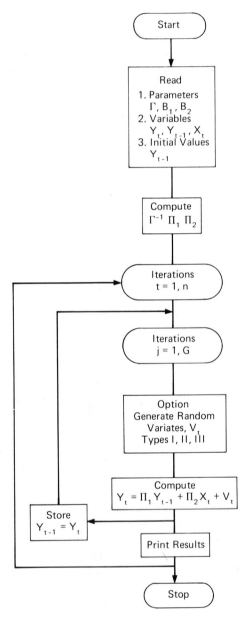

Figure 9-1. Reduced Form Simulation.

where c_t and q_t are the quantities consumed and produced, p_t is price, and y_t and z_t are exogenous variables. A convenient expression for the reduced form of this model can be obtained by rearranging it as

$$-c_t + b_1 p_t + b_2 y_t + u_t^c = 0$$

$$-c_t + b_3 p_t + b_4 z_t + u_t^q = 0$$

or in matrix equivalent

$$\begin{bmatrix} -1 & b_1 \\ -1 & b_3 \end{bmatrix} \begin{bmatrix} c_t \\ p_t \end{bmatrix} + \begin{bmatrix} b_2 & 0 \\ 0 & b_4 \end{bmatrix} \begin{bmatrix} y_t \\ z_t \end{bmatrix} + \begin{bmatrix} u_t^c \\ u_t^q \end{bmatrix} = 0$$

The reduced form follows from inverting the left-hand matrix and using it to multiply both sides of the equation

$$\begin{bmatrix} c_t \\ p_t \end{bmatrix} = \begin{bmatrix} \dfrac{-b_3}{(b_1 - b_3)} & \dfrac{b_1}{(b_1 - b_3)} \\ \dfrac{-b_1}{(b_1 - b_3)} & \dfrac{1}{(b_1 - b_3)} \end{bmatrix} \begin{bmatrix} b_2 & 0 \\ 0 & b_4 \end{bmatrix} \begin{bmatrix} y_t \\ z_t \end{bmatrix} + \begin{bmatrix} v_t^q \\ v_t^q \end{bmatrix}$$

or

$$\begin{bmatrix} c_t \\ p_t \end{bmatrix} = \begin{bmatrix} \dfrac{-b_3 b_2}{(b_1 - b_3)} & \dfrac{b_1 b_4}{(b_1 - b_3)} \\ \dfrac{-b_2 b_1}{(b_1 - b_3)} & \dfrac{b_4}{(b_1 - b_3)} \end{bmatrix} \begin{bmatrix} y_t \\ z_t \end{bmatrix} + \begin{bmatrix} v_t^c \\ v_t^q \end{bmatrix} \tag{9.4}$$

Normally, simulation based on the reduced form would follow by inserting appropriate time series for y_t and z_t, but let us consider the impact of introducing a nonlinearity in the form of a price variable r_t, which reflects the competitive influence of another commodity. Model 9.3 would now appear as

$$c_t = b_1 p_t / r_t + b_2 y_t + u_t^c$$

$$q_t = b_3 p_t / r_t + b_4 z_t + u_t^q \tag{9.5}$$

$$c_t = q_t$$

with its reduced form given by

$$
\begin{bmatrix} c_t \\ p_t \end{bmatrix} = \begin{bmatrix} \dfrac{-b_3 b_2}{(b_1 - b_3)} & \dfrac{b_1 b_4}{(b_1 - b_3)} \\[2ex] \dfrac{-b_1 r_t}{(b_1 - b_3)} & \dfrac{b_4 r_1}{(b_1 - b_3)} \end{bmatrix} \begin{bmatrix} y_t \\ z_t \end{bmatrix} + \begin{bmatrix} v_t^c \\ v_t^q \end{bmatrix}
\tag{9.6}
$$

In this case, note that the lower row of multipliers in the matrix of coefficients now depends on the value of r_t, which varies from period to period. Obviously, a constant inverse or reduced form matrix can no longer be computed and a solution cannot be obtained. Unless the original variable is transformed into a new variable, such a situation would always exist.[21]

Concerning the problem of introducing lagged variables or dynamic equations into a model, the difficulties of solving the reduced form can be shown by now adjusting model 9.3 to reflect dynamic behavior.

$$
c_t = b_1 p_t + b_2 y_t + b_5 c_{t-1}
$$

$$
q_t = b_3 p_t + b_4 z_t
\tag{9.7}
$$

$$
c_t = q_t
$$

The stochastic terms have been omitted to permit a simple derivation of the reduced form multipliers using Kramer's rule. Begin by employing the identity

$$
b_1 p_t + b_2 y_t + b_5 c_{t-1} = b_3 p_t + b_4 z_t
$$

and by gathering terms

$$
p_t(b_1 - b_3) = b_4 z_t - b_2 y_t - b_5 c_{t-1}
$$

The multiplier with respect to z_t, for example, can be found by assuming y_t and c_{t-1} to be fixed or constant.

$$
\Delta p_t(b_1 - b_3) = b_4 \Delta z_t
$$

or

$$
\left[\frac{\Delta p}{\Delta z} \right]_t = \frac{b_4}{(b_1 - b_3)}
\tag{9.8}
$$

The multiplier for the demand variable can be similarly expressed.

$$\left[\frac{\Delta c}{\Delta z}\right]_t = \frac{\Delta c_t}{\Delta p_t} \cdot \frac{\Delta p_t}{\Delta z_t} = b_1 \frac{\Delta p_t}{\Delta z_t} \qquad (9.9)$$

Note that these multipliers, as computed for the first period, correspond to the normal impact multipliers for the same period. If the lagged variable c_{t-1} would always remain fixed, simulation of the reduced form could take place using the impact multipliers over successive periods. The lagged variable, however, does vary, and its effect is to increase the complexity of expression for the multiplier as the solution moves forward in time. The change occurring in the multipliers can be shown by moving the transformed version of 9.7 forward by one period

$$p_{t+1}(b_1 - b_3) = b_4 z_{t+1} - b_2 y_{t+1} - b_5 c_t$$

and solving for the desired multiplier

$$\left[\frac{\Delta p}{\Delta z}\right]_{t+1} = \frac{b_4 - \dfrac{b_5 b_1 b_4}{(b_1 - b_3)}}{(b_1 - b_3)} \qquad (9.10)$$

This operation can be repeated to obtain the multiplier for the next period.

$$\left[\frac{\Delta p}{\Delta z}\right]_{t+2} = \frac{b_4 - b_5 b_1 \left[\dfrac{b_4 - \dfrac{b_5 b_1 b_4}{(b_1 - b_3)}}{(b_1 - b_3)}\right]}{(b_1 - b_3)} \qquad (9.11)$$

That the terms of the numerator become extremely complicated as the multiplier is computed in further periods is obvious. Klein and Evans have shown that this makes simulation using the reduced form less efficient, although this would not necessarily be the case where simulation is carried out for a small number of periods.[22]

Structural Form Solution

Simulation based on the solution of the structural form of the model is presently the best approach to overcoming the difficulties caused by non-linearities or lagged variables. Only now the method of solution requires the use of some iterative procedure. Several such procedures are first examined below, particularly recommended is that of Gauss-Seidel.

Total Step and One Step Methods

Iterative methods which generally can apply to simulating sets of linear equations can be classified as total step or one step.[23] Of the former, the oldest known is Jacobi's method of simultaneous displacement. This method has been superseded by more elaborate gradient methods such as Richardson's, which avoids the previous difficulty of a required predetermined correspondence between equations and unknowns. Gradient methods more recently explored are those of steepest ascent and of optimal strategy. A major criticism of the total step method relates to difficulties in computer application; algorithms for computation are complex and substantial storage space is required.

Economists have concentrated instead on the use of one step methods, of which the Newton and the Gauss-Seidel are the most popular.[24] The Newton method was the first to be applied because it has the distinct advantage of allowing an immediate and direct solution of related systems of equations; the matrix of coefficients derived from the equations can be multiplied directly by the price and quantity variables, the latter being separated into appropriate blocks. Although this permits the resulting model solutions to converge in a very short time, solutions cannot be obtained for models containing nonlinearities more complex than those of products and quotients. Consequently, economists have turned to the Gauss-Seidel method, which can handle nonlinearities and which can provide exact solutions that converge in a very short time.

The Gauss-Seidel Method

Klein and Evans are mainly responsible for the current popularity of the Gauss-Seidel method; and Adams, Behrman, and Naylor have demonstrated its applicability to policy simulation analysis with commodity models.[25] A full understanding of this method requires examining the complete structural form of an econometric model as presented in system 9.1.

$$\Gamma Y_t + B_1 Y_{t-1} + B_2 X_t = U_t \tag{9.12}$$

One can normally simplify the simulation of this model by causally ordering the equations into separate blocks; Figure 9-2 gives an example of a model ordered into three separate blocks. The equations of the *recursive* I block are arranged so that the coefficients of the endogenous variables form a lower triangular matrix. Above the diagonal, the coefficients are zero; all the entries on the diagonal are nonzero while entries below the diagonal may be zero or nonzero. The latter group of nonzero entries can represent

		1	2	3	4	5	6	7	8	9	10	11	12	13	14	15
							Endogenous Variables									
Equations	(1)	1	0	0	0	0										
	(2)	x	1	0	0	0										
	(3)	0	x	1	0	0										
	(4)	0	0	0	1	0										
	(5)	0	0	x	0	1										
	(6)						1	x	0	0	x					
	(7)						0	1	0	x	0					
	(8)						0	x	1	0	0					
	(9)						0	0	0	1	0					
	(10)						0	0	x	x	1					
	(11)											1	0	0	0	0
	(12)											0	1	0	0	0
	(13)											0	x	1	0	0
	(14)											x	0	0	1	0
	(15)											0	0	0	x	1

Figure 9-2. Tableau Describing Causal Ordering in a Commodity Model.

coefficients of lagged variables, exogenous variables, or lower order recursive variables. The equations in the *simultaneous* block contain variables which are to some extent interdependent, and nonzero entries appear above and below the diagonal. The equations in the *recursive* II block also form a lower triangular matrix.

Simulation of a model ordered in this manner begins by first solving the recursive I block of equations. Since the equations have already been ordered such that the solution of a previous equation leads to the solution of a succeeding equation, simulation of this block presents no difficulty. It is only when we arrive at the simultaneous block of equations that the Gauss-Seidel method must be introduced. As indicated above, the coefficients or entries in the matrix corresponding to this block can be zero or nonzero, and the nonzero ones can also contain nonlinearities in the form of endogenous variables.

Klein and Evans show how the solution for a set of equations containing nonlinearities of this form can proceed.[26] Begin with the jth equation of the simultaneous block given in model 9.12 and rewrite it as follows.

$$y_{jt} = f(y_{1t}, y_{2t}, \ldots, y_{gt}; y_{1,t-1}, y_{2,t-1}, \ldots, y_{g,t-1}; x_{1t}, x_{2t}, \ldots, x_{mt}) \quad (9.13)$$

Guess a set of starting estimates (0) to be used for the dependent variables on the right side of the equation; values of the exogenous variables are given.

Solve each equation to obtain a new set of estimates (1) for the dependent variables.

$$y_{jt}^{(1)} = f(y_{1t}^{(0)}, y_{2t}^{(0)}, \ldots, y_{gt}^{(0)}; y_{1,t-1}, y_{2,t-1}, \ldots, y_{g,t-1}; x_{1t}, x_{2t}, \ldots, x_{mt})$$

$$(9.14)$$

One then uses the estimates (1) on the right side of each equation to obtain estimates (2).

$$y_{jt}^{(2)} = f(y_{1t}^{(1)}, y_{2t}^{(1)}, \ldots, y_{gt}^{(1)}; y_{1,t-1}, y_{2,t-1}, \ldots, y_{g,t-1}; x_{1t}, x_{2t}, \ldots, x_{mt})$$

$$(9.15)$$

This procedure can be continued for up to (r) iterations such that

$$y_{jt}^{(r)} = f(y_{1t}^{(r-1)}, y_{2t}^{(r-1)}, \ldots, y_{gt}^{(r-1)}; y_{1,t-1}, y_{2,t-1}, \ldots, y_{g,t-1}; x_{1t}, x_{2t}, \ldots, x_{mt})$$

$$(9.16)$$

where

$$\left| \frac{y_{jt}^{(r)} - y_{jt}^{(r-1)}}{y_{jt}^{(r-1)}} \right| \leq C$$

$$(9.17)$$

The value of r is selected as a critical percentage so that at convergence the finally estimated value doesn't differ from the previously estimated value by more than, for example, $C = 0.1$ or 0.001. When the critical value isn't met, the (r) estimates are placed on the right hand side of each equation and the procedure is continued. Note that the critical value applies to each variable and to each equation until the full set of equations is solved for a particular period. Figure 9-3 features a flow diagram that describes this method in greater detail. The diagram also shows that the simulation advances period by period with the convergent values of the variables y_{jt} becoming the lagged endogenous variables $y_{j,t-1}$ and that the equations and variables can be shocked according to methods specified in the previous section.

Some substitution can take place to help increase the speed of convergence. For example, one could substitute the latest value of $y_{jt}^{(v)}$ into a later equation $y_{it}^{(v)}$ involving y_{jt} at the same iterative step, although this assumes that y_{jt} has been correctly specified.

$$y_{it}^{(v)} = f(y_{1t}^{(v-1)}, y_{jt}^{(v)}, \ldots, y_{gt}^{(v-1)}; y_{1,t-1}, y_{2,t-1}, \ldots, y_{g,t-1}; x_{1t}, x_{2t}, \ldots, x_{mt})$$

$$(9.18)$$

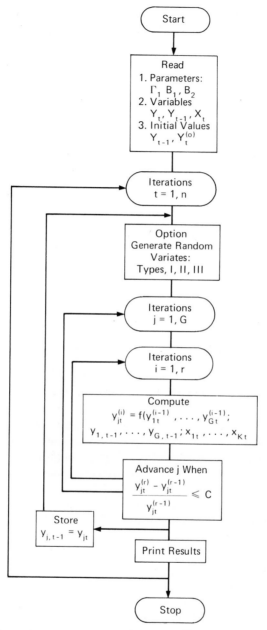

Figure 9-3. Gauss-Seidel Structural Form Simulation.

Once all of the endogenous variables in the simultaneous block have converged, the equations in the recursive II block can be solved in a manner similar to the recursive I block. Only now, all of the values obtained in the prior two blocks are substituted as is necessary in this final block. Should the simultaneous block not converge, however, various remedies have to be considered.

Problems of Convergence

Possibly several factors are responsible for the failure of the endogenous variables to converge in the iterative simulation of the simultaneous block of equations. A model will not converge if one or more equations are incorrectly specified, causing errors in the explained variable to be unreasonably high. Despite appropriate specification, a model still may not converge where the order of equations does not correspond to the lines of economic causation underlying the complete model. If even the reordering of equations does not lead to convergence, then it may be necessary to normalize one or more equations so that certain equations are inverted, resulting in a switching of endogenous variables from the left-hand to the right-hand side of the equation, and vice-versa. Let us consider each of these possibilities in turn.

Misspecification of a model is most easily detected by comparing model specification to the market it represents and by making corrections were possible. Factors reflecting specification error might be poor goodness of fit, autocorrelation in the disturbance terms, or magnitudes and signs of coefficients differing from what could be expected on the basis of *a priori* reasoning. Fisher has suggested one particular method which could be used to solve the specification problem.[27] He presents the view that certain simultaneous models are limiting approximations to nonsimultaneous models in which particular time lags approach zero. Also described are a battery of tests that help to investigate the specification of a model as a whole or any of its submodels. When a model has been correctly specified according to its ability to pass the given tests, and when it truly represents the underlying dynamic system, Fisher would then conclude that the model must converge. Problems of nonconvergence, therefore, can be handled by successively working towards a truer representation of the economic system and applying appropriate tests.

As for the order that equations might follow in a simultaneous model, one can check this by tracing possible lines of economic causation. These lines are obvious in a recursive model where the values of one or more dependent variables must be obtained before proceeding to solve the values of the dependent variable in a succeeding equation. Ordering in a simultaneous model might be determined by examining links through time or market activity. The length of lags in one or more equations might be such that it would be logical in time for such equations to precede others within the iteration period. Similarly, one might also observe the lines of activity that follow from a flow diagram describing the behavior of market participants. Certain decisions may be taken antecedent to other decisions, and this pattern could also be followed.

A final approach to the problem of nonconvergence involves normalizing selected endogenous variables in one or more equations. A practical guide to selecting variables for normalization is to attempt to arrange the equations in the model so that each endogenous variable appears only once on the left-hand side of any equation. A conflict would appear if supply and demand variables, both described by the same data, exist on the left-hand side of separate equations. In such a situation, either equation is a candidate for normalization. The actual method of achieving normalization can be better explained using as an example a simplified version of model 9.12.

$$c_t = f_c(p_t, x_{1t}, \ldots, x_{mt}) \tag{9.19}$$

$$q_t = f_q(p_t, x_{1t}, \ldots, x_{mt}) \tag{9.20}$$

$$p_t = f_p(\Delta s_t, x_{1t}, \ldots, x_{mt}) \tag{9.21}$$

$$\Delta s_t = q_t - c_t \tag{9.22}$$

Demand c_t, supply q_t, stocks s_t, and prices p_t are endogenous variables in the system while the $x_{1t}, \ldots, x_{mt}$ are predetermined. Consider the case where demand is relatively inelastic or constant over a simulation period during which a number of iterations occur. The equations and variables relevant to the adjustment process arising between quantity and price are expressed in the form

$$q_t = f_q(p_t, x_{1t}, \ldots, x_{mt}) \tag{9.20}$$

$$p_t = f_p^*(q_t, x_{1t}, \ldots, x_{mt}) \tag{9.21*}$$

where $\Delta s_t = q_t$. If the relative slopes of the functions resemble those of Figure 9-4 the process of convergence can be described as one of discovering some level of p_t and q_t that satisfies both functions. For the first iteration guess a value for p_t, say $p_t^{(0)}$. Then function 9.20 is solved for $q_t^{(1)}$ and function 9.21* for $p_t^{(1)}$. The latter price now becomes the starting value for a second set of iteration values, $q_t^{(2)}$ and $p_t^{(2)}$. The path describing this process is shown in the upper diagram of Figure 9-4 where the first iteration leads to a solution for f_q giving $q_t^{(1)}$ and subsequently to a solution for f_p^* giving $p_t^{(1)}$. Note that

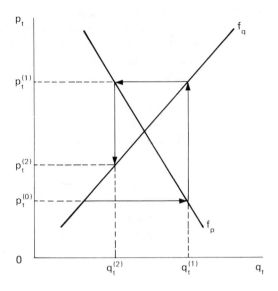

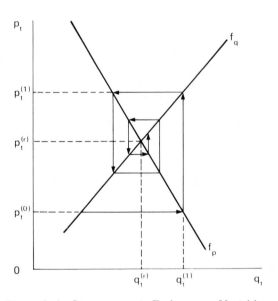

Figure 9–4. Convergence in Endogenous Variables.

$p_t^{(1)}$ and $p_t^{(2)}$ are closer to some potential equilibrium price than are $p_t^{(0)}$ or $p_t^{(1)}$ respectively. After possibly r iterations, price and supply would converge accordingly to final equilibrium values $p_t^{(r)}$ and $q_t^{(r)}$. The movements in prices and quantities by which this would be accomplished appear in the lower part of Figure 9-4.

If the relative slopes or computed elasticities of the price and supply functions are as shown in the upper part of Figure 9-5, it is unlikely that a convergent solution could be obtained for p_t and q_t. Again begin the first iteration with a guess $p_t^{(0)}$. Solution of f_q then yields $q_t^{(1)}$ and solution of f_p^* gives $p_t^{(1)}$. Since $p_t^{(1)}$ is further from the potential equilibrium price than is $p_t^{(0)}$, it is unlikely that a convergent solution can be obtained with the variables as expressed in relationships 9.20 and 9.21*. Klein shows that for every divergent normalization there is a convergent one, and suggests that convergence in a simple model such as the above could be assured by normalizing equations 9.20 and 9.21* as follows.[28]

$$p_t = f_q^{-1}(q_t, x_{1t}, \ldots, x_{mt}) \qquad (9.23)$$

$$q_t = f_p^{-1}(p_t, x_{1t}, \ldots, x_{mt}) \qquad (9.24)$$

This would lead to a reversal of the direction in which one travels along the iterative path. Beginning the first iteration with the value $p_t^{(0)}$ for p_t, the solution of f_p^{-1} gives $q_t^{(1)}$. Similarly, the solution of f_q^{-1} yields $p_t^{(1)}$. Given one more round of iteration, the lower part of Figure 9-5 clearly shows that $q_t^{(2)}$ and $p_t^{(2)}$ are now much closer to equilibrium and that a convergent solution is likely. With respect to the practical problem of obtaining coefficients for a normalized equation, one can either solve for the coefficients by inverting the equation of interest or one can reestimate it.

Validation

The validation of commodity models is discussed within the context of simulation analysis because of the efficiency of this method for generating the time-paths of the endogenous variables of interest. It is also possible to validate a model based on its analytical solution, as shown in Chapter 7, and this approach to validation also is considered. A major difficulty exists in validating commodity and other models in that no analytical basis exists for selecting which validation criteria might be the most appropriate to use in particular circumstances.[29] We attempt to overcome this difficulty as much as possible, first by recommending a group of parametric and nonparametric tests to be used, and second by distinguishing their application in the sample period of estimation from that in the post-sample period.

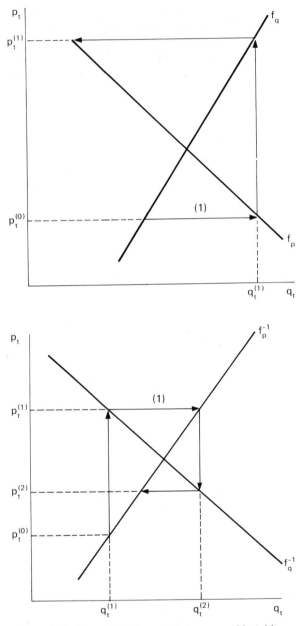

Figure 9-5. Normalization of Endogenous Variables.

Parametric Tests

Parametric evaluation of a commodity model depends on a number of tests related to classical statistical procedures.[30] The tests which have been traditionally applied to measure the forecast error between actual and estimated or simulated observations are single point criteria, such as the mean absolute percentage error and the mean squared error

$$\%E. = \frac{1}{n} \sum_{t=1}^{n} \frac{|y_t - \hat{y}_t|}{y_t} \times 100\% \qquad (9.25)$$

$$M.S.E. = \frac{1}{n} \sum_{t=1}^{n} (y_t - \hat{y}_t)^2 \qquad (9.26)$$

where y_t = actual observation values and $\hat{y}_t$ = forecast or estimated values. Similarly useful is the Theil inequality or U coefficient, which derives from a regression of actual on forcast values and which can also provide information as to sources of error.[31]

$$U = \frac{\sqrt{\frac{1}{n} \sum_{t=1}^{n} (\hat{y}_t - y_t)^2}}{\sqrt{\frac{1}{n} \sum_{t=1}^{n} \hat{y}_t^2 + \frac{1}{n} \sum_{t=1}^{n} y_t^2}} \qquad (9.27)$$

While these methods probably are the post practical for evaluating performance with a historical sample or a small post-sample data set, they fail to define the surrounding probabilistic conditions in a way which would be useful with a large post-sample data set. There are two ways to improve this situation. First, an informative forecast could accompany the point forecasts based on some mathematical statement regarding the probability distributions surrounding these forecasts. This amounts to an interval forecast in which the point forecast is now presented along with an appropriate confidence interval. Second, a decision forecast could be prepared which recommends that the forecast be accepted in relation to some alternative consequence.

For example, consider the case where the policy maker must decide on a certain policy which depends upon the future value y_t^* of the endogenous variable y_t.[32] The future value, of course, is not known and the policy maker could make an incorrect decision. The loss or consequence the policy maker must undergo in such a case is given by the loss function $L(D_i, y_t)$, which describes the loss of selecting decision D_i when y_t turns out to be the true value of y_t^*. One could then form the following rule, which would lead to decision D_i while minimizing the expected loss

$$E[L] = \sum_y L(D_i, y_t) P(y_t^* = y_t) \qquad (9.28)$$

where $P(y_t^* = y_t)$ is the probability that the future value y_t^* will be y_t. In this case the policy maker would select the value y_t^* for which his loss will be minimal. This can also assume the form of an error-cost function in which a policy maker decides to act by not following the best possible forecast. Rather, he selects one forecast from alternative forecasts such that the cost of making forecast errors is minimized.

Nonparametric Tests

In examining nonparametric, or what are termed distribution free tests, a variety of possibilities open up for obtaining different types of information about a model's performance. We discuss only those tests deemed useful from an operational point of view.

Turning Point Errors. A major characterization of a model's performance is its ability to explain the turning points of fluctuations in values of the endogenous variables.[33] There are a number of descriptive variables or statistics which can be used to describe turning point errors. Most often they pertain to the number of turning points missed, the number of turning points falsely predicted, the number of under and over predictions, rank correlations of predicted and actual changes, and various tests of randomness in prediction.

Spectral Analysis. A more precise method for determining how well a model explains cyclical, seasonal, or other forms of periodic behavior is spectral analysis, simply because it is concerned with behavior over all parts of a cycle and not just at turning points. In certain cases spectral analysis also enables us to extend our understanding of the stability properties of a model from the nonstochastic case to the stochastic case. The spectral approach as described in Chapter 5 shifts data analysis from the time domain to the frequency domain through the computation of power spectra, coherence, and phase relationships. At the most simple level, a model's validity can be judged by comparing its cyclical characteristics as determined from the spectra of estimated observations to the cyclical properties the market is known to possess. More elaborate validation criteria include the *spectrum matrix* approach of Howrey and Witherell, and the *spectrum bands* approach of Naylor, Wertz, and Wonnacott.[34] Because these approaches are reasonably complex, further description and comparison are deferred to Appendix B.

Comparative Errors. Validation also can take the form of comparing the forecast errors obtained from the model of interest to the forecast errors achieved from a naive or statistical model or from judgemental or other noneconometric forecasts. As shown by Labys and Granger, naive and statistical models can provide a rigorous standard for most commodity forecast comparisons, especially when using short run data.[35] As a starting point one could begin by comparing forecasts from a model to forecasts generated by naive methods such as "no change," where literally no change takes place in the endogenous variables from one period to the next, $\hat{y}_t = y_{t-1}$, or "same change," where the endogenous variables will continue to change in the same direction and by the same magnitude as the previous change $\hat{y}_t - y_{t-1} = y_{t-1} - y_{t-2}$. Expressed in levels, it becomes a weighted sum $\hat{y}_t = 2y_{t-1} - y_{t-2}$.

Cooper and Jorgenson have shown that a good comparative statistical model which utilizes all available information is an autoregressive process of no more than three lags, $\hat{y}_t = b_0 + b_1 y_{t-1} + b_2 y_{t-2} + b_3 y_{t-3}$.[36] They also show how one can standardize the period of fit and technique of estimation across alternative models prior to comparison. Finally, Labys and Granger, and Naylor, Seeks, and Wichern agree that as a comparative model the Box-Jenkins or the autoregressive integrated moving average model offers several advantages over the above.[37]

Error Decomposition. Haitovsky and Treyz propose that forecast error be decomposed according to components involving (1) the particular equation explaining the variable of interest, (2) the rest of the model, (3) incorrect values of the lagged endogenous variables, (4) incorrect forecasts of one or more of the exogenous variables, and (5) lack of serial correlation adjustments for observed errors.[38] This would enable us to improve a commodity model in a way that would facilitate policy analysis since it would identify model subsectors that transmit error across other sectors. Only simple statistical measures are needed to describe the errors such as mean bias and variance.

Other Tests. Several other tests are available for model validation which are worth considering. Day and Singh demonstrate the usefulness of the information tests proposed by Theil based on the magnitude and direction of estimated changes in the endogenous variables.[39] Fromm and Taubman provide an approach to the multiple response problem in which a model is validated over several successive periods or across several important variables within a single period.[40] The latter case is a particularly difficult one because it requires assigning weights to the different variables as to form a welfare or utility function, and this information is rarely available. Lastly, it should be recognized that statistical criteria are not the sole means of model validation. One may be interested in the discriminatory power of a model relative to the different forms of policy decisions to be analyzed. Or a model may yield valuable information about causal mechanisms in a market which outweighs considerations of accuracy.

Sample Period Criteria

The approach taken in selecting crieteria for validation in the sample and post-sample period is to assume that validation best follows when some combination of parametric and nonparametric tests is applied. Selecting crieria for the sample period begins with the assumption that some final model structure has been reached and that the behavioral relationships contained in the model satisfy conventional tests such as the analysis of variance using the F-distribution, the significance of coefficients based on the t-distribution, and the Durbin-Watson test of autocorrelation. The simplest criteria for determining the validity of a model's output are the single point criteria, including the inequality coefficient, and turning point analysis.

If the model happens to be a dynamic one, an additional criterion is that the model be stable or internally consistent. As explained in Chapter 7, the stability of a model can be judged by analytical solution if the model is linear (or linearized) and nonstochastic. For the case of a linear stochastic model, the spectrum matrix approach described in Appendix B might be used.[41] A simulation solution can also be applied for this purpose if one is interested in observing directly the dynamic cyclical properties of the model. While a simulation solution does not always provide information about stability where an analytical solution already has been applied, the simulation approach provides a rough measure of stability which is convenient, for example, when one is making frequent changes in a model structure.[42]

Post Sample Period Criteria

Here also we are interested in a combination of tests that will evaluate a model's performance. Assuming that actual observations exist and that forecast errors can be observed, the simplest criteria which can be applied are again the single point criteria and turning point analysis. Next in importance is the ability of a model to forecast better than naive or statistical models or judgmental predictions, although a model's usefulness often is in predicting behavior rather than attaining a particular forecast accuracy. Among the more useful models for evaluating comparative errors are the autoregressive or Box-Jenkins models.

Other criteria which can be proposed may not add that much additional information except in circumstances where a model's value rests in predicting particular types of information, or where forecast performance is sufficiently poor to warrant respecification and reestimation of the model. In the first case, for example, spectral analysis can provide information concerning the long run cyclical properties of the model. In the second case, analysis of decomposition error would indicate which aspects of a model's structure or simulation contribute most to forecast error and subsequently must be corrected.

Commodity Experience

Examples of commodity simulation are presented according to the purposes for which simulation is conducted: historical explanation, forecasting or prediction of policy impact, and decision making. Commodity studies examined in this respect include tungsten, coffee, rubber, and tin.

Historical Policy Simulation

Policy simulation analysis applied to the sample period can help to explain the behavior of a commodity market or industry or to explore how the behavior of that market or industry would have changed if other policies or plans had been adopted. An example of the former can be found in Burrows' study of the tungsten industry, which features a model designed to explain the behavior of tungsten prices.[43] That model consists of 25 behavioral equations and one market clearing identity with the corresponding endogenous variables composed of production and consumption in the major countries, also including inventories and prices in the United States. To simulate the model, a "restricted" reduced form is computed from the structural form and the method of Gauss-Seidel applied. Because of the nonlinearities involved, it was reported that considerable experimentation was necessary in normalizing the system to obtain covergence.

The years selected for the simulation corespond to the sample period, 1947–1968. Two types of simulations are reported; the first follows the total form described earlier producing single period or one-period-ahead forcasts and the second follows the final form generating dynamic or evolutionary values. Only a sample of the results obtained can be reviewed here and Table 9-1 summarizes the actual and estimated values for several different tungsten price series obtained from the dynamic simulation. Although no validation criteria are presented in the published study, the close resemblance of the simulated and actual values for prices and other series suggests that the model explains the tungsten market reasonably well.

An example of historical simulation where the goal is to determine market outcomes based on alternative policies can be found in Epp's study of the

Table 9-1. Simulation Results from the Tungsten Model, Actual Versus Predicted Values of Price Series for the Dynamic Reduced Form Solution, 1947–68 (Dollars per Pound)

	PW		PFW		PTI		PHR	
	Predicted	Actual	Predicted	Actual	Predicted	Actual	Predicted	Actual
1947	2.19	1.82	3.88	n.a.	1.23	n.a.	6.46	n.a.
1948	1.80	1.73	3.79	1.26	1.26	1.20	6.42	6.29
1949	1.13	1.41	3.17	3.15	1.28	1.32	5.68	6.07
1950	1.66	1.70	3.14	3.15	1.27	1.32	5.34	6.07
1951	5.01	4.88	5.07	5.23	1.66	1.61	7.12	6.61
1952	3.08	4.28	5.36	5.90	1.76	1.81	8.25	8.74
1953	5.22	3.22	5.72	4.74	1.79	1.76	7.96	5.88
1954	0.53	1.73	4.00	4.44	1.82	1.76	7.00	5.88
1955	2.29	2.22	3.02	3.84	1.76	1.71	4.65	5.24
1956	2.49	2.10	3.80	3.60	1.74	1.71	5.78	5.24
1957	1.50	1.20	3.25	2.67	1.79	1.73	5.29	4.51
1958	0.58	0.74	2.19	2.16	1.76	1.82	3.86	3.72
1959	1.00	0.83	2.16	2.11	1.75	1.81	3.62	3.65
1960	0.60	1.18	2.01	2.11	1.77	1.81	3.47	3.60
1961	0.66	1.07	1.84	2.31	1.78	1.82	3.13	3.33
1962	1.17	0.75	2.06	2.18	1.79	1.82	3.25	3.10
1963	0.87	0.56	2.09	1.76	1.82	1.82	3.34	2.84
1964	1.78	0.93	2.27	1.71	1.82	1.80	3.16	2.89
1965	1.54	1.41	2.47	2.74	1.86	1.83	3.49	3.28
1966	1.88	2.27	2.53	2.83	1.88	1.81	3.34	3.86
1967	2.13	2.50	2.81	2.78	1.90	1.94	4.23	4.69
1968	3.18	2.42	3.39	2.81	1.93	1.94	4.67	4.48

Note: All prices are deflated by the wholesale durables price index.
PW = Price of tungsten.
PFW = Price of ferrotungsten.
PTI = Price of high-speed steel type T1.
PHR = Price of hydrogen-reduced powder.
n.a. = Not available.

Source: James C. Burrows, *Tungsten: An Industry Analysis* (Lexington, Mass.: D. C. Heath & Co., 1971). p. 209.

world coffee market.[44] In this case, the policies to be tested are related to possible terms of the International Coffee Agreement. The simulation analysis is performed with a fifteen equation model of the world coffee market viewed as an oligopoly. Most important of the endogenous variables estimated are the price and export variables influencing coffee revenues of the three grades of coffee traded: Brazilian, mild, and robusta. The policy variables manipulated are the Brazilian support price, export quotas, indicator prices, and production goals.

Results of performing simulation experiments based on the policy variables are presented for the historical period 1958–1965 and for two years

Table 9-2. Simulation Results from the Coffee Model

Support price level	E	Main Effects[a] (E_i) (000,000 dollars)	Contrasts with E_6 as Control $(E_i - E_6)$	Five percent Confidence Intervals, E_6 as Control
Price Effect on Brazilian Revenues				
15¢	E_1	-208	-405	$-415 \leq (E_1 - E_6) \leq -394$
30¢	E_2	-116	-313	$-323 \leq (E_2 - E_6) \leq -302$
45¢	E_3	-30	-227	$-237 \leq (E_3 - E_6) \leq -216$
60¢	E_4	$+49$	-147	$-158 \leq (E_4 - E_6) \leq -137$
75¢	E_5	$+123$	-73	$-84 \leq (E_5 - E_6) \leq -63$
90¢	E_6	$+197$		
Price endogenous E_7		-14	-211	$-221 \leq (E_7 - E_6) \leq -200$
Price Effect on Mild Revenues				
15¢	E_1	-168	-253	$-261 \leq (E_1 - E_6) \leq -244$
30¢	E_2	-70	-154	$-163 \leq (E_2 - E_6) \leq -145$
45¢	E_3	$+6$	-79	$-88 \leq (E_3 - E_6) \leq -70$
60¢	E_4	$+54$	-30	$-39 \leq (E_4 - E_6) \leq -22$
75¢	E_5	$+81$	-4	$-13 \leq (E_5 - E_6) \leq +5$
90¢	E_6	$+84$		
Price endogenous E_7		$+14$	-71	$-79 \leq (E_7 - E_6) \leq -62$
Price Effect on Robusta Revenues				
15¢	E_1	-91	-191	$-197 \leq (E_1 - E_6) \leq -185$
30¢	E_2	-56	-157	$-163 \leq (E_2 - E_6) \leq -150$
45¢	E_3	-20	-120	$-126 \leq (E_3 - E_6) \leq -114$
60¢	E_4	$+19$	-81	$-87 \leq (E_4 - E_6) \leq -75$
75¢	E_5	$+57$	-43	$-49 \leq (E_5 - E_6) \leq -37$
90¢	E_6	$+100$		
Price endogenous E_7		-10	-111	$-117 \leq (E_7 - E_6) \leq -105$

[a] The main effect (E_i) is defined as the mean of factor level i minus the overall mean.

Source: M. L. S. Epps, "A Computer Simulation of the World Coffee Economy," Unpublished Ph.D dissertation, Duke University, 1970, pp. 192–95.

into the forecast period 1966–1967 following an experimental design approach. Table 9-2 summarizes typical results showing the average coffee revenue that stems from changes in the Brazilian support price. The table is so conceived that the main effects of a particular support price level, the difference between each effect and the highest price effect, and the positive main effect of the highest price level are all illustrated. Revenues obtained from all three export grades of coffee are shown to vary directly with the support price, a price of 90 cents per pound yielding the largest revenues.

One other important aspect of historical policy simulation is determining the conditions under which various aspects of market behavior can be stabilized. The Agarwala study of the U.K. agricultural market is interesting in this respect as are the Kofi and Goreux cocoa studies and the lauric oils stabilization example presented later.[45]

Forecast Policy Simulation

Policy simulation analysis applied to a commodity model in the post-sample period can generate a set of forecasts with respect to the important endogenous variables or it can predict different outcomes for those variables related to alternative policy prescriptions. Both these goals are pursued by Behrman in his simulation of the world rubber market.[46] The simulation is based on a sizeable model, which he better handles by decomposing it into an exogenous block, a recursive block, and a simultaneous block. Examples of variables featured in the exogenous block are price deflaters, government rubber stockpiles, and rainfall. The recursive block contains principally the technological change relationships needed to explain the production of synthetic rubbers. The simultaneous block includes relationships explaining market equilibrium such as individual country natural rubber supplies, the demand for natural rubber relative to synthetic rubber, natural rubber stocks, and the real and expected prices of natural rubber.

A series of policy forecasts have been performed based on the simulation of the reduced form of the model; the period of the forecasts extends from 1965 to 1980 where an interesting method of comparing outcomes is used. Given certain growth rates for the exogenous variables based on past market experience, conditional forecasts are used to provide results for the first or basic simulation. Alternative values are then selected for certain exogenous variables based on differing policy assumptions, and a number of alternative simulations prepared. Taken as an example, one set of assumptions deals with the uncertainty surrounding future rubber supplies from Indonesia. Exports are assumed to remain constant for the basic simulation, and then are altered to imply different rates of growth. The actual rates of growth and export levels are shown in the heading of Table 9-3; simulation results for important endogenous variables appear in the body of the table. The different outcomes are subsequently evaluated according to the mean absolute percentage differences experienced by the endogenous variables relative to the values found for the basic simulation.

Simulations designed to determine a set of policies that could stabilize fluctuations of future prices and exports of tin have been carried out by Desai.[47] The basis for the simulations is a four-equation model based on the following

Table 9-3. Annual Percentage Differences and Mean Absolute Differences Between Basic Simulation and Simulations with Alternative Assumptions about Indonesian Total Natural Rubber Supply for Key Variables in the World Rubber Economy, 1965–80[a]

Year	Simulation A $SNI = 738$			Simulation B $SNI = 605\,e^{0.015(t-1965)}$			Simulation C $SNI = 630\,e^{0.025(t-1965)}$			Simulation D $SNI = 643\,e^{0.015(t-1965)}$		
	SN^w	$\dfrac{DS^w}{(DN+DS)^w}$	PN^w	SN^w	$\dfrac{DS^w}{(DN+DS)^w}$	PN^w	SN^w	$\dfrac{DS^w}{(DN+DS)^w}$	PN^w	SN^w	$\dfrac{DS^w}{(DN+DS)^w}$	PN^w
1965	−12.7	2.9	9.8	−6.7	1.2	5.4	−7.8	1.5	6.3	−8.5	1.7	6.7
1966	−5.7	4.7	4.9	−0.7	1.9	0.5	−2.0	2.5	1.7	−2.3	2.7	1.9
1967	−12.9	5.0	11.8	−8.2	2.3	7.5	−9.8	3.1	8.9	−9.8	3.2	9.0
1968	−6.7	5.6	6.7	−2.9	3.2	2.6	−4.6	4.0	4.3	−4.4	4.0	4.1
1969	−12.9	5.8	12.0	−9.5	3.8	8.8	−11.5	4.7	10.5	−11.0	4.6	10.2
1970	−7.4	4.6	7.6	−4.7	2.9	4.3	−6.8	3.9	6.3	−6.1	3.6	5.6
1971	−12.5	5.0	11.2	−10.3	3.8	9.5	−12.7	4.7	11.4	−11.6	4.4	11.3
1972	−7.6	4.1	7.3	−6.1	3.3	5.5	−8.5	4.3	7.7	−7.3	3.8	6.7
1973	−11.8	4.4	11.9	−10.7	3.7	9.9	−13.3	4.7	12.0	−11.8	4.2	10.9
1974	−7.6	3.3	7.4	−7.0	2.9	6.6	−9.6	3.9	8.8	−8.0	3.3	7.5
1975	−11.1	2.9	10.3	−10.9	2.6	10.0	−13.7	3.6	12.2	−11.9	3.0	10.9
1976	−7.6	3.8	7.1	−7.7	3.7	7.0	−10.5	4.7	9.5	−8.6	4.0	7.9
1977	−10.5	3.5	9.6	−10.9	3.5	9.9	−13.9	4.5	12.2	−11.8	3.9	10.6
1978	−7.5	3.3	6.9	−8.2	3.4	7.5	−11.2	4.4	9.9	−9.0	3.7	8.1
1979	−9.8	3.1	8.8	−10.8	3.4	9.6	−14.0	4.2	12.0	−11.6	3.6	10.2
1980	−7.3	3.0	6.6	−8.5	3.3	7.5	−11.6	4.1	10.0	−9.2	3.5	8.1
Mean absolute percentage difference, 1965–1980	9.5	3.8	8.6	7.7	3.1	7.0	10.1	3.9	9.0	8.9	3.6	8.1

[a] SNI = Indonesia Supply, SN^w = World Supply, DN^w = Natural Rubber Demand, DS^w = Synthetic Rubber Demand, PN^w = World Natural Rubber Price.

Source: Jere R. Behrman, "Econometric Model Simulations of the World Rubber Market, 1950–1980," in L. R. Klein (Ed.), *Essays in Industrial Econometrics*, Vol. III, Economics Research Unit, Department of Economics, University of Pennsylvania, Philadelphia, 1971, p. 66.

endogenous variables: tim consumed in tin plate, tin consumed in other uses, secondary tin output, and world tin output. The approach taken in examining policy alternatives was to determine whether a simple output control policy together with a buffer stock could help to stabilize the market price for tin.

That the simulations have been performed by adding shocks of Types I and II to the reduced form of the model is the unique feature of Desai's study. Before the various policy alternatives could be evaluated, a number of test simulations were conducted to determine which forms of shocks and assumptions regarding consumption could lead to the most realistic outcome. Results of these tests indicate that (1) shocks of Type II provide the best dynamic simulation of the market; and (2) the most realistic of the conditional predictions assumed an upward trend in U.S. tin consumption and a downward trend in OEEC and Canadian consumption. Based on these conditions, the final simulations were then performed, so as to minimize tin price fluctuations while maximizing gross tin revenues. Results given in Table 9-4 are for

Table 9-4. Simulation Results from the Tin Model: Mean Annual Revenue and Its Variance Under Alternative Stabilization Plans (£000,000)

Plan	Mean annual revenue	Variance of revenue
A	132.45	419.19
B	120.54	530.74
C	126.68	505.94
D	131.13	494.89

Source: Meghnad Desai, "An Econometric Model of the World Tin Economy, 1948–1961" *Econometrica*, Vol 34 (January 1966) No. 1, p. 121.

the revenues obtained from using four alternative buffer stock and output policies: Plan A assumes stock levels equal to 81,197 tons; Plan B assumes the same stock level with output restrictions; Plan C is the same as B but adds buffer stocks of 20,000 tons; and Plan D increases the buffer stocks of Plan C by 35,000 tons. The period of evaluation of the alternative plans extends 24 years beyond the sample period 1948–1961. The final results suggest that a form of crude output control together with a larger-sized buffer stock could stabilize prices while still achieving substantial revenues.

Lauric Oils Simulation

Methodology

Simulations of the lauric oils model follow from the basic model structure presented in Chapter 6.[48] That model is divided into a recursive block I, a simultaneous block, and a recursive block II, altogether containing fifteen structural equations and seven identities. This same block ordering provides the basis for the simulations with the Gauss-Seidel algorithm applied to the simultaneous block. Other characteristics of the simulations include the use of the nonlinear price equation 6.61, and the adoption of the final form of solution producing evolutionary behavior. Several different simulation experiments have been conducted including historical and short and long run forecast simulations. While the historical and short run forecast simulations are nonstochastic, the long run simulations are stochastic, interposing the effect of random variations in climatic conditions.

It should be added that no problems arose in performing the simulations. Dividing the basic model into separate recursive and simultaneous blocks appears to reflect well the general ordering or pattern that economic forces follow in the lauric oils market. The simulation was stable and convergence in the simultaneous block occurred rapidly, with only three to nine iterations required in any particular year of a simulation run.

Historical Simulations and Validation

Results of simulating the major endogenous variables for the lauric oils model over the period 1960–1967 are reported in Table 9-5 as well as in Figures 9-6 through 9-9. Although several different validation criteria are to be employed in future work on the model, the present results are analyzed only in the form of the mean square error and mean absolute percentage error and a rough comparison of turning points. Table 9-5 shows that the recursive block I of the model explains fairly well the coconut oil and palm kernel oil exports emanating from the different countries. The percentage error of coconut oil exports, as high as 13.21% for Indonesia, is only 3.67%, 6.53%, and 2.95% for the Philippines, Ceylon, and Oceania respectively. Similarly, the percentage error for world palm kernel oil exports is 3.74%. The turning points of the actual and simulated export series also correspond fairly closely for most years up to and including 1967 as shown in Figure 9-6.

Values of the stock and world price variables obtained from simulation of the simultaneous block of the model do not approximate the actual values

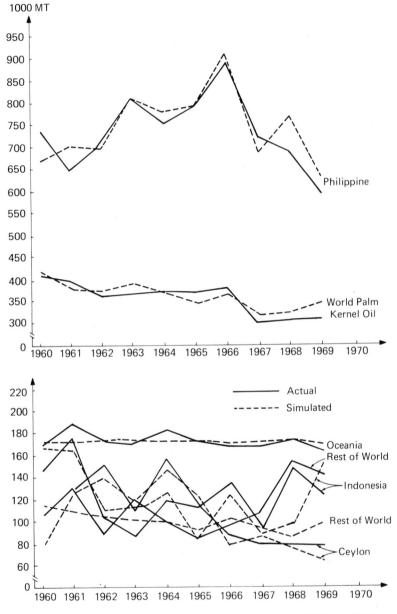

Figure 9-6. Lauric Oil Exports Simulated and Actual Values, 1960–1969.

Table 9-5. Simulation Results from the Lauric Oils Model: Mean Percentage Absolute Forecast Error for Selected Endogenous Variables

Model Variables	% Error (1960–67)	% Error (1968–69)
Recursive Block I		
Philippine Exports	3.67	9.50
Ceylon Exports	6.53	10.80
Indonesia Exports	13.21	23.50
Oceania Exports	2.95	1.70
Rest of World Exports	10.51	43.76
World Palm Kernel Oil Exports	3.74	8.56
Simultaneous Block		
US Stocks	12.95	14.20
UK Stocks	9.13	52.20
EEC Stocks	30.83	3.20
Ceylon Stocks	14.03	11.70
World Stocks	8.50	1.58
Prices	2.91	12.50
Recursive Block II		
US Consumption	2.09	0.10
US Imports	5.19	2.02
UK Consumption	6.72	2.38
UK Imports	6.13	8.85
EEC Consumption	2.76	2.34
EEC Imports	3.95	3.98
Japan Imports	8.68	7.52
Rest of World Imports	5.18	14.00

Source: W. C. Labys, *An Econometric Model of the World Lauric Oils Market*, UNCTAD/CD/Misc.43/Rev.1, United Nations, Geneva, July 1971.

as well as had been expected. However, specifying the stock relationships was difficult and only now is information available which can lead to improvements in a revised model. Consequently, the reported percentage errors are not considered too serious with the exception of the E.E.C. Values found for the U.S., U.K., and Ceylon relationships are 12.95%, 9.13%, and 14.03% respectively. The error of 30.83% recorded for the E.E.C. cannot be explained except in terms of specification difficulties and of the relative inadequacy of this particular data set. The actual nature of the error is reflected in Figure 9-7 which shows an understatement of inventory levels for 1963, 1964, and 1965. Note also in Figure 9-7 that turning points in inventory series for other countries are captured fairly adequately. The world price explanation appears also to be reasonable, with a reported percentage error of only 2.91%. Figure 9-8 shows that all turning points are captured adequately, the exception being a one-period lag in the sharp upturn after 1962.

The lowest percentage errors are found with the consumption and import variables in the recursive block II. Some examples are levels of 2.09%, 6.72%, and 2.76% achieved for the U.S., U.K., and E.E.C. consumption equations respectively. Similar low levels are also found for the import estimates derived from the respective identities. As shown in Figure 9-9 these low errors are reflected in the relatively good predictions of most turning points.

Simulation analysis also has been conducted over the sample period to determine how various export norm policies could have stabilized fluctuations in lauric oils prices.[49] Three different levels of export norms have been selected, centering about the average level of coconut oil exports achieved over the period 1960 through 1969, as reported in Table 9-6. Particular norm

Table 9-6. Coconut Oil and Palm Kernel Oil Net Exports (000 MT)

	1960	1961	1962	1963	1964	1965	1966	1967	1968	1969	1970
Coconut Oil Net Exports											
Phillippines	738	648	708	817	759	797	899	924	690	595	609
Ceylon	75	129	151	110	157	115	87	78	78	68	67
Indonesia	146	175	103	87	120	112	136	96	146	122	99
Oceania	167	189	174	171	184	174	169	170	174	166	170
Sub-Total	1126	1141	1136	1185	1220	1198	1291	1068	1088	961	942
Rest of World	102	125	88	120	100	85	100	108	157	143	147
Total Coconut Oil	1228	1266	1224	1305	1320	1283	1391	1176	1245	1104	1089
Palm Kernel Oil Net Exports	409	394	361	369	373	371	378	296	307	315	322
Total Net Exports	1637	1660	1585	1674	1693	1654	1769	1472	1552	1415	1411

Source: Worlds Oil and Fats Statistics. Prepared by Economic and Statistics Department, Unilever Ltd. for the Congress of the International Association of Seed Crushers; also assorted National Publications. Figures have been adjusted to account for overshipments.

levels chosen were 1,225,000 metric tons, 1,255,000 tons, and 1,275,000 tons respectively. To accommodate the deficiency or excess of lauric oils that would result from operating the schemes, the simulation was operated with stock levels being simultaneously adjusted to reflect additions to or subtractions from actual export levels. The reduction in price levels achieved as obtained

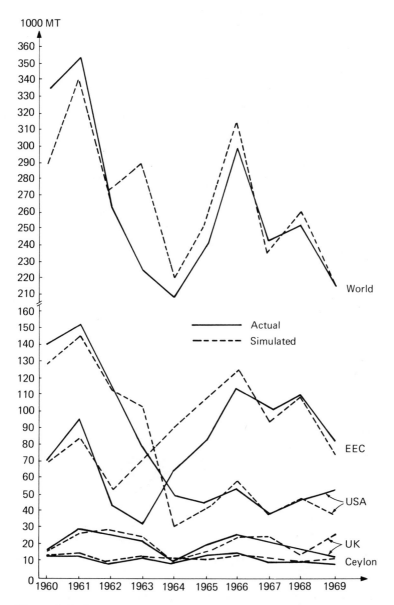

Figure 9-7. Lauric Oil Stocks: Simulated and Actual Values, 1960–1969.

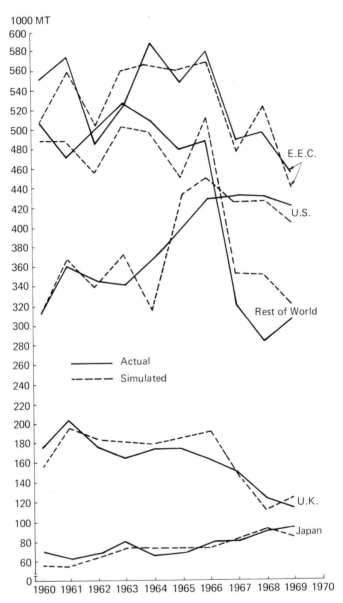

Figure 9-9. Lauric Oil Imports Simulated and Actual Values, 1960–1969.

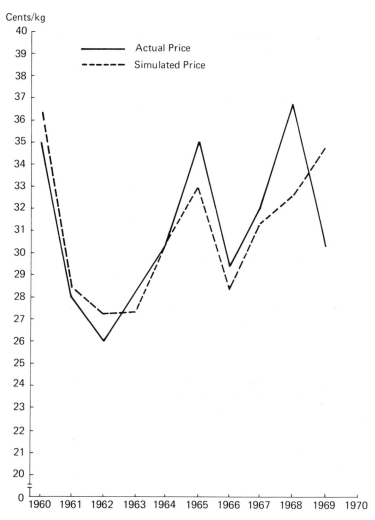

Figure 9-8. Lauric Oil Prices Simulated and Actual Values, 1960-1969.

Table 9-7. Coconut Oil Price Levels. Actual and Norm Estimates, 1960–69[a]

	Actual	Norm I	Norm II	Norm III
1960	35.5	36.2	35.8	35.6
1961	28.0	28.1	27.7	27.5
1962	26.0	27.9	27.5	27.3
1963	27.0	31.9	31.5	31.2
1964	30.4	34.5	34.1	33.9
1965	35.1	35.0	34.6	34.3
1966	29.3	33.6	33.2	32.9
1967	32.1	32.4	32.0	31.8
1968	36.8	34.9	34.5	34.2
1969	30.4	38.9	38.5	38.4
Std. Error	3.24	2.88	2.88	2.86

[a] New York, Crude in Tanks, U.S. cents/kg.

Source: W. C. Labys, *Feasibility of Operating a Supply Stabilization Scheme for the Lauric Oils Market: Returns, Costs and Financing,* UNCTAD/CD/Misc. 41, Geneva, March 1971, p. 13.

Table 9-8. Returns, Costs and Net Gains from Operating Alternative Export Norm Schemes, 1960–69.[a] U.S. $(000)

	Returns	Storage Costs	Handling Costs	Total Costs	Net Gains	Cumulative Stocks[b]
Export norm						
Norm I	−90,734	53,926	317	54,243	−144,977	292,000
Norm II	9,254	27,768	294	28,062	−18,808	48,000
Norm III	71,778	36,118	299	36,417	35,361	—

[a] *Returns:* positive or negative revenues obtained from selling and buying stocks to maintain export norm levels or to achieve the degree of price stabilization required for operating the buffer stock schemes.

Costs: storage and handling costs represent a combination of cost estimates received: storage costs = $2/mt/month = $24/mt/year; handling costs = $0.50/mt.

Net Gains: difference between returns and total costs.
[b] Metric tons.

Source: See Table 9-7.

from the simulated price levels is reported in Table 9-7. Using the standard error of price variations as a rough measure of the amplitude of price fluctuations, the standard errors obtained for prices corresponding to the export norms are shown to be lower than that of the actual prices. The extent to which price swings are dampened, however, is small and improvements in dampening are likely to take place only with further refinement of the export norm mechanism. Revenue computations based on the simulations as reported in Table 9-8 indicate that only a small loss or positive net gains in revenue occur when considering the costs and returns of operating the scheme at different norm levels. Of course these results involve a number of simplifying assumptions, which would be removed in a more complex analysis.

Short Run Forecast Simulation and Validation

Simulated values of the endogenous variables in the historical period become the values of the lagged endogenous variables in extending the simulation to the post-sample years 1968 and 1969. One year ahead predictions are used for the exogenous variables. Of major importance in evaluating the forecast performance of the model is the substantial shift downward of exports in 1968 and 1969.

Table 9-6 shows that levels of copra and coconut oil exports declined from 1,391,000 tons in 1966 to 1,245,000 tons in 1968 and to 1,104,000 tons in 1969. Total lauric oils exports fell back even more sharply from 1,769,000 tons in 1966 to 1,552,000 tons in 1968 and 1,415,000 tons in 1969. This decline for the most part is attributed to setbacks in production caused by unfavorable climatic conditions. The Philippines, for example, suffered a rainfall loss and typhoons not only in 1967 but over the next several years. The dry season in the Philippines lasted as long as five months in 1968 and eight months in 1969.

In addition to typhoons occurring during 1968 and 1969, the production areas suffered two earthquakes of Intensity VI. Ceylon also suffered droughts beginning 1964 which by 1969 exerted a substantial cumulative effect. The combined reduction of exports led to abnormally high copra and coconut oil prices for 1968. These high prices, however, did not extend through the end of 1969 as one might have expected, largely because ample lauric oil stocks existed in the U.S. and in Europe. But such a major shift in the supply function together with an abnormal price situation made it difficult for the model to forecast those two years accurately.

One possibility for improving the model's forecast performance would be to adjust the intercepts of certain relationships in the model, so that they now reflect more accurately the market changes which have occurred. It seemed sensible to adjust the intercepts of the consumption equations such that consumption might follow exports downwards; this was accomplished by subtracting a differential corresponding to a fixed percent of the average of the previous three years' consumption.[a] Stock levels in Ceylon also are sufficiently closely linked to exports that the equation intercept similarly could be adjusted downwards. Other possible adjustments in the model could not be justified as easily, and thus are not made.

Results of the forecast performance of the model simulation for 1968 and 1969 also appear in Table 9-5 and in Figures 9-6 through 9-9. Except for the export levels of Indonesia and the Rest of the World, the export projections from recursive block I show that the model does to some extent reflect the underlying supply factors. For the Philippines and Ceylon in particular, the reduced levels of exports correspond to the decline in rainfall with the percentage forecast errors averaging only 9.50% and 10.80% over 1968 and 1969 respectively. Oceania coconut oil exports and world palm kernel oil exports are predicted with an error of only 11.70% and 3.74% respectively. The sudden rise in exports for both Indonesia and the Rest of the World proved particularly difficult to predict, especially because the increase occurred for reasons other than those accounted for in the explanatory equations.

Reasonably good forecasts are obtained for the variables in the simultaneous block of the model, although the U.S. equation is the exception here. The forecast error achieved for the U.S., E.E.C., and Ceylon stock forecasts amounted to 14.20%, 3.20%, and 11.70% respectively, averaged over 1968 and 1969. The U.K. stock level for 1969 was extremely difficult to predict since stocks reached their lowest level since 1964. The effect of this error, however, was minimal because it did not lead to substantial error in the forecast of world stocks. As shown in Table 9-5 above, the aggregate or world stock level is predicted with an average forecast error of only 1.58% for 1968 and 1969.

The price forecasts appear to have suffered worst from the change in market structure. Although the average forecast error for the years 1960–1967 amounted to only 2.91%, for 1968 and 1969 it rose to 12.50%. It had been hoped that the forecast error would not exceed 5%. The econometric model did not predict the high of 36.8 U.S. cents per kg. which occurred in 1968 nor could it explain the downturn to the 30.4 U.S. cents per kg. reached in 1969. In terms of the price equation used, this appears to be a result of stock levels being relatively too low to force the price downward; in addition, the coefficient on the exports variable also seemed biased downward. In terms of market developments, the actual prices reached also are unexpected on the basis of accepted price theory.

---

[a] Percentages used: $c_t^{us} = -5\%$; $c_t^{ec} = -5\%$; $m_t^{jp} = -10\%$; $m_t^{rw} = -10\%$; and $s_t^{cy} = -20\%$

The level of lauric oil exports in 1968 was slightly higher than in 1967, yet the price rose from 32.1 to 36.8 U.S. cents per kg. Exports fell from 1968 to 1969, yet the price also declined to 30.4 U.S. cents per kg. It is believed that these particular price movements were to some extent the results of shifts in inventory positions within the importing countries. Even under these conditions, the forecast performance for the price model remains adequate. Had price behavior in the simultaneous sector not been interrelated with inventory behavior in the major countries, the forecast error is likely to have been higher.

Since the most important variable in the model to be forecast was the world coconut oil price, a further evaluation of its forecast accuracy has been made using comparative forecast models. The latter include the no change, simple adaptive expectations, and average expectations forms of naive models. As shown in Table 9-9, the price forecasts obtained from the econometric model are slightly superior to those resulting from the other models.

Table 9-9. Coconut Oil Price Forecasts. (U.S. cents per kg.)

	Actual and Forecast Prices		Average % Error
	1968	1969	
Actual	36.8	30.4	—
Econometric model	32.6	34.7	12.5
No change	32.1	36.8	16.9
Simple adaptive expectations	32.2	34.5	13.0
Average expectations	30.7	34.5	13.0

Adjusting the intercepts of the consumption and import equations for the reduction in exports proved to be fruitful and results in Table 9-5 above show low forecast errors. For the U.S., U.K., and E.E.C. consumption equations, forecast errors are only 0.10%, 2.38%, and 2.34% respectively. They are somewhat higher for Japan and the Rest of the World. Roughly similar levels appear for the import variables.

Long Run Forecast Simulation

There are a number of advantages to be gained in utilizing an econometric model based on annual data to provide a long run simulation from five to twenty years. First, the simulations will reflect the ability of a model to reproduce the cyclical fluctuations relevant to the commodity of interest.

Second, the simulations can be used to determine the long run stability of a model given certain shocks or displacements in key exogenous variables. Third, and more related to determining future economic conditions in a market, simulations permit us to evaluate the future state of a market based on conditional forecasts of key variables or based on alternative policy prescriptions.

With respect to the lauric oils market, it would be useful to determine what levels of consumption and prices may be reached over the fifteen-year period 1972 through 1987 given low, medium, and high conditional forecasts for world exports. In order to utilize the present econometric model to produce such forecasts, it is necessary to reconsider the implication of Chapter 5 that the elasticities and cross-elasticities of demand for lauric oils may change when the total export levels of lauric oils exceed 1,500,000 tons per year. However, preliminary tests with the model did not indicate that market behavior differed substantially during such a period. In addition, the simultaneous aspect of the model assures through price adjustment that imports and exports will be in relative equilibrium at the end of each period.

The actual operation of the simulation required substituting low, medium, and high export forecasts for the export estimates normally provided by the equations in recursive block I. The details underlying these forecasts can be found elsewhere.[50] In brief, the low level of total lauric oils exports forecast

Table 9-10. Projections for Lauric Oil Demand Including Rates of Change, 1972–87[a](000 Metric Tons)

Year	U.S.			E.E.C. Countries			World[b]		
	Low	Medium	High	Low	Medium	High	Low	Medium	High
1972	486	492	492	510	527	545	1464	1606	1689
1977	547	561	575	496	526	568	1409	1665	1984
1982	607	624	648	507	536	595	1561	1773	2232
1987	659	684	717	502	552	620	1538	1908	2470
Annual per cent change in growth									
1972–77	2.4	2.7	3.2	−0.6	0.0	0.7	−0.8	0.8	3.2
1977–82	2.2	2.2	2.5	0.6	0.4	0.9	2.0	1.2	2.3
1982–87	1.8	2.0	2.2	0.0	0.9	0.9	−0.5	1.5	1.6
1972–87	2.1	2.2	2.6	0.0	0.3	0.9	0.3	0.8	2.6

[a] Demand figures represent 2 year average taken over indicated and succeeding year except for 1987.
[b] Imports for consumption.

Source: W. C. Labys, "Projections and Prospects for the Lauric Oils," *Journal of the American Oil Chemists' Society* 49 (June 1972), pp. 232A–233A.

**Table 9-11. Price Projections Based on
Export Alternatives, 1972–87**

Export projection level	New York crude oil price ¢/kg.		
	1972	1977	1987
Low	31.7	33.4	32.6
Medium	30.4	28.6	23.1
High	24.6	20.2	13.2

Source: See Table 9-10.

for 1987 is 1,538,000 metric tons; the medium forecast is 1,908,000 tons; and the high forecast is 2,470,000 tons. In addition, the export variables representing each country or region are shocked stochastically to reflect the random variations in climatic conditions resulting from typhoons and droughts. The simultaneous block and the recursive block II of the model are then solved by providing extrapolated values for the remaining exogenous variables in the model.

Table 9-10 summarizes the levels of demand and the annual percentage change in growth of demand forecast for the years 1972, 1977, 1982, and 1987. For both the U.S. and the E.E.C. countries, demand is expected to grow over that period, although the rate of growth in the U.S. will be relatively higher. Rates of growth in world demand will also increase. Should per capita consumption in the developing countries begin to approach that of the developed countries, the rates of growth for the world will be higher. The levels of demand presently forecast as well as the corresponding level of prices, however, are realistic when compared to expectations held by fats and oils experts.

Conclusions

In this chapter an attempt has been made to outline the methods of policy simulation analysis appropriate for use with the reduced form or structural form of econometric commodity models. Only elementary forms of simulation constructions have been considered, but these will hopefully provide a base for more complex applications. Different methods of validating commodity models have also been surveyed. It is possible to improve the validation of commodity models over sample and post-sample periods by employing several parametric and nonparametric tests in combination. Up to now, few commodity models have been validated using criteria any more sophisticated than the simplest point criteria. Notable exceptions in this respect are the several studies which have included analytical solution or the application of spectral techniques. Simulation analysis can probably improve validation where a model is formulated stochastically; however, Howrey and Kelejian have cautioned us of its limitations.

Finally, several different forms of policy simulation analysis have been illustrated using simulation experiments with the lauric oils model. The attempt has been to review some of the different purposes for which policy simulations can be conducted. Although this has included examples of historical explanation, market stabilization and short and long run forecasting, other forms of policy impact studies remain to be considered such as that of decision making and control. The forecast performance of the lauric oils model in simulation is not as good as could be expected, but it is a first generation model whose present purpose has been to illustrate the theories and methods relevant for commodity model building and use.

10 Conclusions

To conclude this monograph by contrasting the available economic and econometric developments with the major remaining problems would be appropriate. In other words, how do the building blocks currently utilized for model construction and application stant up when beset by the difficulties of estimating and using econometric models in general and commodity models in particular? By making this contrast, one can better assess possibilities for both current and future research.

Components of Commodity Models

Substantial progress has been made in recent years since the analysis of commodity demand has shifted from a static to a dynamic approach. Distributed lags, partial adjustment, and the equivalent adaptive expectations are being used increasingly to demonstrate that the response of commodity demand to underlying forces often spreads itself over a number of periods. Yet though the dynamic approach can explain adjustments from period to period, it fails to describe adjustment as a continuous process. The demand for commodities in a continuous framework, nonetheless, can be analyzed using the dynamic differential approach, and methods have been proposed for estimating differential equations directly.

Commodity supply analysis also has shifted to a dynamic approach. Partial adjustment can be applied to determine the supply of commodities produced regularly or on annual basis. It can also be combined with relationships which reflect planting and removal rates to explain the supply of perennial commodities. In describing commodity supply one frequently finds the problem of stochastic disturbances when, for example, unusual weather conditions occur. Such supply behavior can now be simulated by applying probability distributions to the parameters or disturbances of the corresponding relationships. Even better would be to relate supply to a probabilistic function, which attaches weightings to particular outcomes. Since biological and ecological factors frequently influence supply, there is a need to develop supply relationships more closely linked to these factors.

Related to both demand and supply analysis is the problem or correctly identifying patterns of substitutability and complementarity among commodities. There is still no comprehensive analytical method for describing these patterns. Linked to this problem is that of the role played by synthetics in market adjustments for natural commodities. The process of technological change and the diffusion of innovations must be further investigated within this context.

Recent advances in inventory analysis include the flexible accelerator and its buffer stock variant as well as the supply of storage, but these theories must be further tested empirically and new ones devised. The development of the theory of optimal portfolio investment for commodity inventory applications is a possible step in this direction. Commodity inventory behavior must also be examined separately according to the decision making processes of consumers and producers as well as speculators. We should also attempt to incorporate into inventory theory a wider range of factors such as the temporal character of the market and the nature of inventory psychology and expectations.

Commodity price analysis has progressed in so far as explaining short run fluctuations is concerned; less work has been carried out concerning longer run fluctuations relevant to the present models. A relatively successful approach found in dealing with the latter has been the theory of stock adjustment, the supply of storage variant working especially well. Price theory, as inventory theory, must consider a wider range of influences such as market psychology and information, speculation and futures trading, and the composition of the market in terms of the variety of participants.

Complete Commodity Models

As far as complete commodity models are concerned, recent advances center about methods that can be used to estimate not only nonlinear or simultaneous models but also dynamic models, with possible application to systems formulated in continuous time. Commodity models can also be considered beyond an equilibrium framework and developed as process models, trade models, spatial equilibrium models, industrial dynamics models, or general systems models.

Yet there are a number of important problems still to be solved. The most critical of these concerns the gap that exists between the realities of commodity markets and the simplified model descriptions one adopts. Our ability to relate a basic commodity model to other economic and social forces, though improved when taking a systems approach, cannot fully cope with the problem that the structure underlying commodity models changes frequently or that many variables behave stochastically. Also, methods of estimation such as those mentioned above do not work well when a model embodies several complexities all at once, such as nonlinearities, distributed lags, and autocorrelation. Several ways of dealing with these difficulties might be further development of fixed point iterative estimation procedures, extensions of simulation analysis, or applications of control theory. In particular, the latter approach is likely to prove effective in dealing with cross-temporal feedbacks or structural changes.

The problem of inadequate data is a persistent one in commodity model building. We have mentioned the need to increase the quality and quantity of data, especially with respect to accounting systems which include inventory records. As important is the need for data to extend over longer periods of time as well as over shorter data intervals. One means for coping with the commodity modeling problem of short data series or too few degrees of freedom is to use instrumental variables such as can be found in the two stage principal components approach. While most of the data used does emanate from collected series rather than actually controlled experimental design, our ability to deal with such data using the new estimation procedures and missing data algorithms has improved. There is no way that one can deal with the substantial amount of commodity data withheld because of suspicion or secrecy, except to convince private and government statisticians of the overall benefits to be gained from publishing such data.

In further increasing model realism, one problem just beginning to receive attention concerns describing markets of a noncompetitive nature such as monopoly or oligopoly. One approach mentioned has been to formulate the price relationship contained in a noncompetitive model on the basis of the profit maximizing conditions relevant to the market. The possibility also exists of experimenting with different forms of noncompetitive market structures using a simulation modeling approach.

Applying Commodity Models

That commodity models are being applied to new and different situations today underscores the extent to which their use has increased and improved. At first, the goals of commodity model building were historical explanation or prediction. Typical studies included determining how past behavior of a market would have changed given a different set of policies such as those related to price stabilization; predictions also have been made to help optimize purchases for inventories or to evaluate potential investments in commodity production. However, the application of commodity models to policy questions is now being interpreted within the context of welfare analysis. The policy simulation approach can provide the decision maker with different market outcomes based on alternative policies and different courses of action so that he can choose the policies which optimize his goals.

As far as future applications are concerned, the policy simulation approach can be employed with commodity models to provide policy information for use in rate making by federal regulatory agencies. It can also be applied to formulate a commodity model within the context of a systems or sectoral model for use in development planning. With the commodity model cast into a systems framework, development can not only be linked to the growth of one or a group of commodities but commodity activity can also be related to the overall economy or general development goals.[1]

The interconnection of a commodity model with social and biological systems could be of much value in ecological studies attempting to optimize the use of natural resource commodities. Simulations pertaining to control theory could also help us to learn how to better regulate the prices and utilization of these commodities. A final possible application extends to simulation of international markets, especially to determine the impact on country welfare of international business cycles or of inflation and changes in exchange rates.

Since the most difficult aspect of commodity model application is convincing decision makers that model output can reduce uncertainty and enhance their ability to forecast outcomes, further work is needed to demonstrate the validity and worth of these models. For a start, one could better define validation in terms of analytical as compared to simulation model solutions. Another approach would be to consider validation in three distinct stages: determination of model consistency, comparison of model outcomes with those of other models, and evaluation of the model from the point of view of its effectiveness in decision making.[2] And of course, one needs the experience of commodity models operated over the long run. Only a few commodity models have been operated for as long as four or five years, and learning how well these models have predicted in view of structural changes and other difficulties would add to our confidence.

The Future

Econometric commodity models have worked reasonably well given the quality of presently available data as well as the use of techniques similar to those embodied in the nonlinear dynamic models considered here. In as far as the quality of data concerning international commodity markets is not likely to increase substantially in the near future, the methods and developments presented should provide a sound foundation or at least a "tool box" for improving existing commodity models and for constructing additional ones. With respect to domestic commodity markets, however, the quality of data constantly is improving and this enables us to better describe market behavior. Accordingly, theories and methods must be developed and advanced beyond the level found here. Only then will policy analysis be able to include the range of variables and functional relationships necessary to deal with real world complexities. It is hoped that this study will provide a basis from which the necessary advances can be made.

Appendixes

Appendix A

Stability Conditions for First and Higher Order Systems

A first step towards defining the requirements for system stability is to distinguish between a causal system

$$y = f[t - t_0, \overline{Y}(t_0)] \qquad \text{(A.A.1)}$$

and a historical system

$$y = f[t, t_0, \overline{Y}(t_0)] \qquad \text{(A.A.2)}$$

The solution of a causal system is dependent only on the initial conditions (starting values for the variables) and the time that has elapsed since the initial conditions were imposed. A solution to a historical system, on the other hand, is dependent on the exact historical time when the initial conditions were imposed. Our present concern is with a model of the following form related to the historical system

$$F^i[Y_1^t(t) \ldots Y_n^t(t), t] = 0 \qquad \text{(A.A.3)}$$

with initial conditions $(Y_1^{t_0} \ldots Y_n^{t_0})$ such that

$$F^i[Y_1^{t_0} \ldots Y_n^{t_0}, t] \equiv 0 \qquad \text{(A.A.4)}$$

Samuelson defines the stability conditions for such a model in terms of its reaching stationary equilibrium, $Y^0(t) = Y^0$ representing the final equilibrium position.[1] A system is said to be stable if for any $E > 0$ there exists t^0 such that

$$|Y^i(t) - Y^0| < E \text{ for } t > t^0 \qquad \text{(A.A.5)}$$

First Order Systems

These properties and definitions can now be applied to determine the stability conditions of the structural form of a commodity model given by equation 7.8.

$$\Gamma Y_t + \beta_1 Y_{t-1} + \beta_2 X_t = U_t \qquad \text{(A.A.6)}$$

First consider the structural form as a deterministic or exact system so that $U_t = 0$. The corresponding reduced form

$$Y_t = \pi_1 Y_{t-1} + \pi_2 X_t \qquad \text{(A.A.7)}$$

can be considered as a system of first order nonhomogeneous difference equations.

The complete solution to a system of difference equations is $Y_t = \bar{Y} + v_t$, the sum of the particular solution and the homogeneous solution. The $\bar{Y}_t$ vector is the equilibrium value of Y_t derived from the final form, The v_t are deviations from the equilibrium values. To find the particular solution $\bar{Y}_t$, assume $\bar{Y}_t = Y_t = Y_{t-1}$, and $X_t = \bar{X}_t$ such that

$$\bar{Y}_t = (I - \pi_1)^{-1} \pi_2 \bar{X}_t \qquad \text{(A.A.8)}$$

which is the specific case of the final form

$$Y_t = \sum_{\tau=0}^{\infty} \pi_1^{\tau} \pi_2 X_{t-\tau}$$

If $(I - \pi_1)^{-1}$ exists, stability depends on the homogeneous part of the complete solution. The final form can now be extended beyond the particular solution to include the complete solution.

$$Y_t = \pi_1^t Y_0 + \sum_{\tau=0}^{t-1} \pi_1^{\tau} \pi_2 X_{t-\tau} \qquad \text{(A.A.9)}$$

It would be appropriate to simplify the solution by using the deviation $v_t = Y_t - \bar{Y}_t$ and assuming $X_t - \bar{X} = 0$ for all t. Substituting $v_t = \pi_1^t \hat{Y}_0$, the complete solution reduces to

$$Y_t = (I - \pi_1)^{-1} \pi_2 \bar{X}_t + \pi_1^t Y_0 \qquad \text{(A.A.10)}$$

For stability, it is necessary for $\pi_1^t \to 0$ as $t \to \infty$. Only then will Y_t approach $(I - \pi_1)^{-1} \pi_2 \bar{X}_t$ as $t \to \infty$.

Since π_1 is generally a square nonsymmetric matrix, we need a convenient matrix form so it is clear what occurs to π_1^t as $t \to \infty$.[2] This can be done by letting

$$\pi_1 = P \Lambda P^{-1} \qquad \text{(A.A.11)}$$

where Λ is a diagonal matrix of the eigen values or characteristic roots of π_1, i.e., the λ_i. The convenience of this form is that

$$\pi_1^t = P \Lambda^t P^{-1} \qquad \text{(A.A.12)}$$

So if $\Lambda^t \to 0$ as $t \to \infty$, then so will π_1.

The interpretation of the λ_i is quite straightforward. Since the complete solution becomes

$$Y_t = (I - \pi_1)^{-1}\pi_2 \overline{X}_t + P\Lambda^t P^{-1} Y_0 \qquad \text{(A.A.13)}$$

the homogeneous solution will continually grow if any of the $|\lambda_i|$ are greater than 1. Also, if any of the λ_i are complex conjugates in the form $\lambda_i = a_i \pm b_i i$, then $|Z_i| = |(a_i^2 + b_i^2)^{1/2}| > 1$ for stability. The values of Y_t will asymptotically approach $(I - \pi_1)^{-1}\pi_2 \overline{X}_t$ whenever the λ_i are positive and less than one. Oscillating values of Y_t (which alternate between being greater than $(I - \pi_1)^{-1} \pi_2 \overline{X}_t$ and less than it) will occur if the λ_i are either complex or negative.

In a practical sense, we can extract the eigen values or characteristic roots by solving $|I - \pi_1|$ for the λ_i. With a π_1 of dimension 3×3 or less, this could be done by hand, but it is a relatively easy chore to obtain the characteristic roots by computer methods. Stability conditions can then be determined by applying the above rules.

Higher Order Systems

Consider the reduced form of a higher order equation.[3]

$$Y_t = \pi_{11} Y_{t-1} + \pi_{12} Y_{t-2} + \cdots + \pi_{1p} Y_{t-p} + \pi_2 X_t \qquad \text{(A.A.14)}$$

The order of this equation is the highest lag of endogenous variables, p. We now enlarge the system A.A.14 by p vector identities

$$
\begin{aligned}
Y_t &= \pi_{11} Y_{t-1} + \pi_{12} Y_{t-2} + \cdots + \pi_{1p} Y_{t-p} + \pi_2 X_t \\
Y_{t-1} &= Y_{t-1} \\
Y_{t-2} &= \qquad\qquad\quad Y_{t-2} \\
&\ \ \vdots \\
Y_{t-p+1} &= \qquad\qquad\qquad\qquad\qquad\quad Y_{t-p+1}
\end{aligned}
$$

which when condensed becomes

$$\hat{Y}_t = \hat{\pi}_1 \hat{Y}_{t-1} + \pi_2 X_t \qquad \text{(A.A.15)}$$

with $\hat{\pi}_1$ given by

$$
\hat{\pi}_1 = \begin{bmatrix}
\pi_{1,1} & \pi_{1,2} & \cdots & \pi_{1,p-1} & \pi_{1,p} \\
I & 0 & \cdots & 0 & 0 \\
0 & I & \cdots & 0 & 0 \\
0 & 0 & \cdots & 0 & 0 \\
0 & 0 & \cdots & I & 0
\end{bmatrix}
$$

The endogenous variable vector is now

$$Y_t = \begin{bmatrix} Y_t \\ Y_{t-1} \\ \vdots \\ Y_{t-p+1} \end{bmatrix}$$

and the lagged endogenous vector is

$$Y_{t-1} = \begin{bmatrix} Y_{t-1} \\ Y_{t-2} \\ \vdots \\ Y_{t-p} \end{bmatrix}$$

The equation A.A.15 can now be treated as a first order system and solved as before to yield:

$$\hat{Y}_t = \hat{\pi}_1^{p+1} \hat{Y}_{t-p-1} + \sum_{\tau=0}^{p} \hat{\pi}_\tau^1 \pi_2 X_t \qquad \text{(A.A.16)}$$

The stability conditions stated above are applicable to this solution.

Appendix B

Spectral Validation of Commodity Models

The usefulness of performing spectral analysis of data prior to specifying econometric commodity models has been proposed by Labys and Granger.[1] Spectral analysis of the output of such models also can be useful. In particular, it offers several advantages for model validation.[2] First, the information content of spectral analysis is greater than that of the sample means and sample variances associated with point error measures. Second, spectral analysis overcomes the problems of analyzing data that are highly autocorrelated, a phenomenon which invalidates the applicability of classical statistical criteria. Thirdly, examining the spectrum of the simulated series yields information about the dynamic behavior of a model that cannot be obtained in forecast error measures. Finally, spectral analysis permits the construction of confidence bands so that alternative policy decisions can be evaluated by comparing the spectra of the estimated data that conform to the respective alternatives.

In terms of applicability, the spectral approach is most useful for linear or (linearized) nonlinear models which are stochastic and econometrically derived. It also works equally well over the sample or post-sample period, the only reservation for any application being that the output data are of sufficient length and are convertible to a nonstationary form.[3] Of the principal variants of this approach which have been applied to commodity models, these are identified first with the work of Howrey and Witherell, and second with that of Naylor, Wertz, and Wonnacott.

Howrey and Witherell refer to their method of spectral validation as the *spectrum matrix* approach.[4] That is, the internal consistency or dynamic properties of a commodity model can be determined by forming the spectrum matrix of the final form of the model. While the definition and meaning of the final form can be found in Chapter 8, a further requirement of this approach is that the final form be expressed as a rational lag function (operator) of the endogenous and exogenous variables of the model and its structural errors.[5] This would demand that the model defined by 8.1 be rewritten as

$$\sum_{i=0}^{\gamma} \Gamma_i Y_{t-i} + \beta X_t = U_t \qquad \text{(A.B.1)}$$

where $\Gamma_{i=0}$ is a $G \times G$ nonsingular matrix of coefficients of the current endogenous variables, Γ_i are $G \times G$ matrices of coefficients of lagged endogenous variables with a maximum lag of γ, and β is a $G \times M$ matrix of coefficients of the exogenous variables. Y_t, X_t and U_t are as previously given. The introduction of the rational lag operator defined by $LY_t = Y_{t-1}$ results in the following expression

$$\Gamma(L)Y_t = -\beta X_t + U_t \qquad \text{(A.B.2)}$$

251

where $\Gamma(L)$ is the polynomial operator

$$\Gamma(L) = \sum_{i=0}^{\gamma} \Gamma_i L^i \qquad (A.B.3)$$

The final form of A.B.2 which corresponds to the previous form 8.6 can now be written as

$$\Delta(L)IY_t = -g(L)\beta X_t + g(L)U_t \qquad (A.B.4)$$

where $\Delta(L)$ and $g(L)$ are related through the characteristic matrix given by $g(\lambda)F(\lambda) = \Delta(\lambda)I$, and I is a $G \times G$ identity matrix. The solution to the final form is obtained by considering it as a system of linear difference equations with constant coefficients

$$IY_t = K\Lambda^t - \frac{g(L)}{\Delta(L)}\beta X_t + \frac{g(L)}{\Delta(L)}U_t \qquad (A.B.5)$$

where K is a $G \times r$ matrix of constants, and Λ is a vector containing the r characteristic roots of the determinental equation given by

$$\Delta(\lambda) = \delta_0 + \delta_1\lambda + \cdots + \delta_t\lambda^t = 0$$

The first term of equation A.B.5 contains the characteristic roots which explain the stability of the exact part of the model. The second term reflects the influence of the exogenous variables in the form of dynamic multipliers. The final term, representing the vector of the random errors, is the stochastic component to which spectral analysis can be applied to complete the description of the model, Dhrymes[6] has observed that the stochastic component may be divided into a component corresponding to the random process associated with the exogenous variables and a component associated with the structural errors. To simplify the presentation here, only the structural errors are considered.

The stochastic component of the estimated endogenous variables can be observed using *analytical simulation.*[7] Assuming the component to be co-

$$Y_t = \frac{g(L)}{\Delta(L)}U_t \qquad (A.B.6)$$

variance stationary and the model to be stable, Y_t can be described as being generated by a multivariate stationary stochastic process. Recalling the definition of the spectrum given in Chapter 5, the spectrum representation of the stochastic component is

$$Y_t = \frac{g(L)}{\Delta(L)} \int_{-\pi}^{\pi} e^{i\omega t} \, dU(\omega) \qquad \text{(A.B.7)}$$

where $dU(\omega)$ is the kernel of the vector process U_t. To derive the corresponding spectrum matrix, it is necessary to introduce the concept of the transfer matrix $T(\omega)$ obtained by operating on $e^{i\omega t}$ with $\frac{g(L)}{\Delta(L)}$. Since $dY(\omega) = T(\omega) \, dU(\omega)$, the spectrum matrix can be defined by

$$F(\omega) = T(\omega)f(\omega)T^*(\omega) \qquad -\pi < \omega < \pi \qquad \text{(A.B.8)}$$

where $f(\omega)$ is the spectral matrix of the disturbance process. The power spectra of the endogenous variables can be found in the main diagonal of this matrix and the cross-spectra in the off–diagonal elements. Following the assumption that the error process is serially uncorrelated with a contemporaneous variance–covariance matrix Σ, the spectrum matrix can be stated more concisely as

$$F(\omega) = \frac{1}{2\pi} T(\omega)\Sigma T^*(\omega) \qquad \text{(A.B.9)}$$

since in this case $f(\omega) = 1/2\pi\Sigma$. Each element of this matrix gives the squared amplitude or power for a particular endogenous variable as a function of the angular frequency ω.

Examining the power spectra generated from the wool model suggests that commodity models are likely to generate spectra having more diverse shapes than those generated by macroeconometric models.[8] The typical spectral shape which has been specified by Granger appears in the wool study only for the major wool production variables.[9] An inverted typical spectral shape is found for some of the inventory variables and the wool price variable, and a number of consumption variables displayed a U-shaped spectrum. When the frequency characteristics of these spectra are compared to what might be expected on the basis of actual behavior of the variables, a degree of correspondence is found.

The approach taken by Naylor, Wertz, and Wonnacott differs from the above in two respects.[10] First, spectral analysis is performed with the power spectra derived explicitly from data generated by computer simulation experiments. Second, besides interpreting the basic spectra, a number of other tests are proposed. These include: (1) use of simultaneous confidence bands to compare the spectra obtained from simulated data with the corresponding theoretical or true spectra; (2) use of simultaneous confidence bands to compare the spectra of the endogenous variables generated by different computer runs; and (3) use of spectral analysis to calculate the total variance of different series and use of confidence intervals to compare the variance of those series.

The theoretical basis for the direct determination of the spectrum follows from the definition of Chapter 5

$$f(\omega_j) = \frac{1}{2\pi} \sum_{v=-T+1}^{T-1} k(v)R(v)\cos(v\omega_j) \qquad \text{(A.B.10)}$$

where $j = 0, 1, 2, \ldots, m$ is the number of frequency bands to be estimated. Applying confidence bands to discriminate between spectra requires that one define the theoretical or true spectrum as

$$\Phi(\omega_j) = \frac{\sigma_u^2}{T^2} \qquad 0 < \omega < \pi \qquad \text{(A.B.11)}$$

where σ_u^2 is the variance associated with the stochastic error U_t and $T = 1 + a_1 e^{i\omega} + a_2 e^{-2i\omega}$ with parameters a_1 and a_2. If the theoretical spectrum is reasonably smooth, the distribution of $f(\omega_j)/\Phi(\omega_j)$ is approximately χ_k^2 with $k = 2n/m$ degrees of freedom where n is the number of related observations. The confidence bands for $\Phi(\omega_j)$ defined at the 95 percent confidence interval are given by

$$Pr\left[\frac{f(\omega_j)}{\chi_{.025,k}^2/K} < \Phi(\omega_j) < \frac{f(\omega_j)}{\chi_{.975,k}^2/K}\right] = 0.95 \qquad \text{(A.B.12)}$$

The comparison of two spectra utilizing the definition of the confidence interval can be achieved by deriving an F (variance-ratio) statistic of the form

$$F_{k_1\,k_2} = \frac{R_j}{P_j} = \frac{f_1(\omega_j)/\Phi_1(\omega_j)}{f_2(\omega_j)/\Phi_2(\omega_j)} \qquad \text{(A.B.13)}$$

where $R_j = f_1(\omega_j)/f_2(\omega_j)$; $P_j = \Phi_1(\omega_j)/\Phi_2(\omega_j)$; and $k_1 = k_2 = 2m/n$ is the degrees of freedom for each of the two χ_k^2 variates. The desired set of simultaneous confidence bands which would be associated with the 95 percent confidence levels are defined as

$$Pr\left[\frac{R_j}{F_{.001,k_1,k_2}} < P_j < \frac{R_j}{F_{.999,k_1,k_2}}\right] = 0.95 \qquad \text{(A.B.14)}$$

If the two spectra are identical, then $P = \Phi_1(\omega)/\Phi_2(\omega) = 1$.

Interpreting simultaneous confidence bands is such that two spectra representing different series will be significantly similar if the graph of the horizontal line defined by $P = 1$ falls within the set of corresponding bands. All the tests utilizing simultaneous confidence bands as outlined above were performed only in an exploratory study involving the Samuelson–Hicks multiplier–accelerator model.[11] Tests performed with an econometric commodity textile model were limited to utilizing confidence bands to compare spectra of actual and simulated series for the major endogenous variables.[12] Results reported for apparel demand, textile mill products output, textile mill products demand, and investment indicated significant differences between the spectra of actual and simulated series. Furthermore, these differences could be confined to the higher frequency components of the spectra with the simulated values corresponding closely to the actual values in the low frequencies. Only the textile price variable spectra proved to be significantly different throughout the full frequency range.

We can conclude that spectral analysis while not providing a complete measure of validation does yield objective results in evaluating the evolutionary paths followed by the endogenous variables. However, further work is necessary in attempting to validate a model by comparing the spectrum implied by a model to the spectrum estimated directly from the data. Since the spectrum implied by the model depends on the coefficients of the model as well as the cross–spectral matrix of the disturbance process, there is presently no way of determining exactly whether the differences between the model spectrum and the data spectrum result from the coefficients or the disturbance process.

An Inventory of Commodity Models

The following list includes commodity models of an equilibrium, process, trade, industrial dynamics, or systems nature whose description has been published in some form. Several models presently under construction are not reported. Only a few of the models included are fragmentary in the sense, for example, of assuming supply to be exogenous rather than including explicit supply equations. While these models could have been discarded, they have been retained to provide a broader view of modeling activities.

Aluminum

Rasche, R. H. "Forecasts and Simulations with an Econometric Model of the Aluminum Market," Special Report. Wharton Economic Forecasting Associates. Philadelphia, 1970.

Schlager, K. J. "A Systems Analysis of the Copper and Aluminum Industries: An Industrial Dynamics Study." Unpublished M. S. thesis. Massachusetts Institute of Technology, 1961.

Apples

Brandow, G. E. "A Statistical Analysis of Apple Supply and Demand." Penn State Agricultural Economic and Rural Sociology Report 2, University Park, Pa., 1956.

Bananas

Aggrey-Mensah, W. "A Study of the Sydney Banana Market and of Potential Benefits to Producers of Supply Control." Unpublished Ph.D. Dissertation, University of New England, Australia, 1970.

Beef

Langemeier, L., and R. G. Thompson. "Demand, Supply, Price Relationships for the Beef Sector, Post W.W.II Period." *Journal of Farm Economics* (Feb. 1967): 169–183.

Sohn, H. K. "A Spatial Equilibrium Model of the Beef Industry in the U.S." Unpublished Ph.D. Dissertation, University of Hawaii, 1970.

Also see *Livestock*; *Meat*.

Broilers

Lee, T. C., and S. K. Seaver. *A Positive Spatial Equilibrium Model of Broiler Markets: A Simultaneous Equation Approach.* Storrs Agricultural Experiment Station Bulletin No. 417. University of Connecticut, Storrs, 1972.

Fisher, M. "A Sector Model—The Poultry Industry of the U.S." *Econometrica* 26 (1958): 37–66.

Cobalt

Burrows, James C. *Cobalt: An Industry Analysis.* Lexington, Mass.: D. C. Heath and Co., 1971.

Cocoa

Goreux, Louis, M. "Price Stabilization Policies in World Markets for Primary Commodities: An Application to Cocoa." Mimeographed. International Bank for Reconstruction and Development, January 1972.

Kofi, Tetteh A. "International Commodity Agreements and Export Earnings: Simulation of the 1968 Draft International Cocoa Agreement." *Food Research Institute Studies* 11 (1972).

Weymar, F. Helmut. *The Dynamics of the World Cocoa Market.* Cambridge, Mass.: The M.I.T. Press, 1968.

Mathis, Kary. *An Economic Situation Model of the Cacao Industry of the Dominican Republic.* International Programs Info. Rep. No. 69–2, Department of Agricultural Economics and Sociology, Texas A & M University, 1969.

Coconuts

Labys, W. C. *An Econometric Model of the International Lauric Oils Market: Considerations for Policy Analysis.* UNCTAD/CD/Misc.43/Rev.1, UNCTAD, Geneva, 1971.

Librero, Aida R. "The International Demand for Philippine Coconut Products: An Aggregate Analysis." *The Philippine Economic Journal* 10 (1971): 1–22.

Coffee

Bacha, E. L. "An Econometric Model for the World Coffee Market: The Impact of Brazilian Price Policy." Unpublished Ph.D. dissertation, Yale University, 1968.

Epps, Mary Lee S. "A Computer Simulation Model of the World Coffee Economy." Unpublished Ph.D. dissertation, Duke University, 1970.

Wickens, M., Greenfield, J., and G. Marshall. *A World Coffee Model.* CCP.71/W.P.4, Food and Agricultural Organization of the United Nations, Rome, 1971.

Copper

Ballmer, R. W. "Copper Market Fluctuations: An Industrial Dynamics Study." Unpublished M.S. thesis, Massachusetts Institute of Technology, 1960.

Banks, F. E. *An Economic and Econometric Analysis of the World Copper Market.* Cambridge, Mass.: Ballinger Publishing Co., forthcoming.

Behrman, Jere R. "Forecasting Properties and Prototype Simulation of a Model of the Copper Market." Special Report. Wharton Economic Forecasting Associates, Philadelphia, 1972.

Ertek, Tumay, "World Demand for Copper, 1948–63: An Econometric Study." Unpublished Ph.D. dissertation, University of Wisconsin, 1967.

Fisher, F. M., Cootner, P. H., and M. Baily. "An Econometric Model of the World Copper Industry." *Bell Journal of Economics and Management Science* 3 (Autumn 1972): 568–609.

Mahalingsivam, Rasiah. "Market for Canadian Refined Copper: An Econometric Study." Unpublished Ph.D. dissertation, University of Toronto, 1969.

Cotton

Kolbe, H., and H. Timm. *Die Bestimmungsfaktoren der Preisentwicklung auf dem Weltmarkt fur Baumwolle: Eine Okonometrische Modellanalyse.* NR 4, HWWA–Institut fur Wirtschaftsforschung, Hamburg, July 1971.

Dairy

Rojko, A. S. *The Demand and Price Structure for Dairy Products*. Technical Bulletin No. 1168, United States Department of Agriculture, Washington, D.C., 1957.

Wilson, R. R., and R. G. Thompson. "Demand, Supply and Price Relationships for the Dairy Sector—Post–W.W. II. Period." *Journal of Farm Economics* 49 (May 1967): 360–371.

Eggs

Gerra, M. J. *The Demand, Supply and Price Structure for Eggs*. Technical Bulletin 1204, U.S. Department of Agriculture, Washington, D.C. 1959.

Judge, George G. *A Spatial Equilibrium Model for Eggs*. Competitive Position of the Connecticut Poultry Industry, No. 7, Conn. Agricultural Experiment Station Bulletin No. 318, Storrs, 1956.

Roy, Sujit. "Econometric Models for Predicting Short Run Egg Prices." Mimeographed. Pennsylvania State University, University Park, Pa., 1971.

Fats and Oils

Armore, Sidney J. *The Demand and Price Structure for Food Fats and Oils*. Tech. Bulletin No. 1068, Economic Research Service, U.S. Department of Agriculture, Washington, D.C., 1953.

Drake, A. E., and V. I. West. *Econometric Analysis of the Edible Fats and Oils Economy*. University of Illinois Agricultural Experiment Station Bull. No. 695, Urbana, 1963.

Also see *Lauric Oils; Soybeans*.

Feed

Dawson, J., and Alvin C. Egbert. "The Demand for Feed Concentrates: A Statistical Analysis." *Agricultural Economic Research* 17 (April 1965).

Foote, R. J., Klein, J. W., and M. Clough. *The Demand and Price Structure for Corn and Total Feed Concentrates*. Technical Bulletin 1061, Economic Research Service, United States Department of Agriculture, Washington, D.C. 1952.

King, G. A. *The Demand and Price Structure for By-Product Feeds*. Technical Bulletin 1183, U.S. Department of Agriculture, Washington, D.C., 1958.

Fertilizer

Bell, D. M., Henderson, D. R., and G. R. Perkins. *A Simulation Model of the Fertilizer Industry in the United States: With Special Emphasis on Fertilizer Distribution in Michigan.* Agricultural Economics Report No. 189, Department of Agricultural Economics at Michigan State University and Marketing Economics Division, Economic Research Service, U.S. Department of Agriculture, Washington, D.C., 1972.

Fish

Farrell, Joseph E., and Harlan C. Lampe. *The New England Fishing Industry: Functional Markets for Finned Food Fish, I and II.* Agricultural Experiment Station Bulletins No. 379 and 380, University of Rhode Island, Kingston, 1965.

Gas (Natural)

Khazzoom, Daniel J. "The FPC Staff's Econometric Model of Natural Gas Supply in the United States." *Bell Journal of Economics and Management Science* 2 (Spring 1971): 51–93.

Gold

Michalopoulos, C. S., and R. C. Van Tassel. "The Commercial Demand for Gold." *Western Ecomonic Journal* 1971.

Grain

Leath, M. N., and L. V. Blakley. *An Interregional Analysis of the U.S. Grain Marketing Industry, 1966–67.* Technical Bulletin No. 1444, Economic Research Service, United States Department of Agriculture, Washington, D.C., 1971.

Meinken, K. W. *The Demand and Price Structure of Oats, Barley and Soybean Grain.* Technical Bulletin No. 1080, United States Department of Agriculture, Washington, D.C., 1953.

Rojko, A. S., Urban, F. S., and J. J. Naive. *World Demand Prospects for Grain in 1980.* Foreign Agricultural Report No. 75, Economic Research Service, United States Department of Agriculture, Washington, D.C., 1971.

Also see *Feed; Livestock; soybeans; wheat.*

Hides

Cohen, Kalmen. *A Computer Model of the Shoe, Leather and Hide Sequence.* Ph.D. dissertation, Carnegie Institute of Technology, Englewood Cliffs, N.J.: Prentice-Hall, 1960.

Singh, B. "An Econometric Study of Raw Materials in International Trade— A Case Study of Hides and Skins." Unpublished Ph.D. dissertation, University of Pennsylvania, 1971.

Hogs

Harlow, Arthur A. *Factors Affecting the Price and Supply of Hogs.* Tech. Bulletin No. 1068, Economic Research Service, U.S. Department of Agriculture, Washington, D.C., 1962.

Harlow, Arthur, A. "A Recursive Model of the Hog Industry." *Agricultural Economic Research* 14 (1962).

Leuthold, Raymond M. "An Analysis of Daily Fluctuations in the Hog Economy," *American Journal of Agricultural Economics* 5 (Nov. 1969) 849–865.

Meadows, D. L. *Dynamics of Commodity Production Cycles.* Cambridge, Mass.: Wright-Allen Press, 1970.

Zellner, Jr. R. E. "A Simultaneous Equation Analysis of Selected Terminal Hog Markets." Unpublished Ph.D. Dissertation, University of Mississippi, 1971.

Also see *Livestock; meat.*

Iron Ore

Margueron, C. "A Quantitative Analysis of the Supply-Demand Patterns in Iron Ore: The Future Possibilities of Brazil." Unpublished Ph.D. Dissertation, Columbia University, 1972.

Lauric Oils (Coconuts, Copra, Palm Kernels)

Labys, W. C. *An Econometric Model of the International Lauric Oils Market: Considerations for Policy Analysis.* UNCTAD/CD/Misc. 43/Rev.1, UNCTAD Geneva, 1971.

Livestock

Crom, R. J., and W. R. Maki. "A Dynamic Model of a Simulated Livestock–Meat Economy." *Agricultural Economic Research* 17 (1965).

Egbert, A. C., and S. Reutlinger. "A Dynamic Model of the Livestock–Feed Sector." *Journal of Farm Economics* 47 (Dec. 1965): 1288–1305.

Filippello. Nicholas A. *A Dynamic Econometric Investigation of the Japanese Livestock Economy.* Unpublished Ph.D. dissertation, University of Missouri, Columbia, Dec. 1967.

Foote, R. J. "A Four–Equation Model of the Feed Livestock Economy and Its Endogenous Mechanism." *Journal of Farm Economics* 35 (1953): 44–61.

Fox, Karl A. "A Spatial Equilibrium Model of the Livestock–Feed Economy in the United States," *Econometrica* 21 (1953): 547–566.

Hayanga, M. L., and D. Hacklander. "Monthly Supply—Demand Relationships for Fed Cattle and Hogs." *American Journal of Agricultural Economics* 52 (Aug. 1970): 535–544.

Hildreth, C., and F. J. Jarrett. *A Statistical Study of Livestock Production and Marketing.* New York: John Wiley and Sons, 1955.

Kost, W. E. "Trade Flows in the Grain Livestock Economy of the EEC." Unpublished Ph.D. dissertation, Michigan State University, 1971.

Kulshreshtha, S. N., and A. G. Wilson. "An Open Econometric Model of the Canadian Beef Cattle Sector." *American Journal of Agricultural Economics* 54 (Feb. 1972): 84–91.

Nores, Gustavo, A. "Structure of the Argentine Beef Cattle Economy: A Short Run Model, 1960–1970." Unpublished Ph.D. dissertation, Purdue University, 1972.

Maki, W. R. "Forecasting Livestock Prices and Supply with an Econometric Model." *Journal of Farm Economics* 45 (1963): 1670–1674.

Also see *Beef; Feed; Hogs; Meat.*

Lumber

Adams, F. Gerard, and J. Blackwell. *An Econometric Model of the U.S. Forest Products Industry.* Discussion Paper No. 207, Department of Economics, University of Pennsylvania, Philadelphia, 1971.

Gregory, Robinson B. "Estimating Wood Consumption with Particular Reference to the Effects of Increased Wood Availability." *Forest Science* 12 (March 1966).

McKillop, W. L. M. "Supply and Demand for Forest Products—An Econometric Study." *Hilgardia* 38 (1967): 1–132.

Machinery

Beek, F. V. "An Econometric Model of International Trade in Machinery and Equipment." Unpublished Ph.D. dissertation, University of Maryland, 1969.

Meat

Chetwin, John A. "A Model of the United Kingdom Wholesale Meat Market." Mimeographed. Lincoln College, New Zealand, 1965.

Crom, Richard. *A Dynamic Price-Output Model of the Beef and Pork Sectors.* Technical Bulletin No. 1426, Economic Research Service, U.S. Department of Agriculture, Washington, D.C., 1970.

Faure, H. "Étude Econometrique de la Demande de Viande." *Annal du Credoc* (1967): 3–26.

Fuller, W. A., and G. W. Ladd. "A Dynamic Quarterly Model of the Beef and Pork Economy." *Journal of Farm Economics* 43 (1961): 797–812.

Haimerl, Johann. *A Blockrecursive Structural Model of the Cattle, Beef and Veal Market in West Germany.* Sonderhelt 41, Agrarwirtschaft, A. S. Verlag, Hannover, 1970.

Myers, L. H., Havlicek, J., and P. L. Henderson. *Short Term Price Structure of the Hog-Pork Sector of the U.S.* Purdue University Agricultural Experiment Station Bulletin No. 855, Lafayette, Indiana, 1970.

Wallace, T. D., and G. G. Judge. *Econometric Analysis of the Beef and Pork Sectors of the Economy.* Oklahoma State University Technical Bulletin T-75, Stillwater, Oklahoma, 1959.

Yandle, Christopher A. *A Model of the New Zealand Domestic Market for Meat.* Technical Paper No. 7, Agricultural Economics Research Unit, Lincoln College, Canterbury, New Zealand, 1969.

Multicommodity

Alm, H., Duloy, J., and O. Gulbrandsen. *Agricultural Prices and the World Food Economy.* Institute for Economics and Statistics, University of Uppsala, March 1969.

Cromarty, William A., "An Econometric Model for United States Agriculture." *Journal of the American Statistical Association* 54 (1959): 556–574.

Egbert, Alvin C. "An Aggregate Model of Agriculture, Empirical Estimates and Some Policy Implications." *American Journal of Agricultural Economics* 51 (Feb. 1969): 71–86.

Evans, M. K. "An Agricultural Submodel for the U.S. Economy." In *Essays in Industrial Economics—Vol. II*, L. R. Klein (Ed.). Philadelphia: Wharton School of Finance and Commerce, 1969.

Food and Agricultural Organization of the United Nations. "A World Price Equilibrium Model." Projections Research Working Paper No. 3., CCP.72/W.P.3, Rome, 1972.

McFarquhar, A. M., Mitter, S., and G. Evans. "A Computable Model for Projecting U.K. Food and Agriculture." In A. M. McFarquhar, *Europe's Food and Agriculture*. A Comparison of Models for Projecting Food Consumption and Agricultural Production in Western European Countries to 1972 and 1975. Amsterdam: North–Holland Publishing Co., 1971.

Organization for Economic Cooperation and Development. "Agricultural Projections for 1980—A Trial Study for Japan." Mimeographed. OECD, Paris, 1971.

Roy, D. E., "An Econometric Simulation Model of U.S. Agriculture with Commodity Submodels." Unpublished Ph.D. dissertation, Iowa State University, 1972.

Wang, Kung Lee, and R. G. Kokat. *An Inter–Industry Structure of the U.S. Mining Industries*. Information Circular 8338, Bureau of Mines, U.S. Department of the Interior, Washington, D.C., 1967.

Newsprint

Gillion, C. *Newspapers and the Demand for Newsprint*. Research Paper No. 2, Economic Contract Unit, New Zealand, Institute of Economic Research, Wellington, 1969.

Olive Oil

Al-Zand, Osama A. "Olive Oil Trade and Trade Policies in the Mediterranean Region." Unpublished Ph.D. dissertation, University of Minnesota, St. Paul, 1968.

Onions

Suits, Daniel, B. and S. Koizumi. "The Dynamics of the Onion Market." *Journal of Farm Economics* 38 (1956): 475–484.

Oranges (Frozen Concentrated Orange Juice)

Dean, Gerald W., and Collins, Norman R. *World Trade in Fresh Oranges: An Analysis of the Effect of EEC Tariff Policies.* Giannini Foundation Monograph No. 18, California Agricultural Experiment Station, Berkeley, Jan. 1967.

Raulerson, Richard C., and M. R. Langham. "Evaluating Supply Control Policies for Frozen Concentrated Orange Juice with an Industrial Dynamics Model." *American Journal of Agricultural Economics* 52 (1970): 197–208.

Rausser, Gordon C. "A Dynamic Econometric Model of the California-Arizona Orange Industry," Unpublished Ph.D. dissertation, University of California, Davis, 1971.

Peanuts

Mehta, V. "India's Position in the World Peanut and Peanut Oil Markets." Unpublished Ph.D. Dissertation, North Carolina State University, Raleigh, 1972.

Song, Inbum. "Demand Characteristics for Peanuts and the Impact of a Direct Price Support Program on Farm Income, Government Cost and Peanut Consumption." Unpublished Ph.D. dissertation, Oklahoma State University, 1970.

Petroleum

Adams, F. G., and James M. Griffin. *An Econometric-Linear Programming Model of the U.S. Petroleum Industry.* Discussion Paper No. 193, Department of Economics, University of Pennsylvania, Philadelphia, Sept. 1970.

Adams, F. G., and James M. Griffin. "An Econometric Model of the United States Petroleum Refining Industry." In *Essays in Industrial Econometrics— Vol. I,* L. R. Klein (Ed.). Philadelphia: Wharton School of Finance and Commerce, 1969.

Mitchell, A. "The Demand for Texas Refined Petroleum Products: A Study in Econometrics." Unpublished Ph.D. dissertation, University of Texas, Austin, 1972.

Pharmaceuticals

Tsurumi, H., and Y. Tsurumi. *An Oligopolistic Model of a Japanese Pharmaceutical Company.* Discussion Paper No. 22, Queens University, Kingston, Ontario, 1970.

Phosphate

Hee, Olman. *A Statistical Analysis of the U.S. Demand for Phosphate Rock, Potash, and Nitrogen.* Information Circular 8418, Bureau of Mines, U.S. Department of the Interior, Washington, D.C., 1969.

Pork Bellies

Foote, R. J., Craven, John A., and Robert R. Williams, Jr. "Pork Bellies: Quarterly 3-Equation Models Designed to Predict Cash Prices." Mimeographed, Texas Tech. University, 1971.

Zusman, P. "Econometric Analysis of the Market for California Early Potatoes." *Hilgardia* 33 (Dec. 1962): 539–668.

Rice

Nasol, R. L. "Demand Analysis for Rice in the Philippines." *Journal of Agricultural Economics and Development* (1971): 1–13.

Holder, Shelby, Jr., Shaw, D. L., and J. C. Snyder. *A Systems Model of the U.S. Rice Industry.* Technical Bulletin No. 1453, Economic Research Service, U.S. Department of Agriculture, Washington, D.C., 1970.

Rubber

Behrman, Jere, R. "Econometric Model Simulations of the World Rubber Market," in *Essays in Industrial Economics—Vol. III*, L. R. Klein (Ed.). Philadelphia, Wharton School of Finance and Commerce, 1971.

Cheong, T. "An Econometric Model of the Malayan Rubber Industry," Unpublished Ph.D. dissertation, London School of Economics and Political Science, 1972.

Teken, I. B. "Supply of and Demand for Indonesian Rubber." Unpublished Ph.D. dissertation, Purdue University, 1971.

Kolbe, H., and Timm, H. *Die Bestimmungsfaktoren der Preisentwicklung auf dem Weltmarkt für Naturkautschuk: Eine Ökonometrische Modellanalyse.* NR 10, HWWA-Institut für Wirtschaftsforschung, Hamburg, June 1972.

Horowitz, Ira. "An Econometric Analysis of Supply and Demand in the Synthetic Rubber Industry." *International Economic Review* 4 (September 1963).

Shrimp

Gillespie, E. C., Hite, J. S., and J. S. Lytle. *An Econometric Analysis of the U.S. Shrimp Industry.* South Carolina Agriculture Experiment Station, Bulletin No. 2, Clemson, 1969.

Silver

Burrows, J. C., Hughes, W., and J. Valette. *An Economic Analysis of the Silver Industry.* Lexington, Mass.: D. C. Heath and Co., Forthcoming.

Soybeans (Oil, Meal)

Free, Joe W. *The Future of the South in the Soybean Processing Industry, 1970–1975.* Bulletin No. 168, Southern Cooperative Series, Tennessee Valley Authority, November 1971.

Houck, J. P., and J. S. Mann. *An Analysis of Domestic and Foreign Demand for U.S. Soybeans and Soybean Products.* Technical Bulletin No. 265, University of Minnesota Agricultural Experiment Station, 1968.

Houck, J. P., Ryan, M. E., and A. Subotnik. *Soybeans and their Products: Markets, Models and Policy.* Minneapolis: University of Minnesota Press, 1972.

Matthews, J. L., A. W. Womack, and R. G. Hoffman. "Formulation of Market Forecasts for the U.S. Soybean Economy with an Econometric Model." *Fats and Oils Situation* 260 (Nov. 1971): 26–31.

Vandenborre, R. J. *Econometric Analysis of Relationships in the International Vegetable Oil and Meal Sector.* Agricultural Economics Experiment Station Bulletin, No. 106, University of Illinois, Urbana–Champaign, 1970.

Steel

Van Beeck, J. G. "An Econometric Model of Steel Prices in the E.E.C." Mimeographed. Central Planning Bureau, The Hague, 1972.

Friden, L. "Instability of World Trade in Steel: A Study of Price and Quantity Fluctuations, 1953–1968." Mineographed. Institute for International Economic Studies, Stockholm, Sweden, 1969.

Higgins, Christopher I. "An Econometric Description of the U.S. Steel Industry." In *Essays in Industrial Economics—Vol. II,* L. R. Klein (Ed.). Philadelphia, Wharton School of Finance and Commerce, 1969.

Mo, W. Y., and Kung Lee Wang. *A Quantitative Economic Analysis and Long-Run Projections of the Demand for Steel Mill Products.* Information Circular 8451, Bureau of Mines, U.S. Department of the Interior, Washington, D.C., 1970.

Watanabe, T., and S. Kinoshita. "An Econometric Study of the Japanese Steel Industry." Discussion Paper No. 155, Harvard Institute of Economic Research, Cambridge, Mass.: 1970.

Sugar

Bates, Thomas, H., and Schmitz, Andrew. *A Spatial Equilibrium Analysis of the World Sugar Economy.* Gianini Foundation Monograph No. 23, California Agricultural Experiment Station, Berkeley, May 1969.

Tewes, T. "Sugar: A Short-Term Forecasting Model for the World Market, with a Forecast of the World Market Price for Sugar in 1972–1973." *The Business Economist* 4 (Summer 1972): 89–97.

Wymer, C. R. "Estimation of Continuous Time Models with an Application to the World Sugar Market." Mimeographed. London School of Economics and Political Science, 1972.

Sulfur

Hee, Olman. "Industrial Demand for Sulfur and Alternative Inputs." Mimeographed, Bureau of Mines, U.S. Department of the Interior, Washington, D.C., February 1972.

Tea

Murti, V. N. *An Econometric Study of the World Tea Economy 1948–1961.* Unpublished Ph.D. dissertation, University of Pennsylvania, 1961.

Textiles

Den Hartog, H., and M. Fraenkel. "An Econometric Model of the Textile and Clothing Industries in the Netherlands." Mimeographed, Central Planning Bureau, The Hague, 1972.

Miller, Roger L. *A Short Term Econometric Model of Textile Industries.* Discussion Paper No. 118, Institute for Economic Research, University of Washington, Seattle, 1971.

Naylor, T. H., Wallace, W. H., and W. E. Sasser. "A Computer Simulation Model of the Textile Industry." *Journal of the American Statistical Association* 62 (1967): 1338–1364.

Tin

Desai, M. "An Econometric Model of the World Tin Economy, 1948–1961." *Econometrica* 34 (Jan. 1966): 105–134.

Tobacco

Vernon, J., Rives, N., and T. H. Naylor. "An Econometric Model of the Tobacco Industry." *Review of Economics and Statistics* 51 (May 1969): 149–157.

Tung Oil

Matthews, J. L., and W. A. Womack. "An Economic Appraisal of the U.S. Tung Oil Economy." *Southern Journal of Agricultural Economics* (Dec. 1970): 161–168.

Tungsten

Burrows, James C. *Tungsten: An Industry Analysis.* Lexington, Mass.: D.C. Heath and Co., 1971.

Turkeys

Bawden, D. Lee, Carter, H. O., and G. W. Dean. "Interregional Competition in the United States Turkey Industry." *Hilgardia* 37 (June 1966): 1–95.

Vegetables

Shuffett, Milton D. *The Demand and Price Structure for Selected Vegetables.* Technical Bulletin No. 1105, United States Department of Agriculture, Washington, D.C., 1954.

Tramel, Thomas E., and A. D. Seale, Jr. "Reactive Programming of Supply and Demand Relations—Application to Fresh Vegetables." *Journal of Farm Economics* 41 (Dec. 1959): 1012–1022.

Watermelon

Suits, D. "An Econometric Analysis of the Watermelon Market." *Journal of Farm Economics* 37 (1955): 237–251.

Wheat

Hoyt, R. C. "A Dynamic Econometric Model of the Milling and Baking Industries." Unpublished Ph.D. dissertation, University of Minnesota, 1972.

Meinken, K. W. *The Demand and Price Structure for Wheat.* Technical Bulletin No. 1136. United States Department of Agriculture, Washington, D.C., 1955.

Mo, Y. *An Economic Analysis of the Dynamics of the United States Wheat Sector.* Technical Bulletin No. 1395, United States Department of Agriculture, Washington, D.C., 1968.

Vannerson, F. L. "An Econometric Analysis of the Postwar U.S. Wheat Market." Unpublished Ph.D. dissertation, Princeton University, 1969.

Wine

Labys, W. C. "Preliminary Results for an Econometric Simulation Model of the International Wine Market." Mimeographed. Graduate Institute of of International Studies, Geneva, 1973.

Wool

Duane, P. "Analysis of Wool Price Fluctuations: An Economic Analysis of Price Formation in a Raw Materials Market." Unpublished Ph.D. dissertation, North Carolina State University, Raleigh, 1971.

Durbin, S. I. "A Sample Wool Marketing Simulation Model." Unpublished M.Sc. thesis, Massey University, New Zealand, 1969.

McKenzie, C. J. "Quarterly Models of Price Formation in the Raw Wool Market." Unpublished M.Sc. thesis, Lincoln College, Canterbury, New Zealand, 1966.

Witherell, William H. *Dynamics of the International Wool Market: An Econometric Analysis*. Research Memorandum No. 91, Princeton University, Econometric Research Program, 1967.

Bibliography

Demand

Ayanian, Robert. "A Comparison of Barten's Estimated Demand Elasticities With Those Obtained Using Frisch's Method." *Econometrica* 37 (1969): 79–94.

Balestra, Pietro, and Nerlove, Marc. "Pooling Cross Section and Time Series Data in the Estimation of a Dynamic Model: The Demand for Natural Gas." *Econometrica* 34 (July 1966): 585–612.

*Ball, R. J., and Marwah, K. "The U.S. Demand for Imports, 1948–1958." *Review of Economics and Statistics* 44 (Nov. 1962): 395–401.

*Banks, F. "An Econometric Note on the Demand for Refined Zinc." *Zeitschrift für Nationalokonomie* 31 (1971): 105–134.

Bannerji, H. "Analysis of Import Demand." *Artha Vijnana* 1 (Sept. 1959): 259–270.

Barten, A. P. "Consumer Demand Function Under Conditions of Almost Additive Preferences." *Econometrica* 32 (1964): 1–38.

Barten, A. P. "Estimating Demand Equations." *Econometrica* 36 (1968): 213–251.

Barten, A. P. "Evidence on the Slutsky Conditions for Demand Equations." *Review of Economics and Statistics* 49 (1967): 77–83.

Barten, A. P., and Turnovsky, S. J. "Some Aspects of the Aggregation Problem for Composite Demand Equations." *International Economic Review* 7 (1966): 231–259.

Brandow, G. E. *Interrelations Among Demands for Farm Products and Implications for Control of Market Supply.* Pennsylvania Agriculture Experiment Station, Bulletin 680, University Park, 1961.

Brown, T. M. "Habit Persistence and Lags in Consumer Behavior." *Econometrica* 20 (1952): 1–26.

Burk, Marguerita G. "Development of a New Approach to Forecasting Demand." *Journal of Farm Economics* 46 (Aug. 1964): 618–682.

*Byron, R. P. "The Restricted Aitken Estimation of Sets of Demand Relations." *Econometrica* 38 (1970): 816–830.

Choudry, N. K. "An Econometric Analysis of the Import Demand Function for Burlap (Hessian) in the U.S.A., 1919–1953." *Econometrica* 26 (July 1958): 416–428.

Coffin, H. G. "An Econometric Analysis of Import Demand for Wheat and Flour in World Markets." Unpublished Ph.D. dissertation, University of Connecticut, 1970.

---

* Items marked with an asterisk have been quoted in this study.

*Court, R. H. "Utility Maximizations and the Demand for New Zealand Meats." *Econometrica* 35 (1967): 424–446.

Court, L. M. "Entrepreneurial and Consumer Demand Theories for Commodity Spectra." *Econometrica* 9 (1941): 135–162.

Cramer, J. S. "A Dynamic Approach to the Theory of Consumer Demand." *Review of Economic Studies* 24 (1957): 73–86.

DaCosta, G. C. "Elasticities of Demand for Indian Exports—An Emprical Investigation." *Indian Economic Journal* 13 (July–Sept. 1965): 41–54.

Daly, Rex. "The Long-Run Demand for Farm Products." *Agricultural Economics Research* 8 (1956): 73–91.

DeJanvry, A. C. *Measurement of Demand Parameters Under Separability.* Unpublished Ph.D. dissertation, University of California, Berkeley, 1966.

*Dhrymes, P. J., and Mitchell, B. M. "The Econometrics of Dynamic Demand Models." Paper presented at the meetings of the American Economics Association, Detroit, Dec. 1970.

Farrell, M. J. "Irreversible Demand Functions." *Econometrica* 20 (1952): 171–186.

Farrell, M. J. "The New Theories of the Consumption Function." *Economic Journal* 69 (1959).

Ferguson, C. E. and Polasek, M. "The Elasticity of Import Demand for Raw Apparel Wool in the United States." *Econometrica* 30 (Oct. 1962): 670–685.

Foote, R. J. *Analytical Tools for Studying Demand and Price Structure.* Agricultural Handbook No. 146, Economic Research Service, U.S. Department of Agriculture, Washington, D.C., 1958.

Foote, R. J., and Fox, K. A. *Analytical Tools for Measuring Demand.* Agriculture Handbook No. 64, Economic Research Service, U.S. Department of Agriculture, Washington, D.C., 1954.

*Fox, K. A. *Econometric Analysis for Public Policy.* Ames: The Iowa State Press, 1958.

Foytik, J. "Characteristics of Demand for California Plums." *Hilgardia* 20 (1951): 407–527.

Frisch, R. "A Complete Schema for Computing all Direct and Cross-Demand Elasticities in a Model with Many Sectors." *Econometrica* 27 (1959): 177–196.

George, P. S. "Measurement of Demand for Food Commodities in the United States." Unpublished Ph.D. thesis, Department of Agricultural Economics, Univ. of California, Davis, 1969.

George, P. S., and King, G. A. *Consumer Demand for Food Commodities in the United States With Projections to 1980.* Giannini Foundation Monograph No. 26. Berkeley, Calif., March 1971.

Gerra, M. J. *The Demand, Supply, and Price Structure for Eggs.* Techn. Bulletin No. 1204, Economic Research Service, U.S. Department of Agriculture, Washington, 1959.

Girschick, M. A., and Haavelmo, T. "Statistical Analysis of the Demand for Food: Examples of Simultaneous Equations in Structural Equations." *Econometrica* 15 (1947): 79–110.

Goldman, S. M., and Uzawa, H. "A Note on Separability in Demand Analysis." *Econometrica* 25 (1957): 387–398.

Goodwin, J. W., Andorn, R., and Martin, J. E. "The Irreversible Demand Function." University of Oklahoma Agricultural Experiment Station Bulletin No. T.127, Norman, 1968.

*Griliches, Zvi. "Hybrid Corn: An Exploration in the Economics of Technological Change." *Econometrica* 25 (Oct. 1957): 501–522.

Harberger, A. C. "A Structural Approach to the Problem of Import Demand." *American Economic Review* 63 (May 1953): 148–160.

Harmston, F. K. and Hino, H. "An Intertemporal Analysis of the Nature of Demand for Food Products." *American Journal of Agricultural Economics* 52 (Aug. 1970): 381–386.

Heien, D. M. "Structural Stability and the Estimation of International Import Price Elasticities." *Kyklos* 21 (1968): 695–711.

Holmes, R. A. *Estimation of Demand Elasticities for Substitute Foods.* Agricultural Economics Research Council of Canada, Ottawa, 1966.

Holmes, R. A. "Combining Cross-Section and Time-Series Information on Demand Relationships for Substitute Goods." *American Journal of Agricultural Economics* 50 (1968): 56–65.

*Houck, J. P. "A Look at Flexibilities and Elasticities." *Journal of Farm Economics* 48 (May 1966): 225–232.

*Houck, J. P. "The Relationship of Direct Price Flexibilities to Direct Price Elasticities." *Journal of Farm Economics* 47 (Aug. 1965): 789–792.

Houck, J. P. "A Statistical Model of the Demand for Soybeans." *Journal of Farm Economics* 46 (May 1964): 366–374.

Houthakker, H. S. "New Evidence on Demand Elasticities." *Econometrica* 33 (1965): 272–288.

*Houthakker, H. S., and Magee, S. P. "Income and Price Elasticities in World Trade." *Review of Economics and Statistics* 51 (May 1969): 111–125.

*Houthakker, H. S., and Taylor, L. D. *Consumer Demand in the United States: 1929-1970.* Cambridge, Mass.: Harvard University Press, 1966.

Islam, N. "Experiments in Econometric Analysis of an Import Demand Function." *Pakistan Economic Journal* 11 (Sept. 1961): 21-38; 11 (Dec. 1961): 1-19.

Kaliski, S. F. "Some Recent Estimates of the Elasticity of Demand for British Exports—An Appraisal and Reconciliation." *Manchester School* 39 (Jan. 1961): 23-42.

Kemp, M. C. "Errors of Measurement and Bias in Estimates of Import Demand Parameters." *Economic Record* 38 (Sept. 1962): 396-372.

Kemp, M. C. *The Demand for Canadian Imports 1926-1955.* Toronto. University of Toronto Press, 1962.

Koo, A. Y. C. "Marginal Propensity to Import as a Forecaster." *Review of Economics and Statistics* 64 (May 1962): 215-217.

*Koyck, L. M. *Distributed Lags and Investment Analysis.* Amsterdam: North–Holland Publishing Co., 1954.

Krause, L. B. "United States Imports, 1947-1958." *Econometrica* 30 (April 1962): 221-238.

Kreinin, M. E. "United States Imports and Income in the Postwar Period." *Review of Economics and Statistics* 62 (May (1960): 223-225.

*Kreinin, M. E. "Price Elasticities in International Trade." *The Review of Economics and Statistics* 49 (Nov. 1967): 579-582.

Ladd, G. W., and Martin, J. E. *Application of Distributed Lag and Auto-correlated Error Models to Short-Run Demand Analysis.* Iowa Agricultural Experiment Station Research Bulletin 526. Ames, 1964.

Ladd, G. W., and Tedford, J. R. "A Generalization of the Working Method for Estimating Long-Run Elasticities." *Journal of Farm Economics* 41 (1959): 221-233.

*Leamer, Edward E., and Stern, R. M. *Quantatitive International Economics.* Boston: Allyn and Bacon, Inc., 1970.

*Learn, E. W. "Estimating Demand for Livestock Products at the Farm Level." *Journal of Farm Economics* 38 (Dec. 1956): 1483-1491.

Manderscheid, L. V. "Some Observations on Interpreting Measured Demand Elasticities." *Journal of Farm Economics* 46 (Feb. 1964): 128-136.

*Maki, W. R. "Economic Effects of Short-Run Changes in the Demand for Livestock." *Journal of Farm Economics* 39 (Dec. 1957): 1670-1674.

*Mansfield, Edwin. *The Economics of Technological Change.* New York: W. W. Norton and Co., 1968.

Martin, J. E. "Isolation of Lagged Economic Responses." *Journal of Farm Economics* 49 (Feb. 1967): 160–169.

Mattei, Aurelio. "A Complete System of Dynamic Demand Functions." *European Economic Review* 2 (1971): 251–276.

McLemore, Dan L. "Wholesale Demand Functions for Fresh Peaches in Twenty-three Markets." Unpublished Ph.D. dissertation, Clemson University, 1971.

Meinken, D. W. *et al.* "Measurement of Substitution in Demand for Time-Series Data: Synthesis of Three Approaches." *Journal of Farm Economics* 38 (August 1956): 711–735.

Moore, L. "Factors Affecting the Demand for British Exports." *Bulletin of Oxford University Institute of Economics and Statistics* 25 (1963): 343–359.

Morgan, D. J., and Corlett, W. J. "The Influence of Price in International Trade: A Study in Method." *Journal of the Royal Statistical Society* Series A, Part III (1951): 307–358.

Morrissett, Irving. "Some Recent Uses of Elasticity of Substitution—A Survey." *Econometrica* 21 (1953): 41–62.

*Nerlove, Marc. "Distributed Lags and Estimation of Long-Run Supply and Demand Elasticities: Theoretical Considerations." *Journal of Farm Economics* 40 (May 1958): 301–311.

*Nerlove, Marc. *Distributed Lags and Demand Analysis.* Agricultural Handbook No. 141, Economic Research Service, U.S. Department of Agriculture, Washington, D.C., 1958.

*Nerlove, Marc. "Estimates of Elasticities of Selected Agricultural Commodities." *Journal of Farm Economics* 37 (1956): 496–509.

*Nyberg, Albert, J. "The Demand for Lauric Oils in the United States." *American Journal of Agricultural Economics* 52 (Feb. 1970): 97–120.

*Orcutt, G. H. "Measurement of Price Elasticities in International Trade." *Review of Economics and Statistics* 32 (May 1950): 117–132.

Organization for Economic Co-operation and Development, Department of Economics and Statistics. "Statistical Import Functions and Import Forecasting: An Empirical Study of Import Determination in Seven Member Countries." DES/NI/F(66)4, Paris, October 1966.

Parks, Richard W. "Systems of Demand Equations: An Empirical Comparison of Alternative Functional Forms." *Econometrica* 37 (1969): 629–650.

Pasour, E. C., and Schrimper, R. A. "The Effect of Length of Run on Measured Demand Elasticities." *Journal of Farm Economics* 47 (Aug. 1965): 774–788.

Pjarnanson, H. F., McGarry, M. J., and Schmitz, A. "Converting Price Series of Internationally Traded Commodities to a Common Currency Prior to Estimating National Demand and Supply Equations." *American Journal of Agricultural Economics* 51 (Feb. 1969): 189–192.

*Polasek, M., and Powell, A. "Wool versus Synthetics: An International Review of Innovation in the Fibre Market." *Australian Economic Papers* 3 (June–December 1966): 49–64.

Powell, Alan. "A Complete System of Consumer Demand Equations for the Australian Economy Fitted by a Model of Additive Preferences." *Econometrica* 34 (July 1966): 661–675.

Prais, S. J. "Econometric Research in International Trade: A Review." *Kyklos* 15 (1962): 560–579.

Preeg, E. H. "Elasticity Optimism in International Trade." *Kyklos* 20 (1967): 460–469.

Prest, A. R. "Some Experiments in Demand Analysis." *Review of Economics and Statistics* 31 (1949): 33–49.

Purcell, J. C., and Raunikar, R. "Price Elasticities from Panel Data: Meat, Poultry and Fish." *American Journal of Agricultural Economics* 53 (May 1971): 216–221.

Rao, S. V. "Elasticities of Demand for Imports During the Period 1920–21 to 1929–1930. *Artha Vijnana* 2 (Dec. 1960): 307–312.

Reimer, R. "The United States Demand for Imports of Materials." *Review of Economics and Statistics* 46 (Feb. 1964): 65–75.

Rojko, A. S. "Time-Series Analysis in Measurement of Demand." *Agriculture Economics Research* 13 (1961): 37–54.

*Schultz, Henry. *The Theory and Measurement of Demand*. Chicago: University of Chicago Press, 1938.

Scott, M. F. *A Study of United Kingdom Imports*. Cambridge, Eng.: Cambridge University Press, 1963.

Simon, Julian L. "The Price Elasticity of Liquor in the United States and a Simple Method of Determination." *Econometrica* 34 (1966): 193–205.

*Stanton, B. F. "Seasonal Demand for Beef, Pork and Broilers." *American Economic Review* 51 (Jan. 1961): 1–14.

*Stone, Richard. *The Measurement of Consumers' Expenditure and Behavior in the United Kingdom, 1920–1938*. Cambridge, Eng.: Cambridge University Press, 1954.

Strotz, R. H. "The Empirical Implications of a Utility Tree." *Econometrica* 25 (1957): 269–280.

Swamy, D. S. "A Quarterly Econometric Model of Demand for and Supply of Exports." *Indian Economic Review* 1 (April 1966): 79–103.

Theil, H. "The Information Approach to Demand Analysis." *Econometrica* 33 (Jan. 1965): 67–87.

Tolley, G. S., Wang, Y. and Fletcher, R. G. "Re-examination of the Time-Series Evidence on Food Demand." *Econometrica* 37 (Oct. 1969): 695–705.

*Tomek, W. G. "Changes in Price Elasticities of Demand for Beef, Pork, and Broilers." *Journal of Farm Economics* 47 (Aug. 1965): 793–802.

*Tomek, W. G., and Cochrane, W. W. "Long-Run Demand: A Concept, and Elasticity Estimates for Meat." *Journal of Farm Economics* 43 (Aug. 1962): 717–730.

Turnovsky, S. J. "International Trading Relationships of a Small Country: The Case of New Zealand." *Canadian Journal of Economics* 1 (Nov. 1968): 772–790.

Wegge, L. "The Demand Curves From a Quadratic Utility Indicator." *Review of Economic Studies* 35 (1968): 209–224.

*Wold, H., and Jureen, L. *Demand Analysis.* New York: John Wiley and Sons, 1953.

Working, E. J. "What Do Statistical Demand Curves Show?" *Quarterly Journal of Economics* 41 (1927): 212–235.

Wu, De-Min. "An Empirical Analysis of Household Durable Goods Expenditure." *Econometrica* 33 (1965): 761–780.

Yeh, Martin H., and Heady, E. O. "National and Regional Demand Functions for Fertilizer." *Journal of Farm Economics* 41 (1959): 332–348.

Supply

*Abel, Martin E. "Analysis of Seasonal Variation with an Application to Hog Production." *Journal of the American Statistical Association* (1962): 655–667.

*Abeywardena, V. "Forecasting Coconut Crops Using Rainfall Data—A Preliminary Study." *Ceylon Coconut Quarterly* 19 (1968): 161–176.

Akerman, G. "The Cobweb Theorem: A Reconsideration." *Quarterly Journal of Economics* 71 (Feb. 1957): 151–160.

*Ady, Peter. "Supply Functions in Tropical Agriculture." *Oxford University Institute of Statistics Bulletin* 30 (1968): 157–188.

*Arak, Marcelle. "The Price Responsiveness of Sao Paolo Coffee Growers." *Food Research Institute Studies* 3 (1968): 211–223.

Arak, Marcelle. "The Supply of Brazilian Coffee." Unpublished Ph.D. dissertation, Department of Economics, Massachusetts Institute of Technology, 1966.

*Batemen, Merrill J. "Supply Relations for Perennial Crops in the Less Developed Areas." In *Subsistence Agriculture and Economic Development.* Edited by C. R. Wharton, Jr. Chicago: Aldine Press, 1969.

*Bateman, Merrill J. "Aggregate and Regional Supply Functions of Ghanian Cocoa (1956–1962)." *Journal of Farm Economics* 47 (1965): 384–401.

Bateman, Merrill. J. "Cocoa in the Ghanian Economy." Unpublished Ph.D. dissertation, Department of Economics, Massachusetts Institute of Technology, 1965.

Bauer, P. T., and Yamey, B. S. "A Case Study of Response to Price in an Underdeveloped Country." *The Economic Journal* 69 (December 1959).

Bean, L. H. "The Farmers' Response to Price." *Journal of Farm Economics* 11 (July 1929): 368–385.

*Behrman, J. R. *Supply Response in Underdeveloped Agriculture: A Case Study of Four Major Annual Crops in Thailand, 1937–1963.* Amsterdam: North–Holland Publishers, 1968.

*Bermeister, C. A. "Cycles in Cattle Numbers." *The Livestock and Meat Situation* (March 1949).

Bostwick, D. "Yield Probabilities as a Markov Process." *Agricultural Economies Research* 14 (1962).

Breimyer, H. F. "Emerging Phenomenon; A Cycle in Hogs." *Journal of Farm Economics* 41 (Nov. 1959): 760–768.

*Breimyer, H. F. "Observations on the Cattle Cycles." *Agricultural Economics Research* 7 (Jan. 1955): 1–10.

Buchman, Kenneth L. "The Analysis of Changes in Agricultural Supply: Problems and Approaches." *Journal of Farm Economics* 42 (Aug. 1960): 531–551.

*Chan, F. "A Preliminary Study of the Supply Response of Malayan Rubber Estates Between 1948 and 1959." *Malayan Economic Review* 7 (Oct. 1962): 77–94.

Cingolini, Giorgio. "Analysis of the Dynamics of Tree-Fruit Acreage in California's Central Valley." Unpublished Ph.D. dissertation, University of California at Berkeley, 1970.

Coase, R. H., and Fowler, R. F. "The Analysis of Producers' Expectations." *Economica* 7 (Aug. 1940): 280–292.

Cochrane, Willard W. "Conceptualizing the Supply Relation in Agriculture." *The Journal of Farm Economics* 27 (Dec. 1955): 1161–1176.

Dean, E. *The Supply Responses of African Farmers: Theory and Measurement in Malawi.* Amsterdam: North–Holland, 1966.

Dean, G. W., and Heady, E. O. "Changes in Supply Response and Elasticity for Hogs." *Journal of Farm Economics* 50 (Nov. 1958): 845–860.

Est, Vincent I. "Supply Functions Estimated in Demand Studies." *Agricultural Supply Functions.* E. O. Heady (Ed.). Ames: Iowa State University Press, 1961.

Etherington, W. "An Econometric Analysis of Small-Holder Tea Growing in Kenya." Unpublished Ph.D. dissertation, Stanford University, 1971.

*Ezekiel, M. "The Cobweb Theorem." *Quarterly Journal of Economics* 52 (Feb. 1938): 255–280.

Falcon, W. P. "Farmer Response to Price in an Underdeveloped Area— A Case Study of West Pakistan." Unpublished Ph.D. dissertation, Dept. of Economics, Harvard University, 1962.

Farnsworth, H. C., and Jones, W. O. "Response of Wheat Growers to Price Changes." *Economic Journal* 66 (June 1956): 271–287.

*Fisher, Franklin, M., and Temin, Peter. "Regional Specialization and the Supply of Wheat in the United States, 1867–1914." *Review of Economics and Statistics* 52 (May 1970): 134–149.

*French, Ben C., and Bressler, R. G. "The Lemon Cycle." *Journal of Farm Ecomonics* 44 (Nov. 1962): 1021–1036.

*French, Ben C., and Matthews, J. L. "A Supply Response Model for Perennial Crops." *American Journal of Agricultural Economics* 53 (Aug. 1971): 478–490.

Goldberger, Arthur S. "The Interpretation and Estimation of Cobb–Douglas Functions." *Econometrica* (July–Oct. 1968): 464–472.

*Goodwin, R. M. "Dynamical Coupling With Special Reference to Markets having Production Lags." *Econometrica* 15 (1947): 181–204.

Gwyer, G. D. "Perennial Crop Supply Response: The Case of Tanzinian Sisal." Agrarian Development Studies Report No. 3. Wye College, Ashford, Kent, 1971.

Harlow, A. A. "The Hog Cycle and the Cobweb Theorem." *Journal of Farm Economics* 42 (Nov. 1960): 842–853.

*Heady, E. O., and Dillon, J. L. *Agricultural Production Functions.* Ames: The Iowa State University Press, 1961.

Jones, G. T. "The Response of the Supply of Agricultural Products in the United Kingdom to Price." *The Farm Economist* 10 (Jan. 1962): 1–28.

*Kehrberg, Earl W. "Determination of Supply Functions from Cost and Production Functions." *Agricultural Supply Functions.* Edited by E. O. Heady *et al.* Ames: The Iowa State University Press, 1961, pp. 139–151.

*Knight, Dale A. "Evaluation of Time Series as Data for Estimating Supply Parameters." *Agricultural Supply Functions.* Edited by E. O. Heady *et al.* Ames: The Iowa State University Press, 1961, pp. 74–107.

*Kohl, R. L., and Paarlberg, D. "The Short Time Response of Agricultural Production to Price and Other Factors." Purdue University Agri. Expt. Sta. Bul. No. 555, October 1950.

*Labys, W. C. "A Lauric Oil Exports Model Based on Capital Stock Supply Adjustment." *Malayan Economic Review* XVIII (April 1973), No. 1.

*Larson, A. B. "The Hog Cycle as Harmonic Motion." *Journal of Farm Economics* 46 (May 1964): 357–386.

Levhari, David L., and Sheshinski, Eytan. "A Microeconomic Production Function." *Econometrica* (May 1970): 559–573.

Lorie, J. G. "Causes of Annual Fluctuations in the Production of Livestock and Livestock Products." *Journal of Business* 20 (April 1947): Part 2.

Maki, W. R. "Decomposition of the Beef and Pork Cycles." *Journal of Farm Economics* 44 (Aug. 1962): 731–743.

Malecky, J. M. "A Study of Supply Relationships in the Australian Sheep and Wool Industry." Wool Economic Research Report No. 19. Canberra, Australia, 1971.

Mubyarto, R. "The Elasticity of the Marketable Surplus of Rice in Indonesia: A Study in Java–Madura." Unpublished Ph.D. dissertation, Iowa State University, 1965.

*Nerlove, Marc. *The Dynamics of Supply: Estimation of Farmers Response to Price.* Baltimore: The Johns Hopkins Press, 1958.

Nerlove, Marc. "Time-Series Analysis of the Supply of Agricultural Products." *Agricultural Supply Functions.* Edited by E. O. Heady, *et al.* Ames: The Iowa State University Press, 1961.

Nerlove, Marc. "Estimates of the Elasticities of Supply of Selected Agricultural Commodities." *The Journal of Farm Economics* 37 (1956): 286–301.

Nerlove, Marc. "Adaptive Expectations and Cobweb Phenomena." *Quarterly Journal of Economics* 72 (1958): 227–240.

Nerlove, Marc, and Bachman, K. L. "The Analysis of Changes in Agricultural Supply: Problems and Approaches." *The Journal of Farm Economics* 42 (Aug. 1960): 531–544.

*Nyberg, Albert J. *The Philippine Coconut Industry.* Unpublished Ph.D. dissertation, Cornell University, 1968.

*Oury, Bernard. "Supply Estimation and Productions by Regression and Related Methods." *Economic Models and Quantitative Methods for Recessions and Planning in Agriculture.* Edited by E. O. Heady. Ames: The Iowa State University Press, 1971.

*Oury, Bernard. *A Production Model for Wheat and Feedgrains in France, 1946–1961.* Amsterdam: North-Holland Publishing Co., 1966.

*Rausser, G. C., and Cargill, T. F. "The Existence of Broiler Cycles: An Application of Spectral Analysis." *American Journal of Agricultural Economics* 52 (Feb. 1970): 109–121.

Richter, H. V. "Problems of Assessing Unrecorded Trade." *Bulletin of Indonesian Economic Studies* 6 (March 1970): 45–60.

Schaller, W. N., and Dean, G. W. *Predicting Regional Crop Production: An Application of Recursive Programming.* Technical Bul. No. 1329, U.S. Department of Agriculture, Washington, D.C., 1965.

Schultz, T. W., and Brownlee, O. H. "Two Trials to Determine Expectations Models Applicable to Agriculture." *Quarterly Journal of Economics* 56 (May 1942): 487–496.

*Smith, B. B. *Factors Influencing the Price of Cotton.* Technical Bul. No. 50, U.S. Department of Agriculture, Washington, D.C., 1928.

*Stern, Robert M. "Malayan Rubber Production, Inventory Holdings, and the Elasticity of Export Supply." *The Southern Economic Jornal* 31 (April 1965): 314–323.

Stern, R. M. "The Price Responsiveness of Primary Producers." *The Review of Economics and Statistics* 44 (May 1962): 202–207.

Sturt, Daniel W. "Producer Response to Technological Change in West Pakistan." *Journal of Farm Economics* 47 (August 1965).

*Tobin, B. F., and Aurthur, H. B. *Dynamics of Adjustment in the Broiler Industry.* Boston: Harvard University Press, 1964.

*Walsh, R. M. "Response to Price in Production of Cotton and Cottonseed." *Journal of Farm Economics* 26 (1944): 359–372.

*Waugh, F. W. "Cobweb Models." *Journal of Farm Economics* 46 (Nov. 1964): 732–750.

*Waugh, F., and Miller, M. "Fish Cycles: A Harmonic Analysis." *American Journal of Agricultural Economics* 52 (August 1970): 422–430.

Zarembka, Paul. "On the Empirical Relevance of the CES Production Function." *Review of Economics and Statistics* 52 (Feb. 1970): 47–53

Inventories

*Abramovitz, Moses. *Inventories and Business Cycles*. New York: National Bureau of Economic Research, Inc. 1950.

*Allen, S. G. "Inventory Fluctuations in Flaxseed and Linseed Oil, 1926–1939." *Econometrica* 22 (July 1954): 310–327.

Brennan, M. J. "The Supply of Storage." *American Economic Review* 47 (March 1958): 50–72.

Brennan, M. J. "A Model of Seasonal Inventories." *Econometrica* 27 (April 1959): 228–244.

Clower, R. W. "An Investigation into the Dynamics of Investment." *American Economic Review* 44 (March 1954): 64–81.

Clower, R. W., and Bushaw, D. W. "Price Determination in a Stock-Flow Economy." *Econometrica* 22 (July 1954): 328–343.

Cootner, Paul H. "Common Elements in Futures Markets for Commodities and Bonds." *American Economic Review* 51 (May 1961): 173–183.

Cootner, Paul H. "Returns to Speculators: Telser vs. Keynes." *Journal of Political Economy* 68 (Aug. 1960): 396–404.

Darling, Paul G. "Manufacturers' Inventory Investment, 1947–1958." *American Economic Review* (Dec. 1959): 950–963.

Fujino, Shozaburo. "Some Aspects of Inventory Cycles." *Review of Economics and Statistics* 41 (May 1960).

*Goodwin, Richard M. "Dynamic Coupling with Especial Reference to Markets Having Production Lags." *Econometrica* 15 (July 1947): 181–204.

Goodwin, Richard M. "Secular and Cyclical Aspects of the Multiplier and Accelerator." *Income, Employment and Public Policy: Essays in Honor of Alvin H. Hansen*. New York: W. W. Norton and Co., 1948.

Hochman, E., and Lee, I. M. *Optimal Decision in the Broiler Producing Firm: A Problem of Growing Inventory*. Giannini Foundation Monograph No. 29, Berkeley, Calif., June 1972.

Jorgenson, D. W., and Stephenson, J. A. "Anticipations and Investment Behavior in U.S. Manufacturing, 1947–1960." *Journal of the American Statistical Association* 64 (March 1969): 67–89.

Jorgenson, D. W., and Stephenson, J. A. "The Time Structure of Investment Behavior in United States Manufacturing, 1947–1960." *Review of Economics and Statistics* 49 (Feb. 1967): 16–27.

Klein, L. R. "Stocks and Flows in the Theory of Interest." *Econometrica* 18 (July 1950): 236–241.

*Lovell, Michael. "Manufacturers' Inventories, Sales Expectations, and the Acceleration Principle." *Econometrica* 29 (July 1961): 293–314.

Lovell, Michael C. "Inventories and Stability: An Inter-industry Analysis." Unpublished Ph.D. dissertation, Harvard University, March 1959.

Lovell, Michael C. "Factors Determining Manufacturing Inventory Investment." *Inventory Fluctuations and Economic Stabilization.* Joint Economic Committee, 87th Congress, 1st Session, Washington, D.C., Dec. 1961.

Lovell, Michael C. "Buffer Stocks, Sales Expectations, and Stability: A Multi–Sector Analysis of the Inventory Cycle." *Econometrica* 30 (April 1962).

*Lundberg, Eric. *Studies in the Theory of Economic Expansion.* London: P. S. King and Son, 1937.

*Mack, Ruth P. *Information, Expectations and Inventory Fluctuation.* New York: National Bureau of Economic Research, 1967.

Manne, A. S. "Some Notes on the Acceleration Principle." *Review of Economics and Statistics* 27 (May 1945): 93–99.

*Metzler, Lloyd A. "The Nature and Stability of Inventory Cycles." *Review of Economics and Statistics* 3 (Aug. 1941): 113–129.

Mills, Edwin S. "The Theory of Inventory Decisions." *Econometrica* (April 1957): 222–239.

Mills, Edwin S. "Expectations, Uncertainty and, Inventory Fluctuations." *Review of Economic Studies* (1954–1955): 105–110.

Mills, Edwin S. "Expectations and Undesired Inventory." *Management Science* 3 (Oct. 1957): 105–110.

Morehouse, Strotz, and Horwitz. "An Electro-Analog Method for Investigating Problems in Economic Dynamics: Inventory Oscillations." *Econometrica* 18 (Oct. 1950).

Stanback, Thomas M., Jr. "Cyclical Behavior of Manufacturers' Inventories Since 1945." *Proceedings, Business and Economic Statistics Section, American Statistical Association.* Washington, D.C., 1957, pp. 87–95.

*Weymar, F. Helmut. "The Supply of Storage Revisited." *American Economic Review* 56 (Dec. 1966): 1226–1234.

*Yver, R. E. "The Investment Behavior and the Supply Response of the Cattle Industry of Argentina." Unpublished Ph.D. dissertation, University of Chicago, 1971.

Prices

Abel, M., "Price Discrimination in the World Trade of Agricultural Commodities." *Journal of Farm Economics* 48 (May 1966): 194–208.

Alexander, Sydney S. "Price Movements in Speculative Markets: Trends or Random Walks." *Industrial Management Review* 2 (May 1961): 7–26.

Ashby, A. "On Forecasting Commodity Prices by Balance Sheet Approach." *Journal of Farm Economics* 46 (Aug. 1964): 633–643.

*Barro, Robert J. "A Theory of Monopolistic Price Adjustment." *Review of Economic Studies* 39 (Jan. 1972): 17–26.

Bawden, D. L. "A Spatial Price Equilibrium Model of International Trade." *Journal of Farm Economics* 48 (Nov. 1966): 862–874.

Beckmann, M. J. "On the Determination of Prices in Futures Markets." In *Patterns of Market Behavior*. M. J. Brennan (Ed.). Providence, 1965.

*Behrman, Jere R. "Monopolistic Pricing in International Commodity Agreements: A Case Study of Cocoa." *American Journal of Agricultural Economics* 50 (1968): 702–719.

Berry, J. E., Smith, E. D., and Rudd, R. W. "Pricing in Kentucky Fertilizer Markets." *Journal of Farm Economics* 47 (May 1965): 296–310.

Bieri, J., and Schmitz, A. "Time Series Modeling of Economic Phenomena." *American Journal of Agricultural Economics* 52 (Dec. 1970): 805–813.

Box, G. E. P., and Jenkins, G. M. *Time Series Analysis Forecasting and Control*, San Francisco: Holden-Day, 1970.

Brinegar, C. S. "A Statistical Analysis of Speculative Price Behavior." Ph.D. dissertation, Stanford University, 1954.

Broadbent, E. E., Madsen, A. G., and West, V. I. *Pricing Butcher Hogs at Illinois Country Markets*, University of Illinois Agricultural Experiment Station Bulletin 714, Urbana, 1965.

Buse, R. C., and Brandow, G. E. "The Relationship of Volume, Prices, and Costs to Marketing Margins for Farm Foods." *Journal of Farm Economics* 42 (1960): 362–370.

Caine, Sir Sydney. *Prices for Primary Producers*. London: Institute of Economic Affairs, 1966.

Cootner, P. H. (Ed.). *The Random Character of Stock Market Prices*. Cambridge, Mass.: MIT Press, 1964.

*Cootner, P. H. "Speculation and Hedging." *Food Research Institute Studies*. Special Supplement, 1967.

Daly, R. "Demand for Farm Products at Retail and Farm Level." *Journal of the American Statistical Association* 53 (1958).

Dobson, W. D. "A Model for Evaluating Consequences of Changes in Federal Milk Order Pricing Policies." *American Journal of Agricultural Economics* 52 (Nov. 1970): 599–602.

Doll, J. P., and Chin, S. B. "A Use for Principal Components in Price Analysis." *American Journal of Agricultural Economics* 52 (Nov. 1970): 591–593.

Ehrich, R. L. "Cash-Futures Price Relationships for Live Beef Cattle." *American Journal of Agricultural Economics* 51 (Feb. 1969): 26–39.

*Fishman, G. S. "Price Behavior Under Alternative Forms of Price Expectations." *Quarterly Journal of Economics* 78 (May 1964): 281–298.

Frahm, D. G., and Schrader, L. F. "An Experimental Comparison of Pricing in Two Auction Systems." *American Journal of Agricultural Economics* (Nov. 1970): 528–534.

Gray, Roger W. "Fundamental Price Behavior Characteristics in Commodity Futures." *Futures Trading Seminar*, II. Madison,Wis.:Mimir Publishers, 1963.

Gray, Roger W. "The Search for a Risk Premium." *Journal of Political Economy* 69 (June 1961): 250–260.

*Gray, Roger W. "The Seasonal Pattern in Wheat Futures Prices Under the Loan Program." *Food Research Institute Studies* 3 (Feb. 1962): 21–30.

Griliches, Z. "Hedonic Price Indexes for Automobiles: An Econometric Analysis of Quality Change." In A. Zellner (Ed.). *Readings in Economic Statistics and Econometrics*. Boston: Little, Brown and Co., Inc. 1969. Pp. 103–130.

Hacklander, Duane D. "Price Relationships Among Selected Wholesale Beef and Pork Cuts." Ph.D. dissertation. Michigan State University, 1971.

Hawtrey, R. G. "A Symposium on the Theory of the Forward Market, III." *Review of Economic Studies* 7 (June 1949): 196–205.

Heady, E. O., and Kaldor, D. R. "Expectations and Errors in Forecasting Agricultural Prices." *Journal of Farm Economics* 62 (1954): 34–47.

Hee, O. "Tests for Predictability of Statistical Models." *Journal of Farm Economics* 48 (Dec. 1966): 1479–1484.

Hieronymus, T. A. *Uses of Grain Futures Markets in the Farm Business*. Agricultural Experiment Station Bulletin 696. Urbana: University of Illinois, 1963.

Houck, James P. *Demand and Price Analysis of the U.S. Soybean Market*. Minnesota Agricultural Experiment Station Bulletin No. 244, 1963.

Houck, James P. "The Relationship of Direct Price Flexibilities to Direct Price Elasticities." *Journal of Farm Economics* 46 (Aug. 1964): 789–792.

*Houthakker, H. S. "Systematic and Random Elements in Short Term Price Movements." *Proceedings of the American Economic Association* 51 (May 1961): 164–172.

Houthakker, H. S. "Can Speculators Forecast Prices?" *Review of Economics and Statistics* 39 (1957): 143–151.

Ikerd, J. E., and Cramer, C. L. "A Practical Computer Method for Pricing Pork Carcasses and Hogs." *American Journal of Agricultural Economics* 52 (May 1970): 242–246.

Ikerd, J. E., and Cramer, C. L. "Price Signal Refraction in Pork Processing." *American Journal of Agricultural Economics* 50 (May 1968): 224–231.

Irwin, H. S. "Seasonal Cycles in Aggregates of Wheat Futures Contracts." *Journal of Political Economy* 43 (1935): 278–288.

Johnson, D. Gale. *Forward Prices for Agriculture.* Chicago: University of Chicago Press, 1947.

Judge, G. G., Havlicek, J., and Rizek, R. L. "An Interregional Model: Its Formulation and Application to the Livestock Industry." *Agricultural Economic Research* 17 (Jan. 1965).

Judge, G. G., and Wallace, T. D. "Estimation of Spatial Price Equilibrium Models." *Journal of Farm Economics* 40 (Nov. 1958): 801–820.

Kapur, G. P. "Prices and Production in Agriculture." *Indian Economic Journal* 11 (April–June 1964).

*Kendall, M. G. "The Analyses of Economic Time Series Part I: Prices." *Journal of the Royal Statistical Society* Ser. A, 96 (1953): 11–25.

Kottke, M. "Spatial, Temporal, and Product-Use Allocation of Milk in an Imperfectly Competitive Dairy Industry." *American Journal of Agricultural Economics* 52 (Feb. 1970): 33–40.

*Kravis, I. B., and Lipsey, R. E. *Price Competitiveness in World Trade.* New York: National Bureau of Economic Research, 1971.

Labys, Walter C. "Commodity Price Fluctuations: A Short-Term Explanation for Selected Commodities on the American Market." Ph.D. dissertation, University of Nottingham, 1968.

*Labys, Walter C., and Granger, C. W. J. *Speculation, Hedging and Commodity Price Forecasts.* Lexington, Mass.: D.C., Heath and Co., 1970.

*Labys, Walter C., Rees, H. J. B., and Elliott, C. M. "Copper Price Behavior and the London Metal Exchange," *Applied Economics* 3 (1971): 99–113.

Ladd, G. W. "Federal Milk Marketing Order Provisions: Effects on Producer Prices and Intermarket Price Relationships." *American Journal of Agricultural Economics* 51 (Aug. 1969): 625–641.

Larson, Arnold. "Evidence on the Temporal Dispersion of Price Effects of New Market Information." Ph.D. dissertation, Stanford University, 1960.

*Larson, Arnold. "Measurement of a Random Process in Futures Prices." *Food Research Institute Studies* 1 (Nov. 1960): 313–324.

Larson, Arnold. "Price Prediction on the Egg Futures Market." *Food Research Institute Studies* 7 Suppl. (1967): 49–64.

*Leuthold, R. M. "An Analysis of Daily Fluctuations in the Hog Economy." *American Journal of Agricultural Economics* 51 (Nov. 1969): 849–865.

*Leuthold, R. M., MacCormick, A. J. A., Schmitz, A. and Watts, D. G. "Forecasting Daily Hog Prices and Quantities: A Study of Alternative Forecasting Techniques." *Journal of the American Statistical Association* 65 (March 1970): 90–107.

*Logan, S. H., and Boles, J. N. "Quarterly Fluctuations in Retail Prices of Meat." *Journal of Farm Economics* 44 (Nov. 1962): 1050–1060.

Love, H. G., and Shuffett, D. M. "Short-Run Price Effects of a Structural Change in a Terminal Market for Hogs," *Journal of Farm Economics* 47 (Aug. 1965): 803–812.

Mandelbrot, B. "Forecasts of Future Prices, Unbiased Markets and 'Martingale' Models." *Journal of Business Security Prices* 39 Suppl. (Jan. 1966): 242–255.

Margins, Speculations, and Prices in Grains Futures Markets. Economic Research Service, U.S. Department of Agriculture, Washington, D.C., December 1967.

McCain, Wesley G. "Price Effects of Margin Changes in Commodity Futures Markets." Ph.D. dissertation, Stanford University, 1969.

McCalla, A. F. "A Duopoly Model of World Wheat Pricing." *Journal of Farm Economics* 48 (Aug. 1966): 711–727.

McCalla, A. F. "Pricing the World Feed Grain Market." *Agricultural Economic Research* 19 (Oct. 1967): 93–102.

*McKenzie, Philpott B. P., and Woods, M. J. "Price Formation in the Raw Wool Market." *The Economic Record* 45 (Sept. 1969): 386–398.

Mills, Frederick C. *Price-Quantity Interactions in Business Cycles.* National Bureau of Economic Research. Princeton: Princeton University Press, 1946.

*Mills, E. S. *Price, Output and Inventory Policy.* New York: John Wiley & Sons, 1962.

*Muth, John F. "Rational Expectations and the Theory of Price Movements." *Econometrica* 29 (July 1961): 315–335.

*Myers, L. H., Havlicek, J. Jr., and Henderson, P. L. *Short-time Price Structure of the Hog–Pork Sector of the United States.* Purdue University. Agricultural Experiment Station Research Bulletin No. 855. Feb. 1970.

Nerlove, M. "Spectral Analysis of Seasonal Adjustment Procedures," *Econometrica* 32 (July 1964): 241–286.

*Paul, A. B. "The Pricing of Bin Space—A Contribution to the Theory of Storage." *American Journal of Agricultural Economics* 52 (Feb. 1970): 1–12.

Paul, A. B., and Wesson, W. T. "Pricing Feedlot Services Through Cattle Futures." *Agricultural Economic Research* 19 (April 1967): 33–45.

Peston, M. H., and Yamey, B. S. "Inter-Temporal Price Relationships with Forward Markets: A Method of Analysis." *Economica* n.s. 27 (Nov. 1960): 355–367.

Philpott, R. P. *Fluctuations in Wool Prices, 1870–1963.* Agricultural Economics Research Unit, Publication No. 13. Lincoln College, University of Canterbury, New Zealand, 1965.

Powers, M. J. "Does Futures Trading Reduce Price Fluctuations in the Cash Markets?" *American Economic Review* 60 (1970): 460–464.

*Rausser, G. C., and Cargill, T. F. "The Existence of Broiler Cycles: An Application of Spectral Analysis." *American Journal of Agricultural Economics* 52 (Feb. 1970): 109–121.

Samuelson, Paul A. "Intertemporal Price Equilibrium: A Prologue to the Theory of Speculation." *Weltwirtschaftliches* 79 (1957): 181–221.

Samuelson, Paul A. "A Random Theory of Futures Prices." *Industrial Management Review* 6 (June 1965).

*Schmitz, A. and Watts, D. G. "Forecasting Wheat Yields: An Application of Parametric Time Series Modeling." *American Journal of Agricultural Economics* 52 (May 1970): 247–254.

Shisko, Irwin, "Techniques of Forecasting Commodity Prices." *Commodity Year Book* 7 (1965): 30–36.

*Shepherd, Geoffrey S. *Agricultural Price Analysis*, 5th ed. Ames: Iowa State University Press, 1966.

Skadberg, J. M., and Futrell, G. A. "An Economic Appraisal of Futures Trading in Livestock." *Journal of Farm Economics* 48 (Dec. 1966): 1485–1489.

Smidt, Seymour. "A Test of the Serial Independence of Price Changes in Soybeam Futures." *Food Research Institute Studies* 5 (1965): 117–136.

Snape, R. H. "Price Relationships on the Sydney Wool Futures Market." *Economica* 35 (May 1968).

Stein, J. L. "The Simultaneous Determination of Spot and Futures Prices." *American Economic Review* 51 (Dec. 1961): 1012–1025.

Stout, T. T., and Feltner, R. L. *Price Relationships in the Market for Slaughter Hogs in Indiana.* Indiana Agricultural Experiment Station Research Bulletin 746, Lafayette, June 1962.

Takayama, T., and Judge, G. G. "An Interregional Activity Analysis Model for the Agricultural Sector." *Journal of Farm Economics* 46 (May 1964): 349–365.

Telser, Lester G. "Futures Trading and the Storage of Cotton and Wheat." *Journal of Farm Economics* 40 (June 1958): 235–255.

Theil, H. *Applied Economic Forecasting.* Chicago: Rand McNally and Co., 1966.

*Thomsen, F. L., and Foote, R. J. *Agricultural Prices.* New York: McGraw-Hill, 1952.

Tomek, W. G., and Gray, R. W. "Temporal Relationships Among Prices on Commodity Futures Markets: Their Allocative and Stabilizing Roles." *American Journal of Agricultural Economics* 52 (Aug. 1970): 372–380.

Trierweiler, J. E., and Hassler, J. B. "Measuring Efficiency in the Beef–Pork Sector by Price Analysis." *Agricultural Economic Research* 22 (Jan. 1970): 11–17.

Vaile, Roland. "Cash and Futures Price of Corn." *Journal of Marketing* 9 (July 1944).

*Venkateramanan, L. S. *The Theory of Futures Trading.* London: Asia Publishing House, 1965.

Waite, Warren C., and Trelogan, Harry C. *Agricultural Market Prices.* New York: Wiley, 1951.

*Waugh, F. V. and Norton, V. J. *Some Analyses of Fish Prices.* University of Rhode Island Agricultural Experiment Station Bulletin No. 401, Kingston Rhode Island, 1969.

*Weiss, J. S. "A Spectral Analysis of World Cocoa Prices." *American Journal Agricultural Economics* 52 (Feb. 1970): 122–126.

West, D. *Swine Producers' Price Expectations and the Hog Cycle.* North Carolina State University Economic Research Report 10, Raleigh, 1969.

*Working, Holbrook. "Cycles in Wheat Prices." *Wheat Studies of the Food Research Institute* 8 (Nov. 1931).

*Working, Holbrook. "A Random Difference Series for Use in the Analysis of Time Series." *Journal of the American Statistical Association* 29 (1934): 11–24.

Working, Holbrook. *Memorandum on Measurement of Cycles in Speculative Prices.* Food Research Institute, Stanford University, 1949.

*Working, Holbrook. "New Concepts Concerning Futures Markets and Prices." *American Economic Review* 52 (June 1962): 431–457.

Working, Holbrook. "New Ideas and Methods for Price Research." *Journal of Farm Economics* 38 (Dec. 1956): 1427–1457.

*Working, Holbrook. "A Theory of Anticipatory Prices." *American Economic Review* 48 (May 1958): 188–199.

Working, Holbrook. "Price Relations between July and September Wheat Futures at Chicago since 1885." *Wheat Studies* 9 (March 1933): 187–238.

Working, Holbrook. "Price Relations Between May and New Crop Wheat Futures at Chicago since 1885." *Wheat Studies* 10 (Feb. 1934): 183–228.

Working, Holbrook. "Theory of the Inverse Carrying Charge in Futures Markets." *Journal of Farm Economics* 30 (Feb. 1946): 1–28.

Models

*Adams, F. G., Eguchi, H., and Meyer-zu-Schlochtern, F. *An Econometric Analysis of International Trade.* OECD Economic Studies Series, Paris, January 1969.

*Adams, F. G., and Griffin, James M. *An Econometric Linear Programming Model of the U.S. Petroleum Industry.* Discussion Paper No. 193, Department of Economics, University of Pennsylvania, Philadelphia, September 1970.

*Adams, F. G. and J. M. Griffin. "An Econometric Model of the United States Petroleum Refining Industry." In *Essays in Industrial Econometrics—Vol. I.* L. R. Klein (Ed.). Philadelphia: Wharton School of Finance and Commerce, 1969.

*Alm, H., Duloy, J., and Gulbrandsen, O. *Agricultural Prices and the World Food Economy.* Institute for Economics and Statistics, University of Uppsala, March 1969.

*Anderson, T. W., and Rubin, H. "Estimation of the Parameters of a Single Equation in a Complete System of Stochastic Equations." *Annals of Mathematical Statistics* 20 (1949): 46–63.

*Ansoff, H. I., and Slevin, D. P. "An Appreciation of Industrial Dynamics." *Management Science* 14 (March 1968): 383–396.

*Armington, P. S. "A Theory of Demand for Products Distinguished by Place of Production." *IMF Staff Papers* 16 (March 1969): 159–178.

*Arthur, H. B., Houck, J. P., and Beckford, G. L. *Tropical Agribusiness—Structures and Adjustments: Bananas.* Boston: Division of Research, Harvard Business School, 1968.

*Ballmer, R. W. "Copper Market Fluctuations: An Industrial Dynamics Study." Unpublished M.S. thesis, Massachusetts Institute of Technology, 1960.

Bassmann, R. L. "A Generalized Classical Method of Linear Estimation of Coefficients in a Structural Equation." *Econometrica* 25 (1957): 77–83.

*Bates, Thomas H., and Schmitz, Andrew. *A Spatial Equilibrium Analysis of the World Sugar Economy.* Gianini Foundation Monograph No. 23. California Agricultural Experiment Station, Berkeley, May 1969.

Bawden, Lee D. "An Evaluation of Alternative Spatial Models." *Journal of Farm Economics* 46 (Dec. 1964): 1372–1379.

*Bawden, Lee D. "Spatial Price Equilibrium Model of International Trade." *Journal of Farm Economics* 48 (1966): 862–874.

*Behrman, Jere R. "Econometric Model Simulations of the World Rubber Market." In *Essays in Industrial Economics—Vol. III.* L. R. Klein (Ed.). Philadelphia: Wharton School of Finance and Commerce, 1969. Pp. 1–96.

*Behrman, Jere R. *Econometric Models of Mineral Commodity Markets: Limitations and Uses.* Presented at session on Economic Forecasting, Council of Economics, American Institute of Mining, Metallurgical and Petroleum Engineers, New York, February 1968.

Bell, Duran, Jr. *Models of Commodity Transfer.* Giannini Foundation Monograph No. 20, California Agricultural Experiment Station, Berkeley, October 1967.

Bellman, R. *Adaptive Control Processes: A Guided Tour.* Princeton: Princeton University Press, 1961.

Bennion, E. G. "The Cowles Commission's Simultaneous–Equation Approach: A Simplified Explanation." *Review of Economics and Statistics* 34 (1952): 49–56.

*Bentzel, R., and Hansen, B. "On recursiveness and Interdependency in Economic Models." *Review of Economic Studies* 22 (1954): 153–168.

Blankmeyer, E. "Dynamic Portfolio Analysis and Export Stabilization." Unpublished Ph.D. dissertation, Princeton University, 1971.

Bressler, Raymond C., and King, Richard A. *Markets, Prices and Interregional Trade.* New York: John Wiley & Sons, 1970.

*Brundy, James M., and Jorgenson, Dale W. "Efficient Estimation of Simultaneous Equations by Instrumental Variables." Discussion Paper No.

191, Harvard Institute of Economic Research, Harvard University, June 1971.

*Burrows, James C. *Cobalt: An Industry Analysis.* Lexington, Mass.: D. C. Heath and Co., 1971.

*Burrows, James C. *Tungsten: An Industry Analysis.* Lexington, Mass.: D. C. Heath and Co., 1971.

*Burrows, James C., Hughes, W., and Valette, J. *An Economic Analysis of the Silver Industry.* Lexington, Mass.: D. C. Heath and Co., Forthcoming.

*Burt, O. W. "Control Theory for Agricultural Policy: Methods and Problems in Operational Models." *American Journal of Agricultural Economics* 51 (May 1969): 394–403.

*Cochrane, D., and Orcutt, G. H. "Application of Least Squares Regression to Relationships Containing Autocorrelated Error Terms." *Journal of the American Statistical Association* 44 (1949): 32–61.

*Chow, Gregory C. *Optimal Control of Linear Econometric Systems with Finite Time Horizon.* Econometric Research Program Memorandum No. 115, Princeton University, October 1970.

*Chow, G. C., and Fair, R. C. *Maximum Likelihood Estimation of Linear Equation Systems with Autoregressive Residuals.* Research Memorandum No. 118, Econometric Research Program, Princeton University, September 1971.

*Cohen, Kalmen. *A Computer Model of the Shoe, Leather and Hide Sequence.* Ph.D. dissertation, Carnegie Institute of Technology. Englewood Cliffs, N.J.: Prentice-Hall, Inc. 1960.

*Crom, Richard. *A Dynamic Price-Output Model of the Beef and Pork Sectors.* Technical Bulletin No. 1426, Economic Research Service, U.S. Department of Agriculture, Washington, D.C., 1970.

*Cromarty, William A. "An Econometric Model for United States Agriculture." *Journal of the American Statistical Association* 54 (1959): 556–574.

Dawson, J., and Egbert, Alvin C. "The Demand for Feed Concentrates: A Statistical Analysis." *Agricultural Economic Research* 17 (April 1965):

Day, Richard H. *Recursive Programming and Production Response.* Amsterdam: North-Holland, 1963.

*Dean, Gerald W., and Collins, Norman R. *World Trade in Fresh Oranges: An Analysis of the Effect of E.E.C. Tariff Policies.* Giannini Foundation. Monograph No. 18. California Agricultural Experiment Station, Berkeley, January 1967.

*Desai, M. "An Econometric Model of the World Tin Economy, 1948–1961." *Econometrica* 34 (Jan. 1966): 105–134.

*Dhrymes, P. J. *Econometrics*. New York: Harper & Row, 1970.

*Dhrymes, P. J. "Some Aspects of the Estimation of Large Econometric Models." Discussion Paper No. 14, Department of Economics, University of Pennsylvania, Philadelphia, 1971.

*Dhillon, P. *Milk Production and Removal in the Northeast*. New Jersey Agricultrual Experiment Station Bulletin No. 826, New Brunswick, October 1969.

*Duesenberry, J. S., *et al.* (Eds.). *The Brookings Quarterly Econometric Model of the United States*. Chicago: Rand McNally and Co., 1965.

*Duesenberry, J. S., *et al.* (Eds.). *The Brookings Model: Some Further Results*. Chicago: Rand McNally and Co., 1969.

Durbin, J., and Watson, G. S. "Testing for Serial Correlation in Least Squares Regression." *Biometrika* 38 (1951): 159–177.

*Durbin, J. "Testing for Serial Correlation in Least-Squares Regression When Some of the Regressors Are Lagged Dependent Variables." *Econometrica* 38 (1970): 410–421.

Eidman, V. R., Carter, H. O., and Dean, G. W. *Decision Models for California Turkey Growers*. Giannini Foundation. Monograph No. 21. California Agricultural Experiment Station, Berkeley, July 1968.

*Egbert, Alvin C. "An Aggregate Model of Agriculture: Empirical Estimates and Some Policy Implications." *American Journal of Agricultural Economics* 51 (Feb. 1969): 71–86.

*Egbert, A. C. and Reutlinger, S. "A Dynamic Model of the Livestock-Feed Sector." *Journal of Farm Economics* 47 (Dec. 1965): 1288–1305.

*Eisenpress, H., and Greenstadt, J. "The Estimation of Nonlinear Econometric Systems." *Econometrica* 34 (1966): 851–861.

Emmery, M. *The Price Elasticity of the Demand for Wool in the U.K.* Wool Economic Research Report No. 11. Bureau of Agricultural Economics, Canberra, Australia, 1967.

*Epps, M. L. S. "A Computer Simulation of the World Coffee Economy." Unpublished Ph.D. dissertation, Duke University, 1970.

*Evans, M. K. "An Agricultural Submodel for the U.S. Economy." In *Essays in Industrial Economics—Vol. II*. L. R. Klein (Ed.). Philadelphia: Wharton School of Finance and Commerce, 1969.

*Fair, Ray C. *A Short-Run Forecasting Model of the United States Economy*. Lexington, Mass.: D. C. Heath and Co., 1971.

*Fair, Ray C. "The Estimation of Simultaneous Equation Models with Lagged Endogenous Variables and First Order Serially Correlated Errors." *Econometrica* (May 1970): 507–516.

*Fair, Ray C. *A Comparison of Alternative Estimators of Macroeconomic Models.* Research Memorandum No. 121, Econometric Research Program, Princeton University, September 1971.

*Farrell, Joseph E., and Lampe, Harlan C. *The New England Fishing Industry: Functional Markets for Finned Foods Fish, I and II.* Agricultural Experiment Station Bulletins No. 379 and 380, University of Rhode Island, Kingston, 1965.

Filippello, Nicholas A. "A Dynamic Econometric Investigation of the Japanese Livestock Economy." Unpublished Ph.D. dissertation, University of Missouri, December 1967.

*Fisher, Franklin M., "A Correspondence Principle for Simultaneous Equation Models." *Econometrica* 38 (Jan. 1970): 73–92.

*Fisher, Franklin M. *A Priori Information and Time Series Analysis.* Amsterdam: North-Holland, 1962.

*Fisher, F. M. "Generalization of the Rank and Order Conditions for Identifiability." *Econometrica* 27 (1959): 431–447.

*Fisher, F. M. "Uncorrelated Disturbances and Identifiability Criteria." *International Economic Review* 4 (1963): 134–152.

*Fisher, F. M. *The Identification Problem in Economics.* New York: McGraw-Hill, 1966.

*Fisher, F. M. "Dynamic Structure and Estimation in Economy Wide Econometric Models." In *The Brookings Quarterly Econometric Model of the United States.* J. S. Duesenberry, et al. (Eds.). Chicago: Rand McNally and Co., 1965, pp. 589–636.

*Fisher, W. D., and Wadyck, W. J. "Estimating a Structural Equation in a Large System." *Econometrica* 39 (May 1971): 461–466.

*Foote, R. J. "A Comparison of Single and Simultaneous Equation Techniques." *Journal of Farm Economics* 37 (Dec. 1955): 975–990.

*Forrester, J. W. *Industrial Dynamics.* Cambridge, Mass.: M.I.T. Press, 1965.

*Fox, K. A. *Econometric Analysis for Public Policy.* Ames: The Iowa State College Press, 1958.

*Fox, K. A. *The Analysis of Demand for Farm Products.* Technical Bulletin No. 1081, United States Department of Agriculture, Washington, D.C., 1953.

*Fox, K. A. "A Spatial Equilibrium Model of the Livestock-Feed Economy in the United States." *Econometrica* 21 (1953): 547–566.

Friedman, Joan, and Foote, Richard J. *Computational Methods for Handling Systems of Simultaneous Equations.* Agricultural Handbook No. 94. United States Department of Agriculture, Washington D.C., 1955.

*Fromm, G., and Taubman, P. *Policy Simulations with an Econometric Model.* Amsterdam: North-Holland, 1968.

*Gerra, Martin, J. *Supplementary Information on Procedure Used for Major Commodity Groups in Measuring the Supply and Utilization of Farm Commodities.* Agricultural Handbook No. 91. United States Department of Agriculture, Washington, D.C., 1953,

*Goldberger, A. S. *Impact Mutliplers and Dynamic Properties of the Klein–Goldberger Model.* Amsterdam: North-Holland, 1959.

*Goldfield, Stephen M., and Quandt, Richard E. "Nonlinear Simultaneous Equations: Estimation and Prediction." *International Economic Review* 9 (Feb. 1968).

*Griliches, Zvi. "Distributed Lags: A Survey." *Econometrica* 35 (1967): 1–49.

*Griliches, Zvi. "The Brookings Model Volume: A Review." *Review of Economics and Statistics* 50 (1968): 228–231.

Gulbrandsen, Odd. "Prediction Model of Agricultural Products for Sweden." *Models and Simulation.* H. Stockhaus (Ed.). Goteborg: Scandinavian University Books, 1970.

*Haavelmo, T. "The Statistical Implications of a System of Simultaneous Equations." *Econometrica* 11 (1943): 1–12.

*Haavelmo, T. *Statistical Inference in Dynamic Economic Models.* T. Koopmans (Ed.). New York: John Wiley & Sons, 1950.

Harkema, R. *Simultaneous Equations: A Bayesian Approach.* Rotterdam: Rotterdam University Press, 1972.

*Harlow, Arthur A. "A Recursive Model of the Hog Industry." *Agricultural Economic Research* 13 (1962).

*Harlow, Arthur A. *Factors Affecting the Price and Supply of Hogs.* Technical Bulletin No. 1274. Economic Research Service, United States Department of Agriculture, Washington, D.C., 1962.

*Hayanga, M. L., and Hacklander, D. "Monthly Supply-Demand Relationships for Fed Cattle and Hogs." *American Journal of Agricultural Economics* 52 (Aug. 1970): 535–544.

*Higgins, Christopher I. "An Econometric Description of the U.S. Steel Industry." In *Essays in Industrial Economics—Vol. II.* L. R. Klein (Ed.). Philadelphia: Wharton School of Finance and Commerce, 1969. pp. 1–62.

*Hildreth, C. and Jarrett, F. J. *A Statistical Study of Livestock Production and Marketing.* New York: John Wiley & Sons, 1955.

*Holder, S. H. Jr., Shaw, D. L., and Snyder, J. C. *A Systems Model of the U.S. Rice Industry.* Technical Bulletin No. 1453. Economic Research

Service, U.S. Department of Agriculture, Washington, D.C., November 1971.

Hopp, Henry, and Foote, Richard J. "A Statistical Analysis of Factors that Affect Prices of Coffee. *Journal of Farm Economics* 37 (1955): 429–438.

*Houck, J. P. and Mann, J. S. *An Analysis of Domestic and Foreign Demand for U.S. Soybean and Soybean Products.* Technical Bulletin No. 265. University of Minnesota Agricultural Experiment Station, 1968.

*Houck, J. P., Ryan, M. E., and Subotnik, A. *Soybeans and Their Products: Markets, Models and Policy.* Minneapolis: University of Minnesota Press, 1972.

*Hurwicz, L. "Generalization of the Concept of Identification." In *Statistical Inference in Dynamic Economic Models.* Cowles Commission Study. New York: John Wiley & Sons, 1953.

*Johnston, J. *Econometric Methods.* New York: McGraw-Hill, 1972.

*Judge, G. and Takayama, T. *Spatial and Temporal Price and Allocation Models.* Amsterdam: North-Holland, 1971.

King, Richard A. (Ed.). *Interregional Competition Research Methods.* Agricultural Policy Institute Series No. 10, North Carolina State University at Raleigh, 1965.

*King, Richard A., and Foo-Shiung Ho. "Reactive Programming: A Market Simulating Spatial Equilibrium Algorithm." Economics Special Report, Department of Economics, North Carolina State University at Raleigh, February 1972.

*Klein, L. R. "Estimation of Interdependent Systems in Macroeconometrics." *Econometrica* 37 (April 1969): 171–192.

*Klein, L. R. A *Textbook of Econometrics.* New York: Row, Peterson and Co., 1953.

*Klein, L. R. "Single Equation vs. Equation System Methods of Estimation in Econometrics." *Econometrica* 28 (Oct. 1960): 866–871.

*Klein, L. R. and Evans, M. K. *Econometric Gaming.* London: The Macmillan Co., 1969.

*Klein, L. R., and Goldberger, A. S. *An Econometric Model of the United States Economy, 1929–1952.* Amsterdam: North-Holland, 1955.

*Kloek, T., and Mennes, L. B. M. "Simultaneous Equation Estimation Based On Principal Components of Predetermined Variables." *Econometrica* 28 (1960): 45–61.

Kogiku, K. C. "A Model of the Raw Materials Market." *International Economic Review* 8 (Feb. 1967).

*Koopmans, T. C. "Identification Problems in Economic Model Construction." *Studies in Econometric Method.* W. C. Hood and T. C. Koopmans, eds., New York: John Wiley & Sons, 1953.

*Labys, W. C. *An Econometric Model of the International Lauric Oils Market: Considerations for Policy Analysis.* UNCTAD/CD/Misc.43/Revl, UNCTAD, Geneva, 1971.

*Labys, W. C. "Projections and Prospects for the Lauric Oils, 1972–1987. *Journal of the American Oil Chemists Society* 49 (June 1972): 228A–233A.

*Labys, W. C., "Policy Application of Commodity Models: The Case for Lauric Oils." Mimeographed. Rural Development Panel, Southeast Asia Development Advisory Group, Singapore, September 1972.

Ladd, George W. "Effects of Shocks and Errors in Estimation: An Empirical Comparison." *Journal of Farm Economics* 38 (1956): 485–495.

*Langemeier, L., and Thompson, R. G. "Demand, Supply, Price Relationships of the Beef Sector, Post W.W.II Period." *Journal of Farm Economics* 49 (1967): 167–183.

Larsen, R. E. *State Increment Dynamic Programming.* New York: American Elsevier Publishing Co., 1968.

Leath, M. N., and Blakeley, L. V. *An Interregional Analysis of the U.S. Grain Marketing Industry, 1966–1967.* Technical Bulletin No. 1444. Economic Research Service, United States Department of Agriculture, Washington, D.C., 1971.

*Lee, T. C., and Seaver, S. K. *A Positive Spatial Equilibrium Model of Broiler Markets: A Simultaneous Equation Approach.* Storrs Agricultural Experiment Station Bulletin No. 417, University of Connecticut, Storrs, February 1972.

Linnemann, Hans. *An Econometric Study of International Trade Flows.* Amsterdam: North-Holland, 1966.

*Liu, T. C. "A Monthly Recursive Econometric Model of the United States." *Review of Economic and Statistics* 69 (1969): 1–13.

*Liu, T. C. "Underidentification, Structural Estimation and Forecasting." *Econometrica* 28 (1960): 855–865.

Lowenstein, F. "Factors Affecting the Domestic Mill Consumption of Cotton." *Agriculture Economics Research* 4 (1952): 44–51.

*Lyttkens, E., Dutta, M., and Bergstrom, R. "Fix-Point and Iterative Instrumental Variable Methods for Estimating Interdependent Systems." Presented at the Second World Congress of the Econometric Society, Cambridge, England, 1970.

*Malinvaud, E. *Statistical Methods of Econometrics*. Amsterdam: North-Holland, 1966.

*Matthews, J. L., and Womack, A. W. "An Economic Appraisal of the U.S. Tung Oil Economy." *Southern Journal of Agricultural Economics* (Dec. 1970): 161–168.

*Matthews, J. L., Womack, A. W., and Hoffman, R. G. "Formulation of Market Forecasts for the U.S. Soybean Economy with an Econometric Model." *Fats and Oils Situation* 260 (Nov. 1971): 26–31.

*McCarthy, Michael D. "Notes on the Selection of Instruments for Two-Stage Least-Squares and K-Class Type Estimators of Large Models." *Southern Economic Journal*. (Jan. 1971): 251–259.

*Meadows, Dennis L. *Dynamics of Commodity Production Cycles*. Cambridge, Mass.: Wright–Allen Press, 1970.

*Meinken, K. W. *The Demand and Price Structure of Oats, Barley, and Soybean Grain*. Technical Bulletin No. 1080. United States Department of Agriculture, Washington, D.C., 1953.

*Meinken, K. W. *The Demand and Price Structure for Wheat*. Technical Bulletin No. 1136. United States Department of Agriculture, Washington, D.C., 1955.

*Mitchell, Bridger M. "Estimation of Large Econometric Models by Principal Components and Instrumental Variable Methods." *Review of Economics and Statistics*. 50 (May 1971): 140–146.

*Mitchell, B. M., and Fisher, F. M. "The Choice of Instrumental Variables in the Estimation of Economy-Wide Econometric Models, Some Further Thought." *International Economic Review* 11 (June 1970): 226–234.

*Mo, Y. *An Economic Analysis of the Dynamics of the United States Wheat Sector*. Technical Bulletin No. 1395. United States Department of Agriculture, Washington, D.C., 1968.

*Moore, Henry L. "Empirical Laws of Supply and Demand and the Flexibility of Prices." *Political Science Quarterly* 34 (1919): 546–567.

Moore, John R., and Walsh, Richard D., (Eds.). *Market Structures in Agriculture*. Ames: Iowa State University Press, 1966.

*Mosbaek, E. J., and Wold, H. O. *Interdependent Systems: Structure and Estimation*. Amsterdam: North-Holland, 1970.

*Naylor, Thomas H. (Ed.). *Computer Simulation Experiments with Models of Economic Systems*. New York: John Wiley & Sons, 1971.

*Naylor, T. H. "Policy Simulation Experiments with Macroeconometric Models: The State of the Art." *American Journal of Agricultural Economics* 52 (May 1970): 263–271.

*Nerlove, M., and Wallis, K. F. "Use of the Durbin Watson Statistic in Inappropriate Situations." *Econometrica* 34 (1966): 235–238.

*O'Mara, Gerald K. *An Analysis of Alternative Forecast Models for the Broiler Industry: A Summary.* Proceedings of a Workshop on Systems Research in the Livestock Industries. Animal Products Branch, Marketing Economics Division, Economic Research Service, U.S.D.A., Washington, D.C., 1970.

Polak, J. J. *An International Economic System*, London, 1954.

Pyhonen, Pentii. "A Tentative Model for the Volume of Trade Between Countries." *Weltwirtschaftliches Archiv* Band 90 (1963): 93–99.

Prais, S. J. "Econometric Research in International Trade: A Review." *Kyklos* 15 (1962): 560–579.

*Pugh, Alexander L. *DYNAMO User's Manual*. Cambridge, Mass.: M.I.T. Press, 1963.

*Quirk, J. P., and Smith, V. L. "Dynamic Economic Models of Fishing." *Economics of Fisheries Management: A Symposium*. Ad. Scott (Ed.). University of British Columbia, Vancouver, 1970.

*Raulerson, Richard C. *Grower-Oriented Supply and Marketing Policies for Frozen Concentrated Orange Juice*. Agriculture Economic Report 1, Department of Agricultural Economics, University of Florida, Gainesville, Nov. 1969.

*Raulerson, Richard C., and Langham, M. R. "Evaluating Supply Control Policies for Frozen Concentrated Orange Juice with an Industrial Dynamics Model." *American Journal of Agricultural Economics* 52 (1970): 197–208.

*Rhomberg, Rudolf R. "Possible Approaches to a Model of World Trade and Payments." *IMF Staff Papers* 17 (March 1970): 1–28.

Rhomberg, Rudolf R. "A Short-Term World Trade Model." *Econometrica* 34 (1966): 90–91.

*Rojko, A. S. *The Demand and Price Structure for Dairy Products*. Technical Bulletin No. 1168. United States Department of Agriculture, Washington, D.C., 1957.

Rojko, Anthony S., and Mackie, A. B. *World Demand Prospects for Agricultural Exports of less Developed Countries in 1980*. Economic Research Service, Foreign Agriculture Economic Report 60. U.S. Department of Agriculture, Washington, D.C., June 1970.

*Rojko, A. S., Urban, F. S., and Naive, J. J. *World Demand Prospects for Grain in 1980*. Foreign Agricultural Report No. 75, Economic Research Service, United States Department of Agriculture, Washington, D.C., 1971.

Sackrin, S. M. "Income Elasticity of Demand for Cigarettes: A Cross-Section Analysis." *Agricultural Economic Research* 11 (1957): 1–9.

Savage, Richard I., and Deutsch, Karl W. "A Statistical Model of the Gross Analysis of Transaction Flows." *Econometrica* 28 (1960): 551–572.

*Schlager, K. J. "A Systems Analysis of the Copper and Aluminum Industries: An Industrial Dynamics Study." Unpublished M.S. thesis, Massachusetts Institute of Technology, 1961.

*Simon, H. "Causal Ordering and Identifiability." *Studies in Econometric Method.* W. C. Hood and T. C. Koopmans (Eds.). New York: John Wiley & Sons, 1953.

Smith, V. L. "An Experimental Study of Competitive Market Behavior." *Journal of Political Economy* 50 (1962): 111–137.

Steele, Joe L. *The Use of Econometric Models by Federal Regulatory Agencies.* Lexington, Mass.: D. C. Heath and Co., 1971.

*Strotz, R. H., and Wold, H. "Recursive vs Nonrecursive Systems: An Attempt at Synthesis." *Econometrica* 28 (1960): 417–427.

*Sullivan, J. D. and Liu, C. Y. *Hog-Pork Subsector Research: Industry Model.* Proceedings of a Workshop on Systems Research in the Livestock Industries. United States Department of Agriculture, Washington, D.C., 1970.

*Swamy, P. A. V. B., and Holmes, James. "The Use of Undersized Samples in the Estimation of Simultaneous Equation Systems." *Econometrica* 39 (May 1971): 455–460.

*Taplin, Grant B. "Models of World Trade." *IMF Staff Papers* 14 (Nov. 1967): 433–455.

*Taplin, Grant B. "A Model of World Trade." IMF Research Department Memorandum DM/72/14, Washington, D.C., February 1972.

*Taylor, L. D. "The Principal Components—Instrumental Variable Approach to the Estimation of Systems of Simultaneous Equations." Unpublished Ph.D. dissertation, Harvard University, 1962.

*Taylor, L. D., and Wilson, T. A. "Three-Pass Least-Squares: A Method for Estimating Models with a Lagged Dependent Variable." *Review of Economics and Statistics* 46 (1964): 329–346.

*Theil, Henry. *Economic Forecasts and Policy.* 2nd ed. Amsterdam: North-Holland, 1961.

Thompson, R. G., Sprott, J. M., and Callen, R. W. "Demand, Supply, and Price Relationships for the Broiler Sector, With Emphasis on the Jack-Knife Method." *American Journal of Agricultural Economics* 54 (1972): 245–248.

*Tramel, Thomas E., and Seale, A. D. Jr., "Reactive Programming of Supply and Demand Relations–Application to Fresh Vegetables." *Journal of Farm Economics* 41 (Dec. 1959): 1012–1022.

Tyszynski, H. "World Trade in Manufactured Commodities, 1899–1950." *The Manchester School of Economic and Social Studies* 19 (1951): 272–304.

Wallace, T. D., and Judge, G. G. *Econometric Analysis of the Beef and Pork Sectors or the Economy.* Oklahoma State University Technical Bulletin T-75, Oklahoma State University, August 1959.

*Wallis, K. F. "Lagged Dependent Variables and Serially Correlated Errors: A Reappraisal of Three-Pass Least-Squares." *Review of Economics and Statistics* 49 (1967): 555–567.

Watanabe, T. and Kinoshita, S. "An Econometric Study of the Japanese Steel Industry." Discussion paper No. 155, Harvard Institute of Economic Research, 1970.

Waugh, Frederick V. *Demand and Price Analysis, Some Examples from Agriculture.* U.S. Department of Agriculture, Economic Research Service, Technical Bulletin No. 1316, Washington, D.C., 1964.

*Weymar, Helmut. *Dynamics of the World Cocoa Market.* Cambridge: M.I.T. Press, 1968.

*Witherell, William H. *Dynamics of the International Wool Market: An Econometric Analysis.* Research Memorandum No. 91. Econometric Research Program, Princeton University, 1968.

*Wold, H. *Econometric Model Building: Notes on the Causal Chain Approach.* Amsterdam: North-Holland, 1964.

*Zellner, A., and Geisel, M. S. "Analysis of Distributed Lag Models with Applications to Consumption Function Estimation." *Econometrica* 38 (1970): 865–888.

*Zellner, A. and Theil, H. "Three-Stage Least-Squares: Simultaneous Estimation of Simultaneous Equations." *Econometrica* 30 (1962): 54–78.

*Zusman, P. "Econometric Analysis of the Market for California Early Potatoes." *Hilgardia* 33 (Dec. 1962): 539–668.

Stability and Multipliers

*Adelman, I., and Adelman, F. "The Dynamic Properties of the Klein–Goldberger Model." *Econometrica* 27 (1959): 596–625.

*Baumol, W. *Economic Dynamics,* 2nd ed. New York: The Macmillan Co., 1959.

*Domar, E. "Capital Expansion, Rate of Growth and Employment." *Econometrica* 14 (April 1946): 136–147.

*Evans, Michael K. *Macroeconomic Acitvity*. New York: Harper & Row, 1969.

*Foote, R. J. "A Four Equation Model of the Feed Livestock Economy and Its Endogenous Mechanism." *Journal of Farm Economics* 37 (1955): 44–61.

*Frisch, R. "On the Notion of Equilibrium and Disequilibrium," *Review of Economic Studies* (1936).

*Goldberger, Arthur S. *Econometric Theory*. New York: John Wiley & Sons, Inc., 1964.

*Goldberger, Arthur S. *Impact Multipliers and Dynamic Properties of the Klein-Goldberger Model*. Amsterdam: North-Holland, 1959.

*Haavelmo, T. "The Probability Approach in Econometrics." *Econometrica* 5 (1937): 105–146.

*Harrod, R. "An Essay in Dynamic Theory." *Economic Journal* 49 (March 1939): 14–33.

*Hicks, J. R. *Value and Capital.* Oxford: Clarendon Press (1939).

*Howrey, P. and Witherell, W. H. *Stochastic Properties of a Model of the International Wool Market*. Econometric Research Program Memorandum No. 101, Princeton University, June 1968.

*Howrey, P., and Kelijian, H. H. "Simulation versus Analytical Solutions." In T. H. Naylor (Ed.). *The Design of Computer Simulation Experiments*. Durham: Duke University Press, 1969. Pp. 207–231.

*Jury, E. I. "A Stability Test for Linear Discrete Systems Using a Simple Division." *Institute of Radio Engineers* 49 (Dec. 1961).

*Kalecki, M. "A Macro-Dynamic Theory of Business Cycles." *Econometrica* 3 (1935): 327–357.

*Reutlinger, S. "Analysis of a Dynamic Model, with Particular Emphasis on Long-Run Projections." *Journal of Farm Economics* 48 (1966): 88–107.

*Samuelson, P. "Interaction Between Multiplier Analysis and the Principle of Acceleration." *Review of Economic Statistics* 21 (1939): 75–78.

*Samuelson, P. "The Stability of Equilibrium: Comparative Statics and Dynamics." *Econometrica* 9 (1941): 96–120.

*Samuelson, P. "The Stability of Equilibrium: Linear and Non-Linear Systems." *Econometrica* 10 (1924): 1–25.

*Samuelson, P. *The Foundation of Economic Analysis*. Cambridge, Mass.: Harvard University Press, 1947.

*Suits, D. "An Econometric Model of the Watermelon Market." *Journal of Farm Economics* 37 (1955): 237–251.

*Theil, H., and Boot, J. C. G. "The Final Form of Econometric Equation Systems." *Review of the International Statistical Institute* 30 (1962): 136–152.

*Vanderborre, Roger W. "Dynamic Impact Multipliers in Agriculture." *American Journal of Agricultural Economics* 50 (1968): 311–320.

*Zusman, Pinhas. "Dynamic Discrepancies in Agricultural Economic Systems." *Journal of Farm Economics* 44 (1962): 744–763.

*Zusman, Pinhas. "An Investigation of the Dynamic Stability and Stationary States of the United States Potato Market, 1930–1958." *Econometrica* 30 (July 1962): 522–547.

Simulation

Argarwala, R. "A Simulation Approach to the Analysis of Stabilisation Policies in Agricultural Markets: A Case Study." *Agricultural Economics* 22 (Jan. 1971): 13–28.

Amstutz, Arnold E. *Computer Simulation of Competitive Market Response.* Cambridge, Mass.: M.I.T. Press, 1967.

Balderston, F. E., and Hoggatt, A. C. *Simulation of Marketing Processes.* University of California, Institute of Business and Economics Research, Berkeley, 1962.

Balderston, F. E. and Hoggatt, A. C. "Simulation Models: Analytic Variety and the Problem of Model Reduction." *Symposium on Simulation Models.* Hoggatt, A. C. and Balderston, F. E. (Eds.). Cincinnati: South-Western, 1963.

Blunden, G. P., and Krasnow, H. S. "The Process Concept as a Basis for Simulation Modeling." *Simulation* 9 (Aug. 1967): 89–94.

Burdick, Donald S., and Naylor, Thomas H. "Design of Computer Simulation Experiments for Industrial Systems." *Communications of the ACM* IX (May, 1966): 329–339.

Burdick, Donald S., and Naylor, Thomas H. "The Use of Response Surface Methods to Design Computer Simulation Experiments with Models of Business and Economics Systems." In *The Design of Computer Simulation Experiments.* Naylor, Thomas, H. (Ed.). Durham, N.C.: Duke University Press, 1969.

Churchman, C. West. "An Analysis of the Concept of Simulation." *Symposium on Simulation Models.* Hoggatt, Austin C., and Balderston, F. E. (Eds.). Cincinnati: South-Western, 1963.

Cohen, Kalman J. and Cyert, Richard M. "Computer Models in Dynamic Economics." *Quarterly Journal of Economics* LXXV (Feb. 1961): 112–127.

*Cooper, Ronald L., and Jorgenson, Dale W. *The Predictive Performance of Quarterly Econometric Models of the United States.* Institute of Business and Economic Research Working Paper No. 113. University of California at Berkeley, 1969.

Crom, R. J. "Computer Models and Simulation." *Journal of Farm Economics* 36 (Dec. 1964): 1341–1358.

Crom, R. J., and Maki, W. R. "Adjusting Dynamic Models to Improve Their Predictive Ability." *Journal of Farm Economics* 47 (1965): 962–972.

Cyert, Richard M. "A Description and Evaluation of Some Firm Simulations." *Proceedings of the IBM Scientific Computing Symposium on Simulation Models and Gaming.* White Plains, N.Y.: IBM, 1966.

*Dhrymes, Phoebus J., *et al.* "Criteria for Evaluation of Econometric Models." *Annals of Economic and Social Measurement* 1 (July 1972): 291–324.

*Eisner, Mark. *A Researcher's Overview of the Troll/1 System.* Economics Project of the Department of Economics, Massachusetts Institute of Technology, November 1971.

*Evans, Michael K. "Non-Linear Econometric Models." *The Design of Computer Simulation Experiments.* Naylor, T. H. (Ed.). Durham: Duke University Press, 1969: 369–373.

*Fishman, G. S., and Kiviat, P. J. "The Analysis of Simulation-Generated Time Series." *Management Science* 13 (March 1967): 525–557.

Frazier, T. L., Narrie, D. B., and Rodgers, T. F. "Simulation Procedures for Livestock Auction Markets." Georgia Agricultural Experimental Station, *Research Bulletin* 74 (March 1970): 1–44.

Fromm, Gary. "Utility Theory and the Analysis of Simulation Output Data." *The Design of Computer Simulation Experiments.* Naylor, Thomas H. (Ed.). Durham, N.C.: Duke University Press, 1969.

*Fromm, Gary, and Klein, L. R. "Solutions of the Complete Systems." *The Brookings Model: Some Further Results.* Duesenberry, J. S., *et al.* (Eds.). Chicago: Rand McNally, 1969: 363–421.

Fromm, Gary, and Taubman, Paul. *Policy Simulations with an Econometric Model.* Amsterdam: North-Holland Publishing Co., 1968.

Geraci, Vincent J. "On the Simulation of Dynamic Econometric Models." Econometric System Simulation Program Working Paper 37. Duke University, Aug. 1969.

Gross, Donald, and Ray, J. L. "A General Purpose Forecast Simulator." *Management Science* 11 (April 1965): 119–135.

Hartley, O. "The Modified Gauss-Newton Method for the Fitting of Non-Linear Regression Function by Least-Squares." *Technometrics* 3 (1961): 269–280.

Holt, C. "Validation and Application of Macroeconomic Models Using Computer Simulation." *The Brookings Quarterly Econometric Model of the United States.* Duesenberry, J. S., *et al.* Amsterdam: North-Holland, 1965.

*Holt, Charles C., *et al. Program Simulate II.* Social Systems Research Institute. University of Wisconsin, 1967.

*Howrey, E. P. "Selection and Evaluation of Econometric Models." *Computer Simulation versus Analytical Solutions for Business and Economic, Models.* Gothenburg: Graduate School of Business Administration, August 1972.

*Klein, L. R., and Evans, M. K. *Econometric Gaming.* London: The Macmillan Co., 1969.

*Kofi, Tettah A. "International Commodity Agreements and Export Earnings: Simulation of the 1968 International Cocoa Agreement." *Food Research Institute Studies* 11 (1972).

*Labys, W. C. "Commodity Modeling Alternatives for Policy Simulation Analysis: A Case Study of the Lauric Oils Market." *Computer Simulation versus Analytical Solutions for Business and Economic Models.* Gothenburg: Graduate School of Business Administration, August. 1972.

Labys, W. C. "Simulation of a Basing Point System." Unpublished M.B.A thesis, Duquesne University, 1962.

Low, E. M., and Agarwala, R., "An Econometric Analysis of Support Buying in the U.K. Egg Market 1958–1968." Processes of Agricultural Research Symposium on the Use of Models in Agricultural and Biological Research, Berks, 1969.

Maki, W. R., and Crom, R. J. *Evaluating Market Organizations in a Simulated Livestock-Feed Economy.* Iowa State University Agriculture and Home Economics Experiment Station Research Bulletin No. 541. Ames, Oct. 1965.

McKay, Gary C. *A Simulation Model of the Women's Nylon Hosiery Industry.* National Bureau of Standards Report 9318, Washington, D.C., 1966.

McKay, Gary C., and Hughes, Margery T. *Simulation Modeling: An Application to the United States Tufted Carpet Industry.* National Bureau of Standards Report 9319, Washington, D.C., May 1966.

Meier, R. C., Newell, W. T., and Pazer, H. L. *Simulation in Business and Economics*. Englewood Cliffs, N.J.: Prentice-Hall, 1969.

*Meinguet, J. "Modern Relaxation Methods for the Solutions of Systems of Linear Equations of High Order." *Mathematics and Engineering Applications: Some Selected Examples*. OECD Studies Series, Paris, 1965.

Nagar, A. L. "Stochastic Simulations of the Brookings Econometric Model." *The Brookings Model: Some Further Results*. Duesenberry, J. S., *et al*. Chicago: Rand McNally, 1969.

Naylor, Thomas, H. (Ed.). *The Design of Computer Simulation Experiments*. Durham, N.C.: Duke University Press, 1969.

Naylor, Thomas H., Balintfy, J. L., Burdick, D. S., and Kong Chu. *Computer Simulation Techniques*. New York: John Wiley & Sons, 1966.

Naylor, Thomas H., Burdick, Donald S., and Sasser, W. Earl. "Computer Simulation of Economic Systems: The Problem of Experimental Design." *Journal of the American Statistical Association* 62 (Dec. 1967): 1315–1337.

Naylor, Thomas H., and Finger, J. M. "Verification of Computer Simulation Models." *Management Science* 14 (Oct. 1967): 92–101.

*Naylor, Thomas H., Seaks, T. G., and Wichern, D. W. "Box-Jenkins Methods: An Alternative to Econometric Models." Working Paper No. 57. Social System Simulation Program, Duke University, February 1, 1971.

Naylor, Thomas H., and Vernon, John M. *Micro-Economics and Decision Models of the Firm*. New York: Harcourt, Brace Jovanovich, 1969.

Naylor, Thomas H., Wallace, W. H., and Sasser, W. Earl. "A Computer Simulation Model of the Textile Industry." *Journal of the American Statistical Association* 62 (Dec. 1967): 1338–1364.

Naylor, Thomas H., Wertz, Kenneth, and Wonnacott, Thomas. "Some Methods for Analyzing Data Generated by Computer Simulation Experiments." *Communications of the ACM*, November, 1967.

Naylor, Thomas H., Wertz, Kenneth, and Wonnacott, Thomas H. "Some Methods for Evaluating the Effects of Economic Policies Using Simulation Experiments." *Review of the International Statistical Institute* 36 (1968): 184–200.

*Naylor, Thomas, H., Wertz, Kenneth, and Wonnacott, Thomas H. "Spectral Analysis of Data Generated by Simulation Experiments with Econometric Models." *Econometrica* 37 (April 1969): 333–352."

Norman, Morris. "The SIM Model Solution Program." Mimeographed. Economic Research Unit, University of Pennsylvania, 1971.

Orcutt, G. H. "Simulation of Economic Systems." *American Economic Review* 50 (1960): 893–907.

Orcutt, G. H., *et al. Micro–Analysis of Socio–Economic Systems: A Simulation Study*. New York: Harper, 1969.

*Pennington, R. A. *Introduction to Computer Methods and Numerical Analysis*. New York: The Macmillan Co., 1967.

Radford, P. J. "Some Considerations Governing the Choice of a Suitable Simulation Language." Processes of Agricultural Research Council Symposium on the Use of Models in Agricultural and Biological Research. Berks, 1969.

Ronningen, T. S. "Systems Research in Agriculture." *Agriculture Science Review* 6:4 (Fourth Quarter 1968): 1–6.

Sasser, W. Earl, Burdick, Donald S., and Naylor, Thomas H. "A Sequential Sampling Simulation Study of an Inventory Model." *Communications of the ACM* XIII May, 1970.

Sasser, W. Earl, and Naylor, Thomas H. "Computer Simulation of Economic Systems: An Example Model." *Simulation* 8 (Jan. 1967): 21–32.

Shubik, Martin. "Simulation of the Industry and the Firm." *American Economic Review* 50 (1960): 908–919.

Shubik, Martin, Kerstenetsky, Isaac, and Naylor, Thomas H. "Development Models, Simulations and Games." *Revista Brasileira de Economia*. March 1971.

Street, P. R. "An Outline of a Continuous Computer Simulation Model of the Dynamics of Grazing Utilization with Dairy Cattle." Agricultural Economics Society Discussion Paper. University of Reading, Department of Agriculture, 1969.

Sutter, R. E., and Crom, R. J. "Complete Models and Simulation." *Journal of Farm Economics* 46 (1964): 1341–1350.

Tocker, K. D. "Review of Simulation Languages." *Operational Research Quarterly* 16 (June 1965): 189–218.

VanHorn, Richard L. "Validation of Simulation Results." *Management Science* 17 (Jan. 1971): 247–257.

Vernon, John M., Rives, N. W. Jr., and Naylor, Thomas H. "An Econometric Model of the Tobacco Industry." *Review of Economics and Statistics* 51 (May 1969): 149–158.

Wallace, William H., Naylor, Thomas H., and Sasser, W. Earl. "An Econometric Model of the Textile Industry in the United States." *Review of Economics and Statistics* 50 (Feb. 1968): 13–22.

*Wallis, K. F. "Some Recent Developments in Applied Econometrics: Dynamic Models and Simultaneous Equation Systems." *Journal of Economic Literature* (Sept. 1969): 787–803.

Yurow, Jerome A. "Analysis and Computer Simulation of the Production and Distribution Systems for a Tufted Carpet Mill." *Journal of Industrial Engineering* 18 (Jan. 1967).

Notes

1. H. L. Moore, *Forecasting the Yield and the Price of Cotton* (New York: The Macmillian Co., 1917); H. Working, *Factors Determining the Price of Potatoes in St. Paul and Minneapolis*, University of Minnesota Agricultural Experiment Station Bulletin No. 10, Minneapolis, 1922 and H. Schultz, *The Theory and Measurement of Demand* (Chicago: University of Chicago Press, 1938).

2. T. Haavelmo, "The Statistical Implications of a System of Simultaneous Equations," *Econometrica* 11 (1943): 1–12.

3. H. Wold and L. Jureen, *Demand Analysis* (New York: John Wiley and Sons, 1953); W. C. Hood and T. C. Koopmans, Eds., *Studies in Econometric Method* (New York: John Wiley and Sons, 1953); and R. Stone, *The Measurement of Consumers' Expenditure and Behavior in the United Kingdom*, 1920–1938, Vol. 1 (Cambridge, Eng.: Cambridge University Press, 1954).

4. P. Balestra and M. Nerlove, "Pooling Cross Section and Time Series Data in the Estimation of a Dynamic Model: The Demand for Natural Gas," *Econometrica* 34 (1966): 585–612; and S. Ben-David and W. G. Tomek, "Allowing for Slope and Intercept Change in Regression Analysis," Mimeographed, Cornell University 1965.

5. L. M. Koyck, *Distributed Lags and Investment Analysis* (Amsterdam: North Holland Publishing Co., 1954).

6. M. Nerlove, *Distributed Lags and Demand Analysis*, Agricultural Handbook No. 141, Economic Research Service, United States Department of Agriculture, Washington, 1958.

7. H. S. Houthakker and L. D. Taylor, *Consumer Demand in the United States: 1929–1970*, (Cambridge: Harvard University Press, 1966).

8. R. Frisch, "A Complete Schema for Computing all Direct and Cross-Demand Elasticities in a Model with Many Sectors," *Econometrica* 27 (1959): 177–196.

9. G. E. Brandow, *Interrelations Among Demands for Farm Products and Implications for Control of Market Supply*, Pennsylvania Agricultural Experiment Station Bulletin No. 680, University Park, 1961; and A. P. Barten, "Consumer Demand Functions Under Conditions of Almost Additive Preferences," *Econometrica* 32 (1964): 1–38.

10. R. H. Strotz, "The Empirical Implications of a Utility Tree," *Econometrica* 32 (1957): 269–280.

11. S. M. Goldman and H. Uzawa, "A Note on Separability in Demand Analysis," *Econometrica* 32 (1964): 387–398.

12. A. C. DeJanvry, "Measurement of Demand Parameters Under Separability," Unpublished Ph.D. dissertation, University of California at Berkeley, 1966.

13. P. S. George and G. A. King, *Consumer Demand for Food Commodities in the United States with Projections for* 1980, Giannini Foundation Monograph No. 26, California Agricultural Experiment Station, Davis, California, March 1971.

14. *Ibid.*

15. A. P. Barten, "Evidence on the Slutsky Conditions for Demand Equations," *Review of Economics and Statistics* 49 (1967): 77–83.

16. George and King, *loc. cit.*

17. J. C. Burrows, *Cobalt: An Industry Analysis* (Lexington, Mass.: D. C. Heath and Co., 1971).

18. L. R. Klein, *An Introduction to Econometrics* (Englewood Cliffs, N. J.: Prentice-Hall, 1962, pp. 8–82; and R. W. Parks, "Systems of Demand Equations: An Empirical Comparison of Alternative Functional Forms," *Econometrica* 37 (October 1969): 629–50.

19. Koyck, *op. cit.*, pp. 5–39.

20. S. Almon, "The Distributed Lag Between Capital Appropriations and Expenditures," *Econometrica* 30 (1965): 178–196; and Z. Grilliches, "Distributed Lags: A Survey," *Econometrica* 35 (January 1967): 16–49. See also R. C. Fair and D. M. Jaffee, "A Note on the Estimation of Polynomial Distributed Lags" Economic Research Program Research Memorandum 120, Princeton, February 1971; and S. Robinson, "Polynomial Approximation of Distributed Lag Structures," Discussion Paper No. 1, Department of Economics, London School of Economics, June 1970.

21. Nerlove, *loc. cit.*; and M. Nerlove and W. Addison, "Statistical Estimation of Long–run Elasticities of Supply and Demand," *Journal of Farm Economics* 40 (November 1968): 861–880.

22. W. H. Witherell, *Dynamics of the International Wool Market: An Econometric Analysis*, Economic Research Program Memorandum No. 91 (Princeton: Princeton University, 1967), pp. 142–147.

23. Further discussion of this point can be found in C. A. Yandle, "An Econometric Model of the New Zealand Meat Market, *Agricultural Economics Research Unit Technical Paper No. 7*, Lincoln College, Canterbury University, New Zealand, 1970.

24. See Nerlove, *loc. cit.*; and M. Nerlove, "On the Nerlove Estimate of Supply Elasticity: A Reply," *Journal of Farm Economics* 40 (August 1958): 723–728.

25. See Houthakker and Taylor, *op. cit.*, pp. 6–54.

26. This formulation follows from the simplification provided by K. F. Wallis, "Some Recent Developments in Applied Econometrics: Dynamic

Models and Simultaneous Equation Systems," *Journal of Economic Literature*, 1 (1970): 771–796.

27. See E. E. Leamer and R. M. Stern, *Quantitative International Economics* (Boston: Allyn and Bacon, 1970), pp. 56–75; I. Morrissett, "Some Recent Uses of Elasticity of Substitution—A Survey," *Econometrica* 21 (1953): 41–62; K. W. Meinken, A. S. Rojko, G. A. King, "Measurement of Substitution in Demand from Time Series Data–A Synthesis of Three Approaches," *Journal of Farm Economics* 38 (1956): 711–735; and J. Tinbergen, "Some Measurements of Elasticities of Substitution," *Review of Economic Statistics* 28 (1964): 109–116.

28. Brandow, *loc. cit.*; Barten (1964), *loc. cit.*; and George and King, *loc. cit.*

29. Frisch, *loc. cit.*; Goldman and Uzawa, *loc. cit.*; Strotz, *loc. cit.*; Brandow, *loc. cit.*; Barten, *loc. cit.*; and DeJanvry, *loc. cit.*

30. George and King, *op. cit.*, pp. 39–40.

31. M. Wickens, J. Greenfield and G. Marshall, *A World Coffee Model*, CCP 71/W.P.4. A report prepared for the Committee on Commodity Problems, 46th Session, Food and Agricultural Organization of the United Nations, Rome 1971.

32. See R. H. Court, "Utility Maximizations and the Demand for New Zealand Meats," *Econometrica* 35 (1967): 424–446; R. P. Byron, "The Restricted Aitken Estimation of Sets of Demand Relations," *Econometrica* 38 (1970): 816–830.

33. A. Zellner, "An Efficient Method for Estimating Seemingly Unrelated Regressions," *Journal of the American Statistical Association* 57 (1962): 334–368.

34. See, for example, W. C. Labys and C. W. J. Granger, *Speculation, Hedging and Commodity Price Forecasts* (Lexington, Mass.: D. C. Heath and Co., 1970), pp. 138–146.

35. See Witherell, *op. cit.*, pp. 143–165.

36. M. Polasek and A. Powell, "Wool versus Synthetics: An International Review of Innovation in the Fibre Market," *Australian Economic Papers*, 3 (June–December 1966): 49–64.

37. Z. Grilliches, "Hybrid Corn: An Exploration in the Economics to Technological Change," *Econometrica* 25 (October 1957): 501–522.

38. J. R. Behrman, "Econometric Model Simulations of the World Rubber Market," in *Essays in Industrial Econometrics* Vol. III, L. R. Klein, Ed. (Philadelphia: Wharton School of Finance and Commerce, 1969): 1–96.

39. E. Mansfield, *The Economics of Technological Change* (New York: W. W. Norton & Co., 1968).

40. For further explanation of these and other exponential models, see J. Johnston, *Econometric Methods* (New York: McGraw-Hill Book Co., 1972), p. 52.

41. Leamer and Stern, *op. cit.*, pp. 7–18; and F. G. Adams, H. Eguchi, and F. Meyer-zu-Schlochtern, *An Econometric Analysis of International Trade* (Paris: Organization for Economic Cooperation and Development, 1969), pp. 15–28.

42. See Houthakker and Taylor, *op. cit.*, pp. 26–29.

43. H. S. Houthakker and S. P. Magee, "Income and Price Elasticities in World Trade," *Review of Economics and Statistics* 51 (May 1969): 11–25.

44. Houthakker and Magee, *op. cit.*

45. S. J. Turnovsky, "International Trading Relationships for a Small Country: The Case for New Zealand," *Canadian Journal of Economics* 1 (November 1968): 772–790.

46. See, for example, G. H. Orcutt, "Measurement of Price Elasticities in International Trade," *Review of Economics and Statistics* 32 (May 1950): 117–32; M. Nerlove, "Distributed Lags and Estimation of Long-Run Supply and Demand Elasticities: Theoretical Considerations," *Journal of Farm Economics* 40 (May 1958): 301–11; R. J. Ball and K. Marwah, "The U.S. Demand for Imports, 1948–1958," *Review of Economics and Statistics* 44 (November 1962): 395–401; Mordechai E. Krenin, "Price Elasticities in International Trade," *The Review of Economics and Statistics* 49 (November 1967): 579–582; H. S. Houthakker, "New Evidence on Demand Elasticities," *Econometrica* 33 (1965): 277–88; and Houthakker and Magee, *loc. cit.*

47. Orcutt, *loc. cit.*

48. Leamer and Stern, *op. cit.*, p. 31.

49. M. C. Kemp, "Errors of Measurement and Bias in Estimates of Import Demand Parameters," *Economic Record* 38 (September 1962): 369–72; and D. M. Heien, "Structural Stability and the Estimation of International Import Elasticities," *Kyklos* 21 (1968): 695–711.

50. Houthakker and Magee, *loc. cit.*

51. Nerlove, *loc. cit.*; Heien, *loc. cit.*

52. Morissett, *loc. cit.*; T. C. Liu, "The Elasticity of U.S. Import Demand: A Theoretical and Empirical Appraisal," *IMF Staff Papers* 1 (1954); Reuben C. Buse, "Total Elasticities—A Predictive Device," *Journal of Farm Economics* 30 (1952); Ball and Marwah, *loc. cit.*; S. J. Prais, "Econometric Research in International Trade: A Review, *Kyklos* 15 (1962): 560–579; H. Theil, "A Reconsideration of the Keynes-Tinbergen Discussion of Econometric Techniques, *De Economist*, 1963; Krenin, *loc. cit.*

53. See Johnston, *op. cit.*, pp. 300–321.

54. K. A. Fox, *Econometric Analysis for Public Policy* (Ames: The Iowa State Press, 1958).

55. L. R. Klein, "Single Equation vs. Equation System Methods of Estimation in Econometrics," *Econometrica* 28 (October 1960): 866–871.

56. P. Rao and R. L. Miller, *Applied Econometrics* (Belmont, California: Wadsworth Publishing Co., 1971), p. 176.

57. Johnston, *op. cit.*, pp. 300–321.

58. G. H. Orcutt and D. Cochrane, "A Sampling Study of the Merits of Autoregressive and Reduced Form Transformation in Regression Analysis," *Journal of the American Statistical Association* 44 (1949): 356–372.

59. A. Zellner and M. S. Geisel, "Analysis of Distributed Lag Models with Applications to Consumption Function Estimation," Paper presented at the European Meeting of the Econometric Society, 1968; and P. J. Dhrymes and B. Mitchell, "The Econometrics of Dynamic Demand Models," Paper presented at the annual meetings of the American Economic Association, 1970.

60. K. F. Wallis, "Lagged Dependent Variables and Serially Correlated Errors: A Reappraisal of Three-Pass Least-Squares," *Review of Economics and Statistics* 49 (1967): 555–567; and J. D. Sargan, "The Estimation of Economic Relationships Using Instrumental Variables." *Econometrica* 26 (1958). The latter is also discussed in Grilliches, *loc. cit.*

61. Burrows, *loc. cit.*

62. Correspondence, June 19, 1972.

63. Grilliches, *loc. cit.*; and Sargan, *loc. cit.*

64. Witherell, *loc. cit.*

65. F. Banks, "An Econometric Note on the World Zinc Market," Mimeographed, University of Uppsala, 1971; and F. Banks, "An Econometric Note on the Demand for Refined Zinc," *Zeitschrift fur Nationalokonomie* 31 (1971): 105–134.

66. W. C. Labys, *An Econometric Model of the International Lauric Oils Market: Considerations for Policy Analysis* UNCTAD/CD/Misc. 43/Rev. 1, Geneva 1971.

67. A. J. Nyberg, "The Demand for Lauric Oils in the United States," *American Journal of Agricultural Economics* 52 (February 1970): 97–102.

68. J. W. Goodwin, R. Andorn, and J. E. Martin, *The Irreversible Demand Function for Beef* (University of Oklahoma Agricultural Experiment Station Bulletin No. T.127, Norman, 1968).

1. M. Nerlove, *The Dynamics of Supply: Estimation of Farmers Response to Price* (Baltimore: The Johns Hopkins Press, 1958), pp. 66–82; B. B. Smith, "Factors Influencing the Price of Cotton," U.S. Dept. Agri. Tech. Bull. No. 50 (Jan. 1928); L. H. Bean, "The Farmers' Response to Price," *Journal of Farm Economics* 11 (July 1929): 368–385; J. D. Block, *Agricultural Reform in the United States* (New York: McGraw-Hill Book Co., 1929); R. M. Walsh, "Response to Price in Production of Cotton and Cottonseed," *Journal of Farm Economics* 26 (1944): 359–372; and R. L. Kohl and D. Paarlberg, "The Short-time Response of Agricultural Production to Price and Other Factors," Purdue University Agri. Expt. Sta. Bull. No. 555 (October 1950).

2. M. Nerlove, "Time-Series Analysis of the Supply of Agricultural Products," *Agricultural Supply Functions*, E. O. Heady, *et al.* (Eds.) (Ames: The Iowa State University Press, 1961); p. 36.

3. *Cf.* pp. 21–22.

4. B. Oury, "Supply Estimation and Prediction by Regression and Related Methods," *Economic Models and Quantitative Methods for Predictions and Planning in Agriculture*, E. O. Heady (Ed.) (Ames: The Iowa State University Press, 1971), p. 259.

5. Nerlove, *op. cit.*, pp. 45–49.

6. A further explanation of the derivation of supply functions appears in J. Henderson and R. Quandt, *Microeconomic Theory* (New York, McGraw-Hill Book Co., 1971); L. R. Klein, *An Introduction to Econometrics* (Englewood Cliffs: Prentice-Hall, 1962); and E. W. Kehrberg, "Determination of Supply Functions from Cost and Production Functions," *Agricultural Supply Functions*, E. O. Heady, *et al.* (Eds.) (Ames: The Iowa State University Press, 1961); pp. 139–151.

7. E. O. Heady and J. L. Dillon, *Agricultural Production Functions* (Ames: The Iowa State University Press, 1961).

8. J. Johnston, *Econometric Methods* (New York: McGraw-Hill Book Co., 1972).

9. Oury, *op. cit.*, pp. 269–272.

10. *Cf.* p. 48.

11. Nerlove, *The Dynamics of Supply, loc. cit.*

12. Various statistical and technical bulletins of the U.S.D.A.; J. R. Behrman, *Supply Response in Underdeveloped Agriculture: A Case Study of Four Major Annual Crops in Thailand, 1937–1963* (Amsterdam: North-Holland Publishers, 1968); and F. M. Fisher and P. Temin, "Regional Specialization and the Supply of Wheat in the United States, 1867–1914," *Review of Economics and Statistics* 52 (May 1970): 134–149.

13. Nerlove, "Time-Series Analysis. ..." *loc. cit.*

14. R. M. Goodwin, "Dynamical Coupling with Special Reference to Markets having Production Lags," *Econometrica* 15 (1947): 181–204; P. Cagan, "The Monetary Dynamics of Hyper–Inflations," *Studies in the Quantity Theory of Money*, M. Friedman (Ed.) (Chicago: University of Chicago Press, 1956), pp. 25–117; and J. F. Muth, "Optimal Properties of Exponentially Weighted Forecasts of Time Series and Permanent and Transitory Components," ONR Research Mem. 4, (Pittsburgh: Carnegie Institute of Technology, 1959).

15. P. Ady, "Supply Functions in Tropical Agriculture," *Oxford University Institute of Statistics Bulletin* 30 (May 1968): 157–188; M. Arak, "The Price Responsiveness of São Paulo Coffee Growers," *Food Research Institute Studies* 3 (1968): 211–223; M. J. Bateman, "Supply Relations for Perennial Crops in the Less Developed Areas," *Subsistence Agriculture and Economic Development*, C. R. Wharton, Jr. (Ed.) (Chicago: Aldine Press, 1968), pp. 243–253; J. R. Behrman, "Monopolistic Pricing in International Commodity Agreements: A Case Study of Cocoa," *American Journal of Agricultural Economics* 50 (1968): 702–719; F. Chan, "A Preliminary Study of the Supply Response of Malayan Rubber Estates Between 1948 and 1959," *Malayan Economic Review* 7 (October 1962): 77–94; B. C. French and R. G. Bressler, "The Lemon Cycle," *Journal of Farm Economics* 44 (Nov. 1962): 1021–36; B. C. French and J. L. Matthews, "A Supply Response Model for Perennial Crops," *American Journal of Agricultural Economics* 53 (August 1971): 478–490; R. M. Stern, "Malayan Rubber Production, Inventory Holdings, and the Elasticity of Export Supply," *The Southern Economic Journal* 31 (April 1965): 314–323.

16. French and Matthews, *op. cit.*, pp. 478–479.

17. Bateman, *loc. cit.*

18. Equations 3.20–3.30 are reprinted from Clifton R. Wharton, Jr., editor: *Subsistence Agriculture and Economic Development* (Chicago: Aldine Publishing Company, 1969); copyright © 1969 by Aldine Publishing Company. Reprinted by permission of Aldine Publishing Company.

19. M. Ezekiel, "The Cobweb Theorem," *Quarterly Journal of Economics* 52 (February 1938): 255–280.

20. F. W. Waugh, "Cobweb Models," *Journal of Farm Economics* 46 (November 1964): 732–50; Nerlove, *op. cit.*, pp. 49–53; and A. A. Harlow, "Factors Affecting the Price and Supply of Hogs," Technical Bulletin No. 1274, Economic Research Service, U.S. Department of Agriculture, Washington, 1962.

21. M. E. Abel, "Analysis of Seasonal Variation with an Application to Hog Production," *Journal of the American Statistical Association* (1962): 655–667; H. F. Breimyer, "Emerging Phenomenon: A Cycle in Hogs,"

Journal of Farm Economics (Nov. 1959): 760–768; C. G. Haas and M. Ezekiel, "Factors Affecting Hog Prices," Bulletin 1440, U.S.D.A., 1926; A. B. Larson, "The Hog Cycle as Harmonic Motion," *Journal of Farm Economics* 46 (May 1964): 357–386; W. R. Maki, "Decomposition of the Beef and Pork Cycles," *Journal of Farm Economics* 44 (August 1962); pp. 731–743; R. W. Leuthold, "An Analysis of Daily Fluctuations in the Hog Economy," *American Journal of Agricultural Economics* 51 (Nov. 1969): 849–865.

22. H. F. Breimyer, "Observations on the Cattle Cycle," *Agricultural Economics Research* 7 (January 1955): 1–10; C. A. Bermeister, "Cycles in Cattle Numbers," *The Livestock and Meat Situation*, U.S.D.A., March 1949; Maki, *loc. cit.*

23. B. F. Tobin and H. B. Arthur, *Dynamics of Adjustment in the Broiler Industry* (Boston: Harvard University Press, 1964); and G. C. Rausser and T. F. Cargill, "The Existence of Broiler Cycles: An Application of Spectral Analysis," *American Journal of Agricultural Economics* 52 (Feb. 1970): 109–121.

24. F. V. Waugh and M. M. Miller, "Fish Cycles; A Harmonic Analysis," *American Journal of Agricultural Economics* 52 (August 1970): 422–430.

25. Abel, *loc. cit.*; and Waugh and Miller, *loc. cit.*

26. Abel, *ibid.*

27. For further discussion of this approach, see E. E. Leamer and R. M. Stern, *Quantitative International Studies* (Boston: Allyn and Bacon, Inc., 1970), pp. 7–40.

28. Fisher and Temin, *loc. cit.*

29. D. A. Knight, "Evaluation of Time Series as Data for Estimating Supply Parameters," *Agricultural Supply Functions*, E. O. Heady, *et al.*, Eds. (Ames: Iowa State University Press, 1961), pp. 74–107. Other works cited include: R. J. Foote, "A Four-Equation Model of the Feed–Livestock Economy and its Endogenous Mechanism," *Journal of Farm Economics* 35 (1953): 44–61; W. A. Cromarty, "An Econometric Model for United States Agriculture, *Journal of the American Statistical Association* 54 (1959): 556–574; and W. W. Cochrane, *Farm Prices: Myth and Reality* (Minneapolis: University of Minnesota Press, 1958).

30. B. Oury, *A Production Model for Wheat and Feedgrains in France, 1946–1961* (Amsterdam: North-Holland Publishing Co., 1966), pp. 80–154.

31. J. C. Burrows, *Tungsten: An Industry Analysis* (Lexington, Mass.: D. C. Heath & Co., 1971), pp. 138–153.

32. *Cf.* pp. 27–29.

33. Bateman, *loc. cit.*, and French and Matthews, *loc. cit.*

34. Portions of this discussion have been reprinted directly from W. C. Labys, "A Lauric Oil Exports Model Based on Capital Stock Supply Adjustment," *Malayan Economic Review* XVIII (April 1973), No. 1.

35. V. Abeywardena, " Forecasting Coconut Crops Using Rainfall Data —A Preliminary Study," *Ceylon Coconut Quarterly* 19 (1968): 161–176.

36. Ady, *loc. cit.*, and M. J. Bateman, "Aggregate and Regional Supply Functions of Ghanian Cocoa, 1946–1962," *Journal of Farm Economics*, 47 (1965): 384–401.

37. *Ibid.*

38. A. J. Nyberg, "The Philippine Coconut Industry," Unpublished Ph.D. dissertation, Cornell University, 1968.

1. J. M. Clark, "Business Acceleration and the Law of Demand: A Technical Factor in Economic Cycles." *Journal of Political Economy* 25 (1917): 217–235; and M. Abramovitz, *Inventories and Business Cycles* (New York: National Bureau of Economic Research, Inc., 1950).

2. R. M. Goodwin, "Dynamic Coupling with Especial Reference to Markets Having Production Lags," *Econometrica* 15 (July 1947): 181–204.

3. E. Lundberg, *Studies in the Theory of Economic Expansion* (London: P. S. King and Son, 1937); and L. A. Metzler, "The Nature and Stability of Inventory Cycles," *Review of Economics and Statistics* 3 (August 1941): 113–129.

4. R. P. Mack, *Information, Expectations and Inventory Fluctuation* (New York: National Bureau of Economic Research, 1967), pp. 19–23.

5. The form and interpretation of the models as presented here follows from the discussion of M. Lovell, "Manufacturers' Inventories, Sales Expectations, and the Acceleration Principle," *Econometrica* 29 (July 1961): 293–314.

6. E. S. Mills, "Expectations, Uncertainty, and Inventory Fluctuations," *Review of Economic Studies* 22 (1954–55): 15–22.

7. Lovell, *op. cit.*, pp. 303–307.

8. W. H. Witherell, *Dynamics of the International Wool Market: An Econometric Analysis*, Economic Research Program Memorandum No. 91 (Princeton: Princeton University Press, 1967), pp. 103–130.

9. Lovell, *op. cit.*, pp. 295–303.

10. See Chapter 4, W. C. Labys and C. W. J. Granger, *Speculation, Hedging and Commodity Price Forecasts*, (Lexington, Mass.: D. C. Heath and Co., 1970).

11. Abramovitz, *op. cit.*, pp. 127–131.

12. M. Desai, "An Econometric Model of the World Tin Economy, 1948–1961" *Econometrica* 34 (January, 1966): 105–134, and R. M. Stern, "Malayan Rubber Production, Inventory Holdings, and the Elasticity of Export Supply," *The Southern Economic Journal* 31 (April 1965): 314–23.

13. Witherell, *loc. cit.*

14. J. M. Keynes, *The General Theory of Employment, Interest and Money* (New York: Harcourt, Brace, 1936), p. 225; N. Kaldor, "Speculation and Economic Stability," *Review of Economic Studies* 7 (October 1939): 1–27; H. Working, "The Theory of the Price of Storage," *American Economic Review* 31 (December 1949): 1254–62; L. G. Telser, "Future Trading and the Storage of Cotton and Wheat," *Journal of Political Economy* 66 (June 1958): 233–55; M. J. Brennan, "The Supply of Storage," *American Economic*

Review 47 (March 1958): 50–72; and F. Helmut Weymar, *Dynamics of the World Cocoa Market* (Cambridge, Mass: The M.I.T. Press, 1969).

15. The present discussion borrows extensively from the original material presented by Weymar, *ibid.*, pp. 32–7 and 52–3.

16. *Ibid.*, p. 32.

17. Kaldor, *op. cit.*, p. 6.

18. Weymar, *op. cit.*, p. 34.

19. *Ibid.*, pp. 55–92 and J. Burrows, *Tungsten: An Industry Analysis* (Lexington, Mass.: D. C. Heath and Co., 1971), pp. 177–188.

20. R. E. Yver, "The Investment Behavior and the Supply Response of the Cattle Industry in Argentina," Unpublished Ph.D. dissertation, University of Chicago, 1971.

21. D. K. Foley and M. Sidrawsky, "Portfolio Choice, Investment and Growth," *American Economic Review* 60 (March 1970).

22. Mack, *op. cit.*, pp. 272–80.

23. M. Wickens, J. Greenfield, and G. Marshall, *A World Coffee Model* CCP 71/W.P.4. A report prepared for the Committee on Commodity Problems, 46th Session, Food and Agricultural Organization of the United Nations, Rome, 1971.

24. S. G. Allen, "Inventory Fluctuations in Flaxseed and Linseed Oil, 1926–1939," *Econometrica* 22 (July 1954): 310–27.

25. *Ibid.*, p. 314.

26. Witherell, *loc. cit.*

27. See W. C. Labys, *An Econometric Model of the International Lauric Oils Markets: Implications for Policy Analysis*, UNCTAD/Misc. 43 Rev. 1.

28. Several of these points have already been raised in the study of Mack, *op. cit.*, pp. 291–97.

1. An application of spectral analysis and the ARIMA method to commodity price behavior appears in W. C. Labys and C. W. Granger, *Speculation, Hedging, and Commodity Price Forecasts* (Lexington, Mass.: D. C. Heath & Co., 1970). Also see G. P. Box and G. M. Jenkins, *Time Series Analysis, Forecasting and Control* (San Franciso: Holden and Day, 1970); and R. M. Leuthold, A. J. A. MacCormick, A. Schmitz, and D. G. Watts, "Forecasting Daily Hog Prices and Quantities: A Study of Alternative Forecasting Techniques," *Journal of the American Statistical Association* 65 (1970): 90–107.

2. Labys and Granger, *loc. cit.*

3. W. C. Labys, H. J. B. Rees, and C. M. Elliott, "Copper Price Behaviour and the London Metal Exchange," *Applied Economics* 3 (1971): 99–113; J. S. Weiss, "A Spectral Analysis of World Cocoa Prices," *American Journal of Agricultural Economics* 52 (1970): 122–126; and G. C. Rausser and T. F. Cargill, "The Existence of Broiler Cycles: An Application of Spectral Analysis," *American Journal of Agricultural Economics* 52 (1970): 109–121.

4. Labys and Granger, *op. cit.*, pp. 85–87.

5. *Ibid.*, pp. 246–247.

6. I. B. Kravis and R. E. Lipsey, *Price Competitiveness in World Trade* (New York: National Bureau of Economic Research, 1971); H. A. J. Green, *Aggregation in Economic Analysis: An Introductory Survey* (Princeton: Princeton University Press, 1964); and K. Lancaster, "Economic Aggregation and Additivity," *The Structure of Economic Science*, Krupp (Ed.) (Englewood Cliffs: Prentice-Hall, 1966), pp. 201–218.

7. See, for example, H. Working, "Cycles in Wheat Prices," *Wheat Studies of the Food Research Institute* 8 (November 1931); and "A Random Difference Series for Use in the Analysis of Time Series," *Journal of the American Statistical Association* 29 (1934); 11–24.

8. F. L. Thomsen and R. J. Foote, *Agricultural Prices* (New York: McGraw-Hill Book Co., 1952), and Geoffrey S. Shepherd, *Agricultural Price Analysis*, 5th ed. (Ames: Iowa State University Press, 1966).

9. See for example, H. Working, "A Theory of Anticipatory Prices," *American Economic Review* 48 (May 1958): 188–199; and "New Concepts" Concerning Futures Markets and Prices," *American Economic Review* 52 (June 1962): 431–457.

10. M. G. Kendall, "The Analysis of Economic Time Series Part I: Prices," *Journal of the Royal Statistical Society*, Series A 96 (1953): 11–25; and Paul A. Samuelson, "A Random Theory of Futures Prices," *Industrial Management Review* 6 (June 1965).

11. A. Larson, "Measurement of a Random Process in Futures Prices," *Food Research Institute Studies* 1 (November 1960): 313–324; H. S. Houthakker "Systematic and Random Elements in Short-Term Price Movements," *Proceedings of the American Economic Association* 51 (May 1961): 164–172; P. H. Cootner, "Speculation and Hedging," *Food Research Institute Studies*, Special Supplement 1967; R. W. Gray, "The Seasonal Pattern in Wheat Futures Prices Under the Loan Program," *Food Research Institute Studies* 3 (February 1962); and S. Smidt, "A Test of the Serial Independence of Price Changes in Soybean Futures," *Food Research Institute Studies* 5 (1965): 117–136.

12. Labys and Granger, *op. cit.*, pp. 63–87.

13. K. W. Meinken, *The Demand and Price Structure for Wheat*, U.S.D.A. Technical Bulletin No. 1136 (Washington, D.C.: U.S. Government Printing Office, November 1955); R. V. Foote, *Analytical Tools for Studying Demand and Price Structure*, U.S.D.A. Agricultural Handbook No. 146 (Washington, D.C.: U.S. Government Printing Office, 1958); H. F. Breimyer, *Demand and Prices for Meat*, U.S.D.A. Technical Bulletin No. 253 (Washington, D.C.: U.S. Government Printing Office, 1961); and J. P. Houck, *Demand and Price Analysis of the U.S. Soybean Market*, Agricultural Experiment Station Bulletin No. 244, University of Minnesota, 1963.

14. Labys and Granger, op. cit., pp. 11–135.

15. F. H. Weymar, *The Dynamics of the World Cocoa Market* (Cambridge, Mass.: The M.I.T. Press, 1968).

16. L. S. Venkateramanan, *The Theory of Futures Trading* (London: Asia Publishing House, 1965).

17. R. M. Goodwin, "Dynamical Coupling with Especial Reference to Markets Having Production Lags," *Econometrica* 15 (1947): 181–204; M. Nerlove, "Adaptive Expectations and Cobweb Phenomena," *Quarterly Journal of Economics* 73 (May 1958): 227–240; E. S. Mills, *Price, Output, and Inventory Policy* (New York: John Wiley and Sons, 1962); and G. S. Fishman, "Price Behavior Under Alternative Forms of Price Expectations," *Quarterly Journal of Economics* 78 (May 1964): 281–298.

18. This approach to presenting alternative models of price behavior follows that of Weymar, *op. cit.*, pp. 27–31.

19. Breimyer, *loc. cit.*

20. See P. A. Samuelson, *Foundations of Economic Analysis* (Cambridge, Mass.: Harvard University Press, 1961) p. 268; L. R. Klein, "Stocks and Flows in the Theory of Interest," in F. H. Hahn and F. P. Brechling (Eds.), *The Theory of Interest Rates* (London: The Macmillan Co., 1965), pp. 136–151; R. W. Clower, "An Investigation into the Dynamics of Investment," *American Economic Review* 40 (1954): 64–81; and D. W. Bushaw and R. W. Clower,

Introduction to Mathematical Economics (Homewood, Ill.: Richard D. Irwin, 1957).

21. C. J. McKenzie, B. P. Philpott, and M. J. Woods, "Price Formation in the Raw Wool Market," *The Economic Record* (September 1969): 386–398.

22. Equations 5.24–5.28 and the cocoa price equation are reprinted from *Dynamics of the World Cocoa Market* by F. Helmut Weymar by permission of the M.I.T. Press, Cambridge, Massachusetts. Copyright © 1968 by the Massachusetts Institute of Technology.

23. J. F. Muth, "Rational Expectations and the Theory of Price Movements," *Econometrica* 29 (July 1961): 315–335.

24. M. Desai, "*An Econometric Model of the World Tin Economy*, 1948–1961." *Econometrica* 34 (January 1966): 117–121.

25. Discussions of the more important studies in this area can be found in Labys and Granger, *op. cit.*, full text, and "Proceedings of a Symposium on Price Effects of Speculation in Organized Commodity Markets," *Food Research Institute Studies*, Supplement to Vol. VII, 1968.

26. Labys and Granger, *op. cit.*, pp. 89–109.

27. Weymar, *op. cit.* 32–59; Labys and Granger, *op. cit.*, Chs. 4, 5, and 6.

28. See R. J. Barro, "A Theory of Monopolistic Price Adjustment" *Review of Economic Studies* 39 (January 1972): 17–26; and J. C. Burrows, *Cobalt: An Industry Analysis* (Lexington, Mass.: D. C. Heath & Co., 1971).

29. *Ibid.*, pp. 133–184.

30. E. S. Phelps, *et al.*, *Microeconomic Foundations of Employment and Inflation Theory* (New York: W. W. Norton and Co., 1970).

31. See W. C. Labys, *An Econometric Model of the International Lauric Oils Market: Implications for Policy Analysis*, UNCTAD/CD/Mis. 43/Rev. 1, 1971.

32. The need for developing a theory in this form is described in Labys and Granger, *op. cit.*, pp. 259-271.

1. H. L. Moore, "Empirical Laws of Supply and Demand and the Flexibility of Prices," *Political Science Quarterly* 34 (1919): 546–567.

2. Further description can be found in K. A. Fox, *Econometric Analysis for Public Policy* (Ames: The Iowa State College Press, 1958), pp. 7–20.

3. H. Schultz, *Statistical Laws of Demand and Supply* (Chicago: University of Chicago Press, 1928); and H. Schultz, *The Theory of Measurement and Demand* (Chicago: University of Chicago Press, 1938).

4. M. Ezekiel, "The Cobweb Theorem," *Quarterly Journal of Economics* 52 (Feb. 1938): 255–280.

5. J. Tinbergen, *Statistical Testing of Business Cycle Theories* (Geneva: League of Nations Economic Intelligence Service, 1939).

6. T. Haavelmo, "The Statistical Implications of a System of Simultaneous Equations," *Econometrica* 11 (1943): 1–12; and *Statistical Inference in Dynamic Economic Models*, T. Koopmans (Ed.) (New York: John Wiley & Sons, 1950).

7. H. Wold and L. Jureen, *Demand Analysis* (New York: John Wiley & Sons, 1953).

8. K. W. Meinken, *The Demand Price Structure for Oats, Barley, Soybeans, and Grain*, Technical Bulletin No. 1080 (Washington: U.S. Department of Agriculture, 1953); and *The Demand and Price Structure for Wheat*, Technical Bulletin No. 1136 (Washington, D.C.: U.S. Department of Agriculture, 1955).

9. K. A. Fox, *The Analysis of Demand for Farm Products*, Technical Bulletin No. 1081 (Washington, D.C.: U.S. Department of Agriculture, 1953).

10. A. S. Rojko, *The Demand and Price Structure for Diary Products*, Technical Bulletin No. 1168 (Washington, D.C.: U.S. Department of Agriculture, 1957).

11. R. J. Foote, "A Comparison of Single and Simultaneous Equation Techniques," *Journal of Farm Economics* 37 (1955): 975–990; *Analytical Tools for Studying Demand and Price Structures*, Agricultural Handbook No. 146 (Washington, D.C.: U.S. Department of Agriculture, 1958).

12. C. Hildreth and F. J. Jarrett, *A Statistical Study of Livestock Production and Marketing* (New York: John Wiley and Sons, 1955); T. D. Wallace and G. G. Judge, "Econometric Analysis of the Beef and Pork Sectors of the Economy," *Oklahoma State University Technical Bulletin T–75*, Oklahoma State University, August 1959; and Kalmen Cohen, *A Computer Model of the Shoe, Leather and Hide Sequence* (Englewood Cliffs, N.J.: Prentice-Hall, Inc. 1960).

13. D. Suits, "An Econometric Model of the Watermelon Market," *Journal of Farm Economics* 37 (1955): 237–251.

14. Fox, *loc. cit.*

15. L. R. Klein and A. S. Goldberger, *An Econometric Model of the United States Economy*, 1929–1952 (Amsterdam: North–Holland, 1955); A. S. Goldberger, *Impact Multipliers and Dynamic Properties of the Klein–Goldberger Model* (Amsterdam: North–Holland, 1959); J. S. Duesenberry, *et al.* (Eds.), *The Brooking Quarterly Econometric Model of the United States* (Chicago: Rand McNally and Co., 1965); G. Fromm and P. Taubman, *Policy Simulations With an Econometric Model* (Amsterdam: North-Holland, 1968); L. R. Klein and M. K. Evans, *Econometric Gaming* 4 (London: The Macmillan Co., 1969); J. S. Duesenberry, *et al.* (Eds.), *The Brookings Model: Some Further Results* (Chicago: Rand McNally & Co., 1969); and L. R. Klein, "Estimation of Interdependent Systems in Macroeconometrics," *Econometrica* 37 (April 1969): 171–192.

16. P. Zusman, "Econometric Analysis of the Market for California Early Potatoes," *Hilgardia* 33 (Dec. 1962): 539–668; A. C. Egbert and S. Reutlinger, "A Dynamic Model of the Livestock–Feed Sector," *Journal of Farm Economics* 47 (Dec. 1965): 1288–1305; F. H. Weymar, *Dynamics of the World Cocoa Market* (Cambridge: The MIT Press, 1968); M. Desai, "An Econometric Model of the World Tin Economy, 1948–1961," *Econometrica* 34 (Jan. 1966): 105–134; A. A. Harlow, *Factors Affecting and Price and Supply of Hogs*, Technical Bulletin No. 1274, Economic Research Service, U.S. Department of Agriculture, Washington, 1962.

17. F. G. Adams and J. M. Griffin, "An Econometric Model of the United States Petroleum Refining Industry," in *Essays in Industrial Econometrics—Vol. I*, L. R. Klein (Ed.) (Philadelphia: Wharton School of Finance and Commerce, 1969): 93–172; C. I. Higgins, "An Econometric Description of the U.S. Steel Industry," in *Essays in Industrial Economics—Vol. II*. L. R. Klein (Ed.) (Philadelphia: Wharton School of Finance and Commerce, 1969): 1–62; J. R. Behrman, "Econometric Model Simulations of the World Rubber Market," in *Essays in Industrial Economics—Vol. III*, L. R. Klein (Ed.) (Philadelphia: Wharton School of Finance and Commerce 1969): 1–96; and V. N. Murti, "An Econometric Study of the World Tea Economy, 1948–61," Unpublished Ph.D. dissertation, University of Pennsylvania, 1961.

18. W. H. Witherell, "Dynamics of the International Wool Market: An Econometric Analysis," Research Memorandum No. 91, Economic Research Program, Princeton University, 1967; W.Y. Mo, *An Econometric Analysis of the Dynamics of the U.S. Wheat Sector*, Technical Bulletin, No. 1395 Economic Research Service, U.S. Department of Agriculture, Washington, D.C., 1968; W. C. Labys, *An Econometric Model of the International Lauric Oils Market; Considerations for Policy Analysis*, UNCTAD/CD/Misc. 43/Rev. 1,

United Nations, Geneva, July 1971; J. P. Houck, M. E. Ryan, and A. Subotnik, *Soybeans and Their Products; Markets, Models and Policy* (Minneapolis: University of Minnesota Press, 1973); J. L. Matthews, A. W. Womack, and R. G. Hoffman, "Formulation of Market Forecasts for the U.S. Soybean Economy with an Econometric Model," *Fats and Oils Situation*, 260 (Nov. 1971): 26–31; J. L. Matthews and A. W. Womack, "An Economic Appraisal of the U.S. Tung Oil Economy, *Southern Journal of Agricultural Economics* (Dec. 1970): 161–168; and M. L. Hayenga and D. Hacklander, "Monthly Supply–Demand Relationships for Fed Cattle and Hogs," *American Journal of Agricultural Economics* 52 (Nov. 1970): 169–183.

19. See for example, J. C. Burrows, *Cobalt: An Industry Analysis* (Lexington: D. C. Heath & Co., 1971); J. C. Burrows, *Tungsten; An Industry Analysis* (Lexington: D. C. Heath & Co., 1971); and J. C. Burrows, W. Hughes and J. Valette, *An Economic Analysis of the Silver Industry* (Lexington, Mass.: D. C. Heath and Co., 1973).

20. N. A. Cromarty, "An Econometric Model for United States Agriculture," *Journal of the American Statistical Association* 54 (1959): 556–574; M. K. Evans, "An Agricultural Submodel for the U.S. Economy," in *Essays In Industrial Economics—Vol. II*, L. R. Klein, ed. (Philadelphia: Wharton School of Finance and Commerce, 1969): 63–146; and Alvin C. Egbert, "An Aggregate Model of Agriculture Empirical Estimates and Some Policy Implications," *American Journal of Agricultural Economics* 51 (Feb. 1969): 71–86.

21. The following description of the equilibrium model and accompanying econometric methods is based on E. Malinvaud, *Statistical Methods in Econometrics* (Chicago: Rand McNally & Co., 1966): 49–72.

22. T. H. Naylor, "Policy Simulation Experiments with Macroeconometric Models: the State of the Art," *American Journal of Agricultural Economics* 52 (May 1970): 263–271.

23. The following description of the process or industry model follows from F. G. Adams and J. M. Griffin, *An Econometric–Linear Programming Model of the U.S. Petroleum Industry*, Discussion Paper No. 193, Department of Economics, University of Pennsylvania, Philadelphia, September 1970; and J. R. Behrman, *Econometric Models of Mineral Commodity Markets: Limitations and Uses*, Paper presented at Session on Economic Forecasting, Council of Economics, American Institute of Mining, Metaturgical and Petroleum Engineers, New York, Feb. 26, 1968.

24. G. B. Taplin, "Models of World Trade," *IMF Staff Papers* 14 (Nov. 1967): 433–455.

25. R. R. Rhomberg, "Possible Approaches to a Model of World Trade and Payments," *IMF Staff Papers* 17 (March 1970): 1–28

26. F. G. Adams, H. Eguchi and F. Meyer-zu-Schlochtern, *An Econometric Analysis of International Trade*, OECD Economic Studies Series, Paris, Jan. 1969.

27. Rhomberg *op. cit.*, p. 6.

28. P. S. Armington, "A Theory of Demand for Products Distinguished by Place of Production," *IMF Staff Papers* 16 (March 1969): 159–178; and G. B. Taplin, "A Model of World Trade," IMF Research Department Memorandum DM/72/14, Washington, D.C., February 1972.

29. Fox, *op. cit*, pp. 170–211; D. L. Bawden, "A Spatial Price Equilibrium Model of International Trade," *Journal of Farm Economics* 48 (1966): 862–874; and G. G. Judge and T. Takayama, *Spatial and Temporal Price and Allocation Models* (Amsterdam: North–Holland, 1971).

30. A. S. Rojko, F. S. Urban, and J. J. Naive, *World Demand Prospects for Grain in 1980*, Foreign Agricultural Report No. 75, Economic Research Service (Washington, D.C.: U.S. Department of Agriculture, 1971).

31. Other examples of spatial equilibrium trade models include G. W. Dean and N. R. Collins, "World Trade in Fresh Oranges: An Analysis of the Effect of E. E. C Tariff Policies," Giannini Foundation Monograph No. 18, Berkeley, January 1967; and T. Bates and A. Schmitz, "A Spatial Equilibrium Analysis of the World Sugar Economy," Giannini Foundation Monograph No. 23, Berkeley, May 1969.

32. J. W. Forrester, *Industrial Dynamics* (Cambridge, Mass.: M.I.T. Press, 1965), p. 13. A useful critical appraisal of industrial dynamics can be found in H. I. Ansoff and D. P. Slevin, "An Appreciation of Industrial Dynamics," *Management Science* 14 (March 1968): 383–396.

33. See A. L. Pugh, *DYNAMO User's Manual* (Cambridge, Mass.: M.I.T. Press, 1963).

34. R. W. Ballmer, *Copper Market Fluctuations; An Industrial Dynamics Study*, Unpublished M. S. thesis, Massachusetts Institute of Technology, 1960; K. J. Schlager, *A Systems Analysis of the Cooper and Aluminum Industries; An Industrial Dynamics Study*, Unpublished M. S. thesis, Massachusetts Institute of Technology, 1961: and R. C. Raulerson and M. R. Langham, "Evaluating Supply Control Policies for Frozen Concentrated Orange Juice with an Industrial Dynamics Model," *American Journal of Agricultural Economics* 52 (1970): 197–208.

35. D. L. Meadows, *Dynamics of Commodity Production Cycles* (Cambridge: Wright–Allen Press, 1970).

36. See T. H. Naylor (Ed.), *Computer Simulation Experiments with Models of Economic Systems* (New York: John Wiley & Sons, 1971): and *Proceedings of a Workshop on Systems Research in the Livestock Industries*, Animal

Products Branch, Marketing Economics Division, Economic Research Service.

37. H. B. Arthur, J. P. Houck, and G. L. Beckford, *Tropical Agribusiness Structures and Adjustments; Bananas* (Boston: Division of Research—Harvard Business School, 1968). p. 115.

38. *Ibid.*

39. For further discussion see G. C. Chow, "Optimum Control of Linear Econometric Systems with Finite Time Horizon," Econometric Research Program Memorandum No. 115, Princeton University, October 1970; and O. R. Burt, "Control Theory for Agricultural Policy: Methods and Problems in Operational Models," *American Journal of Agricultural Economics* 51 (May 1969): 394–403.

40. Descriptions of these models can be found in Naylor, *loc. cit.*

41. R. Crom, *A Dynamic Price—Output Model of the Beef and Pork Sectors*, Technical Bulletin No. 1426, Economic Research Service (Washington, D.C.: U.S. Department of Agriculture, 1970); G. K. O'Mara, "An Analysis of Alternative Forecast Models for the Broiler Industry: A Summary," and J. D. Sullivan and C. Y. Liu, "Hog–Pork Subsector Research, Industry Model," both in the *Proceedings*, etc., papers cited above.

42. S. H. Holder, Jr., D. L. Shaw, and J. C. Snyder, *A Systems Model of the U.S. Rice Industry*, Technical Bulletin No. 1453, Economic Research Service, Washington, D.C.: U.S. Department of Agriculture, November 1971.

43. T. C. Lee and S. K. Seaver, "A Positive Spatial Equilibrium Model of Broiler Markets: A Simultaneous Equation Approach," Storrs Agriculture Experiment Station Bulletin No. 417, University of Connecticut, Storrs, February 1972; and D. L. Bawden, H. O. Carter, and G. W. Dean, "Interregional Competition in the U.S. Turkey Industry," *Hilgardia* 37 (June 1966): 437–531.

44. T. E. Tramel and A. D. Seale, Jr., "Reactive Programming of Supply and Demand Relations—Application to Fresh Vegetables," *Journal of Farm Economics* 41 (1959): 1012–1022; P. Dhillon, "Milk Production and Demand in the Northeast, New Jersey Agricultural Experiment Station Bulletin No. 826, New Brunswick, October 1969; and R. A. King and F. Hoo, "Reactive Programming: A Market Simulating Spatial Equilibrium Algorithm," Economics Special Report, Department of Economics, North Carolina State University, Raleigh, February 1972.

45. H. Alm, J. Duloy, and O. Gulbrandsen, "Agricultural Prices and the World Food Economy," Mimeographed, Lantbrukshogskolan Institute for Economics and Statistics, Uppsala, Sweden, March 1969.

46. "A World Price Equilibrium Model," Projections Research Working Paper No. 3 for the Committee on Commodity Problems, CC P71/W.P. 3, Food and Agricultural Organization of the United Nations, Rome, October 1971.

47. Arthur, *et al.*, *op. cit.*, p. 139.

48. Matthews and Womack, *loc. cit.*; and Burrows, *loc. cit.*

49. J. P. Houck and J. S. Mann, "An Analysis of Domestic and Foreign Demand of U.S. Soybeans and Soybean Product," Technical Bulletin No. 256, University of Minnesota Agricultural Experiment Station, 1968.

50. Witherell, *loc. cit.*

51. Desai, *loc. cit.*, and T. Ertek, "World Demand for Copper, 1948–1963: An Econometric Study," Unpublished Ph.D. dissertation, University of Wisconsin, 1967.

52. M. Wickens, J. Greenfield, and G. Marshall, *A World Coffee Model* CCP 71/W.P.4., FAO, Rome 1971.

53. C. R. Wymer, "Estimation of Continuous Time Models With an Application To the World Sugar Market," Mimoegraphed, London School of Economics and Political Science, 1972.

54. A useful discussion of alternative forms of model specification can be found in F. M. Fisher. *A Priori Information and Time Series Analysis* (Amsterdam: North-Holland Publishing Co., 1962), and Foote, *Analytical Tools for Studying Demand and Price Structures, loc. cit.*

55. Burrows, *op. cit.*, Chapter 8.

56. Behman, *loc. cit.*

57. J. P. Quirk, and V. L. Smith, "Dynamic Economic Models of Fishing," in A. D. Scott (Ed.), *Economics of Fisheries Management: A Symposium*, University of British Columbia, Vancouver, 1970.

58. Readers interested in a more thorough discussion of causality should consult H. Wold, *Econometric Model Building; Notes on the Causal Chain Approach* (Amsterdam: North-Holland Publishing Co., 1964); R. H. Strotz and H. Wold, "Recursive vs Nonrecursive Systems: An attempt at Synthesis," *Econometrica* 28 (1960): 417–427; H. Wold and L. Jureen, *Demand Analysis* (New York: John Wiley & Sons, 1953): R. Bentzel and B. Hansen, "On Recursiveness and Interdependency in Economic Models," *Review of Economic Studies* 22 (1954): 153–168; E. Malinvaud, *Statistical Methods of Econometrics* (Amsterdam: North–Holland, 1966): Arthur A. Harlow, "A Recursive Model of the Hog Industry," U.S.D.A. 1962: and T. C. Liu, "A Monthly Recursive Econometric Model of the United States," *Review of Economic and Statistics* 69 (1969).

59. For a detailed discussion of the implications of reducing time lags in recursive models, see F. M. Fisher, "A Correspondence Principle for Simultaneous Equations Models," *Econometrica* 38 (Jan. 1970): 73–92.

60. Strotz and Wold, *loc. cit.*, Bentzel and Hansen, *loc. cit.*

61. Schultz, *loc. cit.*; Haavelmo, *loc. cit.*; Wold and Jureen, *loc. cit.*; Cowles Commission Studies include L. Hurwicz, "Generalization of the Concept of Identification," *Statistical Inference in Dynamic Economic Models* (New York: John Wiley & Sons, 1953); and T. C. Koopmans, "Identification Problems in Economic Model Construction," and H. Simon, "Causal Ordering and Identifiability," both in *Studies in Econometric Method*, W. C. Hood and T. C. Koopmans, (Eds.) (New York: John Wiley & Sons, 1953).

62. T. C. Liu, "Underidentification, Structural Estimation and Forecasting," *Econometrica* 28 (1960): 855–865; F. M. Fisher, "Generalization of the Rank and Order Conditions for Identifiability," *Econometrica* 27 (1959): 431–447; F. M. Fisher, "Uncorrelated Disturbances and Identifiability Criteria," *International Economic Review* 4 (1963): 134–152; and F. M. Fisher, *The Identification Problem in Economics* (New York: McGraw-Hill, 1966).

63. These conditions follow from J. Johnston, *Econometric Methods* (New York: McGraw-Hill, 1972), pp. 358–359.

64. Fisher, *loc. cit.*

65. Two exceptions are the comparison of methods provided by Rao and Miller and the discussion of Monte Carlo studies by Johnston, P. Rao and R. L. Miller, *Applied Econometrics* (Belmont, Calif.: Wadsworth Publishing Co., 1971); and Johnston, *loc. cit.*

66. F. M. Fisher, "Dynamic Structure and Estimation in Economy Wide Econometric Models," in *The Brookings Quarterly Econometric Model of the United States*, J. S. Duesenberry, *et al.*, (Eds.) (Chicago: Rand McNally & Co., 1965), 589–636.

67. See Fox, *Econometric Analysis for Public Policy*, *loc. cit.*; Foote, "A Comparison of Single and Simultaneous Equation Techniques," *loc. cit.*; and L. R. Klein, "Single Equation vs Equation System Methods of Estimation in Econometrics," *Econometrica* 28 (Oct. 1960): 886–871.

68. This section follows from Johnston, *loc. cit.*

69. Further discussion of this problem can be found in M. Nerlove and K. F. Wallis, "Use of the Durbin Watson Statistic in Inappropriate Situations," *Econometrica* 34 (1966): 235–238; L. D. Taylor and T. A. Wilson, "Three–Pass Least–Squares: A Method for Estimating Models with a Lagged Dependent Variable," *Review of Economics and Statistics* 46 (1964): 329–346; and J. Durbin, "Testing for Serial Correlation in Least–Squares Regressions

When Some of the Regressors Are Lagged Dependent Variables," *Econometrica* 38 (1970): 410–421.

70. Z. Grilliches, "Distributed Lags: A Survey," *Econometrica* 35 (1967): 16–49.

71. A. Zellner and M. S. Geisel, "Analysis of Distributed Lag Models with Applications to Consumption Function Estimation," *Econometrica* 38 (1970): 865–888.

72. K. F. Wallis, "Lagged Dependent Variables and Serially Correlated Errors: A Reappraisal of Three-Pass Least-Squares," *Review of Economics and Statistics* 49 (1967): 555–567.

73. For further discussion of this problem, see W. D. Fisher and W. J. Wadyck, "Estimating a Structural Equation in a Large System," *Econometrica* 39 (May 1971): 461–466; and P. A. V. B. Swamy and James Holmes, "The Use of Undersized Samples in the Estimation of Simultaneous Equation Systems," *Econometrica* 39 (May 1971): 455–460.

74. T. Kloek and L. B. N. Mennes, "Simultaneous Equation Estimation Based on Principal Components of Predetermined Variables," *Econometrica* 28 (1960): 45–61; L. D. Taylor, "The Principal Components—Instrumental Variable Approach to the Estimation of Systems of Simultaneous Equations," Unpublished Ph.D. dissertation, Harvard University, 1962; P. J. Dhrymes, *Econometrics* (New York: Harper & Row, 1970), pp. 264–272; and F. M. Fisher, *loc. cit.*

75. Kloek and Mennes, *op. cit.*, p. 50.

76. Kloek and Mennes, pp. 54–55.

77. Dhrymes, *op. cit.*, pp. 268–272.

78. Witherell, *loc. cit.*

79. Fisher, *loc. cit.*

80. Z. Grilliches, "The Brookings Model Volume: A Review," *Review of Economics and Statistics* 50 (1968): 228–231.

81. M. D. McCarthy, "Notes on the Selection of Instruments for Two-Stage Least-Squares and K-Class Type Estimators of Large Models," *Southern Economic Journal* (Jan. 1971): 251–259.

82. P. J. Dhrymes, "Some Aspects of the Estimation of Large Econometric Models," Discussion Paper No. 41, Department of Economics, University of Pennsylvania, 1971.

83. B. M. Mitchell, "Estimation of Large Econometric Models by Principal Component and Instrumental Variable Methods," *Review of Economics and Statistics* 50 (May 1971): 140–146; and B. M. Mitchell and F. M.

Fisher, "The Choice of Instrumental Variables in the Estimation of Economy –Wide Econometric Models, Some Further Thoughts," *International Economic Review* 11 (June 1970): 226–234.

84. J. M. Brundy and D. W. Jorgenson, "Efficient Estimation of Simultaneous Equations by Instrumental Variables," Discussion Paper No. 19; Harvard Institute of Economic Research, Harvard University, June 1971; and N. J. Mosback and H. O. Wold, *Interdependent Systems; Structure and Estimation* (Amsterdam: North-Holland Publishing Co., 1970).

85. R. C. Fair, "The Estimation of Simultaneous Equation Models with Lagged Endogenous Variables and First Order Serially Correlated Errors," *Econometrica* (May 1970); 507–516.

86. T. W. Anderson and H. Rubin, "Estimation of the Parameters of a Single Equation In a Complete System of Stochastic Equations," *Annals of Mathematical Statistics* 20 (1949): 46–63.

87. An example of the use of LVR appears in J. E. Farrell and H. C. Lampe, *The New England Fishing Industry; Functional Markets for Finned Food Fish, I and II*, Agricultural Experiment Station Bulletins No. 379 and 380, University of Rhode Island, Kingston, 1965.

88. A. Zellner and H. Theil, "Three-Stage-Least-Squares: Simultaneous Estimation of Simultaneous Equations," *Econometrica* 30 (1962): 54–78.; Brundy and Jorgenson, *loc. cit.*; and Fair, *loc. cit.*

89. L. R. Klein, "Estimation of Interdependent Systems in Macroeconometrics," *loc. cit.*; H. Eisenpress, "Note on the Computation of Full-Information Maximum–Likelihood Estimates of Coefficients of a Simultaneous System," *Econometrica* 30 (1962): 343–348; and H. Eisenpress and J. Greenstadt, "The Estimation of Nonlinear Econometric Systems," *Econometrica* 34 (1966): 851–861.

90. Brundy and Jorgenson, *loc. cit.*

91. G. C. Chow and R. C. Fair, "Maximum Likelihood Estimation of Linear Equation Systems With Autoregressive Residuals," Research Memorandum No. 118, Econometric Research Program, Princeton University, Sept. 1971.

92. R. C. Fair, "A Comparison of Alternative Estimators of Macroeconomic Models," Research Memorandum No. 121, Econometric Research Program, Princeton University, Sept. 1971: and E. Lyttkens, M. Dutta, and R. Bergstrom, "Fix-Point and Iterative Instrumental Variables Methods for Estimating Interdependent Systems," presented at the Second World Congress of the Econometric Society, Cambridge, Eng, Sept. 1970; and Johnston, *op. cit.*, pp. 408–420.

93. A full description of the model can be found in W. C. Labys, *An Econometric Model of the International Lauric Oil Market; Considerations for Policy Analysis, op. cit.*

94. Estimations of the model according to both GLS and 2SPC were performed using a program supplied to the author by M. McCarthy of the Wharton EFA and later revised by M. Schilberg.

Notes for Chapter 7

1. M. Ezekiel, "The Cobweb Theorem," *Quarterly Journal of Economics* (February 1938): 255–280; R. Frisch, "On the Notion of Equilibrium and Disequilibrium," *Review of Economic Studies* (1936): 100–105; T. Haavelmo, "The Probability Approach in Econometrics," *Econometrica* 5 (1937): 105–146; J. R. Hicks, *Value and Capital,* Oxford: Clarendon Press, 1939; R. Harrod, "An Essay in Dynamic Theory," *Economic Journal* 49 (March 1939): 14–33; E. Domar, "Capital Expansion, Rate of Growth and Employment," *Econometrica* 14 (April 1946): 136–147; M. Kalecki, "A Macro-Dynamic Theory of Business Cycles," *Econometrica* 3 (1935): 327–352; P. Samuelson, "The Stability of Equilibrium: Comparative Statics and Dynamics," *Econometrica* 9 (1941): 96–120; P. Samuelson, "The Stability of Equilibrium: Linear and Nonlinear Systems," *Econometrica* 10 (1942): 1–25; and P. Samuelson, "Interactions Between Multiplier Analysis and the Principle of Acceleration," *Review of Economic Statistics* 21 (1939): 75–78.

2. P. Samuelson, *The Foundations of Economic Analysis* (Cambridge: Harvard University Press, 1947) and W. Baumol, *Economic Dynamics* 2nd Ed. (New York: The Macmillan Co., 1959).

3. R. J. Foote, "A Four Equation Model of the Feed Livestock Economy and its Endogenous Mechanisms," *Journal of Farm Economics* 35 (1953): 44–61 and D. Suits, "An Econometric Model of the Watermelon Market," *Journal of Farm Economics* 37 (1955): 237–251.

4. A. Goldberger, *Impact Multipliers and Dynamic Properties of the Klein-Goldberger Model* (Amsterdam: North-Holland Publishing Co., 1959).

5. I. Adelman and F. Adelman, "The Dynamic Properties of the Klein-Goldberger Model," *Econometrica* 27 (1959): 596–625.

6. P. Zusman, "Econometric Analysis of the Market for California Early Potatoes," *Hilgardia* 33 (1962): 539–668; S. Reutlinger, "Analysis of a Dynamic Model, With Particular Emphasis on Long–Run Projections," *Journal of Farm Economics* 48 (1966): 88–107; and W. H. Witherell, *Dynamics of the International Wool Market: An Econometric Analysis*, Research Memorandum No. 91, Economic Research Program, Princeton University, 1967.

7. W. Mo, "An Economic Analysis of the Dynamics of the United States Wheat Sector," Technical Bulletin No. 1395, Economic Research Science, U.S. Department of Agriculture, 1968; and E. I. Jury, "A Stability Test for Linear Discrete Systems Using a Simple Division," *Institute for Radio Engineers* 49 (Dec. 1961): 1948–1949.

8. P. Howrey and W. H. Witherell, *Stochastic Properties of a Model of the International Wool Market*, Econometric Research Program Memorandum No. 101, Princeton University, June 1968; and T. H. Naylor, K. Wertz, and T. Wonnacott, "Spectral Analysis of Data Generated by Simulation

Experiments with Econometric Models," *Econometrica* 37 (April 1969): 333–52.

9. Samuelson, *op. cit.*, pp. 257–83.

10. P. Howrey and H. H. Kelejian, "Simulation Versus Analytical Solutions," in T. H. Naylor, ed., *The Design of Computer Simulation Experiments* (Durham: Duke University Press, 1969), 207–231.

11. *Ibid.*

12. See also Arthur Benavie, *Mathematical Techniques for Economic Analysis* (Englewood Cliffs: Prentice-Hall, Inc., 1972), pp. 237–240.

13. Reutlinger, *loc. cit.*

14. Jury, *loc. cit.*

15. Mo., *loc. cit.*

16. Adelman and Adelman, *loc. cit.*

17. M. Desai, "An Econometric Model of the World Tin Economy, 1948–1961," Unpublished Ph.D. Dissertation, University of Pennsylvania, 1964.

18. Howrey and Kelejian, *op. cit.*, pp. 223–229.

19. W. C. Labys, "Projections and Prospects for the Lauric Oils, 1972–1987," *Journal of the American Oil Chemists Society* 49 (June 1972): 228A–233A.

Notes for Chapter 8

1. A. S. Goldberger, *Impact Multipliers and Dynamic Properties of the Klein–Goldberger Model* (Amsterdam: North-Holland Publishing Co., 1959).

2. H. Theil and J. C. Boot, "The Final Form of Econometric Equation Systems," *Review of the International Statistical Institute*, 30 (1962): 136–152; M. K. Evans, *Macroeconomic Activity* (New York: Harper & Row, 1969); and G. Fromm and L. R. Klein, "Solutions of the Complete System," in *The Brookings Model: Some Further Results*, J. S. Duesenberry, *et al.* (Eds.) (Chicago: Rand McNally & Co., 1969), pp. 362–422.

3. P. Zusman, "Econometric Analysis of the Market for California Early Potatoes," *Hilgardia* 33 (December 1962): 539–668; W. H. Witherell, *Dynamics of the International Wool Market: An Econometric Analysis* Research Memorandum No. 91, Econometric Research Program, Princeton University, Sept. 1967; S. Reutlinger, "Analysis of A Dynamic Model with Particular Emphasis on Long-Run Projections," *Journal of Farm Economics* 48 (1966): 88–107; W. Y. Mo, *An Economic Analysis of the Dynamics of the United States Wheat Sector* Tech. Bull. No. 1395, Economic Research Service, U.S.D.A, April 1968, and R. W. Vanderborre, "Dynamic Impact Multipliers in Agriculture," *American Journal of Agricultural Economics* 50 (1968): 311–320.

4. Theil and Boot, *loc. cit.*

5. Definitions presented below follow those of A. S. Goldberger, *Econometric Theory* (New York: John Wiley & Sons, 1964), pp. 373–376.

6. See also Mo, *op. cit.*, pp. 20–23.

7. An example of the use of delay and cumulative dynamic multipliers can be found in Witherell, *op. cit.*, pp. 174–195.

8. The following discussion follows from that of Reutlinger, *loc. cit.* Also of importance as a reference is P. Zusman, "Dynamic Discrepancies in Agricultural Economic Systems," *Journal of Farm Economics* 44 (1962): 744–63.

9. See Mathematical Appendix B of P. A. Samuelson, *Foundations of Economic Analysis* (Cambridge: Harvard University Press, 1961).

10. A more detailed derivation appears in Zusman, "Econometric Analysis of the Market for California Early Potatoes," *op. cit.*, 636–640.

11. Reutlinger, *op. cit.*, p. 99.

12. *Ibid.*, p. 100.

13. *Ibid.*, p. 103.

14. *Ibid.*, p. 101.

15. See also W. C. Labys, *An Econometric Model of the International Lauric Oils Market: Considerations for Policy Anaylsis*, UNCTAD/CD/Misc. 43/Rev. 1, Geneva: UNCTAD, July 1971.

16. See P. Zusman, "An Investigation of the Dynamic Stability and Stationary States of the United States Potato Market, 1930–1958." *Econometrica* 30 (July 1962): 522–547.

1. L. R. Klein and M. K. Evans, *Econometric Gaming* (London: The Macmillan Co., 1969); G. Fromm and L. R. Klein, "Solutions of the Complete System." in *The Brookings Model: Some Further Results*, J. S. Duesenberry, *et al.* (Eds.) (Chicago: Rand McNally Co., 1969), pp. 363–421; and G. Fromm and P. Taubmann, *Policy Simulations with an Econometric Model* (Washington, D.C.: The Brookings Institution, 1968).

2. T. H. Naylor (Ed.), *The Design of Computer Simulation Experiments* (Durham: Duke University Press, 1969); and T. H. Naylor (Ed.), *Computer Simulation Experiments with Models of Economic Systems* (New York: John Wiley & Sons, 1971).

3. D. Meadows, *Dynamics of Commodity Production Cycles* (Cambridge, Mass.: Wright Allen Press, 1970).

4. C. C. Holt *et al.*, *Program Simulate II*, Social Systems Research Institute, University of Wisconsin, 1967; and M. Eisner, *A Researcher's Overview of the Troll/1 System*, Econometrics Project of the Department of Economics (Cambridge, Mass.: Massachusetts Institute of Technology, November 1971).

5. M. Norman, "The *SIM* Model Solution Program," Mimeographed, Department of Economics, University of Pennsylvania, 1972.

6. K. Cohen, *Computer Models of the Shoe, Leather, Hide Sequence* (Englewood Cliffs, N.J.: Prentice-Hall, Inc. 1960).

7. T. H. Naylor, W. H. Wallace, and W. E. Sasser, "A Computer Simulation Model of the Textile Industry," *Journal of the American Statistical Association* 62 (1967): 1338–1364; J. Vernon, N. Rives, and T. H. Naylor, "An Econometric Model of the Tobacco Industry," *Review of Economics and Statistics* 51 (May 1969): 149–157; F. G. Adams and J. M. Griffin, "An Econometric Model of the U.S. Petroleum Refining Industry," in *Essays in Industrial Dynamics*, Vol. I, L. R. Klein (Ed.) (Philadelphia: Wharton School of Finance and Commerce, 1969), pp. 93–172; and F. G. Adams and J. Blackwell, "An Econometric Model of the United States Forest Products Industry," Discussion Paper No. 207, Department of Economics, University of Pennsylvania, December 1971.

8. M. Desai, "An Econometric Model of the World Tin Economy, 1948–1961," *Econometrica*, Vol. 34 (January 1966), pp. 105–134; J. R. Behrman, "Econometric Model Simulations of the World Rubber Market, 1950–1980," in *Essays in Industrial Dynamics*, Vol. III, L. R. Klein (Ed.) (Philadelphia: Wharton School of Finance and Commerce, 1971), pp. 1–96.

9. M. L. S. Epps, "A Computer Simulation of the World Coffee Economy," Unpublished Ph.D. dissertation, Duke University, 1970; J. Burrows, *Tungsten: An Industry Analysis* (Lexington, Mass.: D. C. Heath & Co., 1971); R. Crom, *A Dynamic Price-Output Model of the Beef and Pork Sectors*, Technical Bulletin No. 1426, Economic Research Service (Washington: U.S. Department

of Agriculture, 1970); and W. C. Labys, *An Econometric Model of the World Lauric Oils Market: Considerations for Policy Analysis*, UNCTAD/CD/Misc. 43/Rev. 1. United Nations, Geneva, July 1971.

10. E. P. Howrey and W. H. Witherell, *Stochastic Properties of a Model of the International Wool Market*, Econometric Research Program Research Memorandum No. 101, Princeton University, June 1968; and T. H. Naylor, K. Wertz, and T. Wonnacott, "Spectral Analysis of Data Generated by Simulation Experiments with Econometric Models," *Econometrica*, 37 (April 1969): 333–352.

11. T. H. Naylor, "Policy Simulation Experiments with Macro–econometric Models: The State of the Art," proceedings of the American Agricultural Economics Association, *American Journal of Agricultural Economics*, 52 (May 1970), pp. 263–71.

12. E. P. Howrey and H. H. Kelejian, "Simulation versus Analytical Solutions," from T. H. Naylor (Ed.), *The Design of Computer Simulation Experiments* (Durham, N.C.: Duke University Press, 1969), p. 207.

13. A. S. Goldberger, *Impact Multipliers and Dynamic Properties of the Klein–Goldberger Model* (Amsterdam: North-Holland Publishing Co., 1959), p. 49.

14. The major study in this regard is I. and F. L. Adelman, "The Dynamic Properties of the Klein Goldberger Model," *Econometrica* 27 (October 1959), pp. 596–625.

15. Most of these problems have been discussed previously by Naylor, *op. cit.*, pp. 265–272.

16. Klein and Evans, *op. cit.* pp. 24–27.

17. Naylor, *loc. cit.*

18. This was originally pointed out by Howrey and Kelijian, *loc. cit.*

19. Adelman and Adelman, *loc. cit.*

20. An example of stochastic solution with the reduced form is given on page 178, using Desai's tin model.

21. An alternative approach to solving this problem using an iterative procedure can be found in Burrows, *op. cit.*, pp. 189–192.

22. Klein and Evans, *op. cit.*, p. 26.

23. For further discussion of the relative advantages and disadvantages of the methods presented here see J. Meinguet, "Modern Relaxation Methods for the Solutions of Systems of Linear Equations of High Order," in *Mathematics and Engineering Applications: Some Selected Examples* (Paris: OECD, 1965).

24. One step methods are further discussed in Holt, *loc. cit.*, and R. A. Pennington, *Introduction to Computer Methods and Numerical Analysis* (New York: The Macmillan Co., 1967), pp. 295–303.

25. Klein and Evans, *Econometric Gaming, loc. cit.*; Adams and Blackwell, *loc. cit.*, and Behrman, *loc. cit.*

26. Klein and Evans, *op. cit.* pp. 28–33.

27. For a discussion of the applicability of this method and the tests involved see F. M. Fisher," A Correspondence Principle for Simultaneous Equation Models," *Econometrica*, 38 (January 1970): 73–92.

28. Fromm and Klein, *loc. cit.*

29. P. J. Dhrymes, *et al.*, "Criteria for Evaluation of Econometric Models," *Annals of Economic and Social Measurement* 1 (July 1972): 291–324.

30. In applying these tests, we assume that some final model has been reached. Appropriate tests to be applied in model selection can be found in E. P. Howrey, "Selection and Evaluation of Econometric Models," in *Computer Simulation versus Analytical Solutions for Business and Economic Models* (Gothenburg: Graduate School of Business Administration, 1972).

31. H. Theil, *Economic Forecasts and Policy* (Amsterdam: North-Holland Publishing Co., 1961). See also E. P. Howrey, L. R. Klein, and M. D. McCarthy, "Notes on Testing the Predictive Performance of Econometric Models," Discussion Paper No. 173, Department of Economics, University of Pennsylvania, 1970; and D. W. Jorgenson, J. Hunter, and M. Nadiri, "The Predictive Performance of Models of Quarterly Investment Behavior," *Econometrica* 38 (March 1970): 213–224.

32. This approach has been proposed by E. E. Leamer and R. M. Stern, *Quantitative International Economics* (Boston: Allyn and Bacon, Inc., 1970), pp. 112–114.

33. H. Theil, *op. cit.*, pp. 112–117.

34. Howrey and Witherell, *loc. cit.* and Naylor, Wertz, and Wonnacott, *loc. cit.*

35. W. C. Labys and C. W. J. Granger, *Speculation, Hedging, and Commodity Price Forecasts* (Lexington, Mass.: D. C. Heath and Co., 1970).

36. R. L. Cooper and D. W. Jorgenson, *The Predictive Performance of Quarterly Econometric Models of the United States*, Institute of Business and Economic Research Working Paper No. 113, University of California at Berkeley, 1969, pp. 19–24.

37. Labys and Granger, *loc. cit.*; and T. H. Naylor, T. G. Seaks, and D. W. Wichern, " Box-Jenkins Methods: An Alternative to Econometric Models " Working Paper No. 57, Social System Simulation Program, Duke University, February 1971.

38. Y. Haitovsky and G. Treyz, "The Decomposition of Econometric Forecast Error," described in Dhrymes, *et al.*, *loc. cit.*

39. R. H. Day and I. Singh, *A Microeconometric Study of Agricultural Development*, Social Systems Research Institute, University of Wisconsin, December 1971.

40. Fromm and Taubman, *loc. cit.*

41. Howrey and Witherell, *loc. cit.*

42. Naylor, *Computer Simulation Experiments with Models of Economic Systems*, *op. cit.*, p. 318.

43. Burrows, *op. cit.*, p. 189–214.

44. Epps, *loc*, *cit.*

45. R. Agarwala, "A Simulation Approach to the Analysis of Stabilization Policies in Agricultural Markets: A Case Study." *Journal of Agricultural Economics* 22 (January 1971): 13–28; T. A. Kofi, "International Commodity Agreements and Export Earnings: Simulation of the 1968 International Cocoa Agreement," *Food Research Institute Studies* 11 (1972) 2; and H. Kim, L. Goreux, and D. Kendrick, "Feedback Stochastic Decision Rules for Commodity Stabilization: An Application of Control Theory to World Cocoa Markets," Development Research Section, IBRD, Washington, D.C., October 1972.

46. Behrman, *loc. cit.*

47. Desai, *loc. cit.*

48. Labys, *loc. cit.*; also see W. C. Labys, "Commodity Modeling Alternatives for Policy Simulation Analysis: A Case Study of the Lauric Oils Market," in *Computer Simulation versus Analytical Solutions for Business and Economic Models* (Gothenburg: Graduate School of Business Administration, 1972).

49. W. C. Labys, *Feasibility of Operating a Supply Stabilization Scheme for the Lauric Oils Market: Returns, Cost and Financing* UNCTAD/CD/ MISC 41, United Nations, Geneva, April 1971.

50. W. C. Labys, "Projections and Prospects for the Lauric Oils, 1972–1987," *Journal of the American Oil Chemists Society*, 49 (June 1972): 228A–33A.

1. W. C. Labys, "Policy Planning with Commodity Models Based on Perennial Tree Crops," Mimeographed, Presented at the Rural Development Panel, Southeast Asia Development Advisory Group, Singapore, September 16–18, 1972.

2. E. P. Howrey, "Selection and Evaluation of Econometric Models," in *Computer Simulation versus Analytical Solutions for Business and Economic Models* (Gothenburg: Graduate School of Business Administration, 1972).

Notes for Appendix A

1. P. Samuelson, *The Foundations of Economic Analysis* (Cambridge: Harvard University Press, 1947), pp. 320–21.

2. See Phoebus Dhrymes, *Econometrics* (New York: Harper & Row, 1970), pp. 567–574.

3. This generalization follows from that of H. Theil and J. C. G. Boot, "The Final Form of Econometric Equation Systems," *Review of the International Statistical Institute* 30 (1962): 136–152.

1. W. C. Labys and C. W. J. Granger, *Speculation, Hedging, and Commodity Price Forecasts* (Lexington, Mass.: D. C. Heath and Co., 1970).

2. This appendix is based on the methodology and results obtained from E. P. Howrey and W. H. Witherell, *Stochastic Properties of a Model of the International Wool Market*, Econometric Research Program Research Memorandum No. 101, Princeton University, June 1968; T. H. Naylor, K. Wertz, and T. Wonnacott, "Spectral Analysis of Data Generated by Simulation Experiments with Econometric Models," *Econometrica* 37 (April 1969): 333–352; and G. S. Fishman and P. J. Kiviat, "The Analysis of Simulation-Generated Time Series," *Management Science* 13 (March 1967): 525–557.

3. Readers not familiar with these terms or with the other spectral definitions presented are referred to more complete accounts of the theory of spectral analysis such as that found in C. W. J. Granger and M. Hatanaka, *Spectral Analysis of Economic Time Series* (Princeton: Princeton University Press, 1964).

4. Howrey and Witherell, *op. cit.*, p. 23.

5. *Ibid.*, p. 18.

6. Phoebus J. Dhrymes, *Econometrics* (New York: Harper & Row, 1970): 525–530.

7. Howrey and Witherell, *op. cit.*, p. 22.

8. *Ibid.*, p. 24.

9. C. W. J. Granger, "The Typical Shape of an Economic Variable," *Econometrica* 34 (January 1966): 150–161.

10. Naylor, Wertz, and Wonnacott, *loc. cit.*; see also G. M. Jenkins and D. G. Watts, *Spectral Analysis and Its Applications* (San Francisco: Holden Day, 1969).

11. *Ibid.*

12. Thomas H. Naylor, William H. Wallace and W. Earl Sasser, "A Computer Simulation of the Textile Industry," *Journal of the American Statistical Association* 62 (December 1967): 1338–1364.

Index

347

350

About the Author

Walter C. Labys is Visiting Professor at the Graduate Institute of International Studies in Geneva, where he teaches econometrics, quantitative methods, and microeconomic theory. His present research interests include the construction of national and international commodity models and their application in market forecasting, policy evaluation, stabilization, and economic development. Among commodities of special interest are the oils and fats group—particularly lauric oils and palm oil—and copper and wines.

Practical extensions of his work have taken a variety of directions. Serving as a consultant to UNCTAD, he has built a model of the international lauric oils market, and is currently applying the model to solving stabilization problems for that market, as requested by the Asian Coconut Community. He is also interested in the construction of commodity development models to be used as a format for development planning. These efforts have involved participation with the Southeast Asia Development Advisory Group and the Economic Development Institute of the World Bank. Other research and consulting activities have included forecasting, gaming, growth, and urban economics with firms such as Unilever, New England Life, Westinghouse and Abt Associates. He was a member of the Department of Economics at the University of Rhode Island during 1971–1972 and at the University of Nottingham during 1966–1968.

Dr. Labys completed his Ph.D. in economics at the University of Nottingham in 1968. A recipient of several academic awards, he earned the M.A. in economics from Harvard University, the M.B.A. in economics and operations research from Duquesne University, and the B.S in electrical engineering from Carnegie-Mellon University. He is the author of *Speculation, Hedging, and Commodity Price Forecasts* with Clive Granger and published in 1970 by Lexington books, as well as of several other papers, and is a member of the Econometric Society and the American Economic Association. Born in 1937, he is married and has two children.